Walls Are Crumbling

JOHN M. OESTERREICHER

FOREWORD BY JACQUES MARITAIN

SEVEN JEWISH PHILOSOPHERS DISCOVER CHRIST

Walls Are Crumbling

THE DEVIN-ADAIR COMPANY · NEW YORK · 1952

NIHIL OBSTAT: John P. Haran, S.J., *Censor librorum*
IMPRIMATUR: ✠John J. Wright, *Bishop of Worcester*
February 20, 1952

64845

296
029 w

Book designed by Walter Miles
Manufactured in the United States of America
by The Colonial Press Inc., Clinton, Mass.

to John Henry Cardinal Newman
a token of gratitude

Foreword *by Jacques Maritain*

FATHER OESTERREICHER IS HIMSELF AN OUTSTANDING WITNESS TO the great movement he studies here in the persons of seven who represent it most significantly—a movement which stirs the minds of many among the sons of Israel and turns them to the true Messias of their people. While reading his beautiful book I thought, not without emotion, of his own intellectual and spiritual history—also of our first meetings in Europe, of the brave battle he led against anti-Semitism in Austria while the Hitlerite abomination was brewing, of the friendship which has bound us, ever since, through such unexpected events, through struggle and painful experience.

Vast learning and profound historical knowledge, inspired by an ardent faith, give a special authority to this scholar's testimony and writings. I should like to say particularly how much I appreciated some years ago the study in which he demonstrated that the expression *perfidia judaica* in the liturgy of Good Friday means "lack of faith [in Christ]," and by no means "perfidy"; and how much I appreciate this present work, devoted to seven eminent contemporary Jewish thinkers whom the Gospel has conquered.

Three of them, I have had the privilege of knowing personally. How can one describe the purity, the light which shone from Edith Stein at the time of her conversion; the total generosity which one felt in her and which was to bear fruit in martyrdom? Attracted by the Church throughout his lifetime, Paul Landsberg died before acting on his final decision to become a Catholic; but, as Father Oesterreicher shows, his thought was entirely oriented toward Catholicism and was nourished by a deep Augustinian inspiration. I admired greatly his intellectual loyalty, his freedom of spirit, and his unbending courage.

Henri Bergson was my first master. My gratitude, my admiration for him have but grown with the years, filling my heart with sentiments even more intense than the enthusiasm which fired Raïssa and me when we studied under him at the Collège de France. Many years ago I criticized what I called "Bergsonism of fact," while insisting on the eminent value of "Bergsonism of intention." But the friendship which he, in his goodness and despite these theoretical differences, showed us during his last years, and which, having

vii

bound us to him, now binds us to his daughter, is one of the great joys of our life. It was he who freed French thought from the deceiving ascendancy of Positivism and led it back to the sense of the absolute. Under the name of *durée* and under an imperfect and misleading conceptualization, he found again the great treasure of metaphysical intelligence, the intuition of being. Nothing could be more beautiful than the intellectual movement by which, in the strength of a watchful conscience and fidelity to the light, he uncovered step by step the great realities of the spirit, until in the end he passed the limits of philosophy and cleaved to the word of the Son of God his heart had heard.

Paul Landsberg and Edith Stein perished in German concentration camps, as did so many Jewish friends whose memories I cherish—such as Manu and Babet Jacob and their aged mother, all three Israelites pure and admirable Christians at heart; Benjamin Fondane, a disciple of Chestov but haunted by the Gospel; and the dear and humble Max Jacob, victim of the concentration camp of Drancy, whose conversion to Christianity has shed its rays on modern French poetry—Father Oesterreicher might well have added him to his gallery had he not reserved it for philosophers.

In all these deaths offered in sacrifice I see the sign of a great reality. In becoming Christians—be it merely in the hiddenness of the soul or be it that they received the sacraments—those of whom Father Oesterreicher speaks or could speak have remained more than ever faithful to Israel and to its vocation. It was during the earthquake of a monstrous persecution, in which Jews and Christians were reunited and set out together toward Calvary, that the wall of separation began to fall in the world, that wall which in spiritual principle Christ did away with: "The two peoples," says St. Paul, "He has made one, He has broken down the wall of separation." But the hardness of the human heart has kept it standing through the ages, and its ultimate downfall will come about only through the supreme catastrophes of history.

I do not wish to minimize the part which Israel's obstinacy has played, ever since the first days of the Church, in the central tragedy of human history. But it is well to remember also the responsibilities of Christians, not only the perpetual persecutions which Israel has had to endure, but also that insensitivity of heart, *cette indélicatesse du coeur,* that unjust indifference and those cruel prejudices which so many Gentile Christians have shown for so long toward the elder people, and which Jules Isaac recently denounced in a book on which we ought to meditate, marred though it is by unfortunate excursions into New Testament exegesis.

Father Oesterreicher rightly underlines the irrepressible zeal, engaging the entire soul and exercised in every domain, which is Israel's by vocation. This is an epoch when all in man's heart seems grown cold, when the absence of the prophetic spirit adds singularly to the misery of the world. May I say that in such an epoch, the sons of Israel in whose souls the walls have crumbled, who have seen the light of Christ, are doubtless called—while contributing humbly and generously to the common work in the "Church of Jews and Gentiles"—to a role of which modern Christendom has particular need? I dedicate this thought to the memory of Emmanuel Chapman, with gratitude to Father Oesterreicher for having paid him homage in his Preface.

The author of the present work gives us today the fruit of studies long pursued with constant care for objectivity, with rare philosophical penetration, and with great love. He has made admirably clear the deep import of the message confided to us by these great minds, into which they put all their anguish, their search, their hope. In the diversity of viewpoints, of doctrines and personal destinies, the seven essays gathered in this volume compose a whole, a harmony unusually meaningful; they bring to our thoughtful attention intellectual themes of high human value and poignant actuality.

Contents

Contents

Preface

THIS IS A BOOK OF HOPE. FOR ALMOST TWO THOUSAND YEARS, JEWS have denied that Jesus is the Messias. For almost two hundred years, modern thought has been a philosophy of denial and contradiction. Finally, rancor has invented the slogan: "Jews lack the power of spiritual thought, they are to blame for the destructive philosophies of materialism." But the seven of this book reverse these trends toward "no," their message being one of affirmation and hope, a sign of a new advent.

"May I bury my son!" exclaimed Rabbi Tarphon, a Jewish teacher of the early second century. "If they [the Gospels] come into my hands, I will burn them, even with the divine Name therein." [1] It is a long, far journey from this fury against the memory of Jesus to the loving confession of Henri Bergson, the great Jewish philosopher of our day: "The gospel is my true spiritual home." Playing upon the word *evangelion,* the "Good News," the tidings of salvation, Rabbi Meir of the second century called the gospel *aven giljon,* "worthless paper, scroll of idolatry," and a few decades later, Rabbi Johanon, varying the gibe, called it *avon giljon,* "scroll of sin, book of iniquity." [2] How unlike this is the cry of the young Jewish thinker, Paul Landsberg, that our world will be swallowed by chaos unless it "takes the Christian revelation for its helmsman."

For centuries Jewish teachers have rejected Jesus' claim to be the Christ, the one and only Saviour of the world; for centuries there has been a conspiracy of silence, so that His Name was not uttered, neither in home nor in house of learning. Jewish unbelief and, no less, Gentile persecution built a wall which kept the Jews from Christ, but now this wall is giving way, His Name is uttered, He is seen again. And this is how seven contemporary Jewish thinkers look on Him. For Bergson He is the unsetting Sun who fires the souls of the mystics, the "great men of the good," who can do nothing without Him. "Whence comes Christ?" he asks himself, and answers: "Surely He comes from above." On his deathbed, Edmund Husserl rejoiced: "What a wonderful day, Good Friday! Yes, Christ has forgiven us everything." "In Him God's being, out-

xiii

side of time and beyond the world, unfolds itself in time and before the world," Adolf Reinach declares, and Max Scheler hails
Him as the very Truth, the Bringer of a new love, the Ransomer
of pain. "Dearest Light," "Thou Two-in-One," Landsberg hymns
Him. Max Picard calls Him "Servant and Sir, Man and God," and
stammers of Him that when, on the cross, His soul and body
were rent in death, He made forever sure the face of man as the
likeness of God. That same cross made Him, for Edith Stein, the
sovereign Spouse, the majestic Lover. With the witness of these
seven, who can doubt that the wall which has stood so long and
seemed unbreakable, the wall of separation from Christ, is crumbling?

Faith in Christ means to the seven—to some more, to some less—a
new vision of the Church. The fulfillment of the Judaism of old,
issue of Christ's thought and design, holder of His spirit, His will
and His means, indeed, Christ Himself extended through the
ages—this is Bergson's vision. Scheler's is of the Church as the communion of salvation, in which men believe together, love together,
worship together, and it is only in this togetherness, he professes,
only in love, that a man can know eternal truth, only in a body
that he can worship in the spirit. For Landsberg the Church is at
once the heir of heresy and the unbowed-to benefactor of our age:
the foundation of law and the idea of science, for instance, we owe
to her, and to her in the end return all the truths that are buried
in errors. In a world of flight, Picard knows the Church to be the
rock of peace; in a world which deflowers the primal phenomena
—life and death, silence and the word, love and marriage—she is
the keeper of the seal of creation. The steep, heaven-piercing
mountain of prayer, from whose heights the winds of sanctity
blow down into the valleys of men—this she is to Edith Stein.
Again an old wall is crumbling, the wall of prejudice against the
Church. Beside the vision of such a man as Bergson, of such a
woman as Edith Stein, the view of the Church as a tyranny is but
a squint.

It is not a little thing that seven modern Jewish philosophers
should, without forethought, without a plan of their own, without directing their efforts toward it, become defenders of Catholic thought and teaching; that they should parallel, confirm, even
enrich it. Creation is not a myth but a fact, they assert unwaver-

ingly. Spirit is no more the offspring of matter, nor mind of the brain, than is the musician of his instrument. Man is not an animal, rather God's image, born to know, to speak, to love, to worship; indeed, he must worship, he must choose between God and idols. Though time is change, it is in time that man, "freedom incarnate," is free to grow toward the Unchangeable. And in the life of man, the immortal, the person, the greatest moment is death. All these affirmations and more, whose denial is the pleasure of "modern thought," the seven found in their painful search for truth. They are sure that truth and the good are objective, not man-made; that contrition is a new beginning; that faith is a summit of knowing; that hope is the very fabric of the soul. Sin and virtue, the fall of man and his redemption, laughed at by small souls, matter to the seven, are cardinal again.

Before the force of their arguments, much of "modern thought" crumbles, is shown up as a "flight from God," as a fever caused by the virus *ressentiment,* as a "philosophy of bad conscience" —such are the verdicts of Picard, Scheler and Edith Stein. They unmask as the greatest lie in history the shout that "God is dead," Christianity bankrupt, and that religion must give way to progress.

G. K. Chesterton has pointed out that nowadays a man says: "I suppose I'm heretical," and looks around for applause, while in former ages, even a heretic was proud to think himself orthodox and the last thing he would have admitted was his heresy. "Heretical" has come to mean "clearheaded," "courageous," Chesterton goes on to say, and "orthodoxy" has come to mean "stubborn" and "wrong." [3] Unfooled by this confusion, the seven, original thinkers as they are, value and seek orthodoxy. Not content with the negations the modern mind substitutes for the old truths, they can all say with Chesterton, some more, some less, that with the utmost daring they have discovered what had been discovered before.[4]

With the crumbling of modern thought, there crumbles also the anti-Semitic cliché, so dangerous to the conscience of Christendom, that the Jews are the protagonists of the modern denial of faith, the advocates of materialistic philosophies, that they are well represented by Marx and Freud. Far from being the prime movers in the war against God, those Jews engaged in it are but latecomers; they are not the makers but the victims of the age, their long-kept "No" to Christ making Jews peculiarly susceptible to the modern "No." Marx and Freud could never have been, except for their spiritual ancestry of Gentile apostates. Marx's "religion is the opiate of the people" could not have been uttered had there not been first the Young Hegelians, Bruno Bauer and Ludwig Feuerbach, one with the watchword that history culminates in the disappearance of religion, the other with his thesis that religion is nothing but man's relationship to himself, that the divine mysteries are nothing but the mysteries of human nature. Without the guesswork and fiction of the evolutionary anthropologists, William Robertson Smith and James Frazer, Freud's *Totem and Taboo* could never have been written. Before Marx issued his ban on metaphysical questions and defined the "socialist man" as the man who does not raise them, Auguste Comte had decreed the same prohibition. And when Freud looked forward to a future in which science would overthrow religion, make an end of the reign of "neurotic illusion," he dreamt his master's dream, Comte's dream of the age of science, in which mankind would be free from the "terror of religion."

What is Jewish in Marx and Freud, and in other Jews who champion naturalistic philosophies, is their zeal. In fact, as St. Paul intimates in his letter to the Romans, zeal is the God-given character of the Jews, graven in them by the thunder of Sinai, by Elias, the prophet of storm and fire, by all the prophets, men of flame.[5] Not even a Jew who makes Communism, science, or literature his god loses this mark, but its only true goal, its only congruous object, is the kingship of God in Christ. And having discovered Him, the seven of this book are true Jews, an authentic voice.

Of this unique phenomenon—the Christian thought of Jewish thinkers—Bergson, Husserl, Reinach, Scheler, Landsberg, Picard and Edith Stein are not the only representatives. There are, among others, the late Emmanuel Chapman, with his work on beauty; Robert C. Pollock of Fordham University, a profound student of St. Bonaventure; Herbert T. Schwartz of St. Xavier's University, who has concerned himself with the philosophy of music. There is Simone Weil, whose *Gravity and Grace* and *Waiting for*

God show her unresting search for the Absolute; drawn to Christ and His Church by her sense of the secret of suffering, still she never fully reached them, because she never went beyond suffering to the mystery of salvation. Among the writings of Annie Kraus there is a striking treatise, *On Stupidity*. Stupidity is a vice, she says, a matter not of the intellect but of the will, or, in the words of St. Thomas, a "habit of the heart," not part of man's natural endowment but a consequence of his fall. To be stupid is to be deaf and dumb toward being and its Giver; it is to refuse to heed, to refuse to receive into the mind, to refuse to do justice to, reality—there can be no true knowledge unless we acknowledge reality's fullness. "The fool says in his heart, there is no God"—this is the beginning of stupidity, the mystery of its birth, just as the beginning of wisdom is the fear of the Lord.[6] Then there is Raïssa Maritain, whose *The Moral Conscience and the State of Nature* is a penetrating essay on the mystery of conscience. In another study, *The Prince of This World,* she writes: "Lucifer has cast a strong though invisible net of illusion upon us. He makes us love the passing moment above eternity, uncertainty above truth. He persuades us that we cannot love creatures except by making gods of them. . . . Not the least of his victories is to convince artists and poets that he is their necessary, inevitable collaborator and the guardian of their greatness." He reigns, and yet the reign has been wrested from him by the cross, the signature of Christ's love. "The pierced hands of the Son are needed to loose the merciful hands of the Father, held captive by our sins, to put in bonds the prince of this world and destroy his principality." [7]

Why then the seven? Some of them are the great philosophers of our day and all of them men of moment, whose work is a contribution that cannot be effaced from the history of ideas. And so much do their lives vary each from the other, so different are their journeys and their nearness to the goal, that even in their failures and their errors they are a miniature humanity. So various are their starting points and their fields of inquiry that they are a little republic of philosophers, their work almost a modern *Summa*. As the thought of philosophers for whom philosophy is not a profession but a condition for life, it is so dyed with the personal that its appeal is to the center of our being. Reading them we know that in philosophy eternity is at stake.

Written for those who would rather think than not, *Walls Are Crumbling* is dedicated to Cardinal Newman, with the hope that for many readers it may do what, thirty years ago, his *Development of Christian Doctrine* did for me. I still remember, as if it had been yesterday, the light, the clarity, the intellectual joy, it brought me; I still remember the words with which it closes, words of which it has been said that they "will be remembered as long as the English language endures." And they may well stand here, for they are, in effect, the appeal of the seven Jewish philosophers who discovered Christ.

"Such were the thoughts concerning the 'Blessed Vision of Peace,' of one whose long-continued petition had been that the Most Merciful would not despise the work of His own Hands, nor leave him to himself;—while yet his eyes were dim, and his breast laden, and he could but employ Reason in the things of Faith. And now, dear Reader, time is short, eternity is long. Put not from you what you have here found; regard it not as mere matter of present controversy; set not out resolved to refute it, and looking about for the best way of doing so; seduce not yourself with the imagination that it comes of disappointment, or disgust, or restlessness, or wounded feeling, or undue sensibility, or other weakness. Wrap not yourself round in the associations of years past; nor determine that to be truth which you wish to be so, nor make an idol of cherished anticipations. Time is short, eternity is long."

J.M.O.

Acknowledgments

FOR THE GENEROSITY AND UNTIRING PATIENCE OF SISTER ADELGUNDIS
Jaegerschmidt, O.S.B., of St. Lioba's Priory, Freiburg i. Br.-Guenterstal, Edmund Husserl's pupil and friend; Mrs. Anna Reinach, of Madrid and Munich; Mrs. Maerit Furtwaengler-Scheler, of Heidelberg, and Mrs. Madeleine Landsberg, of Paris, I cannot be sufficiently grateful. My deep thanks are also due to Miss Jeanne Bergson, of Paris; Mrs. Malvine Husserl, of Freiburg i. Br.; Mrs. Elisabeth Husserl Rosenberg, of Arlington, Mass.; Mrs. Maria Scheu-Scheler, of Garmisch-Partenkirchen; Sister Teresia Renata de Spiritu Sancto, Prioress of the Carmel of Cologne, and Dr. Max and Dr. Erna Biberstein, brother-in-law and sister of Edith Stein. All of them have confided to me their intimate recollections and valuable letters, manuscripts and photographs, to which I owe much in this book. To Max Picard I am indebted for our old friendship and for many conversations in his lakeside home.

May I also express my gratitude to all those whose correspondence, comment and criticism have been of such aid, particularly to the late Maurice Blondel; the late Father Walter Farrell, O.P.; Dr. L. Gelber and the Husserl Archives, of the University of Louvain; Dietrich von Hildebrand, of Fordham University; Jacques Maritain, of Princeton University; Dr. Hedwig Conrad-Martius, of Munich; James V. Mullaney, of Manhattan College; the Right Reverend Wilhelm Neuss, of the University of Bonn; Father J. Reginald O'Donnell, C.S.B., of the Pontifical Institute of Mediaeval Studies, in Toronto; Balduin Schwarz, of Fordham University; the late Père Antonin D. Sertillanges, O.P.; Dr. Rudolf Sobotta, of Bonn, and Mother Kathryn Sullivan, R.S.C.J., of Manhattanville College of the Sacred Heart. The librarians of the Union Theological Seminary in New York City have shown themselves most cooperative.

There are many, many friends who have helped me, more than I can name. But may I pay special recognition to Walter Miles, the designer of the book, whose solicitude has made it his own; to Thomas O'Conor Sloane III, of the Devin-Adair Company, for the care with which he saw it through publication; to Miss Norina Marazzini, who gave countless hours to the typing of the manuscript, and to Miss Mary Ruth Bede, my secretary, without whose devoted assistance the book could not have been brought to completion. Her selflessness has made me her debtor.

For permission to use copyrighted material, acknowledgment is made to the following publishers and editors: from Coventry Patmore's *Mystical Poems of Nuptial Love,* by permission of Bruce Humphries, Inc.; from his edition of the *Poems of Francis Thompson,* by permission of Father Terence L. Connolly, S.J.; from *The Verse in English of Richard Crashaw,* by permission of the Grove Press; from T. S. Eliot's *Collected Poems 1909-1935* and *Murder in the Cathedral,* by permission of Harcourt, Brace and Company, Inc.; from David Gascoyne's *Poems 1937-42,* by permission of John Lehmann, Ltd.; from L. A. Clare's translation of Jacques Chevalier's *Henri Bergson,* and from Orrick Johns' *Wild Plum,* by permission of the Macmillan Company; from the *Poems of Gerard Manley Hopkins,* by permission of the Oxford University Press; from the translation by Sister Mary David, S.S.N.D., of Paul Claudel's *Coronal,* from L. G. White's translation of Dante's *Divine Comedy,* from the translation by C. N. Valhope and E. Morwitz of Stefan George's *Poems,* from Roy Campbell's translation of the *Poems of St. John of the Cross,* and from Julian Green's translation of Charles Péguy's *God Speaks,* by permission of Pantheon Books, Inc.; and from Margaret Chanler's translation of Gertrud von Le Fort's *Hymns to the Church,* by permission of Sheed and Ward, Inc.

Henri Bergson

PHILOSOPHER OF EXPERIENCE

"THE UNIVERSE IS A MACHINE FOR THE MAKING OF GOD." WITH these words, declares Irwin Edman,[1] Henri Bergson brings to a close his *Two Sources of Morality and Religion*. In Edman's quotation, but one word is altered, but one letter dropped, yet the meaning is changed entirely. Bergson's words, written years before the atom bomb threatened to blow to dust our civilization, are these: "Mankind lies groaning, half crushed beneath the weight of its own progress. Men do not sufficiently realize that their future is in their own hands. Theirs is the task of determining first of all whether they want to go on living or not. Theirs is the responsibility, then, for deciding if they want merely to live, or intend to make just the extra effort required for fulfilling, even on their refractory planet, *la fonction essentielle de l'univers, qui est une machine à faire des dieux,* the essential function of the universe, which is a machine for the making of gods."[2]

The universe "a machine for the making of gods" is indeed a startling figure. The universe is likened to a machine, for a machine neither makes nor moves itself; the laws it follows are not of its own design. To Bergson, the world is an instrument in the hand of its Master, who would have men His image and likeness, His partners—"gods." To serve this end is the world's function, its proper office, for the universe is but the "visible and tangible aspect of love and of the need for loving." Man, a creature "capable of loving and of being loved," is the *"raison d'être* of life on our planet," and in creation God undertakes "to create creators, that He may join to Himself beings worthy of His love."[3]

Could there be a more positive recognition of the God who is before all things, on whom all depends and who depends on nothing? It is difficult to conceive that after so unequivocal a statement Edman could have misread the concluding words of Bergson's final work. His grave oversight could easily be used in a futile endeavor to claim for his own skepticism, for the school of vagueness, the philosopher who holds "there is only one truth."[4] Such a misquotation ranks Bergson with those who proudly preach Man the God-maker; it links him, incredibly, with Renan, the false prophet who predicted "the perfect advent of God" through science, "the end of universal progress, a state in which all existing matter will engender a unique resultant, which will be God."[5] Bergson's first writings may indeed have been open to misinterpretation, but never his last book nor, for that matter, his early work in the light of his later. Indeed, it seems to have been the danger of misinterpretation above all that prompted the Church, concerned primarily with the effect of a writing and not with its writer's intent, to list three of his works, *An Essay on the Immediate Data of Consciousness, Matter and Memory,* and *Creative Evolution,* on the Index of Forbidden Books.

That Bergson's philosophy may stand undisturbed in its purity, it may be well to eliminate at once possible confusion, to banish once and for all the ghosts of early misunderstandings which haunt many textbooks and popular essays. When in *Creative Evolution* Bergson likens God to a "center from which worlds shoot out like rockets in a fireworks," when he says of Him that He "has nothing of the already made," some may take these words to mean that his God is "pure becoming," a "God who evolves." But Bergson's thought is this: that God is not a *thing,* but rather "unceasing life, action, freedom." [6] Some time after *Creative Evolution* was published, he himself stated that from his early works, shedding light as they do on the fact of freedom, making tangible the reality of the spirit, presenting creation as a *fact,* "there stands out clearly the idea of a God, Creator and Free, the Author at once of matter and of life." [7] The few words in *Creative Evolution* which speak of God were "but a steppingstone," [8] he said, and that to learn more of God, of Him who speaks to man and to whom man speaks, the good God, Father and Friend, something beyond a biological study was needed: a study of the human heart, penetrating into the depths of man and into the realm that lies beyond him. Hence in the *Two Sources,* the climax of his writings, Bergson can speak more fully and clearly; he can refer to himself as a "philosopher who holds God to be a person." [9]

All shouts of progress notwithstanding, modern man is so deeply disturbed, so disappointed in himself, that he recoils in neurotic fear from the thought that God might be personal, and in this resemble man. He is more at ease with a "Force," a "Something" resembling the electron and, resenting what could be his cure, prefers a mute *It* to *Him* who speaks and demands an answer. Bergson knows, of course, that God is beyond human comprehension, that He is greater than our tongues can tell,[10] but this never leads him to the fashionable confusion that because God is infin-

3

itely above man, He must be far below him. Keener than the protests of those who are so vocal against what they call anthropomorphism is Bergson's horror of gross assimilation of God with man,[11] and he is fully aware that even so exalted an idea and reality as that of "person"—this title of dignity, as St. Thomas calls it[12]—must be stripped of the finite before it can be applied to the Lord. Yet this never brings him to dissolve the Creator in His works. With the Church, he holds to the truth that God is personal, as He is all He is, superabundantly.[13]

In brief, the distortion of the final phrase of the *Two Sources* does more than destroy its meaning; it empties of significance all Bergson's work. Too often has it been his ill fortune to have suffered careless misrepresentation, even granting the room for misunderstanding in his philosophy. Some of his expressions are indeed ambiguous. The title of *Creative Evolution,* for example, could suggest that for him evolution has taken the place of the Creator, but a careful reading shows that it is God who creates in and through evolution, or rather, as the Christian would say, who continues the first act of creation. Evolution is called creative as is an artist, for there is invention, newness, in nature.

Other pitfalls are the defective concepts in which Bergson clothes some of his intuitions. A profound and fruitful grasp of time, of duration, purged his intellectual life and so enriched it that in opposition to those who tried to force the shoreless ocean of reality into the cup of space, he calls movement reality itself.[14] We meet the same overemphasis, the same error, at the close of one of his Oxford lectures: "The more we plunge into [real duration], the more we return in the direction of the principle in which we participate, though it be transcendent, and whose eternity is not one of immutability, but of life: how, otherwise, could we live and move in it? *In ea vivimus et movemur et sumus.*" [15] Indeed, eternity has none of the inertia of matter and all the intensity of life. It is infinite "tension," fullness never to be exhausted, but even so, eternity is changeless, and God, in whom we live and move and are, is "ever in action, ever at rest." [16] For all his overemphasis, Bergson's vision of time leads to intimacy with the real. He sees that inner time is not clock time, that the time in which man lives is not a "thing," not a mere measurement, but a creative principle; it delivers us from the bondage of things already made and frees us for the future, to invent, to enrich and renew ourselves and the world. Truly, time is creative opportunity, grace, the child of eternity,[17] as for Pentateuch and Prophets, the ground where God and man meet. It is in time that man fell, and again, it is in time that man was redeemed.

Bergson's thought is further obscured when its direction is overlooked. His criticism of the idea of nothingness may mislead that reader who neglects to note *whose* idea is criticized, into seeing Bergson as a pantheist. When he finds fault with the notion that Nothing exists prior to all things and that reality is spread out on it "as on a carpet," [18] he is objecting to Spinoza's view of being,[19] but he does not and cannot touch creation-out-of-nothing, the doctrine which teaches that in the first act of creation, God made the world from *no* substratum whatever; that reality is *not* an "embroidery on the canvas of the void";[20] that, in short, the world had a beginning, and God none. Before the universe was, there was nought but God; even to say "before," however, is a concession to our time-bound thinking, because in a sense the world has been "for all time" and is "everywhere," for the *when* and the *where,* time and space, marks of the finite, were created with it. Creation-from-nothing means that Freedom and Love stood at the beginning of the universe.

The work of Bergson suffers, in content and clarity, from his philosophical method, which is "rigorously traced on experience [both inner and outer] and does not permit the statement of a conclusion that in any way whatever goes beyond the empirical considerations on which it is based." [21] When in the eighties Bergson turned to philosophy, he was faced with a "science" that idolized weights and measures, that, in the name of experience, stifled the quest for truth and all deeper understanding. With the very tool of experience—an experience, however, much deeper than that of scientism—he sought to overthrow the idols of the cult. For him, true empiricism purposed "to get as close as possible to the original, to probe more deeply into its life, and by a kind of intellectual auscultation to feel the throbbings of its soul." [22] But in admitting experience as the sole source of knowledge,[23] Bergson crippled his philosophy, being compelled, for example, to discard the rational proofs of God's existence and of the soul's immortality. And there are many things he held with conviction

5

but left unsaid because he had not arrived at them by way of his method.

But whatever the shortcomings and errors of Bergson's philosophy, conscience was the strong guide of his intellectual search. Unlike certain others, he remained faithful to experience, which he considered the only criterion of knowledge, not flinching when he encountered ultimate religious experience. True to his method, he accepted the mystics, trusted them as the men of highest experience, as "bearers of an inner revelation," *porteurs d'une révélation intérieure*. They sense the divine Presence; they see, as it were, the Invisible, hear the Inaudible, clutch the Intangible; they bring evidence of another world, the realm of grace, of which St. John of the Cross is the singer.

Come, end my sufferings quite
Since no one else suffices for physician:
And let mine eyes have sight
Of you, who are their light,
Except for whom I scorn the gift of vision.

Reveal your presence clearly
And kill me with the beauty you discover,
For pains acquired so dearly
From Love, cannot recover
Save only through the presence of the lover.[24]

No longer need we grope in darkness, for "someone has seen, someone has touched, someone knows," [25] Bergson said, and this vision and knowledge, this beckoning, he followed. In *Creative Evolution,* he wished to affirm "nothing that could not in time be confirmed by the tests of biology";[26] in the *Two Sources,* however, he went beyond his earlier conclusions and found Life transcending all the fecundity of earth. While the majority of modern philosophers refuse to see any but the lower rungs of being, Bergson scales the ladder of life. He does not take the part for the whole, the life man shares with beasts and trees for its fullness; to him, the fullness of life is that which makes man partaker of the divine Nature. Hence Père Antonin D. Sertillanges, O.P., likens his thought to "an architecture sister to the cathedrals," and finds Bergson's new spiritualism—spiritualism in its original meaning:

6   *Henri Bergson*

a philosophy which holds the reality of spirit independent of matter—in the greater number of its essential theses, reconcilable with the old.[27]

From Mathematics to Philosophy

Henri Louis Bergson was born in Paris on October 18, 1859, the son of a distinguished musician, whose only fault, Bergson once remarked, was disregard for fame, a fault he himself shared. His father had come to France from Poland, where his ancestors had been Hassidim, followers of Baal-shem-tov, the Jewish mystic, who sought lasting union with God through ecstatic prayer and stressed joy and love as His service. Of his mother, Bergson himself said that she was "a woman of superior intelligence, a religious soul in the most elevated sense, whose goodness, devotion, serenity—I might almost say sanctity—were the admiration of all who knew her." [28]

Bergson's intellectual training began at the Lycée Condorcet, whose classical studies were to leave a strong impress on his mind and later work. So greatly did he excel in them that the Latin elegance of one of his doctoral dissertations won special praise. The literary historian and editor of the *Revue des Deux Mondes*, René Doumic, who had been his schoolmate at the Lycée, welcoming him many years later to the Académie Française, gave a charming sketch of him as a boy: "You were already famous then. You have always been famous. And you know with what intense curiosity everyone looks for the first time upon a famous man or even a famous child; his image is registered forever in the memory. I recall the fragile-looking youth you were in those days, with your tall, slender, slightly swaying figure, with your delicate fair charm, for your abundant blond hair, inclining slightly to red, was then carefully parted on your forehead. That forehead was your most striking feature, broad and bulging, and it might not unfairly be described as huge in contrast with the thinness and refinement of the lower part of the face. The eyes below the arch of that lofty forehead looked out with a slightly astonished gaze, an expression noticeable in reflective persons, unmistakably honest, but veiled and solitary, withdrawn from the outer world and turned within. In your demeanor a good deal of gravity was mingled with much graciousness—a smiling gravity and a simplicity that was not forced, a modesty that was unaffected—and such good

7

manners! You said little, but that little was uttered in a clear, sedate voice, full of deference to your companion's opinion, especially when you were proving to him in your quiet little way, and with that unconcerned air of yours, that his opinion was an absurd one. We had never seen a schoolboy so polite, and that made us regard you as somewhat different from ourselves, though not distant—you were never *that*, and you never have been—but rather, somewhat detached and distinguished. From your whole personality emanated a singular charm; it was something subtle, and even a little mysterious." [29]

To his excellence in the classics, Bergson added an unusual mathematical adroitness, the pride of his school; with the greatest of ease he handled the most difficult problems, among them one of Pascal's, which his professor had not known any other pupil to cope with. When, against all expectation, Bergson decided to devote himself to philosophy, his teacher protested: "A foolish resolve! You might be a mathematician, and you will only be a philosopher. You will have missed your vocation." [30]

In 1878 Bergson entered the École Normale Supérieure, where he studied together with Jean Jaurès, who was to become the leader of Socialism in France. The two got on agreeably though they were entirely different. While the one sought company with whom he could talk, and talk loudly, the other loved seclusion and reflective silence. Many of Bergson's fellow students spent their leisure at the café in discussions and arguments, and urged Bergson to take part; but having sought and won the appointment as student librarian, he preferred to pass almost all his time among books. [31]

In 1881 he earned second place at the *Agrégation de philosophie*. Then, and later as a teacher at the *lycées* of Angers, Carcassonne and Clermont-Ferrand, his study of Herbert Spencer confronted him with a difficulty. Spencer's mechanistic theory seemed at first to meet his demands for exactness, for clearness and precision, and he dreamed of expanding and defining it, of extending it to the whole universe by using all the tools science had to offer. Led, however, by his disciplined mind, by a will never to bend reality to preconception but rather to conform his thought to reality, he found that mechanistic thought did not cover the facts, that it was

8   *Henri Bergson*

unable to solve, particularly, the problem of time. Hence he courageously abandoned Spencer's mechanism and set out anew to search for truth.

Those who held the chairs of philosophy could not, he felt, answer the problems of philosophy—they dwelt either in the suffocating climate of the block universe or in the thin air of "idealism." The "self-effacing" materialists thought all was matter; unable to see the mind, they said it did not exist; man was nothing but a "minded body." Soul there was none, it was at best a name for a bundle of associations; thought but the vapor escaping the crucible of the brain, or nothing more than the energy set free by the impact of little molecules ruled by the despotism of mechanical law. As there was no soul, there could be no freedom, no immortality, no religion, all of which were called dreams and illusions, or relics of man's immaturity, specters of the past, harmful to human progress. There were on the other hand the "self-centered" idealists. To some, the whole world was merely a projection of the mind, each man a sun surrounded, as if by planets, by a universe of his own making. Others maintained that there was no hope of grasping the "thing-as-such"; all man could know was the mold cast upon the world by his mind. Likewise, he could never *know* free will, imperishable life, God, but he could *reason* to them and had to act as though they existed, there being no other foundation for moral life.

Bergson was too sound to be misled by idealism, despite the allurement it exercised for so many. He would not live in the world of "as-if," in which things fade, knowledge is compromised, virtue attenuated. Nor was he tempted to adopt the determinist position, which held sway over many philosophers of the time. The inner life was to him "a *given,* refractory to any reconstruction by the world outside." [32] Brushing aside both doctrines as arbitrary, as hindrances to philosophical thought, obstacles in progress toward truth,[33] he began his work unaided, save for his readiness to learn, his docility under the tutelage of all that is, the ever-renewed effort with which he faced every new problem, the penetration of reality to which he gave almost prayerful attention.

Always giving science its full due, Bergson nonetheless refused to give it more than its due, to worship it as a fetish. Doumic, in his

9

address before the Académie, emphasized this when he said: "In freeing philosophy from the domination which the sciences were unduly exercising over it, you have nevertheless not belied your scientific training. Quite the contrary, in fact. You knew more of science than the philosophers who were your predecessors; and on this account you recognized the sphere and noted its limits better. Where they had but a superficial smattering, you possessed long practice and familiarity. It was your extensive knowledge of the sciences that enabled you to deliver philosophy from a yoke that was only apparently scientific . . . and that for the greater honor and benefit, not only of philosophy, but also of science itself." [34]

Master and Masters

For years Bergson toiled, investigated what science had to offer, selected the pertinent facts, but at the same time sought a direct vision of man's interior life. Then, in his *Essay on the Immediate Data of Consciousness* (1889), he made secure the prize of freedom. The self, infallible when affirming its immediate experience, feels free and says so. But no sooner does it attempt to explain its freedom than it sees itself no longer directly, but refracted through space, and perforce expresses freedom by mechanical symbols.[35] The conscious life of the self, Bergson emphatically declares, is something other than a sum of sensations, feelings and ideas, something beyond an assemblage of psychic states. Consciousness is an indivisible unfolding, and "when we try to cut through it, it is as if we were rapidly passing a blade through a flame; all that we divide is the space it occupies." [36] Not frozen, the states of the living self are in flux; not isolated, they are interwoven like the notes of a melody, for consciousness is a current, a unity. The psychologist who recognizes only associations sees but a shadow of man's self; what he grasps are slices, cross sections of the current. He subdivides the interior life to render its states reproducible, after the manner of physical phenomena, to which the law of causality applies; he makes them amenable to the discipline of language, which expresses what is common to all men but not what is unique, what is personal.[37] This method of his is indeed useful, or may be useful, but its limitations must not be forgotten.

"We are free," says Bergson, "when our acts spring from our entire personality, when they express it, when they bear that indefinable

10 *Henri Bergson*

resemblance sometimes found between the work and the artist." In our daily round, our behavior is indeed for the most part like that of a mechanism. Rising in the morning is such an act: the sounding of the clock, an impression from without, makes us rise because certain sensations, feelings, and ideas have become solidified in our mind. The impression does not stir our entire consciousness, as if it were a stone thrown into water, but merely moves an idea solidified, as it were, on the surface—the idea of rising and going about our daily tasks.[38]

To acts of this kind, to the numerous, though generally insignificant, matters of routine, the associationist theory applies, but never to the relatively few acts which bear the imprint of our personality. "It is a gross psychology, dupe of language, which alleges that the soul is determined by sympathy, aversion, or hate, as by so many forces which press upon it. These feelings, provided that they attain sufficient depth, represent each the entire soul, in the sense that the whole content of the soul is reflected in each one of them. To say that the soul is determined under the influence of any of these sentiments is thus to acknowledge that it determines itself." There is freedom, where the "I" can claim fatherhood.[39]

More than once it has been said that this is spontaneity rather than freedom. In a masterly study, Père Sertillanges defends Bergson against this reproach,[40] marshaling to his support the "heart" of Pascal's Pensées, and Aristotle's striking phrase: "Moral choice is a will-ing reason or a reasoning will, and such a principle of action is a man." [41] He thinks it an error to oppose the intellectualism of St. Thomas to Bergson's "anti-intellectualism," for these designations apply only in the most general manner: St. Thomas is intellectualist in that he makes will dependent on counsel, but he is "anti-intellectualist" in that counsel remains undetermined save for the intervention of the will. St. Thomas and Bergson agree that reason does not determine choice, except when it is itself determined to determine it. In free acts, the determinations by reason and will interchange, an interchange which the unique subject permits and the profound nature of the spirit demands; the celebrated allegory of the halt and the blind is its symbol. The halt advances carried on the shoulders of the blind and, guided by the eyes of the halt, the blind man takes the right road. Such a pair is the human soul, but far more subtle; animated at once by

11

the vision of the mind and the dynamism of the will, it can both direct itself and act. Intelligence is master of deliberation, but not of its exercise, which is voluntary; the will is master of the act, but not of its specification, which is intellectual. Man, through both, is master of both, and hence free. On free will, Père Sertillanges concludes, the doctrine of St. Thomas and that of Bergson are far from hostile; they are on the contrary reconcilable, and Bergson, in a letter to him, accepts his findings.[42]

Again, Raïssa Maritain finds that Bergson established a psychological rather than a metaphysical doctrine of freedom, and states: "On its psychological plane, Bergson's doctrine of freedom is in no way incompatible with the metaphysical conclusions of Aristotle and St. Thomas. It is only when it is presented as a metaphysics of freedom that it reveals its insufficiency. Be that as it may, in the two philosophies the conclusion is the same: it affirms liberty as the characteristic of personality." [43]

Bergson's doctrine of freedom tends to heighten the sense of moral responsibility. Because habit is voluntary in origin, habit—in Thomistic philosophy our readiness, born of repeated acts, to do certain things—partakes of our freedom, as long as it is permitted to continue. But Bergson reminds us how important it is for the depth of our lives to refresh and renew our habits by fresh vision and renewed moral choice. That in most of our daily actions, on the other hand, we are "conscious automata" is to our advantage, for in this we have everything to gain: full freedom for the important tasks.[44] We act mechanically in part, Bergson points out, that we may become more fully human as a whole; it is our dignity, the noble burden we carry, to choose and direct our more or less mechanical activities. Since the fullness of freedom is manifest in those acts stamped by our personalities, we are called upon to cleanse and carve, to mold ourselves. We are, according to the infallible testimony of immediate experience, "creators of our intentions, of our decisions, of our acts, and hence, of our habits, of our characters, of our selves. Artisans of our lives, even artists when we will, we work continually with the material furnished us by past and present, by heredity and circumstances, to form a figure unique, new, original, unforeseeable as the form given by the sculptor to the clay." [45] So wrote Bergson in accepting the Nobel Prize.

But from first to last, we are not sufficient to this challenge; what we need is a "supplement to the soul." These are Bergson's words in another connection. Meditating on man and on his tools as extensions of his limbs and senses, he says that today, when this body has grown out of measure, the soul remains what it was, too small to fill it, too weak to guide it. "What we need are new reserves of moral energy . . . and the body, now larger, waits for a supplement to the soul. The mechanical summons up the mystical." [46] Only grace safeguards our freedom—grace, that mistress who frees in binding us to the Source of life. *Perierat homo per liberam voluntatem: venit Deus homo per gratiam liberatricem,* "by free will man was lost, then by grace the God-Man set him free," says St. Augustine.[47] In going back to our origin, we cease to be slaves to "natural necessities, we shall once more stand erect, masters associated with a greater Master." [48] In the mystics, captives of love, "instruments of God," [49] Bergson finds the highest freedom.

In seeing thus the mystery of freedom, not only the man Bergson but also the philosopher proves himself of the lineage of Abraham, Isaac, and Jacob. From Sinai's "Thou shalt" and "Thou shalt not," to the Prophet's "Return, O Israel, to the Lord thy God," [50] Israel, and with it mankind and every soul, being chosen by God, is called to choose Him. At the beginning of history, man's freedom was summoned by the commandment in Eden, the first bidding to trust and obey; again and again impaired by sin, it is recaptured and brought to fulfillment when the bride triumphantly says: "Now that He is mine, I will never leave Him." [51]

Memory, Suggestion of Immortality

Determinism had tried to shackle the spirit; in the *Immediate Data of Consciousness* Bergson breaks these fetters. In *Matter and Memory,* published in 1897, the year he became lecturer at the École Normale Supérieure, he lays bare the shallowness of a psychology which accredits to the tissues of the brain the magical property of giving birth to thought, accredits to matter some occult power, "mindedness." It is folly to think that, could we behold at a given moment the dance of the atoms which make up the cortex, and had we, furthermore, the "key to psychophysiology," we should know every detail of the corresponding consciousness. There is indeed a close connection between a state of consciousness and the brain, "but there is also a close connection between a coat

13

and the nail on which it hangs, for if the nail is pulled out, the coat falls to the ground. Shall we say then that the shape of the nail gives us the shape of the coat, or in any way corresponds to it?" There is no parallelism between conscious life and the brain at work; "in most cases, the psychical state seems immensely wider than the cerebral state," [52] and the brain is, says Bergson, using a metaphor by others often abused, "no more than a kind of central telephone exchange: its role is to make connections, or to delay them. It adds nothing to what it receives." [53] The office of the brain concerns movements alone—those of the outside world which impinge upon the body, and those of the body which in turn impinge upon the outside world. The brain can affect and be affected by physically present bodies only—an absent body, unable to be perceived, cannot affect it. Hence human memory, in which the physically absent becomes the mentally present, in which the past is brought before us; memory, with its dominion over the gone by, over all the worlds we have known, is no function of the brain; "it is not a manifestation of matter; it is spirit." [54]

Bergson's conclusion is based on scientific facts, on clinical observation; it was his genius that found its way through the jungle of technical material and often distorted theories. Prior to the publication of *Matter and Memory*, Jacques Chevalier points out, the theory of detailed localization of the functions of the brain, which maintains that there are compartments, so to speak, in which are stored all our images with their interrelations, was unchallenged, and it is still widely held.[55] Far from being science, this seems hardly more than prejudiced interpretation of often imaginary data—a perfect example of materialistic bias. The exact study of injuries to the brain shows that in the case of a distinct localized lesion accompanied by a loss of memory, it is not the recollections of a certain period of our lives, nor a group of recollections logically intertwined, which disappear, but those pertaining to one of the senses or to bodily movements. The vanished memories are all auditory, or all visual, or all motor. In truth, the memories do *not* vanish—at least, cerebral pathology gives no indication whatever that they are in any way altered; what are damaged are the nervous pathways, the cerebral links, which permit the memories to manifest themselves. Thus hindered in its use of the brain by cerebral disorders, memory is rendered powerless. There are, it is to be granted, forms of amnesia in which an entire period of life seems obliterated, but it is in just such instances that no precise lesion can be found.

These and similar findings indicate to Bergson that memories are not stored up in the brain, are not a deposit in its cells. The brain but mimes the thought, translates it into action, links it to the outside world.[56] For the present, the body is the trysting place of the spirit and things; it is to the soul what a compass is to the seafarer, orientating it to its surroundings and permitting it to fix its attention upon them. In short, the soul needs the body as an instrument of manifestation, but not as a condition for existence;[57] it uses the body to work and act, but can live without it. Thus survival becomes, if not certain, at least so very probable that the burden of proof rests upon the doubter.[58]

It may be fruitful to recall here St. Augustine's thought on the transcendent character of memory. Present to man's consciousness, according to his *Confessions*, is what is without, and within, and above man. In darkness, he says, I can, if I will, bring forth colors in my memory, and in silence, song. "Great is the power of memory, exceeding great, O my God, a wide and limitless sanctuary. Who can plumb its depths? . . . Great is the power of memory, a thing, my God, before which to tremble, a profound and infinite multiplicity, and this is mind, and this am I. What then am I, O my God? . . . A life various and manifold and boundless indeed." Through all that is kept in memory, "I race and run, and, probe deeply as I can, there is no end. Such is the power of memory, such the power of life in mortal man." [59] Asking himself where in his memory God might dwell, St. Augustine answers: "Why do I seek in what place of memory Thou dwellest, as though there were places in my memory?" [60] His doctrine reaches its height in his treatise *On the Trinity*, where memory, understanding and will—"not three lives but one life, not three minds but one mind, not three substances but one substance" [61]—are seen as a trinity that mirrors the Triune God. For Bergson, memory proves the reality of the spirit and suggests its survival; for Augustine, memory leads beyond itself to God.

Loyal to his principle of affirming nothing that scientific experience could not, in due time, demonstrate, Bergson speaks of the survival of the spirit, and not of its immortality. Science demands,

15

he concludes, the categorical affirmation that the spirit is capable of surviving the body; for certitude of its continued existence, however, and for light on its endless duration, we must, he stresses, have recourse to religion. His philosophical method makes him neglect any metaphysical proof of immortality, and limits him to the assertion that life need not end with the death of the body; but this very weakness serves the truth. The modern mind pretends to be rooted in nothing but experience—how vainly is demonstrated by Bergson's proof that spirit is independent of matter and that the soul can survive the body. He has made clear that those who deny immortality cannot claim the support of science. Let us add that though here and now souls require bodies to communicate with one another, there is nothing at all in science to exclude a state in which souls could commune without the ministry of matter, by their very presence, at a simple glance.

There is absolutely nothing in science to make impossible the beatific vision hereafter. It is an instance of Bergson's modesty as a philosopher that, for the final and unfailing answer, he points to religion. Though "no eye has seen, no ear has heard, no human heart conceived, what God has prepared for those that love Him," [62] Bergson is not among those who would have it that *nothing* awaits man.

From the time of *Matter and Memory,* the problem of immortality never left Bergson. There are the often quoted words from *Creative Evolution:* "All the living hold together, and all yield to the same tremendous push. The animal takes its stand on the plant, man bestrides animality, and the whole of humanity, in space and in time, is one immense army galloping beside and before and behind each of us in an overwhelming charge able to beat down every resistance and clear the most formidable obstacles, perhaps even death." [63] This has often been taken for an encomium of life, a praise of vitality. But what Bergson wants to say is rather that biology hints at an afterlife for man. In reviewing development in nature, he finds a suggestion of unending life, but he feels able to say no more than "perhaps." After his study of the lives of the mystics, however, he will deal with no mere possibility; his question will become: Is the afterlife identical with mystical experience, which is a participation in the divine life? To which his answer will be: It is a probability, a probability capable of being transformed into a certainty.[64] Here the philosopher approaches the theologian who calls the life of perfection *quaedam inchoatio beatitudinis*, the beginning, as it were, of the life of bliss.[65]

Exult, O dust and ashes,
The Lord shall be thy part,
His only, His forever
Thou shalt be and thou art.[66]

Life, Beauty, Grace

As in *Matter and Memory* he reestablishes the essential difference between spirit and matter, so in *Creative Evolution* (1907) Bergson, now professor at the Collège de France, reaffirms that between man and animal. Man can learn exercise of any kind; he can construct any sort of object; in short, he can acquire any kind of motor habit. But in even the best-endowed animal, the ape, this faculty of combining new movements is strictly limited. "In the animal, invention is never anything but a variation on the theme of routine. If it escapes automatism, it is only for an instant, for just the time to create a new automatism. The gates of its prison close as soon as they are opened; by pulling at its chain, it succeeds only in stretching it." While in the animal, vital energy is consumed in the business of remaining alive, it is not so in man, Bergson continues. In man, life is not the captive of the mechanisms it has constructed; unceasingly, he can oppose to old habits, new, making both the body given him and the tools he has added to it serve him as he pleases. There is an abyss between animal and man, that between the closed and the open, the limited and the unlimited; the difference, Bergson concludes, is one not of degree but of nature.[67]

Man is "memory in matter," "freedom incarnate"; he conquers the inert, masters the world about him, moves freely in the midst of constraint. Doubtless, he owes his unique position in the universe to his superior brain, which enables him to build an unlimited number of motor mechanisms; to language, which, offering consciousness an immaterial body, frees it from dwelling exclusively on material bodies; and to social life, which stores and preserves efforts as language stores thought. But brain, language, society are only the "external and various signs of one and the same internal superiority." [68]

This being so, it is disappointing to read that souls are "nothing else than the little rills into which the great river of life divides itself, flowing through the body of humanity." [69] It is Bergson's distinguished service to have rediscovered the spirit, to have emphasized its greatness when it was the fashion to belittle it; it is his merit to have upheld the reality of the person and man's privileged place in nature. But when he immerses man too deeply in cosmic development, he is led not by the force of any scientific data, rather by one aspect of his metaphysics, with its overstress on movement. Aristotle, on the contrary, having refuted the possibility of the soul's arising from the fetus, says that it enters the body, as it were, through a door—that is, from without—and that it alone comes immediately from God.[70] For the perennial philosophy, the soul is a reality not springing *from* the cosmos, but inserted *into* it; not evolved, but in the fullest sense created; made by no agent, but directly by the Lord.[71]

Nonetheless, as he himself states, Bergson hopes to remain within the limits of a true spiritualism, and while claiming for spirit and matter a community of origin within the cosmos, he disavows for them common roots. Spirit (in the language of his dynamic philosophy, that which rises, which makes itself) and matter (that which falls and unmakes itself) are distinct, and are opposed to each other as radically as possible. They have nothing in common, he says, save the initial creative impulse, which appertains neither to the one nor to the other.[72]

The definition of matter as that which unmakes itself is based on the second principle of thermodynamics, which expresses the fact that the total amount of randomness in the universe is increasing, that usable energy tends to run down into used, to be degraded into heat, which in turn tends to be distributed uniformly. This fact shows the energy of the physical world to be finite and poses the question: Whence does it come? The answers of some physicists—that the energy of our solar system comes from some other part of space, or that periods of increase and decrease of utilizable energy succeed each other forever—are indemonstrable and wholly

18   *Henri Bergson*

improbable; they are mere evasions. The origin of energy, says Bergson, "must be sought in an extra-spatial process." [73] Yes, the source of all finite energy must be sought in One who is infinite Energy, ever spending Itself, never spent. But if the beginnings of energy have to be traced to a process outside of space, how much more the genesis of the spirit!

Bergson carefully refrains from calling evolution a fact; he thinks it probable. Frankly accepting the evolutionist hypothesis, he dissents, however, from the Darwinian idea that an automatic elimination of the unfit is the driving power of the development of species. Natural selection and the struggle for life may explain what has perished, but not what has survived.[74] (It is interesting that Darwin himself protested the assumption that he attributed the modification of species solely to natural selection. He deemed it the "most important, but not the exclusive, means of modification." [75]) Outer circumstances are indeed the conditions under which evolution must work, "the forces with which it must reckon," but are not its directing causes. Bergson postulates "an original impetus, an internal push, that has carried life, by more and more complex forms, to higher and higher destinies." [76] This impetus, the *élan vital,* is a current of consciousness which has penetrated matter, bearing within it the causes of the unlike forms in which life manifests itself. At its base it is one, and in the course of evolution has followed three divergent paths: those of vegetative torpor, of instinct, and of intelligence. Intelligence is thus made but a single vector of the movement launched by the *élan vital,* merely an arrow in the sheaf of life,[77] and man is in a way absorbed into the stream of evolution.

Life is accredited with a power it does not possess: the power of giving birth to the spirit. But still, Bergson's thought should not be confused with ordinary biologism. Whatever reservations must be made about the position he gives to life, it is a grave mistake, not to say an injustice, to class his view with that of the so-called "philosophers of life." All they have in common is a name. Nothing could be further from Bergson than Nietzsche's deification of vitality, or Ludwig Klages's war against the spirit, "the adversary of the soul," the spirit which, "mother-murdering," wounds life. He could never think, let alone write, as did Nietzsche, that the most heinous offense is to blaspheme the earth. Nor would he ever condemn, with Klages, civilization and history as evil because in them "waking towers over dreaming, action tending toward permanence over life which comes and goes." [78] There is no *ressentiment*, no malice, in his thought, which sees life as the bearer of the spirit. No doubt, his criticism of concepts as "snapshots" [79] is one-sided, seeing their shortcomings but not the greatness of the faculty which "conceives" the world. It is not, however, the vitalism of the *Lebensphilosophen* which leads Bergson to this criticism, but a genuine repulsion from the abuses of man's intellectual power by an arid scientism, a withered rationalism. For him the mystery of life, the invisible breath that bears all living, comes to light in the maternal love of animals, often so touching, and in the solicitude of the plant for its seed. "This love," he adds, "may possibly deliver us life's secret." [80] Not until he had met a love of which this care is but a reflection and analogy, was he to speak with greater sureness.

Apart from a metaphysics which, too enchanted by movement, is tempted to ignore the thing that moves, and apart from a quite inadequate view on the origin of the spirit, Bergson's intuition of the *élan vital* contains a certain contribution toward the understanding of the universe. Having been given once for all, the vital impetus is finite, the free issue of a free God. And, according to Bergson, nature follows this impulse given her at the beginning, as a poet follows the inspiration he has received. She manifests finality, but does not, he thinks, proceed like a workman with a preconceived plan or the intention of imitating a model. We have to add, however, that it is only when viewed from without that nature does not seem to follow a plan, for it is precisely God's prescience and predetermination—or, to speak more truly, His everpresent vision and will—which guarantee the "genius and originality" of nature. She is "creative," says Bergson, and tends toward freedom, toward the spirit; she searches, feels her way, finding various solutions, and in her prolific unity displays an infinite richness; in her endless variety (to some but a meaningless disorder), she mirrors an overflowing Bounty, a Goodness which communicates Itself.[81]

It is an act of condescension that is manifest in the universe—here Bergson seems to make his own the view on the origin of things expressed by Félix Ravaisson, his predecessor in the Académie des

Sciences Morales et Politiques, who helped prepare the metaphysical revival in France. That which is most striking about the things of nature, Bergson says in his discourse *The Life and Work of Ravaisson,* is their beauty, and that beauty is the more accentuated in the measure that nature ascends from the inorganic to the organic, from plant to animal, from animal to man. Beauty belongs to form, and form is recorded movement. Hence, those forms are most beautiful which are described by graceful movements, says Bergson, quoting Leonardo da Vinci's "Beauty is grace arrested." And he continues: "In all that is graceful, we see, we feel, we divine, a kind of abandon—as it were, a condescension. Thus, for him who contemplates the universe with the eye of an artist, it is grace that is read through beauty, and it is goodness that shines through grace. All things manifest, in the movement recorded by their forms, the infinite generosity of a principle which gives itself. And not wrongly do we call by the same name charm of movement and the act of liberality characteristic of divine goodness." [82] This account of Ravaisson's thought is really the hidden core of *Creative Evolution.*

The Closed and the Open

With the publication of *Creative Evolution* in 1907, Bergson reached the height of his renown, but fame, which corrupts many a man, did not destroy him nor halt his search. He withdrew into near silence and devoted himself, despite the burden of serious illness, to a patient and tenacious study of the origin of religion and morality. From all fields that could possibly shed light on his problem, he gathered data, tested, pondered, mastered them. Then, in 1932, after twenty-five years of painstaking inquiry and profound meditation, he published *The Two Sources of Morality and Religion,* a "classic from the day it appeared." [83]

It deals a damaging blow to all pseudo ethics. In it, Bergson unfolds the difference between the laws of nature and of ethics, and thereby exposes the delusion of those who imagine that from another Sinai, modern science has handed down new tablets. Never can the moral law, whose character is imperative, be drawn from science, which speaks in the indicative, which states facts, or perhaps only probabilities. Declaring: So it is, or so it seems, science is, by its very nature, unable to go further and to formulate a command: Thou shalt, thou shalt not. Bergson bares the rationalist fallacy that morality can be based on pure reason, for not only is obligation independent of our awareness of it and prior to any rational clarification, but reason alone cannot stifle the evil in man. "When philosophers maintain that it should be sufficient to silence selfishness and passion," Bergson says with gentle irony, "they prove to us—and this is a matter for congratulation—that they have never heard the voice of the one or the other very loud within themselves."

The *Two Sources* also unmasks the protest against morality which would have it the mere product of history, an agreement among men like the bylaws of a club. It exposes that pretentious revolt which, having rendered man helpless, makes him servile to the state as the supreme value, the source of all right. Bergson's distinction between closed and open morality shows the abortive, the monstrous character of statism, which, cut off from the highest Source of good, rots from within. Morality cannot be man-made, the fruit of time, for human nature has remained essentially unchanged. Both primitive and civilized man know moral obligation, for obligation is the "irreducible, the ever-present element in our moral nature." [84]

Two forces, according to Bergson, mold our moral standards and gauges: the demands of society and the appeal of great souls—while the one weighs on man, the other draws him. His view of social obligation ought not be mistaken for that of certain modern sociologists. To him, social sense is innate in normal man, like the faculty of speech, and social pressure does not come exactly from without, society existing within each of its members, and man's social sense pressing on his individual self. This natural obligation assumes the form of impulsion, which, though stemming from a society composed of free beings, in a way imitates nature: it imposes habits that play a role similar to that of necessity, it introduces a regularity bearing some analogy to the inflexible order of natural phenomena, and it does all this to assure its own continuance and the continuance of the individual. Hence, social pressure tends to routine, to blind mechanism, and the moral attitude it begets must needs be static and closed. The man formed by it will be absorbed in the task of individual and social preservation, and will thus remain self-centered. He will do no more than is necessary; his is the ethics of the minimum. [85]

But there is, Bergson emphasizes, the other morality, beyond and above social pressure, one of aspiration. It is the morality of the maximum, of the "may" and not the "must," yielding to love and not to fear, not easily reduced to impersonal formulae, rather embodied in privileged persons who walk before us as leaders. "Inspired by their example, we follow them, as it were joining an army of conquerors. They are indeed conquerors: they have broken down natural resistance and raised humanity to a new destiny." They are the men who let themselves be overcome by an onslaught of love, a love "transposing human life into another tone," by a mighty current passing from their hearts to God and flowing back again from God to mankind. Exceptional souls, they sense their kinship with the soul of Everyman; being borne on a great surge of love for all humanity, they cannot remain within the limits of the group nor halt at the solidarity laid down by nature. These "great men of the good," *ces grands hommes de bien,* invite to imitation; though not seeking it, they wield power over men which spans space and time, the power to awaken souls to their innermost life.[86]

The great men of the good exercise this power by their very existence, by a life that is heroic. In the role in which Bergson casts these chosen souls, indeflectible in their pursuit of the good, Père Sertillanges sees vindicated the Catholic doctrine of the veneration of the saints.[87] By following Christ, they spur us to follow them, and in their company Him who cast fire upon the earth. To be a saint is to be a stranger to mediocrity, which is the enemy of a full moral life. "We live to make effort," Bergson exclaims; "we exist the more, the more we are in a state of 'tension.' The moral rule which appears to me the highest and most fruitful is to choose, of two duties, the one that costs the more." [88] It is his conviction that our task on earth is to strive and stake, and that we exist in proportion to our alertness. But his "highest rule" ought not be interpreted as though he thought the most painful and burdensome necessarily the best; rather does it demand magnanimity, the greatest giving of self. Heroism, says Bergson, is the only road to love.[89]

The theory of the two sources of morality affords many striking and most valuable insights, but it does not do full justice to what Bergson calls the "static," and fails to give a true philosophy of obligation. He likens social pressure, the tribute society exacts for its protection and ours, to instinct in the animal world; he calls it a force, a necessity—but what is necessary is not an obligation. It is just where necessity leaves off that obligation begins, for the ends of creation are attained in the natural order by sheer weight; in the moral order, they are accomplished by a free response to value, by a choice that embraces the good, because in the moral order, God, Master and Author of both realms, has renounced nature's coercion in favor of man's dignity. Stopping short of man's full stature, the closed morality is rather a "pre-morality";[90] social pressure precedes true moral obligation. The "impetus of love," however, marking the open morality, in a way surpasses it. The "more or less irresistible attraction" springing from the fervor of the mystics, from the men possessed by the good and sped by love, goes indeed beyond mere duty. This "emotion," the spiritual movement before which obstacles vanish, the stirring of the soul which carries us along lost in utter joy,[91] though never dispensing with moral obligation, yet excels it. Indeed, this flaming aspiration is somewhat analogous to the readiness and docility bestowed on us by the gifts of the Spirit, by those special promptings we owe to the superabundance of God's goodness.[92]

True obligation is something between social "servitude" and mystical surrender; it is the goal of the one and the beginning of the other, master of pressure, servant of love. Neither the weight of the city of men in which we dwell, nor the allurement of the city of God which the mystics bid us enter, constitutes true obligation, which is no more and no less than the binding character of the eternal law reflected in the mind of man. And our freedom must will the law our intelligence recognizes, sometimes by an immediate sympathetic grasp, sometimes by an arduous discursive effort. Rightly repelled, however, by the frigid and haughty goddess the rationalists call reason, Bergson goes so far in his opposition as to dim the light and power of intelligence. It is a consequence of a metaphysics which denies intelligence its proper place that the *Two Sources* cannot present a true concept of moral obligation; that it hardly mentions responsibility, sin, or contrition; that it seems to ignore that change of heart we call penitence, the merit of virtue and the penalty of sin.[93]

Wanting though his moral philosophy may be, its deficiencies are not such as to blind Bergson to the crucial influence of Christianity. He sees clearly that to it is owed man's moral ascent, his decisive advance. In the Name of Jahve, the prophets had demanded that right be done, and "imparted to justice its violently imperative character," or, rather, inserted into history what had always been justice's own. They had thundered in Israel, yet their cry was heard without her bounds when the Church, with Christ's message, carried their word forth from Jerusalem, and those who had preceded Him became His train. "It is their voice we hear when a great injustice has been done and condoned. From the depths of the centuries they raise their protest." [94]

We must thank Christianity that the walls were leveled which separated city from city, man from man, free from slave. "There is nothing more instructive," says Bergson, "than to see how the philosophers have skirted round the [change from the closed to the open morality], touched it, and yet missed it." [95] The Greek philosophers taught indeed the excellence of man, but what they meant was rather the excellence of the Greek, of the man "born free." The full dignity of the person, the equal worth of all men, humanity's common bond, were unknown to them. Reflecting Greek thought, which considered slavery natural, Aristotle, for example, saw in slaves merely animate tools, and called the enslavement of barbarians a form of hunting.[96] There are, further, the noble doctrines that have arisen in China, but their ideal of true manhood, their counsels of reverence, seem to have been conceived for the Chinese community; they display no concern for those beyond its pale. Again, at the dawn of Christianity the Stoics spoke of love for mankind, of the kinship of all men, of the one law that binds them and the common citizenship they hold in the universe.[97] But with significant inconsistency, these dicta were often addressed to men as Roman[98] and enlightened;[99] they were sayings to be relished, not to be taken in earnest, expressions of a dream, impracticable and unreal. There was no life or power in them, so that for St. Augustine, only their ashes survived.[100] But it is an undying fire Christ cast among men: "Mankind had to wait till Christianity for the idea of universal brotherhood, with its implication of equality of rights and the sanctity of the person, to become a working reality." [101]

With experience as his touchstone, Bergson accepts the witness of history that the philosophies could never have achieved what Christianity has brought about: the transformation of man's conscience and, eventually, the embodiment of the rights of man in code and constitution. The systems are pale beside the glow and color of the gospel; they are shadow where it is light. They lingered where they were planted, tarried where they grew, but the word of Christ is "broadcast to the ends of the earth in a message overflowing with love, evoking love in return." The philosophies were not at fault in that they lacked the vigor of the gospel, for they are the thought of men, a human approach toward perfect morality; in the gospel, God breaks His way into the "city," man's narrow domain, and invades his mind. While the philosophies are *logoi spermatikoi*, seeds of truth, in the gospel speaks the Word. Here truth is not merely propounded; it is preached and done— it lives and suffers, and as the drama of infinite Love, the gospel has changed the breath of the world, given it a new emotion. "Spiritual expansion, missionary zeal, impetus, movement, all these are of Judaic-Christian origin." [102]

It seems one of the ironies of history that this emotion can be divorced from the truth that bore it, and so it comes that the enemies of Christianity fight on borrowed zeal, and live unknowing, or rather wishing not to know, on a borrowed heritage. Doubtless, man can believe or disbelieve the gospel, but he cannot altogether escape its air; he cannot act as though it were not.

If the lost word is lost, if the spent word is spent
If the unheard, unspoken
Word is unspoken, unheard;
Still is the unspoken word, the Word unheard,
The Word without a word, the Word within
The world and for the world;
And the light shone in darkness and
Against the Word the unstilled world still whirled
About the centre of the silent Word.[103]

For Bergson, the gospel has lost nothing with the passing of time; it is a continuous spring of morality, a spring peerless and most potent. In two conversations with Jean Wahl of the Sorbonne, he insisted, in almost identical terms, that "Hitler confirms what I said in the *Two Sources*. Through him it is proven that he who is against Christianity is against morality, and that he who is against morality is against Christianity." [104] To restate Bergson's view: It is Life that is the fountain of morality—the life that courses through mankind, and that life with which the souls of the mystics overflow—and it may not be straying too far afield, rather following his thought to its end, to say that the two sources are nature and grace, the life that is man's as creature, the life that is his in and through Christ.

"Totem and Taboo"

The *Two Sources* also proposes a theory of religion, with which the many pedestrian attempts of the day cannot compare. There have been in the past, and there are today, human societies with neither science nor art nor philosophy, "but there has never been a society without religion." "Being coextensive with our species, [religion] must pertain to our structure." [105] It is characteristic of man and uniquely his; he is the religious animal, the only one that worships.

As in the moral realm, Bergson distinguishes in the religious, two kinds: static and dynamic religion. The static he holds to be a work of nature, a shield for the corporate life of society against intelligence, which would disrupt it were it not protected by what is a virtual instinct, man's myth-making faculty. Hence, tribal religion is seen first as a defensive reaction against the "dissolvent powers of intelligence." Left to itself, he says, intelligence would counsel primarily egoism, but nature, being on the watch, creates in "sacred customs" a safeguard.

Another aspect of primitive religion is nature's defensive reaction against man's awareness of his own death, Bergson continues. No other creatures on earth expect to die; they are simply carried along by the momentum of living, clinging blindly to life with an instinctive "confidence" that today will prolong itself into a tomorrow. But man is haunted by the depressing thought that he, like every living thing about him, must end by dying, a knowledge tending to lame the life of the individual and that of society. Nature, then, intent on the progress of life, opposes to the idea presented by intelligence that death is inevitable, the idea of life after death. Primitive man believes in shades or phantoms, but

27

Bergson is at pains to point out that this delusion is one only in part; it is the shape in which naïve imaginations vest immortality that is hallucinatory, and not the idea itself.[106] Man has pictured life after death in bizarre colors, but no notion of it, however deranged, can affect its reality.

Viewed from a third angle, instinctive religion seems to Bergson a defensive reaction of nature against the discouraging gap that intelligence both introduces and apprehends between the initiative taken and its desired outcome. An animal is sure of itself, for the life impulse is optimistic. Man, on the other hand, is conscious of risk, of the unforeseen to which he and his undertakings are exposed, of circumstances on which he depends but cannot govern. Thus the myth-making faculty imagines friendly powers concerned with his success and hostile powers to explain his failures. It is not fear that makes gods, Bergson affirms; superstition has its origin rather in a reaction against fear.[107]

There is truth in this "biological" interpretation of instinctive religion, and the *Two Sources* contains many acute observations on so-called primitive mentality, magic and totemism. But in not allowing intelligence to play its full part, Bergson's theory ignores much of reality. Jacques Maritain has aptly commented that its weakness is like that of certain celebrated aphorisms; their opposites tell a truth equally profound. That "Genius is patience long drawn out," is certainly true, but it is equally, if not more, pointed to say that "Genius is impatience long drawn out." [108] Bergson thinks that the intelligence disheartens man and strikes him with fear, that the powerful instincts of life use the myth-making faculty to sustain the urge to live. Is it not rather life that weighs on man, and his spirit that lifts the burden? There is no rescue from the impression that life is but a "walking shadow, a poor player," save through the spirit, intelligence in the fullest sense, which, discovering the great truths, inspires confidence. Finding the metaphysical certainties, man gains the courage to face life, and it is only on entering the realm of the imagination that this encouragement, this ray of hope, is refracted and often distorted.

In primitive religion, however childish and full of monstrosities it may be, separated by however wide a gulf from true religion, man's religious nature is at work. At the birth of primitive worship stand wonder and trembling, awe and love, and there stands the genius of primitive man, which is the genius of a child. His simplicity, unconfused by the wealth of nature, sees the Maker behind the things He has made and moves. Man's whole being is directed toward the Absolute; his quest for happiness, his search for causes, his conscience, cannot but be orientated to It; at the bottom of even tribal religion is this longing, man's *desiderium naturale* for God, and all the clouds of primitive religion cannot blacken the original light from above.

Mystics, First Among Men

The myths are man's genuine vision deformed, his true reminiscences distorted. Bergson sees in them little more than tales with which we lull children to sleep; they restrain man within the narrow confines of the tribe and give him gods of his own making, his servants rather than his lords. To change man, to awaken him and raise him to the love of all humanity, strength from without is needed, superior to his own. Bergson finds the cradle of "dynamic religion" in the heart of the mystic, who feels himself pervaded by One immeasurably mightier than himself, just as an iron is pervaded by the fire that makes it glow. Though retaining his personal identity, he is united with and participates in the creative effort, which, says Bergson, is of God, if not God Himself. The mystic thus transcends the limitations imposed by matter on the human species, and continues and extends the divine action.[109] His experience is the highest and most positive within the reach of man.[110]

In the mystics, the word comes true that the meek shall inherit the earth.[111] Bergson's evaluation of them as the moral and religious leaders, as *the* leaders, of mankind, disturbs those who would like to think that man's religious development reaches its peak in absence-of-religion. Those who relish the thought that the world, having come of age, has outgrown the "unrealities" of mysticism, are embarrassed, and often conceal their uneasiness behind a smile at the mystics, ranking them among the mentally aberrant. But Bergson, always humble before facts, seeing what is, and not what bias looks for, knows them to be patterns of mental soundness, for all that distinguishes a healthy mind: a bent for action, adaptability to circumstances, firmness combined with suppleness, discernment of the possible and the impossible, the spirit of simplicity which overrides complication, in short, supreme good sense—all these mark the great mystics, a name he reserves for Christian saints like Paul of Tarsus, Teresa of Avila, Catherine of Siena, Francis of Assisi, Joan of Arc. Having named these few, he exclaims with joy at the torrent of sanctity within the Church: "And how many others besides!" [112]

It is true, the mystics talk of visions, ecstasies, raptures—phenomena also found in the insane, and indeed there are morbid states which counterfeit healthy states. A lunatic may imagine himself an emperor and ape Napoleon; therein lies his madness, but this in no way reflects upon Napoleon. Just so, a disordered mind may parody a mystic, and the result will be "mystic insanity." It hardly follows that mysticism is insanity, an error begotten by a perverse logic on a basic misunderstanding. The mystics, says Bergson, consider all extraordinary phenomena "as of secondary importance, as wayside incidents," their one and only goal being the identification of the human will with the divine Will.[113]

Bergson gives an account of the soul's progress toward her goal—union with God. His description, however subdued, cannot hide that he has caught something of the fire that burns in the mystics; unmatched in philosophical literature, here it can be given only in brief. Once shaken to her center, the soul ceases to revolve around herself. She stops, as if to heed a voice; called, she is swept straight onward, not directly perceiving the force that moves her, but feeling an indefinable presence. "Then comes a boundless joy, an all-absorbing ecstasy or an enthralling rapture: God is there, and the soul is in God. . . . Problems vanish, darkness is dispelled; everything is flooded with light." This splendor is not the end of the journey; in ecstasy, the soul but rests for a while, gathering strength to quicken her pace. And her delight does not remain unshadowed; an anxiety hovers over it, for "however close the union with God may be, it could be final only if it were total. Gone, doubtless, is the distance between the thought and the object of the thought . . . gone the radical separation between him who loves and him who is beloved." But though the soul becomes, in thought and feeling, absorbed in God, the will withholds its total surrender, is still outside, and has to make its way to its Liege and Lord.

Aware of this, the soul is disquieted, agitated in repose. This agitation increases, displacing all else, till the soul finds herself once more alone, even desolate, plunged from dazzling light into gloom, groping, she who had soared in joy. "She does not realize the profound metamorphosis which is going on obscurely within her. She feels she has lost much; she does not yet know that this was in order to gain all. Such is the 'darkest night' of which the great mystics have spoken, and which is perhaps the most significant thing, in any case the most instructive, in Christian mysticism." That Bergson understands the import of the "dark night" evidences a real grasp of the mystery of the cross. Immersed in darkness, the soul is subjected to the severest tests, made ready for her goal. All that is not pure enough, not flexible and strong enough, to be turned to God's employment, is thrown off; all that is not fit for His service is rejected and replaced. In pain, she yearns to become God's perfect instrument.

Before the soul was given over to the trials of the dark night, she had sensed God's presence, beheld Him in a symbolic vision, been close to Him in ecstasy, but her will had often cast her back on herself, depriving her of His nearness. "Now it is God who," having taken full possession of her, "is acting through the soul, in the soul; the union is total, therefore it is final. . . . There is an irresistible impulse which hurls her into vast enterprises. A calm exaltation of all her faculties makes her see things on a vast scale only and, in spite of her own weakness, produce only what can be mightily wrought. Above all, she sees things simply, and this simplicity, which is equally striking in the words she uses and the conduct she follows, guides her through complications which she apparently does not even perceive. An innate knowledge, or rather an acquired ignorance, suggests to her straightaway the step to be taken, the decisive act, the unanswerable word. Yet effort remains indispensable, endurance and perseverance likewise. But they come of themselves, they develop of their own accord, in a soul acting and acted upon, whose liberty coincides with the divine activity. They represent a vast expenditure of energy, but this energy is supplied as it is required, for the superabundance of vitality which it demands flows from a spring which is the very source of life. And now the visions are left far behind: the divinity could not manifest itself from without to a soul henceforth replete with its essence." [114]

31

The mystic, outwardly not to be distinguished from other men, has been raised—and here Bergson follows the Apostle—to the rank of *adjutores Dei,* helpers, coworkers of God, *patients par rapport à Dieu; agents par rapport aux hommes,* "patients in respect to Him, agents in respect to men." "The love which consumes him is no longer simply the love of man for God, it is the love of God for all men. Through God and in the strength of God, he loves all mankind with a divine love." This is not the brotherhood urged on us by the philosophers in the name of reason, on the ground that all men share in one rational essence. Before so noble an idea, we needs must bow, but never can it claim our passionate adherence. And if it should, it will be only because we have breathed, in some corner of our civilization, the intoxicating fragrance left there by mysticism. No more than it is a philosophical idea is this mystic love an intensification of some "innate sympathy" of man for man. Only family and society are ordained by nature and correspond to instincts—and do not the social instincts lead societies rather to conflict than to union? When, by chance, family or social feeling overflows, it is a luxury, a kind of game; it can never go very far. "The mystic love of humanity is a very different thing. It is not the extension of an instinct, it does not originate in an idea. It is neither of the senses nor of the mind. It is of both, implicitly, and it is effectively much more. For such a love lies at the very root of feeling and reason, as of all other things. Coinciding with God's love for His handiwork, a love that made all, it would yield, to him who knew how to question it, the secret of creation." [115]

Here the philosopher of experience embraces the center of faith, hymns the heart of the gospel, that God is Love[116] and that our hearts are Love's abode. Solomon and St. Paul come to life in him, who echoes the Apostle's psalm: "Love is the greatest of all," [117] and the King's Song: "Not death itself is so strong as love. . . . It is a fire no floods avail to quench nor rivers to drown." [118] As through a crystal, the mystical tradition of the Church shines through Bergson, the tradition to which *The Imitation of Christ* gives expression:

Love is a great thing and a good,
and alone maketh heavy burdens light,

and beareth in like balance
things pleasing and displeasing.

Love knoweth no measure, but is fervent without measure.
It feeleth no burden; it regardeth no labour;
it desireth more than it may attain;
it complaineth of no impossibility,
for it thinketh all things
that may be done for his beloved
possible and lawful unto him.

Love waketh much and sleepeth little,
and sleeping, sleepeth not.
It fainteth and is not weary,
is restrained of liberty and is in great freedom.
It seeth causes of fear and feareth not;
but as a quick brand or sparkle of fire,
flameth ever upward.[119]

The Augustinian philosopher Père Blaise Romeyer, S.J., pays the religious philosophy of the *Two Sources* an extraordinary tribute: Though never preaching, it cannot help "carry the reader, who often hungers and thirsts unknowingly for religion, toward the living God. It carries the intelligence, which is happy to discover in it . . . an interpretation of the universe sanely and grandiosely optimistic. It carries the heart, drawn and held by the God of the *Two Sources,* who is Love, the creative source of love, the object of love. It carries the will, which freely and generously raises itself whither intelligence and love lead. It carries our whole being toward Him, molding our ways, pervading our lives, transfiguring our deeds." [120]

Because of Bergson's many affirmations that approach the Church's teaching and, above all, in view of his humble praise of the God of Jesus Christ, Père Sertillanges calls Bergson an "apologist from without." In a picture perhaps overbold, the great Thomist compares his role to that of John the Baptist. In the modern desert, void of God, Bergson sounds a call, preparing the ways of the Lord.[121] He heralds the judgment of the modern bias against the truths of religion and, though a man of reserve, crowns

33

his philosophy by reiterating the ecstatic assertion that divine Love is not a thing of God, but God himself; that God "needs" us that He may love us; and that we are called to complete the work of love. Of those who taught him so, the great mystics of the Church, he says that "they have blazed a trail along which other men may pass. They have, by this very act, shown to the philosopher the whence and whither of life." [122]

The burden of gratitude never chafed Bergson. Not for a moment would he forswear his debt and that of all the world. He once remarked to Jacques and Raïssa Maritain: "All the good that has been done in the world since Christ, and all the good that will be done—if any more will be done—has been and will be wrought through Christianity." [123] This was said on one of the visits of Jacques and Raïssa Maritain, his former pupils, paid to Bergson in the late thirties. It is well known that after the appearance of *Creative Evolution,* Jacques Maritain severely criticized Bergson, but now he is happy to call Bergson's reconciliation with him—so "significant for the history of Bergson's thought and his position toward Thomism"—"one of the great consolations of my life." And in looking back over their lives and reliving, as it were, the metaphysical despair which was all the philosophers of the Sorbonne had left them and which had brought them close to suicide, Raïssa Maritain calls Bergson the gift of divine Providence. "It was then," she rejoices, "that the pity of God caused us to find Henri Bergson." [124]

Jacques Chevalier too records a saying of rare value. When they discussed in what measure Christianity is classic, Bergson, himself a champion of classical education, declared: "One would have to find out why it was the soul formed by Greco-Latin civilization that was best prepared to receive Christianity. But I think we should risk belittling it were we to tie it to one or another tradition. Christianity transfigures everything it touches, simply in rendering it Christian." [125] In an era when many small minds, nursed by Christian spirituality, think it great to belittle it, Bergson, a Jew, exalts it. His candor does not permit him to be tinged in the slightest by that resentment so marked among modern thinkers. Schopenhauer's grudge against the blessedness of hope, Nietzsche's rancor against the divinity of suffering and pity, or the repugnance Aldous Huxley and his school feel toward the

Saviour in the flesh, never enter his heart. He makes no attempt to flee, in time or space, the lasting Christian reality, or to evade its demand by giving undue prominence to Greek or Eastern thought. Of Plotinus he says that he went as far as ecstasy, but never reached the point at which contemplation overflows into action, action which is charity. Of Buddhism he remarks that although not ignoring love, it "lacked warmth and glow, it knew nothing of the complete and mysterious gift of self." [126] To Bergson the experience of Catholic mystics is the measure; it only is complete and absolute, and with it all religious experience must be confronted.

A Faith Buried in the Heart

It seems scarcely in accordance with his own findings that Bergson, at one point in the *Two Sources,* considers mysticism to be "drawn straight from the very wellspring of religion, independent of all that religion owes to tradition, to theology, to the Churches." One wonders why he should think it necessary in his argument to "leave aside"—and that in the name of a philosophy confined to "experience and inference"—"revelation which has a definite date, the institutions which have transmitted it, the faith that accepts it." And one is taken aback to read: "At the origin of Christianity there is Christ. From our standpoint, which shows us the divinity of all men, it matters little whether or no Christ be called a man. It does not even matter that he be called Christ." [127]

These statements, which appear at first glance to undo Bergson's apologia, can be rightly appraised only if one keeps in mind that the *Two Sources,* although the last written expression of his thought, does not represent his final thought in every detail; that his writings do not necessarily manifest his full personal convictions, even at the time, but only those he thought his philosophical method allowed him to assert; and finally, that his consideration for those who would not walk all the way with him suggested to him a certain reserve. So must be understood his surprisingly brief dismissal of the unrelenting question of who Christ was and is. It would be incongruous to suppose that he, an untiring searcher after truth, was himself indifferent as to whether or no the divine fullness dwelt in Christ; rather is he speaking, in this particular passage of the *Two Sources,* for the ears of the hesitant.

He seems to meet the doubter on his own ground when he says that "those who have gone so far as to deny the existence of Jesus cannot prevent the Sermon on the Mount from being in the Gospels, with other divine sayings. Bestow what name you like on their author, there is no denying that there was one." Neither is there any escape from His challenge—is not this what Bergson hopes to convey? He says of the great mystics that they but imitate and continue "what the Christ of the Gospels was completely." [128] Thus, He is the Source of their life, infinitely higher than they.

Several friends who knew Bergson well witness that this was truly his view, so that we need not suppose—we *know*—how greatly Christ, His life, His passion and glory, mattered to him. Georges Cattaui writes that in one of his many conversations with him between 1932 and 1938, he wished to know the true interpretation of Bergson's thought in the *Two Sources* that all the merits of the Christian mystics come to them from Jesus alone: "When I asked him with some insistence, he confided to me that he believed in the divinity of Christ." [129] Another witness is Père Sertillanges, to whom he said not long before his death: "It is evident that the Christ is superhuman. He sprang up among men, a fact entirely new, although I think this fact and the fact of Christianity would not have been possible were it not for what anteceded them in the history of Palestine." To which Père Sertillanges remarked that this was indeed Christ's own teaching, and that Christianity was Israel's religion unfolded. "That is the way I understand it," continued Bergson. "When I ask 'Whence comes Christ? What is the source of this superhuman fact?' I tell myself that surely He comes from above. This is, I think, what you call 'grace.'" Père Sertillanges amended this to "grace of union"; he said that Christ so touches God that the divine and the human unite in His one Person, and that it is this that is meant by the word "Incarnation." Whereupon Bergson in turn confessed: "To this theology I have no objection. It exactly extends what I have said myself." [130]

Further evidence is a letter Bergson wrote in 1939 in memory of Charles Péguy: "Great and admirable figure! He was carved of the stuff of which God makes heroes and saints: heroes—for from his first youth Péguy had no other concern than to live heroically; saints—did he not share with them the conviction that no act is insignificant, that every human action is grave and resounds throughout the entire moral world? Sooner or later, *il devait venir à Celui qui prit à son compte les péchés et les souffrances de tout le genre humain,* he had to come to Him who took upon Himself mankind's sins and sufferings." [131] In the *Two Sources,* sin was not once mentioned; here it is not only mentioned but so great is its weight that it has to be carried by One sinless and all-pure. So grievous is man's suffering that Christ wished to make our pain His own. Undeniably, to the Bergson of this letter, Christ is the Saviour whose love embraces *tout le genre humain,* all of mankind; whose passion is blessed, infinitely fruitful.

Jean Wahl relates an episode concerning this letter. He inquired of Bergson why, in speaking of Christ, he had written "Him," *Celui,* with a capital letter. And this was his answer: "Do you think that one can speak of Him as of a man?" (Or, "as of any other man?"—Professor Wahl does not remember which expression Bergson used, but he is quite right in thinking that in this context their meanings are about the same.) Bergson continued: "At that moment [of Christ's coming], something happened in humanity which came from without and above humanity. I realized this in reading the great mystics. So beautiful a movement, the most sublime in humanity, cannot have come save from a divine principle." [132] Elsewhere, speaking of Bergson's last months, so sorrowful, so filled with anxiety over the fate of France and the future of the world, Jean Wahl says that he had with him as guide the spiritual world of the mystics, the word of the "God of the prophets, the God of Jesus, the One who was to him the God Jesus, whom he recognized and adored outside of any church, thinking that he, bearer of all the world's philosophy, could do no better than the humble believer in a village church." [133]

This testimony is most valuable, but it ought to be worded more precisely. (Professor Wahl himself later amended his statement: "True, he was, in a strict sense, outside of any church. But at that time, I did not know that he wanted to see the Church beside him, and what I wrote must therefore be completed and even rectified." [134]) It was indeed outside the Church, but only through her, that Bergson found the God who is Love, and he worshiped Him, though not within, still with her—he found Him *through* the Church, for she is the custodian of the gospel and the nurse of the saints, and he worshiped *with* her, as she grew increasingly vital to him. He valued highly Cardinal Newman's *Development of Christian Doctrine*,[135] which suggests that, with Newman, he came to see the dogma of the Church as a sign not of "petrifaction" but of growth, as a token of fecundity and life. He came to see that the doctrine of the Church is the word of Christ made manifest, the seed become a tree, the bud an open flower, its full power and glory, at first concealed, now unfolding.

Édouard Le Roy, Bergson's successor at the Collège de France as well as in the Académie Française, speaks of a discussion he had with Bergson after the publication of the *Two Sources*. In his opinion, he told his master and colleague, a completion of the study was called for, on two points particularly: the problem of evil and sin, on the one hand, and on the other, of the relationship between static and dynamic religion, between the closed and the open—that is, of the Church, that spiritual mutuality which embodies them both. There arose then, Le Roy relates, the question of the fall of man, its mode and consequences. Bergson recognized that it posed itself inevitably, but added that he had not spoken of it in the *Two Sources* because he had not yet arrived, along the line of his method, at an answer which satisfied him, and he inquired of his friend how he pictured to himself such a fall. When Le Roy gave him a summary sketch, Bergson listened, as always, with deep attention; for a moment he was silent and then asked: *Est-ce orthodoxe?* "Is this orthodox?" He asked it, Professor Le Roy underlines, in a voice which betrayed a concern, never to leave him, for "an adherence, without reserve or equivocation, to doctrines and institutions that go beyond the domain of pure philosophy." [136]

At his last meeting with Père Sertillanges, Bergson called the Church *le prolongement du Christ,* Christ extended, "at bottom, the same fact," an open society, universal in spirit and tendency, thus keeping the inspiration of her Christ and, in her catholicity, independent of ethnic conditions and social and political contingencies. Deploring the division among Christians, he said that the Protestants were in the wrong in breaking off from the trunk of the tree; in doing so, they lost life-giving sap. They have beautiful souls among them, but they have no mystics, no supermen, so numerous in the Catholic Church. And he added: "For me, the saint is the true superman, of whom Nietzsche showed but a counterfeit." [137]

This was in 1940. Père Romeyer tells of the immense joy that filled his soul when, in a discussion they had as early as 1933, Bergson confessed his belief in the Mystical Body of Christ: "I feel fully convinced of His [God's] existence, and even of the divinity of the complete Mystic who was the Christ of the Gospels. My intimate belief goes further yet: since this Christ, who revealed to the world the existence of the God of love, wanted to live perfectly and to teach powerfully the religion of the Sermon on the Mount, His sojourn on this earth called forth a sequel. It was fitting that a universal social authority, issue of His thought and His design, a Church, by institution holder of His spirit, His will and His means, should—after He returned to the bosom of the Father—continue Him in this world as long as men shall live. Only thus could the mysticism of the Gospels, when passing from Christ to the Christians, keep itself substantially pure. Since He had to mount again to His Father before the end of the world, Jesus Christ had to institute the Church." At this point Bergson asked himself: "Is this pure reasoning?" and replied: "No, since it emanates from the experimental content of the mystical testimonies. And this content is as opposed to the churches of human invention as it is in harmony with faith in a Catholic Church, unique in fact as in right. . . ." "Is this, then, what you hold of Christian mysticism," Père Romeyer inquired, "that the divinity of the Catholic Church is linked to the divinity of the Christ of the Gospels?" "Yes," Bergson answered simply.[138]

These avowals of faith in Christ and His Church reported by the Dominican and Jesuit philosophers, were made in private, in the intimacy of friendship. Bergson's reason for not declaring publicly his inner belief in the Church was, in his own words: "I should not like to advance too far, lest it be said, 'He was a Catholic beforehand; his pretended method was but a detour to his intended goal.' Furthermore, at a moment when all spiritual forces are greatly needed, I should not dare discourage those outside the Church who manifest a high morality and labor for the spread of moral values; I should not dare discourage them by insisting on the necessity of the Church." His belief in Christ was likewise almost always hidden in his heart and never uttered in public; he explained his reserve: "I should be fearful of lessening the impact of my results, which have no value—if they have any— save by virtue of their independence of the faith, and the way in which they nonetheless go to meet it. . . . I should not like it to be said: 'This is what he was aiming at all along.' In truth, I did not aim at anything, and it is not my fault if all good roads lead to the gospel." [139]

Bergson's caution stemmed from his regard for others; his fear was that he might harm more than help men of good will. The Christian must deeply respect this nobility of character, though he cannot forget that the kingship of truth and the sovereignty of love may demand the sacrifice of even such tender concern, as the majesty of God demanded of Abraham the readiness to sacrifice his son. However, at the time the *Two Sources* was written, it was not caution that made Bergson ignore the necessity of the Church in the life of the mystics; it would seem that as yet he was not fully aware of it. Indeed, it must have taken him years of prayer, meditation, and inner struggle before he could see a truth so repugnant to men of our age.

All that the mystics are, they are through the Church, as rivulets drawing from that mighty stream whose fountainhead is Christ. They could not know the incomprehensible and ineffable God were it not for Him, the "revelation which has a definite date," and Him they could not hear were it not for the Church, who is His voice resounding till the end of time. It is she who communicates to them aspiration for union with God, as it is her dogma which—far from stifling the inner life—enkindles it. Because their path is beaconed by the light of faith, the mystics can proceed on the arduous journey to direct experience of God. And when they tell of their experience, they do not *borrow* the language of religion, as Bergson says in the *Two Sources;* they speak their mother tongue. They themselves evince their dependence on the redemptive work of Christ, continued in the Church. The beginning and growth of their inner life is owed, they themselves attest, to the sacraments, those vessels of love in which matter, otherwise retarding the movements of the Spirit, becomes His chariot. They are no less bound to the Church by obedience, knowing her authority to be the warrant of their freedom. Fearing illusion, fearing their own will, they accept, even seek direction, and bow willingly to the word of their confessor. Far sooner would they renounce any spiritual favor than separate, in thought or deed, from the body of the Church, of which they glory to be but members. It is the evidence of the mystics, not faith, that demands of the philosopher humbly attentive to experience that he recognize the cardinal role of the Church. But not only the mystics depend on her; she is the hearth of our civilization, and if her liberties be curtailed, all the world suffers.

It was along these lines that Père Sertillanges reasoned in his memorable conversation with Bergson, who judged the argument so important that, contrary to his habit of never altering, once published, the text of a long-considered work, he promised that the next printing of the *Two Sources* would acknowledge, though without leaving the philosophical order, the office of the Church.[140] Death, however, took the pen from his hand. At the time the two philosophers exchanged their thoughts on the Church as the mother of mystics, Bergson was ill, as indeed he had been for a long time, with a painful and crippling arthritis. Although he was confined to an invalid's chair, although he was emaciated, almost completely immobilized, suffering unspeakably in sleepless nights, his mind remained fresh, his judgment and memory lucid, his command of language singular. When he spoke, it was with the air of a patriarch; his words were paced, they had the clarity and beauty of his written style, they shone with the detachment that humbles itself before truth. Suffering had been his companion for many years; still, his death was sudden. He died of pneumonia on Saturday, January 4, 1941.

The Philosopher's Testament

Bergson was not a member of the Church when he died, but he was a Christian *in voto*. On the morning of what was to be his last day, a priest-friend, Chanoine Lelièvre, was called. But France was occupied then by German troops, communications were difficult—when Chanoine Lelièvre arrived, Bergson was gone; he could do no more than recite the prayers for the dead and bless his body.[141]

As Bergson was not able to make the addition to the *Two Sources* which he had offered, so there are other things he left unsaid. Neither his books nor his conversations preserve his deepest word;

41

it must have been spoken in his colloquy with God, for his was a meditative nature. As a young teacher at Clermont-Ferrand, he walked daily the same familiar paths, where no new sights or sounds could rupture his companionship with the things of the mind. It was there, where he liked to pace the Place d'Espagne and walk through the vineyards, that he conceived the *idée maîtresse* of his philosophy.[142] Though of brilliant mind, he was not given to many words; in fact, the only type of man to whom he felt a thorough aversion was *homo loquax,* who thinks he understands a thing when he can talk about it.[143] Bergson himself tells of his first meeting with William James in 1903. Each philosopher knew the other in his writings; they had written to one another and their mutual sympathy had grown with the years— yet when they met, they exchanged greetings, and then there were some moments of silence. Nor was the silence broken till William James asked: "How do you see the religious question?"[144] A lover of silence and thought, Bergson was fitted to be at home in the spiritual world. For many years before his death, he read the gospel daily, and called it *mon climat de vie,* the clime where his spirit rested, the atmosphere in which his soul rejoiced. And toward the end of his years he retired from every public activity, in order, as he said, "to put an interval between his life and his death."[145]

When Père Sertillanges, taking leave of Bergson, told him: "We pray for you a great deal, and we hope also to pray with you. For a man who speaks as you have done of the things of God and the great souls is evidently a man who prays," he answered—and these were to be his last words to his confrère—"You are good; you have done me good."[146] Though the veil of modesty guarded his spiritual life from the eyes of the world, Père Sertillanges, in calling him a man of prayer, did not go beyond Bergson's own philosophical method, beyond his teaching that true knowledge comes by affinity, that profound understanding bespeaks kinship. Earlier in the day, Père Sertillanges had said that he had no need to assure him of his admiration and affection, but that there was one thing he had never told: that he prayed much for him. Whereupon Bergson replied: "Oh, for that I thank you with all my heart." And he took the hands of his friend and held them to his breast.[147] Mindful of the necessity of prayer, he had asked in his testament the assistance of the Church, that she might speak for him when his lips were mute. His wish was that *she* should utter his final words on earth. It is thus she speaks when she buries one of her children:

Out of the depths I cry to Thee, O Lord;
Lord, hear my voice.

.   .   .   .   .

My soul waits for the Lord
more than watchmen wait for the dawn.
More than watchmen wait for the dawn,
let Israel wait for the Lord,
For with the Lord there is mercy.[148]

And she begs: "May Christ, who has called thee, receive thee, and may the angels lead thee into the bosom of Abraham." [149]

Some years before, in his last will and testament, as published by Madame Bergson and dated February 8, 1937, Bergson had declared: "My reflections have led me closer and closer to Catholicism, in which I see the complete fulfillment of Judaism. I should have become a convert, had I not seen in preparation for years (in great part, alas, through the fault of a certain number of Jews entirely deprived of moral sense) the formidable wave of anti-Semitism which is to sweep over the world. I wanted to remain among those who tomorrow will be persecuted. But I hope that a Catholic priest will be good enough to come—if the Cardinal Archbishop of Paris authorizes it—to pray at my funeral. Should this authorization not be granted, it will be necessary to approach a rabbi, but without concealing from him, nor from anyone, my moral adherence to Catholicism, as well as my express and first desire to have the prayers of a Catholic priest." [150]

What is most striking in his will is Bergson's love for the Jewish people and for the Church. It was, however, not the flesh but the spirit that forged his link with Israel. That, in a way, he answered its ancient vocation has been set forth by no less a one than Étienne Gilson at his reception into the Académie Française on the 29th of May, 1947. "Those who recall their debt to him—the highest joys of the spirit and the sureness that after the Criticism of Kant and the Positivism of Comte, metaphysics remained pos-

43

sible—will never weary in their fervent gratitude," he said of his former teacher, speaking in the name of the multitude of souls to whom he was a finger to faith. "The classical problems, condemned by others as vain, lived again in his thought and imposed themselves imperiously on ours. They were declared insoluble; he showed them inexhaustible. . . . How we loved him! this prophet bedewed with the word of a God whose Name he would not pronounce for so long, restrained by the most noble scruples. Whither he went, whither he led us then, in 1905, he himself did not know. But thirty-four years later he could write me: 'Religion, which was, as it were, immanent in my first reflections, in my first conclusions, has in the end become manifest. I ask myself how I could not have perceived at once, clearly, what now appears to me in full light.' Thus, on the slopes of the very Montagne Sainte-Geneviève, on the border of the very Rue Saint-Jacques . . . two steps from the very Couvent des Jacobins where once Thomas of Aquin taught—there, after a silence of so many centuries, the metaphysics of Genesis and Exodus dared take tongue again. Jahve was given back to us, the God who calls Himself: *I Am;* that God who, once we had found again His Presence, was much later to clarify for us the profound meaning of Thomistic metaphysics, the Creator who creates creators. . . . Let us admire here a miracle of fidelity, wholly radiant with the divine: the deposit confided to Israel for so many centuries was restored to us through Israel." [151]

Bergson's decision to postpone his baptism would be greatly misunderstood were it assumed that he, the philosopher of the open morality, obeyed a racial impulse or acknowledged that blood has a higher claim than truth. His apprehension was not that baptism was a betrayal of the Jewish people, for his bond with Israel was not first one of the body but of the spirit. Though ever gentle, he could judge severely those Jews "from whom all aroma of their spiritual heritage seemed to have evaporated," so that in his testament he deplored that anti-Semitism was increasing "in great part through the fault of a certain number of Jews entirely deprived of moral sense." When he wrote these words he foresaw the terrible wave of anti-Semitism which was to cover Europe, but he could not foresee its diabolical heights, the abuse and torture and death it would mean; else he would have guarded himself in advance against those who might misuse his words. The debt to the lineage of patriarchs and prophets was too great, he thought, ever to be forgotten by a Jew, and he knew Israel's dignity to be exalted, enhanced, enriched, in the Church. For a long time, he had remained almost indifferent to Judaism, and only through Christ did he take cognizance of his part in the old Israel; Jesus alone awakened his fidelities. His own heart, touched by the sufferings of all men, made him sensible of Israel's woes, but the compassion he expressed in his testament was given him by the Christ of tears.[152]

With excessive humility, he seemed to think his public conversion would be of little service to the Church, because his great age and ill health might, in the eyes of many, nullify his testimony. He also feared to pain his Jewish brethren, so deeply humiliated, to hurt them by what they would misconstrue as desertion in the hour of trial, and dreaded that he might, rather than lead them to Christ, alienate many still further. Though he desired with all his heart to be of the Church, he did not see it as an obligation. In a matter of such gravity to his soul, a matter of eternity, a man of his rare integrity would surely have followed his obligation, had he recognized it. As it was, he owned but a desire, strong and deep, and this desire, with the joy of its fulfillment, had to be sacrificed, he felt, in the face of the misery Nazism was to vomit upon his people. That he did not know himself in duty bound to become a member of the Church he himself recognized as the Christ walking through the ages, continuing His work of redemption, was probably due to a defect in his philosophy; it lacked a clear concept of the nature of obligation itself, and its "empiricism" could not give him the rational support he needed in his dilemma.[153]

We sorrow at Bergson's failure to seize what would have been the crowning of his life—a failure which shows the strength of ideas and the sad power of an erroneous or (as in the case of Bergson's) a deficient philosophy. We sorrow that he did not cross the threshold, but we feel he wrestled much, and rejoice that, to the limits of his vision, he followed the dictates of his conscience. In the cardinal decisions of the soul, child cannot stand for father; still, when Jeanne, Henri Bergson's sculptor-daughter, received the sacrament of rebirth, with his consent, though after his death, and when she confessed: *Quelle merveilleuse joie,* "What wonderful joy to be a Catholic," [154] surely she revealed what was in her father's heart.

As the Church calls her own not only the faithful but also the "learners" on their way to the font, so she can claim Bergson, for all that he was not, strictly speaking, a catechumen. What St. Ambrose expressed of the Emperor Valentinian, who died during his catechumenate: *Hunc sua pietas abluit et voluntas,* may be said, we hope, also of Bergson: "His piety and will washed him clean." [155] At all times it is the Holy Spirit who cleanses, the Spirit moving the waters of regeneration, moving also hearts to contrition and the pure love of God, satisfying and sanctifying souls of thirsting faith. "We know that there is a baptism of desire," Père Sertillanges writes, concluding the account of his conversations with Bergson. "I do not doubt that God has this soul." [156] Likewise the Swiss theologian, Monsignor Charles Journet, affirms that as far as it is for mortal men to know a judgment which is God's alone, we dare to say that Bergson was of those of Christ's sheep who, alas, are not yet within the fold; that he was truly linked to the Church by desire and by the ascent of his whole life.[157] Monsignor Journet speaks in the spirit of the encyclical of Pius XII, who, so warmly remembering those who are outside but "unknowingly related to the Mystical Body in desire and resolution," calls them home.[158]

When death came to Henri Bergson, he was far from the city which had seen his triumphs, for all his life he was a pilgrim, he had known himself to be *en route*.[159] His burial was as simple as could be, only a few being present while the body of the renowned philosopher, "the pride of the Academy," [160] was carried to the grave. He had been professor at the Collège de France, a member of the Académie des Sciences Morales et Politiques and of the Académie Française, Grand Officer of the Legion of Honor and a member of the Council of the Order; he had been president of the League of Nations Committee for Intellectual Cooperation and a recipient of the Nobel Prize; thousands and thousands had sat at his feet, hundreds of thousands had read his books, but only some thirty saw him to his last resting place. This is as it should have been, for the strength of his life did not rest on the honors he received; its greatness consisted in his abandonment to truth, in his devotion to what *is*. He began his intellectual work in the chilling air of Spencer's thought, but boldly discarded mechanist philosophy when he saw that it contradicted reality. He was led not by prejudgment or predilection but by the problems posed him and the answers he found, heeding the invitations of truth and sitting down before it like a child. What he attributed to the artist was also his own—"a kind of detachment from life"; "as it were, a virginal manner of thinking." [161]

Thus Bergson moved step by step toward Him he had not sought, so that in the end he could say: "The gospel is my true spiritual home. Nothing Christ says of Himself surprises me, nothing disappoints me." [162] There was no word of Christ he deemed impossible, none too great or too small, or that he would have wished altered. What had long appealed to him in Christianity was *le goût du concret spirituel, le sens des personnes humaines à sauver,*[163] that it does not dwell in abstractions but is life, spirituality most concrete, that it sees men as persons to be saved and saves them. He had come, Madame Bergson tells us, to "regard Catholicism with a *growing* sympathy." [164] He understood the Church ever better; he felt ever nearer her and wished her to be near to him. Thus he begged her prayers, asked that she accompany his soul into a land of experience altogether new.

The last words of the *Two Sources,* the bold figure, "The universe is a machine for the making of gods," is a metaphor of assent to the doctrine of the Church, meeting the thought of St. Thomas that the elements of the universe work in concert for man's eternal bliss. For unless bodies serve Him as an occasion, God does not bring souls into being, although they are directly created by Him and for Him, although they are superior to the stars. Too feeble to be pure spirits, souls need a sort of base drawn from the cosmos, and the whole cosmos labors to give it to them that it itself may reach its goal: the consummation of the number of the elect. *Omnia intendunt assimilari Deo,* the Angelic Doctor says; in seeking their own perfection, all things tend to become like unto God. All being tends toward love, its *raison d'être;* all conspires, and the end of this conspiracy is the multiplication of worlds infinitely greater than the world itself, of human persons, each an epitome of the material and spiritual creations, each a theater where freedom triumphs over necessity, each called to be God's assistant.

"It is of all things the most Godlike to be God's coworker," St. Thomas exclaims with Dionysius.[165] Bergson's metaphor is clearer still in the light of two pictures he had chosen for his room.[166] The almost bare walls bore two engravings of great masters, both representing the elevation of the purest of creatures and her clothing in glory—the Assumption of the Blessed Virgin.

Edmund Husserl

ACOLYTE OF TRUTH

"SEE MY NEW TESTAMENT?" SAID EDMUND HUSSERL MORE THAN once to favorite students. "It is always on my desk, but I never open it. I know that once I open it and read it, I shall have to give up philosophy." [1] He made this admission in his later years, at a time when his teaching was evoking response in many brilliant minds. Not that he thought for a moment his philosophy incompatible with Christianity, quite the contrary; but he gave himself wholly to his philosophy, making it the sum and substance of his life. Thus he feared it would rank but second were he to follow Christ.

In his youth he had not even glimpsed Christ's sovereignty. The Bible, he first discovered at the University of Leipzig—a fruit of his friendship with the mathematician Gustav Albrecht and Thomas Masaryk, the future founder and first president of Czechoslovakia. Husserl was moved by the Psalms and the Prophets, stirred by the New Testament, but in no way did he recognize Christ's total demand. At that time, as a student of seventeen in his first term at the University, he approached a minister, New Testament in hand: "On the basis of this book, I should like to be baptized." He wished no interpretation of Scripture, no further profession of faith, but only to be received as a Christian as he understood it. But it was not until ten years later, on his twenty-seventh birthday, that he was finally baptized, though in much the same spirit, in the principal Lutheran church of Vienna.

At Leipzig, Husserl had been influenced by Masaryk, who at that time had moved away from the Catholic Church, the faith of his youth, and now adhered to a truncated Christianity, the "religion" of the nineteenth-century intellectual. As his later writings were to show, Masaryk discarded all that transcended reason, so that to him religion was man's answer to the riddle of eternity, an answer given by the human heart and mind, man's knowledge the one authority, and the books of the Bible merely testimonies of a phase in man's religious development. Masaryk saw Christ as a great figure only, as an ideal, which made him exclaim: "Jesus, not Caesar"; a teacher best and most dear, whose pure religion of humanity it was man's duty to realize.[2]

At the University of Vienna, Husserl, then in his early twenties, was much affected by Franz Brentano, a priest who had left the

Church, not, as is commonly thought, because of, but rather on the occasion of the pronouncement of the dogma of papal infallibility. To Brentano, Jesus was "one of the greatest prophets," "a great teacher of morality," while the Old Testament was "an outmoded legacy of a barbaric time." Hence he counseled one of his young Jewish friends that to remain a Jew was "to cling by social inertia to the relic of a dead past," and was "contrary to the spirit of freedom and enlightenment." "Not only Jesus," he wrote him, "but also the greatest and most progressive of the prophets before him, resolutely went beyond the idea of a chosen people and, highminded, looked upon it as a narrow one. Therefore away with it, and with all the other old rubbish!"[3] This was the thought, crudely expressed, of many of the "progressive" minds of the last century. The Old and New Testaments were not the way of salvation, one in figure, the other in truth. Rather were the books of Moses and those of Israel's history thought to be the expression of an undeveloped tribe; and the Gospels merely one step forward in the advance of humanity. Baptism was not the sacrament of rebirth, incorporation into the Mystical Body of Christ, but rather entry into Western society, and to decline it was not to deny Jesus as the Christ but—oddly enough—to refuse to be one with the Enlightenment.

Though Brentano's counsel to his young Jewish friend was given some years after Husserl was baptized, there can be little doubt that this was the kind of influence he brought to bear on Husserl. Husserl's chosen reading also showed that at the time of his baptism he believed in the Gospels not as revealed truth, as God's word to man, but rather as the record of the most beautiful life and singular wisdom of the man Jesus. The religious authors who impressed him most in his young days were David Friedrich Strauss and Ernest Renan. In his "Christmas Eve," Robert Browning describes a lecture by Strauss, "the hawk-nosed, high-cheekboned professor," yet it needs no poet's mockery—Strauss' weak and confused thought itself shows the higher criticism ridiculous: that school which tried to make Scripture harmless by deleting the extraordinary, which found in it everywhere foreign influences but could detect nowhere the finger of God.

So, he proposed inquiring first
Into the various sources whence

This Myth of Christ is derivable;
Demanding from the evidence,
(Since plainly no such life was liveable)
How these phenomena should class?
Whether 't were best opine Christ was,
Or never was at all, or whether
He was and was not, both together—
It matters little for the name,
So the Idea be left the same.
Only, for practical purpose' sake,
'Twas obviously as well to take
The popular story—understanding
How the ineptitude of the time,
And the penman's prejudice, expanding
Fact into fable fit for the clime,
Had, by slow and sure degrees, translated it
Into this myth, this Individuum—
Which, when reason had strained and abated it
Of foreign matter, gave, for residuum,
A Man!—a right true man, however,
Whose work was worthy a man's endeavor:
Work: that gave warrant almost sufficient
To his disciples, for rather believing
He was just omnipotent and omniscient,
As it gives to us, for as frankly receiving
His word, their tradition—which, though it meant
Something entirely different
From all that those who only heard it,
In their simplicity thought and averred it,
Had yet a meaning quite as respectable:
For, among other doctrines delectable,
Was he not surely the first to insist on
The natural sovereignty of our race?

To this confusion, Browning himself gives the answer:

Morality to the uttermost,
Supreme in Christ as we all confess,
Why need we prove would avail no jot
To make Him God, if God He were not?
What is the point where Himself lays stress?

Does the precept run "Believe in Good,
In Justice, Truth, now understood
For the first time?"—or, "Believe in ME,
Who lived and died, yet essentially
Am Lord of Life?" [4]

With Strauss, Renan asserted that much of the Gospels' narrative
was mythical: the product of the enthusiasm of Christ's earliest
followers, the outgrowth of the people's Messianic expectations,
or the embellishment of plain facts. In the arbitrary way of those
who prate of the scientific method and in the dogmatic manner
of those who reject dogma, he went so far as to declare that the
few things certain about Jesus were these: He existed; he was
from Nazareth; there was charm in his preaching; he left profound
sayings deeply engraved on the minds of his hearers; his chief disciples were Peter and John; he excited the hatred of the orthodox Jews, who succeeded in having him put to death by Pontius
Pilate; he was crucified outside the gate of the city; and shortly
afterward it was believed that he had been restored to life.[5]

This was Renan's capricious dogmatism, but there was, and there
is, not the least scientific justification for calling these the only
historical facts about Jesus and doubting all else. Husserl, not a
knower of men, too gentle to distrust, may have been deceived by
the air of martyred righteousness with which Strauss and Renan
went about their arguments. Like Strauss, Renan denied miracles
and divine intervention. "We reject the supernatural," he wrote,
"for the same reason that we reject the existence of centaurs and
hippogriffs; and this reason is, that nobody has ever seen them"—
and this not a page after he professed his belief in "the hidden
Soul of the Universe." [6] To Renan's rejection of the supernatural,
his own grandson, Ernest Psichari, was to reply when, before his
conversion, he wrote in his *Voices Crying in the Wilderness:*
"When I ponder the problem of faith, none of the difficulties
raised by modern exegesis succeeds in impressing me. The so-
called 'contradictions of the synoptic Gospels' serve only those
who, from the very first, and without examination, have decided
to deny the supernatural. Ignorant as I am, I know well that such
miserable discussions could never convince anyone of anything
whatsoever." And he added: "I know Thee, O my God, because
it pleased Thee to make Thyself known. I know Thee by that

53

which is unknowable in Thee, I know Thee by Thy unknowable mysteries which are the Holy Trinity, the Incarnation, the Redemption. Those are the proofs which Thou hast deigned to send me." [7]

Ernest Psichari well understood that the liberal theologians were not what they claimed to be, liberators, but looters. They had thought the future would prove them right; Strauss, for example, had the temerity to appeal to the tribunal of time. "Time will show," he ended his *Life of Jesus*, "whether by the one party [his own, those who in the name of science would fit Christianity to the Procrustean bed of their fancy] or by the other [those who upheld a Christianity unbroken], the Church, Mankind, and Truth are best served." [8] And time *has* shown. A straight line leads from those who would eliminate from the world God's miraculous intervention to those who would deny God's love altogether, who, like Martin Heidegger, make Him an absent God. It was this philosophy, which built metaphysics not on the glad wonder of being but on the anguished experience of nothingness, which treated nothingness almost as the creator of things, which spoke of man as *der Platzhalter des Nichts,* the tenant of nothingness, as flung into the world and abandoned there,[9] that made Heidegger the servant of Nazi nihilism and a tool for the persecution of his old teacher, Husserl. All those who wish today to degrade men are the legitimate heirs of those who wished yesterday to depose Christ.

Husserl, however, very much a child of his time in all things not his immediate philosophical field, had no inkling where "liberal theology" would lead. Nor did he see through the higher criticism of Julius Wellhausen, his colleague at the University of Goettingen, whose writings held his interest. Like many of his contemporaries, Husserl took as a search for truth the attempt of the higher critics to dissect the books of the Bible and to deny them all unity. Not that everything they ever said was wrong, for even a blind hen must now and then pick a grain of corn, but their refusal, almost as a matter of principle, to accept the traditional authorship, and their penchant for seeing patchwork everywhere, for thinking Scripture a motley collection from anonymous sources, were in reality symptoms of a general disease. For the mania to dispossess, the preference for the nameless, the distrust of antiquity, the arbitrary decisions as to what writers of the past thought and felt and wrote—all these were not confined to the field of Scripture. Édouard Tournier, the famous Greek scholar of the second half of the nineteenth century, started by finding in the *Ajax* of Sophocles passages unworthy of the great poet, and in the end rejected the entire tragedy. When he died, he had come to doubt the authenticity of all seven of the Sophoclean plays, and begged pardon of God and men for having edited spurious classical tragedies.[10] This is the tendency of higher criticism, to eat itself up, and no parody could make the point more clearly than this true tale.

But Husserl was taken in by the writings of Strauss and Renan, as he was also by those of Tolstoy. Though there is breadth in *War and Peace* and goodness and piety in his *Folk-tales,* Tolstoy's confession of faith was only a shadow of the Christian creed: "I believe in this: I believe in God, whom I understand as Spirit, as Love, as the Source of all. I believe that he is in me and I in him. I believe that the will of God is most clearly and intelligibly expressed in the teaching of the man Jesus, whom to consider as God and pray to, I esteem the greatest blasphemy." Thus echoing the indictment of Caiphas, Tolstoy wished nonetheless to be thought of as a Christian. To love one another was the whole gospel, the true life, he said; but added—with what bathos!—that the root of all evil was resistance to evil, or property, and that the three horrors, "the trinity of curse," were drunkenness, meat eating, and smoking. His *Gospel in Brief* ends: "And bowing his head, he breathed his last." Jesus died, but did not rise; He is dead—what lives on is the impact of His personality on others. Because Tolstoy belittled matter, he could not admit the resurrection, the triumph over decay, the elevation of matter to the freedom of the spirit.[11]

In a marvelous satire on the creed of Tolstoy and other liberals, Vladimir Soloviev spoke of a new religion founded on the eastern steppes of Russia. The followers of this faith called themselves "Hole-drillers," because it was their ritual to drill a middle-sized hole in a wall in some dark corner of the house, put their mouths to it, and repeat earnestly: "My house, my hole, do save me." Never before had the object of worship been reduced to such utter primitivity. But the error of the Hole-drillers was at least a truthful error, for though they were absolutely mad, they deceived no one, calling the house they worshiped a "house," and the hole they drilled a "hole." Soon, however, the religion of the Hole-drillers underwent a process of evolution. It was transformed —it retained its former weakness of religious thought and its narrowness of philosophical interest, but completely lost its truthfulness. The "house" was now called "the kingdom of God on earth," and the "hole" received the name of "the new gospel." But this sham gospel, Soloviev concluded, compares with the true gospel as does a hole drilled in a beam with a living tree.[12]

The new evangelists, denying the past resurrection of the One and the future resurrection of all, rob the world, Soloviev charged, of the triumph of the good. In the resurrection evil meets an answer, in that it serves to enhance the power of the good and its victory. Death is stronger than mortal life, but the resurrection to eternal life is stronger than either. The kingdom of God is the kingdom of life triumphant. In it rests all the work of Christ; in it is realized His love for us and ours for Him. If all struggle for the good comes to nought in death, if death is the conqueror, if there was no resurrection of Christ and shall be none of all flesh, then the new evangelists' talk of the kingdom of God is nothing but words, nothing but an arbitrary and purposeless euphemism for the kingdom of death.[13]

It was the shell of Christianity without its substance that the various liberal schools retained. In a spirit of protest, they had rejected its fullness, but what was to them fall and loss was Husserl's gain. Coming of a Jewish family with little religious tradition, even this impoverished Christianity enriched his life. A Christian to whom Christ is but a man, however great, has turned his back on truth; a Jew, however, who loves the Man Jesus is on his way to it. Yet what Christianity really means first dawned on Husserl in his sixties, it seems, in the years following the first World War, when he read the works of Kierkegaard. The greatest thinker risen in Protestantism, Søren Kierkegaard was the one who stripped it of its pretensions. To him Luther was the hero of mediocrity, who encouraged, for example, the marriage of priests as a concession to concupiscence. He was "a confused head" who threw off burdens, the very opposite of an apostle; while an apostle expresses Christianity in God's interest, Luther expressed it in the interest of man, taking man's part against God. Without giving thought to Strauss, and long before Renan wrote, Kierkegaard nonetheless exposed liberal Protestantism; "Christianity without the following of Christ is merely mythology, poetry," he said. Indeed, the new evangelists had called a myth all that made Christ unique, and thus His "hard sayings" became easy, even trivial. But God did not let Himself be born, Truth did not come into the world, in order to make trivial remarks. Christ was crucified, but "it is not usual in this trivial world to apply the death penalty for making trivial remarks." For Kierkegaard, Christianity without belief in the Incarnation is flat, or rather nonsense. God-made-Man was to him *the* mystery, or, to speak his language, the great paradox. In Christ heaven invades earth, eternity breaks into time, so that violating all rules of grammar, He can say: "Before Abraham came to be, I am." [14]

In all his reading of Kierkegaard, Husserl never really came to grips with his thought. To one of his students who found him in the University library, bent over one of Kierkegaard's books, he said: "I can accept everything of his—except the paradox." [15] It was at this time, too, that Husserl became interested in the theology of Karl Barth and his school, although it had little appeal to him. All his life he remained a son of the Enlightenment and an admirer of Goethe, tolerant, and disinclined to engage himself. Religion he considered a "private affair," an attitude strangely inconsistent with his vigorous pursuit of truth. He did not worship publicly; following the mistaken notion of "inwardness," the misinterpretation of the gospel which locates the kingdom of heaven only in the heart of man, he declined common prayer. Having breathed the atmosphere of individualism: that to pray is "to be alone with the Alone," Husserl thought that significant prayer could be only in one's inner room. But God is not "the Alone," nor is man. Mankind is a community, and praying together is loving together—a truth that has guided the Israel of both the Old and the New Covenants. In the corporate worship of the ancient as well as of the New Israel, the whole creation, visible and invisible, joins; "Bless the Lord, all things the Lord has made" [16]— this Old Testament canticle opens the Church's thanksgiving after Mass. But in the common worship of the Church, more than creation sings; "there sounds together from east to west the chorus of Christ." [17]

Husserl never fully perceived the meaning of the Church, though in his last years he saw her glory more than before. Once, at supper with several of his Catholic colleagues of the University of Freiburg, he took part in a conversation on religion. The theologian Engelbert Krebs spoke of the sacraments, of the wealth, the beauty of Catholic doctrine and life. Whereupon Husserl said with a tone of appreciation: *"Ja, ja, lieber Herr Kollege,* ah yes, you Catholics sit at a festive table." Father Krebs was quick to rejoin: "Well, *Herr Geheimrat,* why don't you sit down with us?" "Oh, it's not so easy," and his colleagues remember that he spoke with a sigh, as one who would say: "If only I could!" [18]

An Unexpected Heir

Edmund Husserl was born on April 8, 1859, in Prossnitz, a town in Moravia, then part of the Austro-Hungarian Empire. He received in Vienna and Olmuetz the wide and balanced training the *Gymnasia* of Europe afford, but his record was not unusual; his classmates seem to have thought of him as a sleepyhead. There were but two subjects in which he excelled, mathematics and the natural sciences; thus, when in 1876 he entered the University of Leipzig, he studied physics, mathematics, and astronomy. He also attended lectures on philosophy by Wilhelm Wundt but they failed to arouse his interest. In 1878 he transferred to the University of Berlin, where there were some of the great mathematicians of the day, Leopold Kronecker, Ernest Eduard Kummer, and Karl Weierstrass. They considered number, not space, the fundamental concept of mathematics; geometry, for them, was derived from arithmetic, and not vice versa; quantities were first expressed in integers and not in measures. It was these mathematicians who taught Husserl exact and disciplined thinking, at the same time that the lectures of Friedrich Paulsen awakened his sense of philosophy.

In 1881 Husserl went to Vienna to continue his mathematical studies; there, two years later, he received the degree of Doctor of Philosophy, having submitted a dissertation on the calculus of variations. For a short time he worked as assistant to Weierstrass in Berlin, but soon took the decisive step of returning to Vienna in order to study philosophy under Franz Brentano, whose personality was to leave a deep mark on him. Many years later, he told of the mighty head on the lean frame, the lined face telling of much mental struggle, the boldly curving nose—how all these, so out of the ordinary, held his attention. Every one of Brentano's movements, he wrote, as well as his eyes, which looked ever inward and upward, bespoke a man who felt urged to a great task. His language was elevated but simple, earnest but unaffected; when he spoke in his gentle voice, with his priestly gestures, he appeared, Husserl recalled, like "a seer of eternal truths and a herald of another world." [19] Once a priest, forever a priest, the Church teaches, and Brentano's manner seemed to reflect.

In Brentano's philosophy too, there remained much of his Catholic past. Although he did not subscribe to the Thomistic theory of knowledge, he kept its concept of intentionality. "Every psychological phenomenon is characterized," he said, "by what the scholastics of the Middle Ages called the intentional or mental in-existence of an object," which he, however, liked to term "relation to a content," "direction to an object," "immanent objectivity." In an idea *something* is ideated, in judgment *something* acknowledged or denied, in love *something* loved, in hate hated, in desire desired—in short, consciousness is always consciousness of *something*.[20] Although the concept of intentionality, in a way the common possession of all genuine philosophy, underwent considerable change on its way from the scholastics to Brentano, and again from Brentano to Husserl, nonetheless Brentano, and through him Husserl, owed it to St. Thomas.

According to St. Thomas, we are able to reach beyond ourselves in order to participate in the being of other things; not, of course, in the way they possess it themselves, but in the way proper to the mind, intellectually, immaterially. Because in knowledge we can extend ourselves, St. Thomas speaks of *in-tentio,* of *in-tendere,* "to stretch forth." [21] A kinship, a communion of being, links things knowable and us, the knowers; it is because they come forth from God, the First Knower, and are His thoughts, that things can be known to us. Things which are merely knowable and cannot themselves know, are constricted, says St. Thomas, confined within themselves, whereas the nature of knowers is open and wide. A thing merely knowable possesses only its own form (in scholastic language, the form is that which makes the thing what it is), while a knower can take into himself the form of the thing he knows. Thus the image and likeness of things known are in the knower, and so, potentially, the whole, rich universe; therefore, St. Thomas says with Aristotle, "the soul is in a sense all things." [22] "The ultimate perfection the soul can attain is, according to the Philosopher [Aristotle], that in it be inscribed the whole order of the universe and its causes." [23] Man, privileged to know what surrounds him, man, so generously endowed, shares in the wealth of being, so that here too the Gospel words hold: "To him who has shall be given, and he shall have abundance." [24]

Intentional existence—to St. Thomas the indwelling in the knower of the thing known—was applied by Brentano to the whole range of "psychological phenomena," and made their characteristic mark. In later years, Husserl was to discard the concept of in-existence, teaching instead that an object was "intentionally present" to consciousness. He also differed with Brentano on the thesis that all psychological experiences are intentional, saying that sensations, for instance, were not; it is not the sensations which are seen, but the thing. No matter how I turn a box, and so have before me its several planes at various angles, I see one and the same box; I *intend* the same object. With Brentano, however, Husserl maintained that consciousness is consciousness of *something*, and maintained it against the shallow and flat notion held by many of his contemporaries that feelings, for example, were merely conditions, with no necessary relation to any object. It is unthinkable, Husserl said, that one should be pleased without something pleasing; neither can there be desire without something which is desired, nor can there be consent without an object to which consent is given. All these are intentions or, as Husserl called them, "acts." There are differences in intention and therefore differences in consciousness, but never is there consciousness without an intended object.

This is by no means a complete account of Husserl's thought on intentionality. Its significance goes much further, for intentionality is a relationship only persons can attain, distinguishing the full life of the spirit from life unleavened by the spirit. As the meaningful relation to an object, intentionality differs from instinct, which is blind to meaning; it is also unlike a state such as fatigue, which, though having a cause, may be said merely to exist, a brutal fact, in itself meaningless, and not communicating with an ob-

60   *Edmund Husserl*

ject. Contrariwise, intentionality is luminous, does justice to the world, and establishes a dialogue between subject and object. In joy, longing or love, man addresses himself to objects; in knowledge, objects address him. Such is the world of intentionality: man speaks to objects and they to him, and this colloquy between man and world echoes that in the beginning was the Word, and that in and by the Word the universe was created. Hence intentionality, the meaningful contact between subject and object, relentlessly disavows the modern neglect of the object, which says: To be convinced is all that matters, of what one is convinced matters not; it disavows that attitude which applauds enthusiasm, careless of its object, whether St. Francis' fire for God or Stalin's lust for power; which admires zeal as such, whether it be to save or to destroy.

Husserl's "turning to the object," as it has been called, made possible for many a rediscovery of the world—that it was *there,* having dimension and scope. The philosophy of the last century had depleted the world till it was shorn of content, "body," significance, and even being, making it ever thinner and thinner. All Descartes wished to start from was his mind, thoughts independent of things; innate ideas were his norms. He thought, and therefore he was; his thoughts existed, and hence God, and hence the world. After Kant had been "aroused" from his "dogmatic slumbers," he was left with nothing but criticism, and it is not chance that his main works are three *Critiques.* God, freedom, and immortality could and ought to be thought, but could not be known; all we perceive of the world was but appearance, so that the phenomenal world, bodies in space and time, would vanish were our minds to vanish. This trend toward emptying the world reached its nadir in Hans Vaihinger's "As-If," in which nothing was real, nothing true, no shred of human knowledge left. To him, human knowledge was a vast web of fictions, unverifiable, not an image of reality but merely a convenient means for man's biological preservation.

Before this low was reached, however, Husserl had spoken. Reinstating philosophy in its true domain—philosophy which had become a subsection of psychology—reclaiming the objectivity of truth, he prepared the way for modern philosophy to regain respect for reality, reverence for that which is. Here Husserl's work meets the perennial philosophy. He himself stated that it was the scholastic concept of intentionality, transformed by Brentano into a basic concept of psychology, which alone made phenomenology possible.[25] Though he stressed the *"transformed* concept"—and rightly, for the difference between the two philosophies should not be minimized; nor should Husserl's original understanding of intentionality, his great contribution to philosophic thought, be ignored—still, St. Thomas was the far-off parent of this vision: things were seen again, truth was honored.

From Arithmetic to Logic

It was in the same period, in the middle eighties, that Brentano introduced Husserl to Bolzano's thought, but it was not until later, after he had read Hermann Lotze's *Logic,* that Husserl's eyes were opened to Bolzano's significance. Priest, mathematician, and philosopher, Bernard Bolzano was outstanding in many ways, combining sharp intellect with tender conscience and deep piety. During the first decades of the nineteenth century he had taught at the University of Prague, where some of his social and political ideas brought him into conflict with the state authorities; compelled to retire, he bore the blow with the patience and manliness of a priest. In his day a great influence among his students, his work was all but forgotten at the time Husserl first began to read him.

Clarity was Bolzano's great aim; of the method of Hegel, his contemporary, he said that it was disastrous drivel.[26] The writings of Fichte, Schelling, and other German idealists were unbearable to him, for "nothing," he said, "is thought clearly; one plays with mere pictures, and every similarity, however superficial, is pronounced an identity." [27] Once he presented a friend with a portrait of Kant, not, he said, as a sign that he shared the opinions of that renowned philosopher, but rather in order that every look at it might remind his friend of one of his life's tasks: by the dissemination of clear concepts to undo, as best he could, the desperate confusion which Kant, all unforeseeing, had caused by his philosophy.[28] To Bolzano, philosophy was the science of the objective relationships among truths. "We make it our task to penetrate as far as possible into their ultimate foundations in order to become wiser and better." [29]

Bolzano was firmly convinced, of course, of the existence of a supreme moral law, objective, reigning independently of man, though, strangely, he seems to have thought it even above God; he was probably led to this overstress by his revulsion against moral relativity. His theory of knowledge, too, fought relativity, being built on three chief concepts: proposition-in-itself, presentation-in-itself, truth-in-itself. The "in-itself" was the immaterial essence of things, that spiritual something which lies behind phenomena; not grasped by our senses nor through our concepts, but found by intuition; existing independently of anything human or earthly; thought by God. Of the three, the towering concept was truth-in-itself—to Bolzano, a sentence which stated a thing as it was, regardless of whether that sentence had ever been thought or spoken by anyone.[30] Much in Bolzano's writings is contestable, but in a day when the absolute was scorned, when all was considered relative, his certainty that truth and the good were objective, above space and time, made him share in their timelessness.

Many years after his death in 1848, Bolzano's philosophy bore fruit in the mind of Husserl. There are those who see in Husserl's philosophy a mere extension of Bolzano's; there are others who belittle the link that ties the two. Both err. Husserl himself declared that he received "decisive impulses from Bolzano," whom he called "one of the greatest logicians of all time," and whose main work, *Theory of Science,* he thought "left far behind everything the world literature had to offer on the systematic treatment of the elements of logic." He praised its scientific rigor, its purity of presentation, its many original and fruitful thoughts, and concluded that it was "on Bolzano's work that logic must build itself as a science; from this work logic must learn what it needs: mathematical sharpness in distinctions, mathematical exactness in theories." [31]

Husserl wrote this appreciation of Bolzano, believer in objective truth, in 1900. He had begun his philosophical career, however, under the spell of the then prevailing view which made psychology the basis of all philosophy. In 1886, on Brentano's counsel, he went to the University of Halle, where he became an assistant to Carl Stumpf, and a year later, *Privatdozent.* There he published, in 1891, his *Philosophy of Arithmetic,* in which he examined the first principles of mathematics. Number, he saw dependent on plurality, and plurality arising, by means of reflection or abstraction, from a concrete totality. Any object can be united with another object, or with several others, and thus be counted: for example, certain trees; sun, moon, earth, and Mars; a feeling, the moon, and Italians. In all these instances, he said, we can speak of a totality, of a plurality, and of a definite number.[32] We unite these objects by a psychical act, which he called "collective connection," whose linguistic expression is "and." Thus, totality and plurality have their origin in the mind, in the act of knowing; and the connection, or as he called it, the "togetherness" of things is psychological and does not bespeak an objective relationship between them.

At this time, when Husserl wrote his *Philosophy of Arithmetic*, his world was built from psychical contents by psychical acts. It was a mental, not a real world; of the real world, in which things are, and are related, he held that nothing can be stated, all knowledge being confined to psychical phenomena or presentations of things. It is indeed an innocent pleasure, countered one of Husserl's principal critics, to call the moon a presentation, so long as one does not come to fancy that one can, by psychological acts, move the moon, not to speak of bringing it into being.[33]

Soon, however, Husserl himself realized that he was a victim of what the same critic called a widespread philosophical sickness. That he was in time able to recover was due, in no small degree, to the influence of Brentano and Bolzano, who had in turn been dependent on the philosophical tradition of the Church. To say this, is no attempt to force on Husserl a philosophic genealogy; rather is it a matter of historic record. He himself was aware of this debt, as he showed when he answered the accusation that his "pure logic" brought back "the old and useless lumber of scholasticism," with the forthright stand: "The objection that what is involved here is a restoration of scholastic-aristotelian logic, on whose insignificance history has spoken, need not disturb us. Perhaps someday it will turn out that the discipline in question is by no means of such little scope nor so poor in deeper problems, as the reproach would have it. Perhaps the old logic was only a very incomplete and clouded realization of the idea of pure logic; but for all that, as a beginning, as a first attempt, it is excellent and merits respect. It may also be asked whether the contempt for traditional logic is not an unjustified consequence of the moods of the Renaissance, whose motives can no longer touch us. . . . The polemics of the Renaissance were empty and fruitless; in them passion spoke, not insight." [34]

The Vanity of Idols

In the *Prolegomena to Pure Logic,* the first volume of his *Logical Investigations,* published in 1900, Husserl renounced adherence to any theory which would have reason depend on something not rational, on something relative to the human species, to man's psycho-physical constitution, to the workings of his mind, or to some stage in his development such as a cultural epoch. These views, which Husserl subsumed under the name of "psychologism," reduce the laws of logic—and in consequence all truth, religious, moral, and otherwise—to a merely human mode of thinking, to subjective experiences or psychical processes. His criticism of these views showed him bold, for his philosophical foes were many. Though they had little in common, though their doctrines often contradicted one another so that they gave the spectacle of a *bellum omnium contra omnes,* a war of all against all,[35] they were united in one thing: their denial of objective knowledge. Characteristically kind, however, Husserl turned the edge of his criticism by confessing to the zeal of the newly converted. "Against nothing," he cited Goethe, "is one more severe than against an error recently renounced." [36]

He *was* severe, and rightly so, for he knew that psychologism was built on air. No charge against a theory, and particularly against a theory of logic, he said, could be more serious than that it violates the very conditions that make a theory possible. And these conditions are twofold: those within the mind of the knower, and those arising from the nature of the theory. First, to know is to judge, and judgment does not merely claim to have attained truth, but is also certain that this claim is justified. But if the knower is never and nowhere able to experience this certitude, if in all his judgments he lacks that evidence which distinguishes judgment from blind prejudice and gives him the luminous certainty of having the truth, he cannot reasonably hold a theory. Second, a theory is an objective body of propositions linked as grounds and consequences. But when a theory denies the laws governing the linkage of propositions, when it maintains that terms like "theory," "truth," "proposition," "object," "property," "relation," and others are without consistent meaning, it nullifies itself. Psychologism does exactly this. Offending against these two basic conditions, it is not only false but absurd from the very start.[37]

Protagoras' saying that man is the measure of all things[38] expresses the relativist slant of mind, which is the mark of psychologism. "Man" here may mean the individual thinker or all mankind. If the former, truth is for anyone what appears true to him, so that what is true for one may be false for another. "Impertinent skepticism," Husserl branded this view, in which knowledge and truth are relative to the subject who happens to be judging, and he doubted that this impertinence had ever been seriously defended. On the other hand, Husserl went on, modern philosophy was so strongly bent toward anthropologism—the kind of relativism which understands "man" in Protagoras' dictum not as the individual but as the species—that it was exceptional to find a thinker who knew how to keep himself free of its errors.[39] Hardly anyone could guard himself against the infection of psychologism, he exclaimed, though it is a theory which labors under the greatest absurdities. Sober, precise, unanswerable—such are the arguments he heaped upon it.

First, to say that for each kind of being, truth is that which must be thought true according to *its* constitution, *its* laws of thought makes no sense; for the same proposition could then be true for one species and false for another. The meaning of the words "true" and "false," however, makes it impossible for anything to be at once false and true. Thus the thesis of the relativist contradicts the meaning of the very words he uses for its assertion.

Second, if the relativist contends that there are beings for whom the principle of contradiction (that a thing cannot *be* and *not be* at the same time) and the principle of the excluded middle (that between two contradictory statements there can be no middle ground; if one of them is denied, the other must be affirmed) do not apply, he means either that for them there are propositions which do not accord with these laws of logic, or else that their actual thinking is not *psychologically* governed by them. This last would in no way be odd, for we ourselves are just such beings. As to the first, Husserl replied, either these beings understand the

66   *Edmund Husserl*

words "true" and "false" as we do—but then, there could be no rational talk about the principles not applying, since they pertain to the meaning of the words as *we* understand them, and never in all the world would we call anything true or false save by their measure; or else, these beings use the words "true" and "false" in an entirely different sense—in which case the dispute becomes merely verbal. If, for instance, what we call "propositions" they call "trees," the principles indeed do not apply, for their meaning has been destroyed. A total change of the meaning of the word "truth"—this is all relativism amounts to; it changes the meaning of the word, while still using it in the sense determined by the principles of logic—in the one and only sense we all use it when we speak of truth.

Third, to base truth on the constitution of a species is to base it on a fact, and thus to give it the character of a fact, which is always individual and temporal; and again, this is absurd. For one must not confuse the content of a judgment with the individual act of judging. My act of judging that two times two equals four, is, no doubt, determined by many causes—that I have eyes and ears, that I was taught to count, and so on. No such factors, however, determine the judgment itself, the truth, "two times two equals four," which is one and the same, no matter who says it.

Fourth, if man's constitution is the source of truth, it follows that if this constitution were to cease to exist, truth also would cease to exist. But to say, "There is no truth," is the same as saying, "It is true that there is no truth," which is a logical impossibility. That mankind should come to an end is, however, logically possible; it may indeed be factually false, but it is certainly not absurd. Hence the relativist would have a logically possible antecedent lead to a logically impossible conclusion, which, said Husserl, is preposterous.

Fifth, if all truth is dependent on the existence of a given species, so also is the truth that this species exists, from which we must conclude that the species is *causa sui*. That a species could be its own cause becomes manifestly absurd when we consider that this species might cease to exist. The relativist would tell us then that *now* the species is the cause of its own *non*-existence. Here we journey, Husserl remarked, from nonsense to nonsense.

Lastly, the relativity of truth brings with it the relativity of the world's existence, since truth and the object of truth are bound up together. If truth is made subjective, there can be no world as such, but only a world for this or that species of being. This might suit some people very well, said Husserl, but the situation would seem somewhat graver to them were they to realize that they too, with their consciousness, form part of this relative world. Once consciousness is made relative, even statements like "I am" or "I experience this or that" have no stable, no true meaning. Furthermore, if truth were relative, and were it to happen that there were no beings so constituted as to acknowledge the world, there would be no world. The whole psychologistic thesis becomes stranger still when one stops to think that some change in the animal species on whose constitution the truth of the world is supposed to depend would then bring about a change in the world; but each animal species is at the same time said to be the evolutionary product of the world. Here we have a pretty game: man evolves from the world, and the world from man; God creates man, and man God.[40]

Husserl was not one to think of himself as another Daniel, to whom the Lord said: "Thou man of desires, understand the words that I speak, and stand upright." [41] Indeed, in temperament he was far from that eager young prophet of Israel but, like him, he showed up the vanity of idols; as Daniel trapped the priests of Bel in their own footprints, so Husserl the relativists.

The Logical Absolutist

In his battle against psychologism, Husserl did not count his task done with holding up to view its absurd consequences; he also uncovered its source in three prejudices. The first prejudice is this: The rules which govern all psychical activity are founded psychologically, and therefore the norms of knowledge must be also. But, Husserl countered, the laws of logic are not norms, directions for correct thinking, rules to which one ought to conform that one's thoughts may be valid; neither does the fact that they can be used as norms make them so, since any general truth, psychological or otherwise, can be used to formulate a norm of correct judgment. For example, the truth that if every A is a B, and S is an A, then S is also a B, can be recast as a precept: All who judge that every *A* is a *B,* and that a certain *S* is an *A,* should also judge that this *S* is a *B.* This fact, that any general truth, whether psychological or not, can yield a rule of correct thinking, assures us that there exist rules of judgment not based on psychology. The laws of logic certainly are not; they are autonomous, self-evident truths, principles which need not be proven, standing "as axioms at the summit of all deductions." [42]

The second error is a confusion of content and method. In order to justify his first prejudice, the psychologist asks: What are understood by presentation and judgment, conclusion and proof, truth and possibility, and so on, if not psychical phenomena? If this were so, Husserl wrote, pure mathematics would be a branch of psychology. It is true, he continued, that sums arise from addition and products from multiplication, and that these and other mathematical operations are psychological. But although mathematical *concepts* are psychological in origin, mathematical *laws* are not psychological, not dependent on man's constitution. To count, "one, two, three, four, five," is a psychological act, occurring in time; the numbers 1, 2, 3, 4, 5, however, are nonempirical, nontemporal in character, and it is with these that arithmetic concerns itself. The same distinction holds for logic: Logical concepts have indeed a psychological origin, but the laws of logic, the principle of contradiction, for instance, do not grow out of psychical experiences. Whoever would have it so is guilty of the fallacy of accident, which argues from some accidental character as if it were essential and necessary: The food you buy, you eat; you buy raw meat; therefore you eat raw meat. Because the laws of logic are experienced, and experience is psychological, the psychologist assumes that the laws are psychological; but he mistakes *what* is "intended" for the *way* in which it is "intended." [43]

The third delusion identifies evidence and the feeling of evidence. Truth is said to reside in judgment alone, and evidence to be a peculiar feeling which somehow guarantees it. Truth does not reside in judgment, however, Husserl countered, but in itself. And evidence is not a feeling, accessory to judgment, tacked on to it by chance or by some law of nature, not at all a psychic mark; it is the very experience of truth, in which the judger becomes conscious that his judgment is correct and in conformity with truth.

69

Evidence is the awareness of harmony between meaning and that which is meant, of perfect correspondence between the assertion and the fact, and thus it is the final, ultimate fulfillment of "intention." Where there is evidence, the object is "intended" exactly as it is given, exactly as it is present; so present is it in the experience of evidence that we can say: Here truth is seen, grasped, comprehended. No doubt, the subjective feeling of evidence is favored by many psychological factors, such as attention, concentration, mental freshness, practice; but this in no way renders evidence itself psychological, nor does it gainsay its objectivity. The basic condition for the feeling of evidence is that evidence presents itself. An erroneous feeling of evidence is of course a deception; distorted though it may be, it is nonetheless a feeling *of* evidence, and bespeaks that evidence as such does exist and is prior to any feeling. "The feeling of evidence," Husserl said, "has no essential condition other than the truth of the judgment to which it pertains. As it is self-evident that where there is nothing, nothing can be seen, so is it self-evident that where there is no truth, there can be no insight into truth, in other words, no evidence." [44]

Standing against the psychologism of his day, Husserl spoke of himself as a "logical absolutist," [45] as *ein logischer Alltagsmensch,* an everyday man in matters of logic,[46] for to him the denial of objectivity was sheer insanity, while its defense was common sense. With an eye on Epicurus and Hegel, who rejected the principle of contradiction, he said sarcastically that genius and madness were perhaps alike in this: there might be madmen who denied the laws of logic—and still one must admit that they were men.[47] Again and again he called the prejudices and fancies of psychologism *widersinnig,* nonsensical, but was careful to point out that he used the word without coloring, as a scientific term.[48] Literally, these prejudices make no sense. Husserl knew that the laws of logic are lasting, enduring, unchanging, the same for every individual and species, untouched by circumstance or time.[49] No psychic event can render knowledge error, or error knowledge, just as no psychic event could ever accomplish that the color red before me be the pitch of middle C, or that the lower of two notes be the higher.[50] The laws of logic are not empirical, not merely averages, of which there could be said: No rule without exception. On the contrary, they are exact, self-evident, given to us by insight.

Husserl's main argument follows classical lines, recalling the vigorous reasoning of Plato, Aristotle, St. Augustine and St. Thomas. In the *Theaetetus*, Socrates declares that it is absurd to say no one ever deems anyone else mistaken, and yet that this is the absurdity implied by Protagoras' "Man is the measure of all things." The best of the joke, Socrates continues, is that since Protagoras admits the opinions of all men to be true, he acknowledges his own opinion to be false. Thus he undoes his own philosophy.[51] Aristotle, in his *Metaphysics,* also shows how untenable is the relativist's position: If all opinions are true, then all opinions must be at once true and false, so that the same thing must both be and not be. Such a view destroys itself, for "he who says everything is true makes even the statement contrary to his own true, and therefore his own not true." [52] St. Augustine says: "Everyone who knows that he is in doubt about something, knows a truth; and, in regard to this, that he knows, he is certain. Therefore, he is certain about a truth." [53] After them, St. Thomas, terse as steel, writes: "That there is truth is self-evident: Who denies that truth exists, concedes that truth exists, for if truth does not exist, it is true that 'truth does not exist.' But if there is one thing that is true, then truth must be." [54]

Truth is absolute: this is Husserl's answer to the psychologists. They would have it relative, dependent on those who think it, so that the law of gravitation, for instance, would not have been true until Newton discovered it. But truth is not born from the knower. "What is true," declared Husserl, "is absolutely true, true in itself; truth is identically one, whether it be grasped by man or monster or angel." [55] It cannot be assigned this or that place in time, not even duration through all of time; it is beyond and above it.[56]

The nature of a truth never varies, whether it be known or not. "Every truth in itself remains what it is and keeps its ideal existence; it is not 'somewhere in the void,' but a valid unity in the timeless realm of ideas." To this realm belong all the truths into whose validity we have insight or at least a founded supposition, and all that is valid, though we may not yet know it or may never know it.[57] Distinguished from these ideal truths are all assertions on temporal events; their realm is that of matter-of-fact. Truth and being, said Husserl, are both "categories" in the same sense, and obviously correlative;[58] they are *a priori* given together and inseparable from one another. Nothing can *be* unless it is determined as this or that, but *that* it is, and is so determined, is truth in itself, the necessary correlative of being in itself.[59] In the words of Husserl, truth is "an identity, the complete agreement between what is meant and what is given," *adequatio rei et intellectus*.[60]

Thomas and the Truth

Husserl was right and clear when he demolished psychologism, but his own discussion on truth does not have equal clarity and precision. It might illumine the problem if we set the thought of St. Thomas, still so little known, side by side with that of Husserl. There are still many, though fewer today than yesterday, who think that he is called the Angelic Doctor not for his integral purity and inexhaustible patience but for his inquiry into the question of how many angels could dance on the point of a pin. He never wrote on any such question, nor is it likely that he ever gave it a thought, for it is merely the farcical statement of his problem of angel and place, of the meeting of spirit and matter, put up to ridicule by an age which no longer understood its depth. Yet that angels dance is a metaphor of what was truly St. Thomas's belief, that the life of pure spirits, their contemplation of truth, is never-ending joy—a certainty lost to our age which, itself insipid and bored, can conceive contemplation only as boredom.

Long before Husserl spoke of truth as *adequatio rei et intellectus,* the equation of reality and mind, of thing and thought—a description attributed to the tenth-century Jewish philosopher Isaac Israeli—St. Thomas had made it his own. He knew indefinable the majesty of truth, in whose service he spent his life, and in humility borrowed the words of another.

Isaac Israeli's description of truth he preferred to others' because of its brevity and fullness: It gives a place to both world and mind, linking one to the other; it speaks of truth in its fullest meaning, as the truth in us and above us, for *intellectus,* the knowing mind, can be understood as our own or as that of the Creator. All things in nature lie between divine and human knowledge, and are called true in so far as they conform with the one and the other.[61] God's knowledge of them is the well of their being, *scientia Dei est causa rerum;* [62] His knowledge of things does not derive from things, rather do they issue forth from His knowing them. Hence we can draw truth only from God, in whom it dwells, for all things carry His imprint, bear His design, and therefore tie us to Him. "Our ideas come from above even when they come from below, as the image of the sun in the sea comes in reality from the sun, though it comes from the sea. Our knowledge is an ideal reflection, as all beings are a real, of an Absolute, at once ideal and real." [63]

We need the senses which mirror the world, and the intellect which throws light upon its images, says St. Thomas, so that the universal may stand out from the particular, and that we may pass from phantasm to concept. Here on earth our concepts cannot be formed without senses and imagination, which lend themselves as mother to the work of the fathering intellect. And it is because of this intellect—*quasi quaedam similitudo increatae veritatis in nobis,* a likeness in us of the divine Mind, of uncreated Truth—which immediately grasps first principles, that God is in a special sense the Author of our knowledge. "There are in us to begin with seeds of all knowledge, first concepts of the intellect, known immediately . . ." [64] "Thus, in a certain way all knowledge is originally given us." [65] So St. Thomas holds, and he concludes: "God is preeminently the cause of man's knowledge, for He marked the soul with the light of the intellect, and He set His seal upon it in its knowledge of first principles, which are, as it were, the seeds of knowledge." [66] Among these first principles are: One cannot at the same time affirm and deny the same thing; good is to be done and evil avoided; every whole is greater than each of its parts.

The mind's inner light is God-given, so that one can almost say that in it God speaks to us;[67] and this is the actual, the ultimate origin of our certitude. But it is not only by adverting to the divine likeness of our mind that we can have confidence in it, for St. Thomas stresses again and again that this assurance is natural to man, and hence sufficient to itself: "What is naturally given to reason is certain to be true, so true that we cannot so much as think it to be false." [68] Even if we doubt this certitude, we do so only by dint of our reason, and even if we deny or ridicule truth, we use the faculty God gave us, so true is it that the assent to first principles is at once an assent to objective truth and to our own nature, which is ordained to it.[69] Hence St. Augustine counseled:

Intellectum valde ama, "Greatly love the intellect," [70] to which St. Thomas and all Catholic philosophers reply: I do, and in all of them the Church speaks.

St. Thomas's trust in the soundness of man's mind is serene: the intellect, he says, tends toward truth. But it is significant that his *Quaestio* on truth in the *Summa* is preceded by one on God's knowledge and by another on ideas. He agrees with St. Augustine that "the doctrine of ideas is so potent that no one can be wise without insight into them." [71] But he is equally determined that there is not, as Platonists have thought, a store of innate ideas in the soul, nor reminiscence of ideas existing in themselves; they are not an intermediate kingdom interposed as another world between God and this world. [72] Rather, ideas are, in God the Maker, examplars of all things He makes, and in God the Knower, likenesses of all things He knows, whether made or not. [73] Thus all things have in Him their firm foundation, so that Père Sertillanges, comparing this vision of the world with the relativist notions of so many moderns, can say that St. Thomas's vision is as if drawn by Michelangelo in a hand heavy but sharp, in lines broad but clear, while the modern notions are much like the paintings of Carrière, which no sooner rise from the mist than they fall back into it again. [74]

The ideas are in God, one with His essence, and whatever distinctions among them our intellect is compelled to make, they are comprised in His simplicity. [75] They are His knowledge of things, one and all-surpassing; and thus their manifoldness is not in Him but in His creatures, which, according to His loving will, reflect Him in many ways and divers degrees. The transcendental truth is one, and everything is true in so far as it is related to this one first truth. [76] Further, every truth is eternal, but only in God. [77] Likewise, universals, which are beyond space and time, are indeed everywhere and always, but they are not eternal save in the Mind which is eternal. [78] St. Thomas answers the contention that created truth has neither beginning nor end—of what is true today it has always been true that it will be, and will always be true that it was—by declaring again that this is so only in the First Cause. [79] Created truth is not absolute, for truth is a relationship between thing and mind, *adequatio rei et intellectus.* Hence, there can be no truth unless there is knowledge, nor can there be truth unless there is being. A truth which precedes itself as one that will be, or outlasts itself as one that was, is a fiction, unless there is something to be known and someone to know it. The thing to be known need not necessarily exist actually, provided that it exist in its causes. Thus, the truths of things are eternal in the will and might of their Creator.

Suppose the impossible: that there were being, but no mind to know it; then there would be being, but no truth. Both being and mind *are,* however, and truth is the relation of one to the other.[80] It does reside in things, but primarily in the knower. Hence the knower is neither a dreamer without a world, nor merely its recorder; his thoughts are not concocted out of whole cloth with no link to reality, nor are they the wrigglings of a seismograph. St. Thomas thus exalts the objectivity of knowledge, and at the same time gives the thinking subject a dignity which outranks anything the subjectivists at their best could imagine.

As firmly as St. Thomas upheld the power of man's mind, just as firmly did he insist on its limitations. Nor was his tranquil certainty that the intellect reaches toward truth disturbed by his admission that "our manner of knowing is so weak that no philosopher could perfectly investigate the nature of even one little fly." [81] It was his belief in God that shielded him against both despair and presumption, against the dethronement of reason which condemns it to crawl on the ground and eat dust, and no less against the arrogance claiming for reason the strength to explore all heaven, to disclose all mysteries. Gladly he acknowledged the need for faith, and it was faith which taught him that truth, revealed truth, is not only to be known, but to be lived. His voice joined the psalmist's: "Thy kindness is before mine eyes, and I *walk* in Thy truth." [82] He experienced St. Paul's saying, so startling in its directness: *"Doing* the truth in charity, we grow in all things in Christ." [83]

St. Thomas, the philosopher, can go no further than that man's intellect tends toward truth. St. Thomas, the Christian, however, believes that Truth sought man, came to him, and was made Flesh; and that Truth-made-Flesh still seeks man, lost in labyrinthine ways, come to a standstill in a blind alley; still calls to be heard, no matter how thick the walls of man's deafness. And when he stands before Truth offering Himself as food and drink in the sacrament of love, St. Thomas sings:

Credo quidquid dixit Dei Filius,
Nil hoc verbo Veritatis verius.

Gerard Manley Hopkins and Richard Crashaw, among others, took up his song, writing each his own paraphrase:

What God's Son has told me, take for truth I do;
Truth Himself speaks truly or there's nothing true.

Faith is my force; faith strength affords
To keep pace with those powerful words.
And words more sure, more sweet than they
Love could not think, truth could not say.[84]

Word and World

The year 1900, in which Husserl's *Prolegomena to Pure Logic* first appeared, was epoch-making for philosophy. Against man's craft to deny and distort, here sanity prevailed over prejudice, man's steady light over psychologism's will-o'-the-wisp. It was a triumph for logic, and thus, ultimately, a triumph of the Logos, the Word by whom all is made, the Reason and Meaning of all things visible and invisible. Much in our lesser word, much in language, varies with age, use and culture, and obeys no lasting rule; but its core reveals a higher law, points to the Logos, the eternal Word. No matter how gravely a man lies, as long as he speaks at all he cannot altogether escape truth, for if he but open his mouth, it is to confess the great truths. When he says "I am," he grants the existence of the person; when he says "I will," he admits his freedom; when he says "I hope," he professes, knowingly or not, the providence of God. Consequently, the materialist, the determinist, the atheist, who say—and since they cannot shed their human nature, they must say—"I am," "I will," "I hope," give the lie to their philosophies. Critical of Heraclitus for saying that one could not step into the same river twice, Cratylus, the only thoroughgoing skeptic, thought that one could not do it even once. To speak at all, he knew, was to acknowledge the objectivity of truth; therefore he deadened the word in himself, kept mute, and only moved his finger.[85]

Language is fastened to truth; the human word mirrors the Word of God. One can ask how German or Latin or Chinese expresses the existential proposition that something is or is not, such as "God exists," "There are men who call themselves agnostics"; how they express the categorical proposition, when something is directly stated in verbal form, such as "Who sings well prays twice," or "The heaven's wide circuit speaks the Maker's high magnificence"; and how the hypothetical proposition, in which two propositions are linked by "if–then" or "either–or," such as "If the mists were dispersed from our hearts, then we could see things invisible to mortal sight," "Christianity is either the way of salvation or the most gigantic of frauds." We can ask how German or Latin or Chinese expresses the plural, the possible and probable, the negative. But all these questions could not be asked *meaningfully* were there not foundations and laws *a priori* to all empirical modifications, were there not an ideal structure which every actual language garbs in a different way. And indeed there is a "pure grammar," Husserl stated in the second volume of the *Logical Investigations.*[86]

In this second volume of Husserl's main work, first published in 1901 and in a revised edition in 1913, he sought an objective theory of knowledge, a pure phenomenology of the experiences of knowledge and thought. Of its six *Investigations,* the first is devoted to "Expression and Meaning," the second to "Universals and Abstraction," the third deals with "Wholes and Parts," the fourth with "The Idea of Pure Grammar," the fifth is a study of "Intentional Experiences and Their Contents," and the sixth, entitled "Elements of Phenomenological Elucidation of Knowledge," is concerned with, among other things, the levels of knowledge, with sensibility and understanding, with perception and intuition. From these *Investigations* and from Husserl's later writings, phenomenology emerges as a philosophical method which seeks the road to true and valid knowledge, and whose appeal is to "things themselves."

"To go to things themselves" is its oft-repeated supreme rule—to go to them and ask them what they themselves tell of themselves, and consequently to win certitudes which in no way result from preconceived theories or from accepted but unverified opinions. This rule entails two principles. First, we must abstain from all presuppositions, so that nothing is considered definitely attained which is not apodictically justified. Since there are to be no pre-judgments—for what knowledge must turn to are the *Urgegeben-heiten,* that which is originally given and lies before all theories —not even the exact sciences can be taken for granted.[87] Second, we need what Husserl called *Wesensschau,* eidetic intuition. Eidetic intuition does not mean seeing the essence of a thing in a single glance or in a sudden overpowering illumination; rather is it an insight earned by painstaking labor, by rigorous work, by putting aside all accidentals and lifting out the essential, the *eidos.* Only after this work has been done can one rest in the vision of essences. That this grasp of essences is called *Schau,* vision, is of course metaphorical, bringing to mind St. Thomas's "We adopt the terms of sensible cognition for intellectual cognition, above all those which belong to sight, the noblest among the senses, the most spiritual, and therefore the most akin to the intellect. And it is because of this that intellectual cognition itself is called vision." [88]

The "intuition of essences" is gained, according to Husserl, not by comparing many objects and abstracting from them their essential qualities; instead, a true intuition of one object reveals its essence. To this intuition is assigned what St. Thomas assigns to the intellect, *est enim intelligere quasi intus legere,* to understand is to read the "within" of being, to decipher the inner nature of things.[89] Husserl called it "the principle of principles" that all underived, originally given data are an authoritative source of knowledge. "Everything which presents itself in intuition in primordial form (in, as it were, *bodily* reality), is simply to be accepted as what it gives itself to be, but only within the limits in which it gives itself." [90] And further: "In phenomenology one must have the courage to accept in the phenomenon, without any twisting, what really presents itself to mental insight, exactly as it presents itself, and to describe it honestly." [91] What is demanded of the philosopher, and of every man who wishes to know, is courage and submission, a mind selfless and open to truth, a soul without guile.

The Phenomenological Eye

Phenomenology is therefore the *logos legon ta phainomena,* the science which reads phenomena as they are. One might say of it what Nietzsche said of philology, that it is "the art of reading well

. . . of being able to read facts without falsifying them by interpretation, without losing, in the desire for understanding, care, patience and finesse." [92] Perhaps no one has made so vivid the original aim of phenomenology as Adolf Reinach, Husserl's first coworker; Husserl himself said that "he was among the first who could understand, creatively and perfectly, the peculiar meaning of the phenomenological method and could view its entire philosophical range." [93]

In 1914, before a study circle at the University of Marburg, the stronghold of neo-Kantianism, Reinach discussed phenomenology. In his interpretation, straightforward and fresh, he said that what marks the phenomenologist is not adherence to a system of propositions, but the phenomenological eye. His is an attitude, a way of philosophizing, a way demanded by the problems of philosophy, differing greatly, therefore, from the manner in which we look around and find our way through life, and even more from the manner in which we work, and must work, in most sciences. In daily life we are practical: we see objects and we do not see them, that is, we see them less or more clearly, and what we see of them depends in general on our needs and purposes. We find it laborious to learn really to see—truly to see, for instance, the colors which strike upon our retina. Far more difficult for us is to grasp the qualitative structure of our psychic experience, that experience which is not without, like the sensible world, but within us. It is little enough the average man notices of it. He is aware, of course, of joy and pain, love and hatred, longing and nostalgia, but these are only rough segments of a realm of infinite nuance, for even the poorest inner life is too rich for its possessor to grasp. But here too we can learn to see, and for the average man it is art first of all which teaches him to see what he ignored before. The difficulties of philosophic vision mount when we turn to time, space, or number. We stand in space and time, we speak of them, we define them, we handle numbers and their rules, and this is sufficient for our practical life; but still their essences remain remote, so that we have to say with St. Augustine: "If no one asks me what time is, I know; but if I wish to explain to him who asks, I know not." [94]

It is a grave error and disastrous to think that our usual remoteness from objects, which is so hard to overcome, has been wiped out by science. By their very nature, certain sciences avoid the direct intuition of essences; they content themselves with definitions and deductions from definitions, as is their right. Other sciences, however, are by their nature committed to a direct grasp of essences, but have in their actual development so far shirked this task. Of these, psychology's failure is the most significant and the most appalling. Today's psychology has not even succeeded in winning clarity about its supreme and defining essence, the nature of the psychic, for it is by no means true, as some try to make us believe, that the difference between the psychic and the nonpsychic is created by our act of defining and fixing their boundaries. On the contrary, our defining and fixing must follow the essential distinctions between the psychic and the nonpsychic, distinctions which are not invented by science but are given and actually met with. What is part of the stream of our inner life, what belongs to the self, like feeling, willing, perceiving, differs in its nature from all that is not part of the stream of consciousness, such as houses or numbers. When I see a colored object in the outside world, then that object, with all its qualities, is obviously physical. My perception of it, however, my turning to it, the attention I give it, the joy I feel about it, my admiration, in short everything that is an activity or state or function of the self, are psychical. Modern psychology, on the other hand, treats colors, sounds, and odors as if they were part of our consciousness and not just as foreign to us as the most massive trees. Of course, not all psychologists have so misunderstood the sphere of the psychic, but only very few have understood their task: the pure grasp of essences.

Wishing to imitate the natural sciences, most psychologists "reduce" our many inner experiences to as few as possible, but in truth they merely falsify and impoverish our consciousness. As the result of a series of "reductions," they propose, as the chief essences of consciousness, feeling, willing, and thinking, or perceiving, judging, and feeling, or some other inadequate division. If any one of the vast, uncountable number of experiences is not comprised within their framework, it is perforce reinterpreted to make it fit. There is, for example, forgiveness, a unique, wonder-striking act, which rises from the depth of our soul. It is certainly not a perception; therefore it has been called a judgment—the judgment that the injustice suffered wasn't really so bad, or perhaps wasn't an injustice at all—exactly the circumstances in which one cannot meaningfully forgive. Or it has been said that it is the cessation of a feeling, the evaporation of anger; as if forgiveness were not something affirmative, something in its own right, much more than a mere forgetting or fading away. Descriptive psychology ought not to try to copy natural science; that is not its sphere and it does it but feebly, explaining away its very object, our experiences, tracing them always to something else. Is not its office rather to shed light on our inner life and lead us closer to it, to make the whatness of our inner experiences—often viewed by us as if we were outsiders, mere onlookers—ultimately clear, graphic, and visible, *anschaulich?* [95]

Insight into essences, Reinach continued in his lecture on phenomenology, is demanded not only in psychology but in other disciplines as well. And what must be seen is not only the essence of what occurs countless times, but also the essence of what is by its nature unique. The historian, for instance, takes pains to bring the unknown to light and the known into full focus; his goal and methods are of course his own, but he shares with the psychologist the difficulty of portraying an event adequately, in its singularity, as well as the temptation to evade full reality and to make instead some construction of his own. *The* evasion, *the* construction, of the age is "evolution." It is made a fundamental assumption of every discipline; it is talked about in lecture hall and market place, but no one asks what it is that evolves. Scientists, and their army of followers with them, anxiously look for the milieu, the environment, of a thing, so as not to be compelled to analyze the thing itself, and imagine they show the essence of a thing when they show its genesis or its consequences. [96]

Examples are legion for Reinach's thesis that for many today the "how" has displaced the "what," indeed, *is* the "what." For instance, because the events of childhood, its blows and caresses, help to shape conscience, conscience is said to be nothing but the result of childhood experiences. Further, conscience is judged not on its own wonder, but only on some of its secondary effects: health, happiness, loyalty to the state. Another instance is religious conversion, which often occurs at a crucial period: in youth, in an emotional crisis, during a severe illness, or after a great loss. At once it is attributed to one of these stresses, which are, in fact, not causes but occasions only. They do not force a conversion, rather do they jar complacency, so that the attention, no longer scattered among a thousand details of daily living, can now be gathered upon the whole of life. Who before had sought escape from the hard metaphysical facts now finds himself face to face with them. Modern theories of education, too, are at times derivative, as if a survey of educational methods, from the Australian aborigines through Plato to Montessori, could settle the problem. More often the theory is pragmatic, and education is considered adequate if only it fulfills the so-called needs of the times. There are few indeed who start by asking, "What is man?" "What is a child?" "Why do we educate?" and who only then proceed to the dependent question "*How* shall we educate?" Again, language, the limbs of truth and love, our means of expressing the whatness of things, by which the "I" seeks and finds the "thou," begins in each man's life with his infant babblings, and doubtless began in the life of mankind with expressions less rich and refined than ours. Forthwith, the essence of language is ignored and in a twinkle declared to be the advanced mumblings of the child and of primitive man.

The analysis of essences begins, of course, with words and their meanings, Reinach went on. It is no mere chance that Husserl's *Logical Investigations* starts with an analysis of the concepts "word," "expression," "meaning," and so on, for the first task is to master the incredible equivocations which clutter philosophical terminology. Husserl puts his finger on fourteen different meanings of "perception," for instance, and still does not exhaust the many others, mostly undifferentiated, which play a role in philosophy. Such distinctions are reproached with being captious and "scholastic," but unjustly, countered Reinach. And he could have added that "scholastic" means "hairsplitting" only to those who have lost the art of distinction; so cardinal is this art in philosophy that a small but obvious distinction, Reinach continued, may, if overlooked by the philosopher, lead to the overthrow of a whole philosophical theory.

The analysis of words and their meanings is but a beginning, Reinach pointed out; what it must lead to are things themselves, to which direct access is, of course, possible even without the help words give us. To put it another way, what philosophical analysis must lead to are essences, *Wesenheiten*, and their laws. The laws to which essences are subject hold good by virtue of the nature of the essences, which are as they are not accidentally but necessarily,

82 *Edmund Husserl*

which cannot be otherwise. To make clear what is meant by laws rooted in essences: that we cannot will without an object, *nihil volitum, nisi cogitatum,* is of inner necessity; but that we tire when we work is only of the factual order. Another illustration of these laws, which spring not from man's whim but from the nature of things: it is the nature of love to move toward the beloved, seeking a union which does not end. Though the true lover never loves on condition that he be loved in return, yet love itself, of inner necessity, calls for an answer. The *lover* must never force a response to his love; still his *love* demands it, and hence, in fidelity to his love, he will not relinquish the hope of a response. Further, the stronger the love, the greater the readiness to sacrifice. And love mounts according to the height of its object: if it does not rise above the physical plane, it may be intense but it is not sublime, for no love can be exalted unless its beloved is.[97]

That there are laws rooted in essences, such as these laws of love, is clearly of fundamental importance in every man's life and equally of great moment to philosophy, whose task is to lay them bare in their purity and thus arrive at the core of things. Philosophy must unveil the *a priori* truths. It is not Kant's concept that Reinach had in mind when he spoke of the *a priori;* indeed, he called Kant's restriction of the *a priori* disastrous.

The *a priori,* Reinach insisted, is rooted not in the mind but in things themselves, *in Sachverhalten;* it is rooted not in thinking but in being. Nor is universal consent the warrant of *a priori* truth, for it exists, no matter whether all or many or none recognize it. Neither are *a priori* truths necessities of our thinking, though indeed all who wish to think aright must follow them. Such necessity to thought is by no means a sufficient mark of the *a priori,* for if I am asked which occurred first, the American Revolution or the Civil War, I find it necessary to think of the Revolution as the earlier—and this is a matter of *empirical* knowledge. Necessity *does* play a role in the *a priori,* only it is not a necessity of thinking, rather one of being. That two objects lie side by side somewhere in space is accidental, for the two could be, without doing violence to their natures, at any distance from one another. A straight line is the shortest distance between two points: to say that this also could be otherwise is absurd, however, since it is the nature of a straight line to be the shortest distance.

83

Primarily, the *a priori* has nothing whatever to do with thinking or knowing, a truth Reinach demanded we see in all its sharpness lest we be deceived by the specious problems and curious constructions that clutter up the mansions of philosophy.[98]

The world of essences and their laws is open to us anywhere and always, Reinach exclaimed. To grasp them, one intuitive act is sufficient, an act that can be accomplished at any time and any place. At any moment, and without my having to go to some particular spot in the world where I may find orange, yellow, and red, I can convince myself, if only I bring their essences into clear view, that orange lies between yellow and red. All objects without exception, even the sensible, such as sounds and colors, have their whatness, their essences, and all follow *a priori* laws. This becomes clearer, Reinach went on, when we turn to psychic phenomena, especially to the link between motive and action, which as a matter of course we seek in daily life and again in the historic disciplines. We understand that from this or that attitude or experience there may, or may have to, spring this or that action. We understand, *not* because we have experienced again and again that people with a given attitude act in a given way, so that we are able to predict: This man will most likely act as they have done. Rather does motive itself give us this understanding, which no naked empirical fact can ever yield. The historian who follows a motivation or the psychiatrist who pursues the course of an illness—both understand even a novel development, because they are guided by the connections between essences, although they have never formulated them and may even be unable to do so.[99]

Everywhere, not only in the world of the soul but even in the world of nature, we must discard the attitude of natural science, with its defined and limited goals. We must discard it, Reinach insisted, however hard we find it, and brace ourselves to grasp phenomena in their purity, to toil without prejudice and preconception toward their essences: the essences of weight, extension, and matter, of light, color, and sound. In this we do not oppose natural science, rather we create the foundations which make its structure understandable. This analysis of essences which phenomenology proposes has opened new fields of exploration in the realms of both matter and spirit, and has shed new light on old problems, particularly on that of knowledge. We all speak of

84 *Edmund Husserl*

knowledge and mean something by it; but should this meaning be not precise enough, we can orientate ourselves by some instance of assured knowledge, and the simplest example is the best. Whatever instance we take—the knowledge that joy fills our hearts or that we see green, or that sound and color are not the same—in every case we see the whatness of knowledge, which is a receiving, a taking in and making one's own of the thing that presents itself.[100]

This was what he wanted to impress most emphatically, Reinach concluded his lecture. Phenomenology wishes to break with theories and constructions, and strives for a return to things themselves, to a pure, unalloyed intuition of essences. But this intuition is not thought of as a sudden inspiration and illumination; on the contrary, great exertion is needed to pierce the remoteness which stands between ourselves and objects, if we are to understand them clearly and luminously. Though we must be wary of many possible deceptions and of many wrong roads our thoughts could travel, phenomenological intuition can lead us closer and closer to the essences of things. To use Plato's image, it is the end of that labor in which the soul's chariot mounts toward heaven that she may see the ideas.[101]

The Bold Ways of God

Phenomenology truly sharpened philosophical sight and widened its field. Indeed, Reinach, and with him Husserl, whose mind he interpreted in his Marburg lecture, were sure that till their time philosophy had not fulfilled its most significant task: to unveil the laws of essences. Their impetuous judgment becomes understandable when one remembers how little they knew of the richness of St. Augustine and how much less of St. Anselm, St. Thomas, St. Bonaventure, and other medieval philosophers; that they were therefore pioneers, discoverers, or rather rediscoverers of a land forgotten by our time, things themselves. Not only did they bring back to modern thought, on the one hand, a good it had lost, the vision of reality, but on the other hand they enriched Catholic philosophy.

If the phenomenological analysis, to which Husserl gave the impetus, is received by Thomism and given a home, Thomism will be the winner, the Louvain philosopher, René Kremer, predicts.

In the ordinary presentation of Thomistic philosophy, he says, concrete description occupies little space. It is clear, however, that a realist philosophy such as Thomism, in which the individual, the concrete, is the *existent,* must attach value to a precise description of the object grasped. Abstract analyses and deductions always presuppose a certain knowledge of the concrete from which they are drawn, and are valid only in so far as they interpret the concrete correctly and are exactly applicable to it. There is, indeed, progress in making explicit what was only implicit; and a concrete analysis, methodical, probing, going to the core, helps avoid the danger of verbalism, which always menaces a highly abstract philosophy.[102]

That Husserl's intuition is not so alien to the thought of St. Thomas as it may seem is the thesis of Alfons Hufnagel. First, for St. Thomas, the end of all discursive reasoning, however laborious, is the simple acceptance of truth, the resting in it, and the peace which comes with its possession.[103] Moreover, St. Thomas holds that the first principles—for instance, that what is true cannot at the same time be false, that every thing has either being or not-being, that the whole is greater than any of its parts, or that good is to be done and evil avoided—are known *per se;* the intellect grasps their truth immediately, without need of reasoning, in a shining clarity of perfect evidence. But since the principles are known intuitively, their terms—being, the whole, the good—must be known intuitively as well, Hufnagel states.[104] Again, whenever St. Thomas calls the whatness of a sensible thing the *primum cognitum,* the first thing known, he is referring to the intuition of its spiritual content.[105] Hufnagel points also to St. Thomas's analogy between the intellectual cognition of essences and the sensible cognition of individual things: very much as the eye needs no *discursus,* no running to and fro, to see a stone, for it has its image within it, so the intellect grasps, without discursive reasoning, the essences of those things whose images are in the knower.[106]

Whatever the similarities between phenomenology and Thomism, the one great kinship between Catholic thought and phenomenology springs from the latter's motto: To go to things themselves. If the philosopher looks at things as they are, he will read the *Ipse pinxit* of the Creator. If he listens to them without prejudice, undeceived by his self-will, he will hear God speaking through them, and more and more marvel at and cherish them as the thoughts of God made manifest. Thus he receives the world anew from the hands of God and shares in the vision of Adam, who saw the work of creation not as the scientist but as the poet sees it, not in the exact order of time but according to the inner order which binds together all that is. He sees the cosmos as Adam saw it, summoned into being by God the Lord and bearing the seal of His benediction: When He looked upon it, He saw that it was good. When the philosopher penetrates the life of the soul, when, to take Reinach's example, he goes to the core of forgiveness, he will discover that to forgive is not to forget nor to look away from evil, but to transform evil into good. He will grasp that it is to give up the claim of justice, to wipe out debt, and to slay guilt so that innocence may rise again. He will seek forgiveness then and not find it, save in Christ; rather, he will never truly grasp forgiveness unless he prays with David: "Have mercy on me, O God, according to Thy great mercy";[107] unless he listens to Christ telling of the prodigal son, and looks up into the face of Him who hangs upon the cross.

As a philosopher, Husserl did not follow his thought to this end. Instead, in a strange deviation, he turned aside to a new subjectivism, demanding of the philosopher a retreat from the outer into the inner world, which he imagined would yield absolute certitude. But of most of the things of this world we can have no absolute certitude; no effort of ours, however gigantic, can change our metaphysical position or raise our humanity to the level of the angels. As a rule, we cannot arrive beyond moral certitude, which makes our life truly human—that is, at once humble and daring—and which suffices us that we may be true and good. Still, the Husserl of later years thought absolute certainty attainable by a withdrawal into the world of consciousness, a method he suggested in his *Ideas* and developed fully in his *Cartesian Meditations*. Without denying or even doubting the objectivity of the world, he required that the philosopher abstain from all judgment about it, that he enclose it in parentheses. This bracketing Husserl called *epoche* or "phenomenological reduction." Thus to his "eidetic reduction," which leaves behind the naïve and merely natural attitude, which discards the genetic, historic, or pragmatic approach, he added the "phenomenological reduction," which reduces things to "pure phenomena," to correlates of our consciousness.

In partial explanation of his final philosophical method, Husserl remarked to one of his Catholic pupils: "Man's life is nothing but a way to God. I am trying to reach this end without theological proofs, methods, or aids, in other words, to get to God without God. I must, as it were, eliminate God from my scientific thinking in order to pave a road to God for those who, unlike you, do not have the security of faith through the Church." And he added: "I know that this procedure might be dangerous for myself, had I not deep ties to God and belief in Christ." [108] Husserl must have considered his notion of leading others to God without God an endeavor of genius, a mental feat performed in a spirit of heroic sacrifice, when, as a matter of fact, never had he been more commonplace, more dated, more attuned to the spirit of the nineteenth century, which in puerile bravado claimed for itself the power that is God's, which made a fetish of the "presuppositionless." God, the eternal, the ever-present, of whom the psalmist says: "If I ascend into heaven, Thou art there; if I lie down in the netherworld, Thou art present. If I take the wings of the dawn and dwell in the uttermost parts of the sea, even there Thy hand shall lead me: and Thy right hand shall hold me" [109]—this God was relegated to the status of a "presupposition."

Husserl often felt that his turn to subjectivism was misinterpreted, maintaining that there were not ten men on earth who understood the true sense of this latest stage of phenomenology;[110] hardly did he realize that this alone condemned his retreat into the world of consciousness, for he who had wished to lead so many to truth had allowed his philosophy to become a private affair. Edith Stein, at one time his assistant, says of Husserl's self-imposed enclosure in the world of immanence that it came as a complete surprise and provoked unending discussion in the circle of his students. It was perhaps this very opposition to the beginnings of his new idealism, she thinks, that pushed Husserl still further in the same direction; it drove him to concentrate on justifying his new thought and to make it more and more the heart of his philosophy, a position it had not held when first appearing in the *Ideas*.[111]

Harvard's John Wild considers Husserl's lapse into irrealism a consequence of his neglect of metaphysics. Because Husserl saw only the logical contradictions of psychologism, without penetrating to the deeper, ontological errors, he fell into this ethereal but nonetheless clearly marked psychologism of the "transcendental or phenomenological ego." [112] In Dietrich von Hildebrand's opinion, Husserl's setting aside the full world for a part, for man's consciousness, poses a puzzle—and what can account for it save a subtle fear? A momentous discovery had been granted him in his *Logical Investigations*. Undisturbed by the chorus of those who denied the objectivity of truth, he dared proclaim it, but seemed to lack the strength to persevere.[113] Before a soul's secret, shyness is called for; before its intricacy, diffidence. For who can be sure of his own steadfastness and thus speak without trembling? Still, one cannot help thinking that, brave at the outset, Husserl later came to fear his own courage, for a consistent search after truth uncut might have led him, as it did so many of his students, to acknowledge Christ not only in the privacy of his heart but in the open forum of philosophers.

However, Husserl's "phenomenological reduction" will doubtless be forgotten while his real achievement and merit remain. His later subjectivism, a weak postscript to the body and strength of his work, can in no way detract from the still untold good his *Logical Investigations* has brought to others. Husserl's place in the history of thought shows that God's ways, here as so often, are bold, His paths adventurous. Through the centuries the Church has upheld the constancy of truth, which Plato and Aristotle teach, which Scripture tells in silent certainty: "O Lord God, Thou alone art God, and Thy words are truth." [114] What philosophers are called on to define, Scripture need not expound, radiating it throughout in the clear and simple light of revelation. This twofold legacy of Greece and Israel, of reason and of life, is the very breath of the Church, who says with St. Augustine: "A happy life is joy in the truth; this is joy in Thee, who art Truth." [115] At a time when many outside the Church denied the objectivity of truth, this trust was handed down through her doctors, Augustine and Thomas, to two priests, Bolzano and Brentano. Though one was tried severely and the other left her, they retained the trust and passed it on to a young Jew, still fettered by psychologism. And it was this Jew who was chosen, years later when his fetters

89

were broken, to bring freedom to others, who was made an acolyte of truth.

The Valor of Faith

"They dread entering the hell of complete skepticism," Husserl complained of the Thomists of his day, when they would not accept his "phenomenological reduction." "They dread entering it in order to show the teleological foundations of truth. They dread eliminating, if only for a moment, revelation, dogma, and God Himself from their thinking." He was right indeed. Knowing God's majesty, a Catholic philosopher *is* fearful; he does not dare eliminate from his thinking Him who Is. Husserl, however, seemed to be fearful lest he lose himself in finding God's fullness, and this fear it was which for so long kept him from reading Scripture. But in his last years, when Nazism's hatred shadowed his life, when he recognized more and more that he lived *sub specie aeternitatis,* Husserl turned often to the New Testament. Sitting in the sun one morning in the spring of 1936, he read the Gospels, remarking afterward: "Today two suns have shone on me." On New Year's Eve, 1934, during a visit from Soror Adelgundis Jaegerschmidt, O.S.B., his one-time pupil and by then his family's friend, he recalled that many years before, when he was gravely ill, Edith Stein had sat at his bedside and read aloud to him from the New Testament. Immediately, Sister Adelgundis offered the same service should he ever need her, and Husserl replied: "Oh, I can well see that you will be present when I die, and that you will read aloud from the New Testament as I enter eternity."

In Husserl's religious thinking, as it appears from his conversations with Sister Adelgundis, the profound and the superficial were, sad to say, often side by side. He could realize: "Grace is the freedom of God," and in the same breath add: "Man draws near to God not by grace but by his own continuous struggling." He could make the deep observation: "The monk—and, after all, each Christian—walks a high and narrow ridge. It is easy for him to fall, but he can rise again. And it is not that he denounces the world, rather does he see it in God." A moment later he spoke of piety becoming a hurry and bustle of "pious" exercises, and on other occasions of "religious" people's discrediting religion because their devotion was merely make-believe, a convention or superstition, and of the Church's great prayers being empty unless permeated by personal conviction. All this is quite true. Yet one wonders what spurred Husserl to see so often the shadow instead of the light. As a thinker he must have known that abuse never defiles right use; neither does it alter the essence of a thing in the least, doing harm only to itself.

In his last years Husserl at times felt drawn to the Catholic Church, and once remarked that were he forty years younger he might well try to enter her. "But you see," he continued, "I am now so old, and all my life I've done everything very thoroughly, so that I should have to spend at least five years on each dogma. You may figure out then to what age I should have to live to finish." Husserl seems to have thought it necessary to "examine" the dogmas as one does scientific hypotheses. But to do so is to judge the Judge, to try the word of God, forgetting that it is the word of God which tries us. It is the barren attempt to shift the center of being and truth from where it is to where we should like it, from God to ourselves. By its very nature, the assent to revealed truth cannot be the result of years of scientific investigation, for faith is at once God's gift to man and man's gift of himself to God. Its hour every hour, its time all and any time, confined to no age, faith cannot be born too soon or too late.

A search of all pertinent fields establishes beyond reasonable doubt that Christ really lived and died; that the house of Annas and Caiphas was as described in the Gospels; that the Sanhedrin's sentence was unjust; that at the time of Christ's crucifixion Pontius Pilate was Rome's governor of Judea, and many more facts relating to Christ's death. Reflection can show that His passion was bitter, but never that it was blessed, as the Christian believes; that it was pain and martyrdom, but never that it was love. Even the most painstaking investigation is utterly impotent before the mystical dialogue of Julian of Norwich: "Then said our good Lord Jesus Christ, 'Art thou well paid that I suffered for thee?' I said, 'Yea, good Lord, gramercy. Yea, good Lord, Blessed mayst Thou be.' Then said Jesus, our kind Lord, 'If thou art paid, I am paid; it is a joy, a bliss, an endless liking to Me that ever suffered I passion for thee; and if I might suffer more, I would suffer more.' " [116]

There are indeed some religious truths reason can attain, and there are numerous details connected with others, such as the authenticity of the Gospels or the relation of the Roman liturgy to Israel's worship in Temple and synagogue, on which reason has a voice, a right to speak. Man's intellect, further, discerns the credibility of the truth to be believed and calls for faith. Faith, however, transcends the power and leaps the frontiers of reason; it is not based on man's own findings, far less on his own likings, but on witness: on Christ, on His infinite knowledge, a knowledge indwelling and underived; on the Church, His tongue; on the patriarchs and prophets, on the apostles, on the saints and mystics, on the knowledge they received—faith is based on authority, on the authority of God who has revealed Himself, God the all-true. A whole night Peter fished in vain, but in the morning when hope was gone, when another attempt seemed futile, even foolish, he was told: "Launch into the deep!" [117] What he obeyed was not an unconscious urging, not a blind inner force, not his own knowledge, little and vague, nor any long-pursued investigation—naught save Christ's bidding. "At Thy word," he said, and filled his barque and that of John. It is this luminous authority which gives faith its certainty. "Far greater is man's certainty about the things he hears from God infallible, than that about the things he sees with his own fallible reason." [118]

No lengthy research, such as Husserl imagined, is required to yield to God's authority, to the Voice which speaks in the Church, in Scripture and in her dogmas. Were such detailed investigation needed, faith would be the prerogative of scholars, but like love, it is glory offered to every man. The exhaustive study of the Church's doctrine, which Husserl would have liked to undertake had his years permitted, could never of itself have compelled his assent. An unprejudiced exegesis of Scripture, a search of the Christian tradition, a comparison of the Church's teaching with that of other Christian bodies, confirm her claims, but they do not necessarily beget faith. Without readiness to believe, such scrutiny leads at best to admiration of the Church's doctrine for its beauty and splendor, for its logical consistency, for the comfort and peace it gives or even for the disquiet and movement it incites. But if worst comes to worst, a cold investigation ends in what St. James called the "faith of demons." [119] The devils "believe" and shrink from God in terror: they cannot but observe the manifest signs of revelation, yet their will, recoiling from the good and displeased at what the intellect perceives, refuses to bow.[120]

The created intellect is compelled to see, but never can it be compelled to believe. If he is to believe, man must part with his preference for self-made myths over revelation, break his inner resistance to a truth which seeks him total and undivided, spur his nature, a coward, to brave response. In faith his freedom is at work, his will, his courage, for his entire self is committed and he is wed "for better for worse, for richer for poorer." Ruth's is the language of faith, Newman says: "Whithersoever thou shalt go, I will go; where thou shalt dwell, I will dwell. Thy people my people; thy God my God." [121] One cannot find faith without prayer, and it must be a clamor like John Donne's:

Batter my heart, three-personed God, for you
As yet but knock, breathe, shine, and seek to mend;
That I may rise and stand, o'erthrow me; and bend
Your force to break, blow, burn, and make me new.
I, like an usurped town to another due,
Labor to admit you, but oh, to no end.
Reason, your viceroy in me, me should defend,
But is captived, and proves weak or untrue.
Yet dearly I love you, and would be loved fain,
But am betrothed unto your enemy;
Divorce me, untie or break that knot again;
Take me to you, imprison me, for I,
Except you enthrall me, never shall be free,
Nor ever chaste, except you ravish me.[122]

Surrender and Sanctuary

When Hitler came to power, Husserl was barred from the University of Freiburg im Breisgau, even from its grounds, by Martin Heidegger, its rector, once Husserl's assistant. Fearful, many friends avoided him, but there was one place where he was always a welcome guest, the Benedictine priory of St. Lioba, Sister Adelgundis' convent. There Husserl seems to have come a little closer to understanding the Christian's surrender. The life he saw contradicted the common and convenient opinion that surrender was but the escape of cowards; rather was it manifest as the glad venture of the coward turned valiant, as the end of mediocrity. Husserl's first visit to St. Lioba was in 1934, when, struck by its atmosphere and absorbing its peace, he remarked: "This is another world, a world apart, standing outside this evil time—almost heaven." A year later he returned, to be present when his pupil and friend took her final vows. Having studied the ritual beforehand, he followed the ceremony with the closest attention.

First the choir of professed Sisters chanted the invitation: "Come, ye daughters, hearken unto me; I will teach you the fear of the Lord, says the Lord. Draw near Him; His light will be in you and your face will not be confounded." To this the Sisters who were to make their final vows replied: "Behold, with all our hearts we come." Then the officiating prelate turned to them: "What do you ask?" "The mercy of God and joyful stability among the Sisters of St. Lioba," they answered. "Is it your will to renounce the world and all its pomp forever?" "We so will." "Is it your will to vow lasting obedience, chastity and poverty?" "We so will." "God began the good work in you; may He perfect it," the prelate prayed, and begged that they who so willingly gave themselves to Him might be wise and humble, radiant in obedience, undismayed under reproof, earnest and serene, most godly in pity, firmly rooted in peace, fervent in prayer and mighty in mercy.

Husserl was stirred by this undodging, unpaltering surrender, and even more by the Sisters' mystical burial and rising, which concluded the ceremony. After signing and reading aloud the chart of profession, they all sang, their arms first outstretched, then crossed: "Uphold me according to Thy word and I shall live; let me not be confounded in my hope." While they were prostrate on the floor of the chapel, the choir chanted: "I am dead, and my life is hid with Christ in God. I shall not die but live, and tell the works of the Lord." Then the prelate prayed that the newly professed might at all times love and seek the straight and narrow way which they had chosen; he gave them their cucullas, garments which were to mark their monastic state, protect their salvation and start them on the road of sanctity. Placing wreaths on their heads, he said: "Receive this sign of Christ and be made His bride; cleave to Him and your crown will be everlasting." Once more the Sisters joyfully confessed their choice: "The kingdom of this world and all the panoply of this aeon have I despised for the

94 *Edmund Husserl*

love of our Lord Jesus Christ, whom I have seen, whom I have desired, in whom I have believed, whom I have loved." After the ceremony, when Husserl met Sister Adelgundis in the library to congratulate her, he was moved to tears. Suddenly he clutched at his heart and fainted; coming to himself, he said with a little smile: "I was overjoyed, it was too much for me, it was too beautiful."

In 1937 he fell ill of pleurisy and patiently suffered great pain. One day he declared: "From the days of my youth I have struggled against all forms of vanity, and now I have almost overcome them—professional vanity too, the respect and admiration of pupils, without which no young teacher can work. Before my death I should have liked to turn to the New Testament, the way Newton did, and read nothing else. What a beautiful evening of life that would have been!" How could he have been so unaware that first things must come first? "Having done my duty as a philosopher," he continued, "I could feel free now to do what would help me to know myself, for no one can know himself who does not read the Bible."

On Holy Thursday, 1938, feeling his death approaching, he asked his nurse: "Can one really die well?" "Yes, in perfect peace," she replied. "But how?" "Through the grace of our Saviour, Jesus Christ," said the nurse, and read to him the psalm: "The Lord is my shepherd." When she came to the words: "Though I should walk in the valley of the shadow of death, I fear no evil, for Thou art with me," Husserl interrupted her: "Yes, that is what I mean! I want Him to be with me. But I do not feel His nearness." His nurse next read the hymn:

Take Thou my hands and lead me. . . .
Alone my footsteps falter
  Or straggle wide;
Lord, who my life canst alter,
  Be Thou my guide. . . .
Full oft methinks Thou hidest
  Thy wondrous might;
Still to my goal Thou guidest
  Me through dark night.

"Yes, so be it," Husserl returned. "What else could I want? You must pray for me."

When he awoke the next morning, his wife greeted him: "Today is Good Friday." "What a wonderful day, Good Friday!" he said. "Yes, Christ has forgiven us everything." The same evening, when he complained to Sister Adelgundis that he was still alive, she tried to strengthen him by recalling Christ's death on the cross. "God is good," she said. "Yes," he returned, "God is good, but incomprehensible. It is a great trial for me . . ." Unable to end the sentence, his hands moved toward one another as if he wished to fold them in prayer. After a while he went on: "There are two movements which continually seek one another, meet, and seek again." To which Sister Adelgundis added: "Indeed, heaven and earth meet in Jesus. God draws near to man in Christ." "Yes," said Husserl, "He is the analogy between . . ." Again his words were incomplete, but Sister Adelgundis, trying to interpret this fragmentary and imperfect expression, spoke of Christ, the Bridge between time and eternity, of Christ the Mediator, and of our redemption through Him. "Yes, so it is," Husserl agreed. He rested awhile and at last raised his arm as if to ward off some frightening vision. Asked what he saw, he whispered: "Light and darkness—much darkness, and again light." It is as if Husserl here anticipated the soul's vision in purgatory, where pretense and self-deceit fall away, where the soul is face to face with reality, seeing itself and its own darkness in the light of truth. Remorseful at the sight of itself, its purgation begins. As the light of God shines upon the soul, a piercing vision of evil casts it into a night of sorrow over its indifference, sloth, tepidity, ingratitude, over all its sins on earth; but it emerges from this night of sorrow to be made "light in the Lord." [123]

For days Husserl lay in a light slumber, silent even during his waking hours. But on April 27, 1938, he suddenly turned to his nurse: "I have seen something wonderful. Write it down quickly!" When the nurse returned with a notebook, Husserl was dead. If a man, even articulate and in complete command of his words, can never be fully known, how much more a mystery is the man about to die, whose tongue is nearly stilled. During the final days, it may be that weakness obscures his mind, or it may be that the opposite is true, that the mind stands at the summit of clarity, its vision no longer interrupted by the shadows of inhibition and the darkness of resistance. And so Husserl's last hours remain a riddle, his last remarks impenetrable. It is not for us to say whether his faith was still circumscribed, unable to leap the boundaries of his time and of his self, or whether, with ultimate courage and generosity, he embraced at last the entire Christ.

Several months after Husserl's death, the Belgian Franciscan, Father Herman L. Van Breda, went to Germany to save Husserl's manuscripts, with which he was later to establish the Husserl Archives at the Catholic University of Louvain. Once in Freiburg, he discovered that Madame Husserl was in danger from the Nazis; he rescued her and found her refuge in a Belgian convent. While in Belgium during the war years, Madame Husserl was received into the Church. After the war, she spent some time in New England, and now lives again in Freiburg. There, whenever her health permits, she walks, leaning on a cane and the arm of her nurse, to holy Mass. Thus the Church has taken under her protection what Husserl left behind, his thought and his love.

Adolf Reinach

SEEKER OF THE ABSOLUTE

64845

"IT WAS REALLY REINACH WHO INTRODUCED ME TO MY *Logical Investigations,* and in an excellent way," Husserl once said lightly and yet in earnest.[1] That the master should have learned the full significance of his own work from one of his followers is startling, but Husserl had thought and written in the solitude of his study, almost a philosophical recluse, and so was little aware of the crisis his book would cause and the benefits it would bring. In the wasteland of German philosophy in the late nineteenth century, he was isolated from other thinkers, and his *Logical Investigations* received scant notice till its discovery by three young philosophers of Theodor Lipps's circle in Munich, Johannes Daubert, Alexander Pfaender, and Adolf Reinach. Their response and understanding were needed to make Husserl fully conscious of his contribution, and it was particularly Reinach, first his pupil and soon his peer, whose gift of penetration brought its wealth to light.

For many years Husserl and Reinach worked closely together, yet their labors ended very differently. Near the close of his long life, rich in work and recognition, Husserl said that his goal was that of the Church: to lead men to eternity, but that his route there was through philosophy. Sadly he added: "All I have written thus far are only preliminary studies, a setting forth of methods. Unfortunately, in the span of a life one does not get to the things that are essential, to the real heart of the matter." [2] He felt himself still a beginner, though he had almost reached the biblical fourscore. Reinach, on the other hand, was torn from a life of unusual promise at the age of thirty-three. His few studies, collected after his death, make but one volume of 461 pages, and while the philosophy of religion he planned during his last years would, from all indications, have been outstanding, it was never to be written. Save for his friends and students, the philosophical world hardly realized the original thinker he was, so that one might imagine he accomplished little. Quite the contrary, "being made perfect in a short space, he fulfilled a long time," [3] for in his last years, still in the morning of his life, he found Christ, a faith knowing no reservation, abounding in strength and joy; he found infinitely more than he had expected when first he turned to philosophy.

Much in Reinach's life prepared him for the hour of faith, not least, his intellectual cleanliness. Language tells the man: Reinach's style was utterly simple, a rare thing among German philosophers, simple with a simplicity which rose from inner mortification. Never would he acknowledge a thought as legitimate until it became as transparent as crystal, until it was perfectly rounded, rid of the roughness with which it first appeared. He always worked with great intensity, put his whole self into his teaching; then, mind and body exhausted, he spent the evening at dominoes with his wife, telling her each time the same stories and exchanging the same little jokes. It was from a sense of responsibility, from an unbending honesty of mind, from an awareness of the gravity of thought, that his vigor sprang. Combining the scientist's calm and care with the rapture of the artist, minuteness with horizon, labor never lessened his joy in truth, for to think was for him to stand in wonder.

Unsheltered and Fearless

Adolf Reinach was born on December 23, 1883, of a distinguished Jewish family ranking side by side with the patricians of Mainz, the ancient episcopal see of western Germany. Every phase of Europe's cultural tradition was visible in this Rhenish city's Romanesque, Gothic, Renaissance, and Baroque architecture. The Jews are said to have come there in the train of Roman legions, not long after the birth of Christ, documents a thousand years old establishing their long residence. As elsewhere, so in Mainz, their tale is one of extremes, protection and quiet alternating with persecution or expulsion. At Reinach's birth, the times were peaceful and prosperous; his father, for instance, was a well-known industrialist and his grandfather the mayor of the city.

Reinach's interest in, indeed, passion for philosophy began in his early youth. As a schoolboy in a particularly dull Greek class, he was transported when he heard of Plato's concept of eternal truth, and at sixteen, when he was about to start his dancing classes, he was teased in the family circle: "What are you going to do with a girl? You'll never learn to dance." "Pooh!" he said, "I'll just talk of Plato and I'll floor her." Much of Reinach is in this brief retort, his amiability in the gentleness and humor with which he took the banter, his openness in the attention he gave to both past and present, to ideas and people. Never bookish, he was always alive to the full range of reality.

After his schooling in the humanities, Reinach studied philosophy in Munich, under Theodor Lipps, and received his doctorate in 1906. Because his family insisted on a *Brotstudium*, studies leading to a profession, he read law at the University of Tuebingen and was admitted to the bar in 1907. He never practiced, however, moving instead to Goettingen, where in 1909 he qualified for teaching philosophy at the University and began his work at Husserl's side. His prediction at the age of sixteen came true a hundredfold; his first lecture on Plato took his students off their feet by its strength, fire, and depth. Though he himself was later embarrassed at his boldness in treating such a theme with what he thought insufficient learning—for he demanded of himself not only an intuitive grasp but detailed knowledge, not only enthusiasm but marksmanship—those who heard it still spoke, years afterward, of what it had meant to them.

The most dependable of friends, Reinach was, in the words of the Old Testament, one "who loves at all times," [4] and whoever was in need could count on his response. His reverence for all creation and, in particular, his respect for every human being gave him an insight into the secret and inexpressible center of men, made him their tender and understanding "confessor," so that they opened their hearts and brought him their sorrows, often without knowing it, and, again not knowing how it came about, left him strengthened. He knew the word, gave the counsel and comfort that were needed, because he was kind; but his kindness was not the easy intimacy, the outgoing warmth which returns to its giver, rather a sense for what went on in others. With them he felt and sorrowed, and yet his feelings were, in a way, objective and disinterested, which made the load on him all the heavier. As he suffered with others, so he suffered from his own imperfections, above all from the metaphysical burden of existence. The difference between himself and others, he once remarked, was that they needed a reason to be sad, while he needed one to be merry.

Reinach's sadness was not of the outer man, caused by some exterior want, for he possessed all that makes for a full human life. He and his wife were deeply happy in their marriage and no friction shadowed their love; an exceptional kinship tied him to his brother and sister; not only were his students devoted to him, but what is more, gratefully he saw that his words shaped them and helped them achieve their full stature. But these joys could not lull him into false ease. Though he was open to the world, deeply interested in all that went on, gay in gay company, "he was an unsheltered man," *er war ein ungeborgener Mensch,* as Hedwig Conrad-Martius wrote in her introduction to his collected works.[5] Long before he spoke the language of a Christian, he knew that man was exiled with Adam, menaced and exposed; that "things" were in disorder and did not simply "straighten themselves out." Yet he never allowed the heaviness of heart which accompanied this awareness to weigh on others; neither did it leave him until he was given the Christian's hope.

Again, though of quiet courage, fearless of danger or death, Reinach knew fear on a much deeper plane. He dreaded error, and still more, falsehood; and confided to one of his friends that there were times at night when he felt something "gray," impersonal, and frightful, coming toward him, an experience he could imagine a possible source of pantheistic illusion. Any desire to be lost in a gelatinous world, to be dissolved into a mass lacking form, color, and distinction, to be drowned in a state of endless stupor, to be sustained not by the living God—Person caring for person—but by the dreary, unconscious, and loveless expanse of nature, was a witchwork abhorrent to his whole being.

As a philosopher, Reinach often warned: *Man muss keine Angst vor den letzten Gegebenheiten haben,*[6] "One must not be afraid of the ultimate realities." The future was to prove that he spoke not only as philosopher but as man: as he never feared truth, he was not afraid of meeting God.

The Reality of Law

Reinach's legal studies, which had seemed to him of little philosophical interest, became significant when, in a sudden flash, he saw that law had part in the eternity of truth. The study presenting his delighted discovery, *The a priori Foundations of the Civil Law,* published in 1913, is perhaps the most original and far-reaching of his writings. Positive law, he wrote, is in continual flux. Hardly any regulation of the positive law found in one code is not missing from some other, and there is assuredly none which could not be supposed as missing. What is decisive in the development of laws are a period's moral views and, even more, its economic requirements. While the mathematical truth, 2 times 2 equals 4, in no way depends on man's will or insight, nor on the age in which it is pronounced, statements of the positive law—for instance, that a creditor may transfer his claim without consent of the debtor—are valid today but may have had no validity yesterday and may have none tomorrow. Here, evidently, there is no question of the eternity of truth, for the law passes this and similar regulations in order to meet certain economic situations; hence they are purposeful and in this sense can be called "right," but in other eras contrary regulations may have been, or may come to be, just as "right." [7]

From this, most modern jurists conclude that all the concepts and maxims of law are the creations of lawmakers, with no existence outside the positive law. Some of these jurists admit the bare possibility that from the statutes of a given code there may be won by induction a few general principles, which remain in force, however, only so long as does that particular code. There are those who declare the concepts of law mere conventions by which society has agreed to live, conveniences without intrinsic cogency, like the yard and the inch, or the arbitrary though useful division of the day into hours, minutes, and seconds. Again, by others the fundamentals of law are called mere fictions: when a man draws up a deed, wishing to transfer a hundred acres of land to another, the giving, it is said, does not occur in reality, but only in the minds of the donor and the beneficiary. No new relationship between person and thing is established, no new rights are acquired; relationship and rights are merely imagined by those concerned and accepted by society as if truly existing. Likewise a promise, this third group asserts, creates no true obligation for the one who makes it, and effects no true claim for the one to whom it is made. Both obligation and claim, according to these modern philosophers of law, have as little real existence as do the mythical figures of Greece.

These theories are to law what psychologism is to truth. Their authors are termites, who eat the living wood of the tree, leaving but the bark; they kill the soul of the law and present us with a corpse. Common sense, the original insight of every man, knows naturally that truth *is,* and that the foundations upon which positive law is built have their existence in the realm of right, *jus,*

Adolf Reinach

Recht—not in man's will or fancy. A man must have lost this innocence of mind to doubt that truth and *jus* are objective; an age must have been despoiled of man's native approach to the universe to conceive of juridical entities as its own inventions.

No wonder, then, that Reinach, who always sought the authentic human approach, who tried to find again, purged and perfected, the innocence of mind our age has lost, was not deceived by the attempt to make of *jus* a fiction. He establishes that positive law does not create juridical concepts, but rather uses them; that a promise, with its consequent obligation and claim, that ownership and donation, exist, just as numbers or trees exist apart from man's understanding and previous to any positive legislation. To call these entities creations of the lawmakers is not only wrong but nonsensical, just as absurd as to call the founding of the German Reich the creation of historians.[8]

That a chair is placed in one corner of a room and not in another is a particular and accidental fact. It is in that corner because whoever arranged the furniture preferred it there, and it may be moved to another corner if he wishes, remaining always subject to his control. However, that a claim once relinquished ceases to exist is necessary and universal, for it is rooted not in the will or whim of man but in the nature of claims. Juridical entities, Reinach sums up, follow *a priori* principles, principles in no way esoteric but simple and self-evident. Of course, the makers of the positive law act with full freedom; they are not confined to the bare statement of the *a priori* principles. Though a promise, a deed of donation, a last will and testament are, by their very nature, binding, the positive law may limit that binding force by ruling that only a written and notarized promise or deed, that only a witnessed will, are to be upheld by the courts. The lawmakers are free to make such restrictions in accordance with the standards of their time and its economic requirements (which, one must not forget, are human requirements), in order that they may fulfill their task of maintaining order and forestalling abuse and confusion. Further, they may—indeed, must—provide for situations not covered by *a priori* principles, and are therefore free to determine, for example, that a treaty with a foreign power must be ratified by at least two thirds of the Senate. The authority they wield is the greatness of their office, but their sovereign freedom in no way invalidates the principles, which are, in fact, laws of essences and therefore indestructible, unchangeable, and proof against man.[9]

Next Reinach, a Socratic teacher, leads his reader step by step into the juridical realm. When a man promises another a gift or a favor, he says, a singular effect is brought about, different from the effect of news told or of a request made. The promise immediately begets a peculiar bond between the two, by virtue of which one may demand, and the other is obliged to give, what has been promised. By its very nature, this bond admits of whatever duration may be assigned to it, yet from its beginning it tends toward dissolution and reaches its natural end when the promise is fulfilled. It may expire—less naturally, so to speak—if he to whom the promise was made renounces his claim or if, the nature of the promise permitting, the other retracts it.[10]

All this may strike us, Reinach continues, either as obvious or as remarkable. There are things which are obvious in that everyone knows them, has passed them a thousand times, and may pass them another two thousand. But it may happen that our eyes open suddenly to something long known, that we see for the first time the uniqueness and singular beauty long hidden from us by the dust of the ordinary. So it is with what we know, or think we know, as a "promise." When a promise is made, something new enters the world: a claim is born, and an obligation. Now, just what are these entities? Surely they are not *nothing,* for how could a "nothing" be renounced or revoked or fulfilled? Still, we cannot group these entities under any of the familiar categories. Since they do not come under the headings of physiology or physics, one might be tempted to call them psychological, experiences of the claimant and obligor. But do not some claims and obligations last unaltered for years? Can the same be said of any experience? Moreover, a claim and obligation have just as full an existence whether or not the subject experiences them, whether he is awake or asleep, conscious or unconscious. Again, Reinach goes on, we cannot group them, or any other juridical entities, with ideal objects, since it is the essential mark of ideal objects, of numbers, concepts or propositions, to be outside time; claim and obligation, on the contrary, arise, endure a while, and then are no more. Thus, neither psychological nor ideal, they seem to be temporal objects of a very special kind, which has so far gone unnoticed.[11]

In showing juridical entities to be "temporal objects of a special kind," Reinach establishes that the juridical is a realm in itself—which should not surprise us, for the wide world of reality has room in it for many realms. Nevertheless, the juridical is often insufficiently distinguished from the moral, for, though the two realms are not identical, they do indeed overlap. Juridical obligations and claims spring from the free acts of persons, from a promise given and accepted, for instance. Moral obligations and claims, however, do not depend on the will of the persons concerned; they do not have their origin in decisions made for that very purpose. A moral right, the moral right to oppose a totalitarian regime, for example, is rooted in the dignity of the human person, and the moral claim one has on the help of a friend arises from the peculiar bond of friendship. Further, juridical, but never moral, rights and claims may be transferred to others. Again, a man who possesses a moral right may decide not to use it, yet he cannot abolish it, for only what has been set down by one's free will can be erased by a free act.

The juridical realm is not the moral realm; it has its own dignity or, to speak the language of some phenomenologists, its own *logos*. On the other hand, the two realms are not opposed, having much in common. The law must be shaped by moral principles, the criminal much more than the civil, for it deals with guilt, the violation of the moral order. There can be no doubt that a law would be wrong were it to legalize sin, so-called mercy killing, for instance, where self-pity for one's own grief at the sight of suffering disguises itself as mercy, where the life of an incurable man is valued no more than that of a useless horse. Equally unjust is a law which deprives a man of one of his natural rights, as does an edict on sterilization, in which the state assumes the power of laying down who should and who should not fulfill God's bidding to be fruitful. The link of the civil to the moral law is less close. Whether a city should be governed by a mayor or a manager, for example, is not directly related to the commandments; it is a problem of discovering which is more to the purpose. Still, the moral problem does enter: Which serves better the common good?

There is another difference between the juridical and the moral realms. The function of the first is rather limited: to create conditions for a life of goodness, but not to create the life of goodness itself. Morality, however, the life of goodness, extends into the world of thought, into the invisible depths of the soul, into a sphere so vast, its parts so minute and delicate, that laws can neither encompass it nor grasp them. Love is the dearest virtue and hate the foulest sin, but the laws of the state cannot enforce the one nor punish the other. For all that, the excellence of the moral realm does not eclipse the juridical.[12]

Juridical entities, such as "promise" and "contract," merit better understanding; Reinach therefore introduces the concept of "social acts." There are certain human acts which are marked by the subject's inner activity, such as making a resolution or a decision, preferring one thing to another, forgiving, praising, reprimanding, asserting, questioning, bidding. Immediately one sees them fall into two groups. Making a decision, to take an instance of the first, is an internal act, remaining within the soul of him who decides, needing no publication to be accomplished. Of course, the decision may be stamped somehow on a man's features and his movements, or he may choose to tell of it, but outer manifestation is in no way necessary to the act of decision.

Quite different are the acts of the second group, which require, besides the subject, another to whom the act is directed. They include experiences in which the actor and the one to whom the act is directed are identical, such as self-esteem, self-hatred, and self-love. Other acts of the second group have for their hallmark a relation to another person: I cannot envy or forgive myself; likewise, a bidding is always to another. But while the act of forgiveness, though directed to another, may be reserved in the recesses of my heart, the command can never be a mere inner turning to another. It must be published; it impinges on another and enters his personal world. By its nature a command requires that it be heard, and never would we give a command were we certain that the one commanded could not notice it. It does happen, indeed, that a command is given and not heard, but if it remains unheard, its purpose is unfulfilled; an arrow may fail to find its mark, but still the bow was bent that it might be found.[13]

Shame, anger, love may be mirrored in one's face, but this reflection is only accidental. A social act, however, is necessarily both inward and outward, having both soul and body, so to speak, and although its embodiment may vary—a command may be expressed by eye, hand, or voice—its expression is essential and always voluntary. What holds true for giving a command holds equally for requesting a favor, asking a question, giving an admonition, telling news, or making a promise; hence all of these are social acts, spears thrown to pierce the soul of another, lodging there. The "psychologists" describe a promise, for instance, as an utterance of purpose or will, but if it is addressed to another, an utterance of the will— "I will do this"—is, in fact, a social act; it is, however, a communication and not a promise. A promise is neither an inward act of the will nor its utterance, but an act with a character and effect entirely its own: its nature is to engender claim and obligation. Were one to call a promise an utterance of the will, one should have to call a question an utterance of doubt and a request an utterance of desire—patently misleading definitions. No, the world of juridical relations is not created by impotent utterances of the will, but by social acts which follow definite and unalterable rules of their own.[14]

Throughout his study on *The a priori Foundations of the Civil Law,* Reinach shows that the world of *jus,* of "right," is real and objective, and that those who see it as a system of fictions are themselves isolated, separated from reality. Tempted, therefore, to peer at the realm of law through one end or the other of a telescope, they cannot see its true dignity, but see it either gigantic or dwarfed: either they worship the laws of the state as the supreme source of life, or else they despise them as the ultimate evil, making them the last word of God or the whisperings of the devil. The juridical realm is neither, yet it *is* of God, the Framer and Ruler of the universe, who so made man that law is an essential part of his life, for he is a world *in* himself but never a world *to* himself. He is a person, a being conscious and free, able to say "I," master of his acts, at no time merely a means to an end. At the same time he is a neighbor, living with and for others, his life affecting theirs, and theirs his. Hence every man is unique and yet ordained toward catholicity; "No man is an island, entire of itself; every man is a piece of the continent, a part of the main."[15] There is between persons a field of the spirit, which social, and therefore juridical, acts can traverse; through them, fellowship is established and worlds are bridged. Needless to say, the juridical realm is not unlimited; it is earthbound, for in heaven, the land of the blessed, there are no rights and no laws, but the perfect freedom of perfect love.

Persons, not Puppets

Reinach insists that the *a priori* foundations of the civil law be not confused with the natural law,[16] and he is right, for while the former are indicative, the latter is imperative. The concept of natural law has come to us by the streams of antique thought and the river of revelation. The great philosophers and poets of antiquity spoke of it, none more compellingly than Sophocles, whose Antigone challenges the tyrant, Creon: "I did not think thy decrees were of such force that thou, a mortal man, could override the unwritten and unfailing laws of heaven. For not of today nor of yesterday, but of forever is their life, and no one knows the hour of their birth." [17] This heritage of Greece and Rome was transformed by the gospel, the Good News, which called all men to be sons of God and heirs of heaven, forever raising the dignity of man, adding, as he himself cannot do, "a cubit to his stature." [18] Greek thought did not go beyond the Hellenic world, nor Roman beyond the frontiers of the Empire, but St. Paul saw Jew and Gentile under one obedience, bound by the same moral precepts: the Ten Commandments were the unwritten law of the Gentiles. He said of them: "Though not having the law [given to Israel on Sinai] they do *by nature* [by the light of their intellect] the things that are of the law; not having the law, they are a law to themselves." [19]

The Church has always seen in the natural law rays of the divine goodness striking upon the human mind—not that every man requires a special revelation or enlightenment. Just as he can chop wood without giving thought to the Creator, though there would be no trees and no men without Him and no swinging of the axe without His lending strength, so he can recognize much of the natural law, much of the Decalogue, without turning to the true, living God, the God of Israel. Still, St. Thomas here applies the verse: "The light of Thy countenance, O Lord, is sealed upon us";[20] still, the natural moral law is an imprint of the divine Mind on ours, our share, our grasp of the eternal law, *participatio legis aeternae in rationali creaturae*.[21] In the eternal law, there speak God's wisdom and goodness, there speaks God Himself. His nature is the rule of our lives, as the Church prays in the collect of

110   *Adolf Reinach*

the eighth Sunday after Pentecost: "Grant us, O gracious Lord, we beseech Thee, always to think and to do the things that are right. May we, who cannot exist without Thee, be strengthened to live *secundum Te*, according to Thee."

Man is living according to the natural law if he remains true to his God-given nature and destiny, if he fulfills all the precepts deriving, necessarily and essentially, from the supreme rule: do good and avoid evil. It is for man to search out and to find these precepts, as well as the rights that accompany them. That he has often been mistaken about them in no way contradicts the reality of the natural law, no more, as Maritain has said, than a faulty addition voids the precise rules of mathematics; no more than the notion of primitive tribes that the stars are holes in a tent spanning the sky denies the stars' existence, or disproves or even weakens astronomical principles.[22] Here too man can err: since he must look for the natural law to discover its demands, he can also look away; on the other hand, his eyes may be closed through no fault of his own, for the lamp of the gospel was, and is still, needed to illuminate natural law. Never are man's dignity, his rights and obligations, fully clear unless we see them with the eyes of Christ.

Reinach's thesis on the *a priori* foundations of the civil law is not identical with the Catholic doctrine of the natural law, but the two run parallel and are one in this: that man is not a puppet but a person. Only where there are persons are there rights and obligations, and only persons can accomplish social acts. In a fit of temper, I see my neighbor as a mere object; I make of him or her an "it," almost a thing. But when I give a promise or sign a contract, the other is a "you"; he and I are partners; he is not merely an object, but another subject.

Catholic tradition and Reinach agree, too, that the world is not a fog, dispersing at man's approach, fleeing his touch, but that it is lucid, at least for those who have not dug themselves into dungeons. Reinach's world is one of meaning, one of laws and therefore of unity, for where there are obligations, there is cosmos— whatever is binding also binds together. In *The Flies,* Jean-Paul Sartre has Orestes address Jupiter: "What is there between you and me? We slip past one another like two ships, without touching. You are a god, and I am free. We are equally alone. . . .

There is nothing in heaven any more, no good, no evil, and no one to give me orders. I am condemned to have no law but my own. . . . Every man must contrive his own way." [23] Long before Sartre preached this philosophy of "heroic" despair and spiteful loneliness, long before he ever spoke, Reinach refuted him.

Is it mere chance that this insight into the foundations of law was given to a Jew? No, even the modern Jew, who is so tenuously bound to Israel's past, is still of the people who stood at Sinai. Out of the lightning and the thunder, the Jews were told as they received the Law: "You have seen how I have carried you upon the wings of eagles, and have taken you to Myself." [24] Again, the Ten Commandments were prefaced by a reminder of all God had done for His people: "I am the Lord thy God, who brought thee out of the land of Egypt, out of the house of bondage." [25] The token of His guidance, the Law—with its civil regulations, criminal statutes, ritual ordinances, and moral precepts—became the very fabric of Israel's existence. On the one hand, it quickened and gladdened the people[26] so that they could say: "I rejoice in the ways of Thy precepts as in all riches," [27] and on the other, it held up a mirror to their transgressions, rebuked them, cried their need for redemption. Thus the Law was a weeping, as it were, for the Saviour, a tutor to Christ,[28] in whose love it was fulfilled. Not sufficient to itself, the Law of the Old Testament asked a question but did not give the answer; Reinach, truly a Jew in this, did not content himself with law, but followed it to its Giver. With all his soul he felt what was Israel's first experience in the desert and should have been her final experience in Christ: that God is provider and protector, rock and shield, ever near; that He is immediate, not tomorrow, not "just around the corner," but now and here.

Christ, the Core of Music

Christ comes like a thief in the night[29]—there is an element of suddenness in every religious experience, in every conversion a surprise. One cannot plan them, but their ground is prepared by what a man is, by what he thinks, feels, wills, by what he does and omits and how he suffers, in short, by all that enters and leaves his soul, and by how he filters it through reverence and love. The way for religious experience and conversion can be prepared, but when they are genuine, they transcend all that went before them,

112   *Adolf Reinach*

for they are the work of grace. Grace needs nature for its vessel, and is itself nature's fill; transforming and ennobling, it is the knighting of nature.

"Knighting" is a pale word for man's crossing his own frontiers, for his translation wrought by grace; there was already nobility in Reinach before God's love conquered him. Many of his philosophical contemporaries regarded the works of a man like St. Augustine as "trash," one of his colleagues dismissing the saint: "Be off with your St. Augustine! I don't want to be bothered with him. Only the other day I told my students that I wouldn't allow him and his puerile interpretations even into a seminar of beginners." Reinach, however, knowing greatness when he met it, admired the thinker Augustine and pored over his treatment of time in the last three books of his *Confessions*. Even as a young philosopher, when he had little understanding for St. Augustine's tears over his sins, for his hymning of God's mercy and majesty, Reinach did not dispose of them as "stuff and nonsense"—the fashion to disdain and ridicule religion never impressed him. Writing of social acts and their need to be heard, for example, he said that in a society of beings who perceived each other's experiences directly, without the medium of the senses, social acts require no body. In the midst of a discussion on the *a priori* foundations of the civil law, he did not hesitate to give as an instance of such purely spiritual acts silent prayer, the prayer that speaks to God without the help of tongue and lips.[30]

As keen as his sense for greatness was his sense for beauty, particularly his understanding for music. Music was to him not a drifting into twilight but an aspiring to an ever brighter realm; in this slow and plodding world a winged idiom giving witness to another land; for all its subjectivity, an objective, metaphysical language. St. Augustine sees in music, in its number, measure, and movement, the instrument with which the Maker of all fashioned heaven and earth.[31] This, too, is the vision of the poets; John Dryden, in his "Song for St. Cecilia's Day," speaks of the bidding of the Creator as the power of music:

> *When Nature underneath a heap*
> *Of jarring atoms lay,*
> *And could not heave her head,*

The tuneful voice was heard from high,
  Arise, ye more than dead!
Then cold, and hot, and moist, and dry
In order to their stations leap,
  And Music's power obey.

The fullest accord of the melody of creation is man:

From harmony, from heavenly harmony
  This universal frame began:
  From harmony to harmony
Through all the compass of the notes it ran,
The diapason closing full in Man.

For Richard Crashaw, to *be* is to sing. Summoning lute and harp and all creatures, he writes:

I have authority in Love's name to take you
And to the work of Love this morning wake you;
  Wake; In the Name
Of Him who never sleeps, All Things that Are,
  Or, what's the same,
  Are Musical.[32]

If music is woven into the texture of being; if, like wisdom, it was possessed by the Lord in the beginning of His ways; if it was set up from eternity, before the earth was made, and the depths, and the mountains and rivers; if it was present when He prepared the heavens and set a law to the waters and balanced the foundations of the earth; if it was with Him forming all things, playing before Him, His delight, at all times[33]—it must speak of God and be a way to Him. All beauty shares in the divine Beauty, yet, like any other work of art, a piece of music may mar this participation if it becomes "independent," if it parts from its source. When it is primarily a means of self-expression for an artist who is all centered in himself, reveling in his own emotions, it tells more of the composer than of God. Reinach felt—though many disagree with him —that this was true in the case of Brahms, of whose music he said that "in it Brahms lamented his dearth of inspiration." One day at a concert, he turned to his wife: "Do take a look at them, these unhappy boys and girls, completely at loose ends with themselves.

114 *Adolf Reinach*

How Brahms hushes them into a pseudo redemption! And behind it all is hopeless misery." [34]

Seeking in music not the sleep of oblivion, but an ever wider awakening to the little trinity of the beautiful, the good, and the true, Reinach chose for his first mentor Beethoven, whose music, more than any other, shames by its greatness the mediocre, vulgar, and frivolous, sweeps away sloth and half-heartedness, and urges the soul to be centered not in, but above itself. Dietrich von Hildebrand, Reinach's pupil, has pointed out that more than Beethoven's life is mirrored in his work: man's metaphysical situation and his great hunger for God. Beethoven gives voice not merely to the difficulties of any one man, rather to man's hardship on earth and to his blessed destiny. And in all this, he is like Jacob wrestling with the angel, not ceasing till he is blessed. Speaking *to* God with such ardor, his music necessarily speaks *of* Him, and reveals more of the land of grace than his mind could understand or his tongue tell.[35]

Beethoven is often pictured as a titan, earthy in his strength, a rebel against feudalism or even against the eternal order. True, he had an ardent sense of justice, he was indignant at the abuse of power, and when his hot temper was aroused he could rage; still he was not a rebel. His soul was tormented; but there was no love of chaos in it, no twist making him cling to grief, rather much warmth and tenderness. "You see my innermost being," he called on God in his famous will, *Das Heiligenstaedter Testament,* "You can see it, You know that my heart loves and longs to be kind to my fellow men." [36] Fire flames through Beethoven's music, but not the hoarded fire of Zeus which Prometheus' cunning stole; it is the fire God's gladness deeded to men, the fire Christ cast on the earth that it burn, run, and never die.[37]

In Beethoven's works, the raging of the elements, man's many sufferings and his struggle, are portrayed, but always are they resolved in peace, and it must have been this that stirred Reinach. The heavy sorrow of the funeral march in the *Eroica* gives way to the sprightliness and mirth of the scherzo; then in the harmony of the finale, sorrow is transformed into a Pauline confidence: "I can do all things in Him who is my strength." [38] In the *Fifth Symphony* man first shouts defiance at what seems inexorable fate;

then of his own strength he finds a—passing—serenity. But he remains a prey of things and of his passions, till he rises in jubilant hope, hope that is not confounded.[39] The thunderstorm of the *Pastoral Symphony*, which makes an end of the merrymaking of the countryside, of the placid playing of the brook and the singing of the birds, is not the end, though for a moment it seems to engulf all life; the symphony ends rather in the shepherd's glad and grateful song that the threat is past and that not one sparrow is forgotten in the sight of God.[40] "O God, the glory of these woods!" Beethoven once exclaimed. "In the heights there is quiet, quiet to serve Him. Each tree in the open seems to say to me, Holy, Holy!" [41]

In the *Ninth Symphony*, harassed man grasps first at wild exuberance, then retreats into melancholy, only to be overtaken by a restless temper, almost despairing. But suddenly the baritone enjoins: "Friends, no more these sounds. Let our tune be pleasing and more joyful," and he sings of "joy, spark from flame divine." The joy he praises is love's, is heaven's daughter, which makes brothers out of strangers, plights friend to friend and man to wife. Who thus embraces his brethren feels that his embrace is not his own: its strength and delight give witness that above the tent of stars there dwells a loving Father.[42] Titanism, the counterfeit of divine strength, brands our age and is therefore read into Beethoven's music. But what really made the *Ninth* possible was the mystery of the Upper Room; what truly resounds in it is St. Paul's canticle of that love without which a man, be he poet or philosopher, even prophet or martyr, is an empty noise.[43]

The matchless character of Leonore is another of Beethoven's hymns of love. No other opera than *Fidelio* extols a love so pure, so heroic, and yet so simple and unassuming, a love of the spirit, of patience and unbroken loyalty, of hope in darkness and of sacrifice which never slows or wearies, a love which "sustains, believes, hopes, endures, to the last." [44] Leonore's message is one of single-hearted faith, artless as a child's: "Be still! Whatever you hear or see, forget not that a Providence reigns over us." That the world, though threatened by chaos, is lighted by promise, runs through the whole opera; the earth, for Beethoven, borders hell and heaven—sin is strong but redemption stronger.

The work of redemption is renewed and the end of each man and of all the world is shaped in the Mass. Comparing Beethoven's *Missa Solemnis* with other orchestral masses, Von Hildebrand calls it "Catholic from first to last as is hardly another, though there are many composed by men who lived more fully in the supernatural realm. But no other man was so great a composer and so ultimately artist that he could give adequate musical expression to the highest there is beneath heaven and on earth." [45] Surely a heart must be dulled if it is unmoved by the adamantine conviction of Beethoven's *Credo in unum Deum,* by his glad stress on *homo* in *et homo factus est,* by the jubilant shouts of the *resurrexit,* by the mounting expectation of the *et vitam venturi saeculi* with its never-ending *Amen.* Later in Beethoven's great mass, "before and at the *Benedictus,* when the violins sing, it is as if heaven were bending down; when the *dona nobis pacem* resounds, as if mankind, fully conscious of its station before God, were looking up to Him, pleading; here, indeed, if anywhere in art, one can say: It is the phase, the passage of the Lord." [46] Though Reinach has left us no such comments, may this not have been the effect of Beethoven's works on him? Do we venture too far when we say that as he listened to him, the Lord went by, unseen, and touched his soul?

Even deeper was Reinach's love for Bruckner. He forewent no opportunity to hear his works, even if it meant going to another city; he abandoned himself to their power, trusting their maker, who never thought of his art as other than a gift. A man humble and perfectly chaste, without envy or guile, who blessed and prayed for his enemies, was singularly fitted to be an instrument of eternal Beauty. His strength welled from the liturgy of the Church and his music is meditation become melody; when he composed he gazed upward trembling and rejoicing, and often tunes came to him in hours of prayer. On the scores of some of his manuscripts he inscribed *Omnia ad majorem Dei gloriam,* "All things to the greater glory of God"—in his childlike candor dedicating them, as he used to say, to the "dear Lord." *Der liebe Gott,* the dear and loving God, was the One from and for whom he lived. And once, on hearing mention of death and judgment, he remarked: "When some day the dear Lord calls me before Himself and asks, Where are the talents I gave you? I'll show Him the score of my *Te Deum,* and He will be a gracious Judge." [47]

Parts of Bruckner's symphonies are rugged; to some early critics this seemed lack of form. But Reinach was not deceived; eagerly he entered the mysterious world of Bruckner's symphonies, with their slow and solemn pace, their intense religious atmosphere, their resolute faith. Of their genuine pathos it has been said that its counterpart in literature is this passage of St. Augustine: "I asked the earth, and it answered me, 'I am not He'; and whatsoever are in it confessed the same. I asked the sea and the deeps, and the living, creeping things, and they answered, 'We are not your God; seek higher than we.' I asked the moving air, and the whole air with its inhabitants answered, 'Anaximenes was deceived; I am not God!' I asked the heavens, the sun, moon and stars; 'Nor,' say they, 'are we the God whom you seek,' and I answered to all the things which stand about the doors of my flesh, 'You have told me of my God, that you are not He; tell me something about Him!' And with a loud voice they cried out, 'He made us!' My questioning them was my thought on them; and their beauty was the answer." [48]

Like God's sovereignty, His goodness is a theme of Bruckner's symphonies, and who dare say how much of his portrayal found its way into Reinach's soul? Rising from "faintheartedness and confusion," as Bruckner himself described a passage of his *Third Symphony,* man realizes his high mission and resolves to accomplish it. Suddenly he blenches from the greatness of his task, but he is heartened by fanfares of courage. Only in cleaving to one mightier than he, can he win his struggle, and he has no other ally, the *Third Symphony* tells, but God. "Thou art with me—to know Thee is to live, to serve Thee to reign," [49] is likewise the breath of the grandiose conclusion of the *Fifth Symphony,* at once so prayerful and heroic that it has been called the symphony of faith. Its religious mood is evoked by the solemn tone of the orchestra, which Bruckner, here and in other works, converts into one great organ. For the mighty hush of the organ in the Austrian abbey of St. Florian was his first musical experience, and its memory always remained with him, so that his work was art born of worship.

This is never clearer than in Bruckner's *Te Deum.* Like the clamor of bells, the hymn begins: "We praise Thee, O God," proclaiming irresistibly: "All the earth doth worship Thee." When the "Holy, Holy, Holy," is sung, heaven and earth adore together in hallowed awe, their adoration growing ever greater, new multitudes joining their praise, till they shout: "Full are the heavens and the earth of the majesty of Thy glory." Then the hymn extols the work of redemption and implores: "We beseech Thee, therefore, to help Thy servants." In a passage of supernal beauty, a violin carries the prayer heavenward, and there the voice of the tenor abides, as it were, in the heights of bliss, remembering the Blood of Christ, writ of redemption and promise of glory. Hence the choir dares to plead for mercy, and with a ringing and transfigured "In Thee, O Lord, have I hoped," the hymn comes to its crowning finale; first intoned by the solo voices, then made strong by the whole choir and full orchestra, it concludes with the all-surpassing "I will not be confounded forever." [50]

This is the world into which Bruckner introduced Reinach. In one of his classes at the Vienna conservatory, Bruckner, whose invincible faith could not so much as imagine unbelief, laid his hand gently on the head of a Jewish pupil and asked: "Tell me, how can you really believe the Messias has not yet come?" May this not have been the question Bruckner's music suggested to Reinach's soul?

The splendor of Bruckner's *Te Deum* could never have come to be without the living faith which sings in it; Haydn's *Creation* could not laud the Creator had his own eyes not seen His Name everywhere; and Handel's *Alleluia Chorus*, his "I know that my Redeemer liveth" and "The trumpet shall sound" cannot be divorced from the trust and joy in Christ which composed them. Even more truly, none of them could have sung without the objective faith they hymn. Likewise, the music of Beethoven's *Missa Solemnis* cannot be lifted from its text, from the truths it unfolds; Mozart's *Requiem* could never implore everlasting peace were not eternal life with Christ offered to man, and were there not the painful possibility of wasting the offer; Bach's *Passion According to St. Matthew* could never have been without the historic suffering of Christ—its beauty follows on His love.

Not only religious music lives on Christ; all the great music of the Western world owes its existence to Him. It could not have grown without the seeds He planted, without the wealth of new emotions

His love begot. There would have been no great composers free to create, for their natural genius would have remained fettered had He not redeemed man and unlocked his heart. Hence, all great music asks Bruckner's question, and this gentle and persistent asking prepared Reinach for the answer. It is a sign of Reinach's *anima naturaliter catholica,* of his soul naturally Catholic, which grasped the gamut of reality and gave each thing its true measure, that his ear was open to Beethoven and to Bruckner; but it was more than natural catholicity which in the end made him find Christ, the Core of music.

So great was the happiness Christ brought His Virgin Mother that her joy burst forth in song.[51] When He entered the world, it was amidst the hymning of angels who greeted Him as the Glory of God and the Peace of men,[52] and on the eve of His passion, parting from His disciples, leaving them the sacrament of His love, He Himself chanted the Hallel.[53] Faith unloosed the tongues of His early followers in "psalms and hymns and spiritual music," [54] and this was precisely their work in the eyes of a pagan, Pliny the Younger: that before start of day they were wont to gather, *carmen Christo quasi deo dicere,* to sing praise to Christ as to a god.[55] At the end of ages, when Christ will come again to claim His own and to disperse the cloud which hides Him from human eyes, the trumpet will announce Him.

So when the last and dreadful hour
This crumbling pageant shall devour,
The trumpet shall be heard on high,
The dead shall live, the living die,
And music shall untune the sky.[56]

Music shall proclaim the end of this world and the beginning of a new heaven and a new earth.

Christ is the Core of all earthly music, because He is the divine Word, the Word spoken in silence, without tone or sound, yet with the roar of thunder and the whisper of harps. He is "the infinite Hymn that ever resounds in the Father's Bosom and ever ravishes the Father, the living canticle that rises up from the depth of the Divinity." [57] He is the Son in whom the Father is well pleased,[58] His Delight, His eternal Melody, the Music that fills heaven.

The Experience of the Absolute

"The soul, of course, is not preexistent and indestructible, as Plato thought; created by a special act of God, it could also be destroyed by one. On the other hand, death is no indication that with it everything comes to an end," Reinach said as a young teacher in Goettingen. Never would he have called himself an agnostic or an unbeliever, yet till the day of his conversion he was not a man of faith. As early as his student days in Munich, he had great reverence for Christianity, sensing that "there, all 'classic' lines converge," that to it every truth tends. But reverence is not faith. In a conversation at Goettingen with a favorite student, Reinach went so far as to say: "The Trinity is the only acceptable concept of God." [59] But to have a "concept of God" is not the same as believing in Him, for faith does not stop at concepts, says St. Thomas, nor at words as conceptual signs; it reaches for nothing short of reality itself, and conceptual signs are but the means by which it arrives there.[60] So long as we view God from where we are, from our own little world, our view bears in it the constant danger of parallax; in faith, however, we see the world and ourselves, to some degree, with the eyes of God. Merely to think about Him is an attempt to make the Infinite finite, but to believe in Him is the rise of finite man to the Infinite; merely to reflect on Him is to put God at our mercy, at the mercy of caprice, but to believe is to put ourselves at His mercy, at the mercy of Mercy.

It is this infinite difference between the idea of God, God pondered, considered and discussed, accepted or dismissed, and the living God who enters our lives; between God thought, and God revealing Himself, speaking, being heard, loving, being loved; it is this infinite difference that made Pascal cry out: God is not the God of philosophy but of Abraham, Isaac, and Jacob.[61] The man who has nothing but a "concept of God" remains distant and unshaken, while the man of faith is set afire by a kiss of grace, engaged, pledged; his whole being gives witness to the divine mystery, knows the joy and pain of truth, for he is at peace and yet anxiously stretches forward to see God face to face. A mere concept of God is without movement, bringing neither delight nor suffering; faith, however, is a matter of life and death, and no amount of thought alone can evolve into it. Never is the Christian the product of an inner evolution.

When Reinach declared: "The Trinity is the only acceptable concept of God," he had as yet no faith. All he meant was that if God is, He must be superabundant Life, but this is far truer than he realized. The Christian who professes the Triune God knows that God is not mute, that He need not go outside Himself to say "Thou," that He thinks and speaks of Himself in the eternal Word, the Son begotten by the Father, and that the Embrace uniting Both is the Holy Ghost, all Three distinct yet One; that He who is in heaven, in inaccessible light, is not alone but abounds in fellowship. His Oneness is not solitude but the infinite interchange of infinite Truth and Love, beyond the realm of arithmetic, beyond the realm of human experience. Incomprehensible is the living God, who blasts our attempts to encompass Him, to conceive Him according to our own image; to think Him other than that is to have lost all perspective.

For years Reinach remained in the outer court of faith: the purity of his philosophical approach, his refusal to compromise with falsehood, his lack of prejudice, his openness, his reverence—all these were disposing his soul for the gift. But it was not till 1915, the second year of World War I, after he had been at the front for several weeks, that he wrote to his wife, who, some months before, had herself met her Damascus: "The first weeks were terrible; then, God's peace came to me too, and now all is well." To Dietrich von Hildebrand he wrote a little later: "I must tell you of a change which has come over me, a change to the very roots of my being." The change was indeed radical; from the moment of which he speaks, Reinach saw everything in a new light. When he left for the war, he was prompted by his sense of duty and love of country; now, he realized that on this earth, more is at stake than the interests of nations—the lasting lot of every man; and the war became for him the wild setting in which men had to fight out the one great struggle of their souls' submission to God.

Having allowed his conversion to mature and prove itself for a good year, Reinach wrote to his wife: "My plan is clear before my eyes; naturally, it is very modest. I should like to start from the inner experience of God, the experience of being sheltered in Him, and shall be content to show that 'objective science' cannot gainsay it. I should like to expound the full meaning of this experience, to show how far it can claim objectivity, to demonstrate why it is a genuine cognition, though of its own kind; and finally, to draw the conclusions. Of course, a presentation like this has nothing to offer to him who lives in God's sight. But it can steady the one who wavers, who lets the objections of science confuse him, and it can lead onward him whom these objections have stayed from walking to God. To do such a work with humility is most important today, far more important than to fight this war. For what purpose has this horror if it does not lead men closer to God?" [62]

This letter was written on May 23, 1916, from a quiet zone in France where, from April to June, Reinach tried as philosopher to examine his religious experience. The question that never left him was how the new undoubtable knowledge which God's grace had given him was related to the philosophical truths he had hitherto realized and taught; how the one truth, which revealed itself to men of good will, was related to the many truths that could be seen by everyone. Among his few possessions returned to his home after his death at the front, were notes on many scraps of paper, all trying to see clearly the newness that had captured his soul.

In the course of his analysis, there returned again and again the concept of the absolute. As it unfolded its importance and fecundity, he decided to set it at the head of his book, and began to draft the first section, which, though fragmentary, is still the only lengthy account of his thought during this period. As found in this world, or as thinkable within its frame, love, goodness, gratitude, trust, dependence, weakness, vary in strength and height, he wrote. It is impossible to think of confidence in a man or of gratitude toward him without the realization that they can be heightened. Confidence in or gratitude toward God, however, though increasable in strength, cannot be raised in height, in quality, for no higher gratitude or confidence is possible or even conceivable than that directed toward Him. And of course, there neither is nor can be a love or a goodness higher and stronger than that we attribute to God. If infinity be taken in its full sense, there is no infinite number, no infinite space, for it is their very nature to be capable of increase, but no one who has ever plunged into the idea of God's love can say that it can grow in breadth or length or height or depth.

Reinach goes on to ask what distinguishes our earthly love from our love for God, so that while the one stretches toward infinity, the other holds infinity within itself. On the other hand, what do they have in common to justify our speaking of one and the same content, though divine love has for its object absolute fullness, and earthly love is essentially and forever fastened to insufficiency and defect? [63]

We need only remember the gratitude we owe another man, and then let gratitude toward God flood our hearts, to find in their so different directions the infinite difference between infinity and finitude. In acts which relate men to men, a definite direction may inhere: there is a friendship that looks up and one that bends down, there is hatred of superiors and also hatred of inferiors. Sometimes these directions are accidental, at other times essential: benevolence, for instance, in contradistinction to goodness, is necessarily directed downward, while comradeship is always among equals. [64]

Any relationship toward God, however, must be absolutely upward. We look up to Him, but our looking up to Him is entirely different from our looking up to men, for a relationship to another human being, no matter how highly placed, is never such that a still higher relationship could not be conceived. Steep though the pinnacles may be on which the mighty of this earth stand, God thrones in heaven, dwells in absolute height. Our metaphysical station before Him, that of the absolute "below" facing the absolute "above," demands certain interior attitudes, dependence, trust, and love; and excludes others as meaningless —one cannot be benevolent or good to God. Confronted as we are with God, the Absolute, our metaphysical situation not only forms and directs our interior attitudes; the inner experience of being absolutely secure in His hands, which may flood the heart of the unbeliever, leads him to God, and since the experience is absolute, to God reigning in absolute majesty. [65]

Hence we can speak, Reinach continues, of absoluteness in a three-fold sense: God exists in absolute height; religious experience is therefore directed toward absolute height; and connected with this formal absoluteness is that of the material content, the consummation of trust, gratitude, and love. There is a rationale among these three senses, a passing by inner motivation from one to the other. To the One who is supreme, to whom our experience rises, we owe absolute fullness of love; if, on the other hand, absolute confidence inspires us, it must seek its intentional object in absolute height.[66]

Opposed to the absolute is the earthly, that which can be increased without end and is therefore imperfect through all eternity. Though these two worlds are a chasm apart, there is at the same time a close kinship between them. At times we do encounter in this world a dim and imperfect likeness of the world above; both there and here we find goodness, love, wisdom. But always there is an abyss: the absolute, having in itself, impossible of increase, all wealth, all fullness, is quite other from that which exists in degrees, in poverty mounting and falling. No matter how far it rises, the earthly can never attain the realm above, indeed, it cannot even come near; be the love a man gives another the greatest possible, still it cannot compare with love for God.[67]

The earthly realm is the world of nothing, some, and many, of more and less, the world of becoming, of change, of growth and decay, while the realm above is the world of unlimited wealth, of fullest fullness, of the sheer *all*. Yet—and this is the most precious gift with which God has blessed us—we who stand in time and space, in the world of imperfection, can grasp that which is above. Not only do we grasp it, but its absolute fullness is, in a measure, reflected in those of our acts which have the other world for their object. We experience God, are conscious of our dependence on Him, love Him, and this dependence, gratitude and love are not relative; they cannot be heightened as can relationships among men, rather are they of an absolute quality. Thus earthly life receives a heavenly content, and this is as it must be. For, when the supernal realm is grasped by a responsive act, by an act such as adoration, which responds to the infinite, the absoluteness of its content corresponds to the absoluteness of its object. These are indeed dry theoretical expositions, Reinach confesses, but buried in them is the priceless center of our lives, which alone can sustain us. Thrown to and fro, swept up and down by hopes and disappointments, expectation and fear, love and hatred, gratitude and

revenge, hemmed in by the more and less of all social relationships, we have in the absolute a domain inviolable, a support
which never fails.[68]

Bringing his paper to a close, Reinach discusses how our earthly
religious experiences, which, like everything earthly, swing between imperfection and perfection, can partake of the absolute.
Distinguishing the content of a religious experience, he says, from
the way its content makes itself felt, we recognize the absoluteness of the one, love of God, for instance, and the relativity of the
other, our momentary emotion. To take an analogy from human
relationships: We may experience the great pity we know to be
another's due, but only in a small way. Here also the "absoluteness" pertains to the content of our experience, not to its manner.
In the manner, too, of our experience, there can be something,
however, which corresponds to "absoluteness," which is expressed
in terms like "completely filled" or "utterly permeated." It is just
this utterness which is often lacking: I may know of some great
misery and truly sympathize, feel it as the great misery it is; still
I do not feel it in proportion to the greatness of the misery, in a
way which penetrates all the levels of my consciousness. And since
we are in the sphere of the relative, this disparity can also be re
versed: At an impressionable moment, I may be overcome with
joy, although the event which occasions it is small and unimpor
tant. In either case, the weight of the "how" of my feeling does
not correspond to the weight of its "what." [69]

Is an absolute weight of experience possible for man? We recol
lect ourselves in prayer, shutting out all distractions that we may
give to our oblation the absolute weight it claims; still we know
that even at our deepest moments, we are found wanting. Perhaps,
Reinach concludes, no other than the Son of God can feel and
pray: "Thy Will be done," in its last depth. But though no abso
lute weight of experience is accorded us, there does remain open
to us the infinite "what" of our religious experience, and this is
our bridge to the realm of the absolute.[70]

We walk this bridge in piety. In one of his notes, which was dated
May 10, 1916, and found after his death, Reinach limned its na
ture, at the same time giving a vivid picture of his own soul turned
toward heaven: "Description of piety, (a) the opening of oneself

receptiveness, (b) the *absolute* direction upward, upward to an absolute above, symbolized in the look to the sky."

Things Seen New

None of his notes written in the din and mud of war speaks explicitly of Reinach's inner life, nor does his paper on the absolute—still, they show that its core was the experience, the knowledge and feeling of sealed shelter, of a home in God, *restloser Geborgenheit in Gott.* This made of Reinach, a Jew by blood, a Jew according to the spirit,[71] tying him to the Old and New Testaments, with their glad news for the house of Israel and for all those who are raised to its dignity,[72] that God Himself is their Keeper. Two images, more than others, describe Him thus: the shepherd and the mother bird. The joy of David's ever-living words: "The Lord is my shepherd, I shall not want," [73] resounds through the Old Testament till it meets its fulfillment in Christ, the Good Shepherd, who gave His life for His sheep.[74] Moses remembered the great deeds of God: "As the eagle enticing her young to fly, and hovering over them, He spread His wings: and has taken Israel and has carried him on His shoulders." [75] And even when Christ had to mourn Israel's refusal to accept the haven He offered, He said still: "Jerusalem, Jerusalem . . . how often would I have gathered together thy children, as the hen gathers her chickens under her wings!" [76]

There is no doubt that Reinach, who before his conversion had ached to the groans and travail of all creatures, knew afterward God's "wings for refuge, His faithfulness for watch and ward," [77] and even through his philosophical notes there shines joy in his liberation and tranquillity. Now he saw God's loving finger everywhere; "Each thing bears the imprint *through God,* time and space included," reads a note of June 22.

What creature, O sweet Lord,
  from praising thee can stay,
What earthly thing but filled with joy,
  thine honour doth bewray.[78]

Now too Reinach realized the immense difference between mere immortality and everlasting life in God. On April 27 he remarked: "There is a specifically religious view of immortality which does not base its conviction on the nature of the person but on that of the soul sheltered and abiding in God." The full significance of trust and gratitude impressed itself on him. "To real life," he wrote on May 11, "we get only by way of living, burning confidence"; and on the 21st: "Before God there is only sheer dependence, and so is there only sheer, absolute thankfulness. Absolute thankfulness cannot be felt to another human being, for there is no human gratitude that cannot be surpassed." Then he remarked that it is proper to this absolute thankfulness toward God that it is not gratitude "for something." This is precisely the spirit of the Gloria of the Mass: "We give Thee thanks for Thy great glory." Though we need, of course, to thank God for each of His benefits, though we cannot do without being grateful for them, our thanksgiving reaches its zenith in the praise that He is, and is as He is.

Reinach's thirst for truth was not quenched by his having found God; if anything, it was quickened. But never did he rank first the postulates of science and demand that religious reality conform with them, rather the opposite. An instance is his note of April 28 on "the antinomy of prayer's being granted." Man's activity in prayer and God's activity in answering were primary to him, and he left it to the law of causality (as some scientists conceived it) to square with them. "My prayer that the onrolling avalanche may not strike me and my hope to be heard—how are they to be reconciled with the single determination of all natural events? Astounding! If the avalanche swerves by, perhaps because of some stones, I feel that my prayer has been heard—even though the stones were there all along, and though this outcome could consequently have been figured out beforehand. Is my experience therefore an illusion, or does one wish to 'save' the experience, as Schleiermacher seems to do, by saying that God foresaw everything and heard the prayer in advance? Or are we here brought face to face with an enigma, caused above all by our notion of time, which we all too readily imagine absolute, a notion we must strike out? First and foremost, we must leave intact the meaning of religious experiences! Even though it leads to enigmas. Perhaps it is just these enigmas that are of the highest value to knowledge. God's mercy has given me my life anew—that is the deep unseen background; in this world, it is accomplished by the grain of sand which turns aside the avalanche. Through prayer, I am in contact with this ultimate background of the world. Granted, prayer is in time, and the answer must follow on it, and it is in the same dimension of time that the avalanche rushes down. And still . . ."

It is through prayer, says Reinach, that we are in contact with the "ultimate background of the world," with God, the Beginning and the End, and petition is not so much an asking for favors as it is a "yes" to His wisdom and power. God is not a "filler-in" but All-in-all, and to turn to Him only as a last resort is to miss the deepest significance of petition, for His help is not merely something added to close up the gaps in our own strength—our whole existence is from, through, and toward Him. Only when man is lovingly aware, therefore, of his continuous dependence on God is he truly himself, and only when he receives God's gifts, glad that they are from God's hands, do they become his full possession. At every instant the laws of nature are the servants of the Creator, and they are man's friends too, servers of his salvation, if he is one with God's will. They become his masters, however, and he their sport, when he tries to face them alone. If the divine purpose is his first care, if he seeks first the kingdom of God and His justice, all the things he needs will be given him; all around him, men, things, events, conditions, which at times seem to threaten him, organize themselves in a new way, as his helpers. They assume a new "figure," a new meaning—or rather, man, his heart in harmony with God's will, gives them out of his new heart a new meaning, their true, divinely intended meaning; he recognizes them as the ministers of God's providence.[79]

Before his conversion, faith had seemed to Reinach of little moment to philosophy; now, it was not only the center of life but the very foundation of knowledge. Among the thoughts he jotted down in France, there is this little note dated June 1916: "Schopenhauer thinks that could one *know,* faith would be ridiculous," to which Reinach added: "Almost the opposite." Faith is no inferior substitute for scientific knowledge; rather does it acknowledge and glory in the mystery of God and His world, a mystery which science often tries to conceal. Reinach wrote on April 28: "As we are awe-struck by the immeasurable depth of being and compare with it what our knowledge achieves or might achieve, we grasp that the inscrutability of being is both necessary and desirable for us." Other of his notes also show our utter need of faith;

on April 27: "A scientific ethics [Reinach probably had in mind an ethics that sought to ingratiate itself with the natural science, that sought to be itself an "exact science"] is entirely incapable of laying down certain ultimate truths, for instance, that in this sinful world it is better to forgive than to punish. But perhaps there are in ethics 'open doors' to religion. One has only to think of the concept of punishment. Or perhaps also of the problem of justice." June 23: "In regard to the transcendent world, the human person is pure receiving; in regard to this world, both receiving and giving."

On a note dated May 14, Reinach quoted from Georg Simmel: "The quiet, certitude, and edification given by religion do not come, of course, from the transcendent; rather does the soul, on passing through the station of faith in God, draw them from within itself." [80] After Simmel's "of course," Reinach put an exclamation point, to cry out against this naturalistic prejudice, against blind spot and bias masquerading as self-evidence, against this denial of the uniqueness of religion. Whoever knows, he protested, the unique phenomena of religious quiet, certitude, and edification, knows Simmel's dictum to be untenable. To assume that the soul, and not God, is the source of her own religious life is to assume that a poor man could give of his own poverty to himself, and then be rich.

The Infinite Wonder of Christ

Few books were to be had on the battlefield, and among them were some works of Simmel and of a few other liberal philosophers of religion—wherefore Reinach's comment on him. His true and constant companions, however, were the *Confessions, The Imitation of Christ*, the New Testament, and the Roman Missal. In a note of May 16 he quoted St. Augustine: "In a good book, God Himself speaks to us," [81] and Thomas à Kempis: "Search not who spoke this or that, but mark what is spoken. Men pass away, but the truth of the Lord remaineth forever. God speaks to us in sundry ways without respect of persons." [82] In his notes he marked particularly the eighth chapter of *The Imitation of Christ*, "That Too Much Familiarity Is to Be Shunned," which says: "Lay not thy heart open to everyone; but treat of thy affairs with the wise and such as fear God. . . . We must have charity toward all, but familiarity with all is not to be counseled." Meditating on it, he asked, on May 16, whether great intimacy was not something we should offer to God alone.

When Reinach read the New Testament, the majestic figure of Christ demanded his eyes, his faith. "When we call Jesus' teaching beautiful, when we laud and magnify His doctrine, we do so absolutely," he wrote on June 16; "The 'wonderful!' He inspires cannot be transcended." No spiritual message from East or West, ancient or modern, can surpass the Beatitudes, no explanation plummet their depth. The parable of the Prodigal Son has no like in beauty, the Last Discourse no equal as testament of love. There is no prayer peer to the Lord's Prayer, simple and all-inclusive, fitting within a few words all things from the greatest to the least. And nowhere else can sayings be found with the finality of "No man can serve two masters," [83] or of "What does it profit a man, if he gain the whole world and suffer the loss of his own soul?" [84]

Jesus is the Blessing Abraham foresaw and rejoiced in,[85] the Saviour of whom the prophets spoke, Son and Lord of David, the One greater than Jonas, greater than Solomon,[86] or, in the words of Léon Bloy, the Jew of Jews.[87] Yet to say this of Him is wholly different from saying of a man that he is the Greek of Greeks or the Englishman of Englishmen. What in others is the result of conditions, in Him is freedom: no mark of His people or of His time can circumscribe Him. "Doubtless," Reinach wrote on May 18, "one can point out historic and national limitations in every man; not so in Jesus." Again and again his mind returned to the limitlessness of Christ. Under the date of May 16 there is this crisp remark: "There is no Life, no History of Jesus." No *Life of Christ* can encompass Him; though little by little He unveiled His wisdom and power, He had no "history," no psychological development, no growth of Messianic consciousness. "Did you not know that I must be about my Father's business?" [88] His first recorded words reveal His sovereignty pure and simple.

On May 9 Reinach wrote: "It is evident that we cannot ascribe 'character' to Christ, no qualities at all, either good or bad. True, in looking at Him we behold acts of love, of kindness, and of mercy, but to call Him kind, not to mention compassionate, is an anthropomorphism; it forces Him into our mold. To have qualities is the way of man but not of God." Here Reinach seems to

131

overshoot his mark in indignation at the moderns, the new Arians of liberal Protestantism, who like to see nothing but Christ's human compassion. To speak of Christ's kindness is not anthropomorphism, for He is truly Man. Still, His Person is divine, and it is in this sense that Reinach continues: "Since Christ lacks entirely what one calls 'personal features,' it is difficult, if not impossible, to paint or sculpture Him, and indeed, all pictures of Christ either tell nothing, or represent the emotion of a particular moment, His suffering, for example, but never the wholeness of His Person. It is hard to say what one feels before the whole Christ: in Him God's Being, outside of time and beyond the world, seems to unfold itself in time and before the world." [89]

Reinach's "seems" is a sign not of doubt but of marvel, that marvel an old English verse sings:

Wit is a-wonder, and reason out-ran,
How maid is mother, and God is man.
Leave thy search, and believe the wonder;
God is the Lord, and skill goeth under! [90]

With Christ the Infinite in mind, Reinach asks, in a note of June 16, whether "character" does not imply that a man has the defects of his qualities, whether it does not spell ethical finitude. Does not a lasting inclination to some commendable act often make a man incapable of doing its psychological opposite? Fixed tendencies, set habits, or "strong points"—whose inflexibility must not be confused with the firmness of virtue, of love, for instance—follow a mechanism, utterly foreign, of course, to all that is divine, and because of this mechanism, at times they hinder more than help the inner life of the soul. A "strong-willed" man may be so set in his "determination" that he is "unable" to yield even when he ought, a uniformly "good-natured" man will be yielding when he should be firm. All things earthly spell finitude, even beauty, wisdom, holiness. The works of Giotto, Michelangelo, Raphael, Duerer, Gruenewald, Rembrandt, or Rouault are each, for all their greatness, but the segment of a circle; Plato's excellence and Aristotle's in some measure account for their shortcomings. And though the saints have the greatest dower of catholicity, still, what singles out St. Benedict among his fellow saints, what sets apart

St. Francis of Assisi, what makes St. Dominic himself, also confines them.

How concisely Reinach put this in a jotting of May 10! "Character bespeaks restriction. This restriction is not without consequence, for it is his restricted character which determines a man's reactions to the events of the world, one way or another. It is obvious, however, that Christ experiences events and takes His stand toward them exactly as their purest and deepest contents demand. His Person is perfect fullness." [91]

Of Water and the Spirit

This and all the other notes were written in the spring and early summer of 1916, amid the spiritual solitude of military life, in muddy fields and somber trenches, where faith was almost literally "a lamp to his feet and a light to his path," [92] where his days were illumined by naught but the certainty that Christ is "God of God, Light of Light, true God of true God; begotten not made; of one substance with the Father." [93] In the beginning of the same year, before he began to write his notes, many months after his inner conversion, Reinach was home on a furlough. At once his wife, Anna Reinach, urged that since they both had come to believe in Christ, they should be baptized together, and suggested that they receive the sacrament from the hands of a Protestant minister.

Sped by an overwhelming desire, Anna Reinach thought that by approaching a Protestant minister, she and her husband could receive baptism without delay, as simply as did the Ethiopian in the *Acts of the Apostles*. "See, here is water," he said to Philip. "What hinders me from being baptized?" and was answered: "If thou dost believe with all thy heart, thou mayest." [94] They did believe with all their hearts, in the Father, Son, and Holy Ghost, she reasoned; nothing, therefore, ought to keep them from the water which gives life. Her husband gladly consented and took all the necessary steps. But a few hours before they went to church, he was suddenly very much disturbed. "I am terribly afraid I am doing wrong in being baptized this way," he said, and after a pause, added: "I fear that I want to be baptized now by a minister because I am not yet ready for the Catholic Church." To this his wife replied: "You are not precluding anything. Once we are in communion with Christ, we shall see where He will lead us. No matter what the price, let us enter; I cannot wait any longer."

After he was baptized, Adolf Reinach rejoiced to have been reborn of water and the Holy Spirit, to have become one with Christ. Though baptized by a minister, he did not consider himself a member of the Protestant community nor did he take part in its worship or life, for he still was and wanted to be on the way. But never on earth did he enter the Church; in November 1917, a year after his baptism, he was killed in Flanders.

As if to tell aloud along which road he had walked, as if to tell that every pilgrimage finds in the Church its home, his wife, his sister, his brother and sister-in-law with their children, and many, many of his friends and pupils, entered the Church one by one, his sister and one nephew choosing the monastic life. The day before his sister joined the Benedictine nuns of Mont Vierge in Wépion, Belgium, the Prioress addressed the chapter: "Tomorrow, we shall have the great joy of welcoming to our community a new member, who is, even according to the flesh, a sister of Our Lord."

Max Scheler

CRITIC OF MODERN MAN

PHILOSOPHY MUST BE QUEEN OR SLAVE: QUEEN OVER SCIENCE when she is handmaid to faith, she becomes its slave when she has the audacity to pose as faith's mistress—so wrote Max Scheler in 1917 in his essay *On the Nature of Philosophy*. Seeking to lift the spirit till it touches the realm of being, seeking to pierce the veil that hides the deepest in things, philosophy leads to a loving participation in their essence by way of knowledge. Hence philosophy *is* knowing and the philosopher a knower, Scheler writes, but to say, as is the vogue, that its dealings are with no more than the knowledge of things and that their essence is none of its concern, rests on no intellectual ground. It is pride, he asserts, which makes a philosopher maintain that philosophy can never lead into the precincts of essence, for he fears that there he would have to recognize that the nature of the Prime Being may demand another, and a more adequate, way of participation than knowledge. Indeed, it might happen that the strict consequence of his philosophical thinking enjoin on him a free subordination to this higher way; he may even be bidden to bring his self, with his inquiring reason, a willing sacrifice to this fuller but nonphilosophical sharing which the Prime Being, by its very nature, might claim. Only pride can say that, no matter what this nature may prove to be, it will refuse this sacrifice; only prejudice can assert that all being has solely the character of an object, and that knowledge alone can partake of it.[1]

True, God was for Aristotle the "Thought of Thought," and the philosopher therefore the perfect man, his path the highest of human existence. But Christ came, and no longer could God, the Prime Being, be seen as a mere object of thought, for He acts, He loves, His Being is creative and merciful goodness. Hence acting *with* Him, loving *with* Him, became the gate to participation in the Prime Being, and philosophy, loyal to logic, rejoiced to minister to faith in Christ, in whom this participation was perfect and was union. The sage had to move to second place, below the saint, and the philosopher to subject himself to the lover of God. Over and above its ancient dignity as queen of science, philosophy gained a dignity far more excellent, that of willing handmaid to the Saviour, a blessed handmaid, for "blessed are the poor in spirit." And in this glad service, philosophy obeyed no strange usurper; rather did it express its true autonomy, fulfill its highest freedom.[2]

But today philosophy is no longer seated thus between faith and science. Having shattered this true relationship, it has set itself above religious truth only to bow low before scientific hypotheses. This reversal, an instance of a general overturn of values, Scheler calls the "revolt of the slaves in the intellectual realm." It seems a paradox that when philosophy limited itself it was unlimited; now that it admits no confines, it has no territory of its own. When it was preamble to faith, it knew it could penetrate to the roots of being; but now that it is subservient to one or the other science— geometry, physics, psychology—there is nothing it is sure of seeing. This is as it must be, says Scheler, for truth is such that it falls prey to the darkness within man unless it humbles itself before the Primal Light.[3]

In philosophy Plato saw moving the wings of the soul, Scheler recalls, the soaring upward of the whole of the human person. To the great philosophers of antiquity, philosophy was a transcending of the spirit, implying a moral approach: the conquest of merely practical—that is, ultimately, selfish—attention to the world. Scheler's view is close to this when he says that it is always our willing and doing which underlie our mistaken values; that it is always, somehow, wrong practice which drags down our consciousness of values and their ranks to its own level. We must learn to will and to do what is good, more or less blindly, before we can see the good, and will and do it with insight. For wisdom dwells in "virtue, the greatest of all monarchies." [4]

It is characteristic of man's natural view that he takes his little world for all the world, his immediate milieu for the universe, be this milieu the particular surroundings of an individual, of his race, of his people, or the general surroundings of natural man as part of his species. That his mind may rise above them and participate in being as it is in itself, says Scheler, the philosopher must relinquish, in principle, all that is merely relative to the vital sphere or to himself as a living creature. For only by forsaking his milieu, the tangibles and intangibles of everyday, can he reach philosophy's true domain. Scheler insists that there can be no philosophical knowledge without love, humility, and self-mastery. In loving the absolute Value, the absolute Being, the spiritual person breaks through the shell of his surroundings; humbling his natural ego, he is led from accidentals to the whatness of the world; mastering the many impulses that go hand in hand with his sense perception, he looses the fetters of his concupiscence and is led from mere opinion toward adequate knowledge.[5]

Scheler's insistence that the purity, measure, strength, and growth of our philosophical knowledge are tied to virtue, that the theoretical and moral worlds are essentially and eternally knit together,[6] continues the line of Christian philosophy. St. Thomas indicts pride as a hindrance to knowledge, for the man who delights in his own excellence soon tires of the excellence of truth.[7] And St. Augustine says, though of religious knowledge, that those who do not seek truth with all their hearts will not find it, but that from its lovers it cannot hide. They must heed: "Ask and it shall be given you, seek and you shall find, knock and it shall be opened to you," and: "Nothing is covered that shall not be revealed." In all this quest, it is love that asks, love that seeks, love that knocks, love that unveils the eyes, and love it is that gives perseverance in the truth. Again he says: "Let love be in you, and the fullness of knowledge must follow."[8]

As Scheler stood in the Christian tradition when he bound together virtue and knowledge, so also he echoed the Old Testament. There the man of God can say that his understanding, discernment and wisdom are greater than his elders' and teachers', because he has kept God's law.[9]

A Heart Restless and Divided

Much of Scheler's work shows the love for the absolute and the humility before the objective world which he demands. His was an unusual mind, to which all things spoke, so awake that every and any circumstance served and stimulated his thought. He was a philosopher not only in the study or the classroom but at all times; every remark of his, whether in the coffee shop or at a ball, in the theater or on the street, bore a philosophical note, betraying a genius that went directly to the uniqueness of every situation and lifted out its general significance.[10]

Socrates spoke of himself as a "gadfly" and a "midwife"; Scheler, to describe his way of thinking and of presenting his thought, called himself a puppeteer. His philosophical equipment—the world and his head—he had always with him, as a strolling player his little theater. The vagrant mummer needs no preparation, no atmosphere, none of the appurtenances of the big theater, nor did Scheler require any special setting; given an ear, he became creative and set his ideas dancing. He might be seated with a companion, his head canted to the side, watching on the unfolded stage of his mind the drama of the world. He looked aslant at his puppets' play, which was his own, and always with half an eye for the listener—or better, the spectator. And again and again, by an interjected *Wie?* or *Nicht wahr?* he assured himself of his companion's attention and of the effect of his play. It was truly magic; in an instant he could transform his surroundings and fill the room with his ideas; he made present the things of which he spoke and visible what is often called "abstract." What he called forth from the realm of spirit came, and now and then there gleamed in his eye an unchastened joy that he was so obeyed.[11]

However, what made Scheler so powerful also made him vulnerable; his genius was his weakness. His spoken word had strength and freshness, the dew of the spirit was on it, but his written style was sometimes clumsy, so that he said of himself: "The word I have but not the sentence." [12] He was indeed lavishly gifted; ideas came to him without labor, flaming in his mind like lightning, and it was this immense fecundity that persuaded him to neglect, even to disdain, intellectual toil. Seldom would he spend the effort to verify his references, to sift and weigh his thoughts, to examine and test them on every side, but rather moved on to new problems. Some of his intuitions on love, to give an instance, were profound, but his presentation is never complete, never rounded, giving always only one aspect, almost to the exclusion of others. He showed little care for his sources; quoting, for example, the words of St. Paul: "Beggars enriching many, paupers possessing all things," [13] he attributes them to St. Francis of Assisi.[14] Nor had he much concern for the consistency of his own thought. In his *Formalism in Ethics* he says: "Knowingly to will evil as evil is entirely possible," adding that he does not "subscribe to the saying of Thomas Aquinas, *Omnia volumus sub specie boni*, 'We will all things under an aspect of good.' " [15] (The pairing of these two sentences suggests that Scheler did not fully understand this principle; indeed, not a few of his objections to St. Thomas are based on misunderstanding.) Some years later, however, in an essay *On the Task of German Catholics after the War,* he said, and without accounting for his change of mind: "Evil is but a consequence of a free act of the will performed *sub specie boni.*" [16]

Here is another example of his inaccuracy. In *Sympathy, Its Essence and Forms,* he writes: "St. Francis was a sworn enemy of scholasticism and its doctrine of the aristocratic-hierarchic order of being." [17] Nearly every word in this sentence is mistaken. How great was St. Francis' awe for wisdom is seen in his childlike reverence for the written word, for whenever he found a scrap of writing on the road, he picked it from the dust and preserved it with care. Once he was told, partly in jest, that a paper he had thus saved was from a pagan author, and he replied that it mattered not, for all words, of pagans or of others, stemmed from God's wisdom and spoke of God, from whom are all good things. It was his very love of wisdom that made him abhor learning for its own sake and the universities of his time as seats of haughtiness and error.[18] This hostility to "learning as a ware" Scheler distorts into enmity to scholasticism, to which alone he ascribes a doctrine held in the Church long before scholasticism was born. Moreover, the context of Scheler's remark seems to indicate that he had in mind Aristotelian thought, which at the time of St. Francis had not become part of scholastic philosophy.

Many a page and many a thought of Scheler is marred by such want of discipline, all the more startling in its contrast with the virtues he knew necessary for the philosophical act. This discrepancy was rooted in an inner disharmony, a discord not to be understood save through the reverence every soul merits. He saw, and saw again, and saw anew, where others passed blindly; inundated with impressions, he was always tempted to trust them too far, to surrender to them, and it was often their novelty that appealed to him, who in a way stayed always a child. His relationship with the world remained too much one of wonder, one of wanting to know it. But infinitely more is asked of us—to rest and persevere in the known, to be permeated by truth and given to it lovingly, to mortify ourselves for its sake, to conform our wills and adjust our lives to the light we see. All this was difficult for Scheler, for in his early youth he had been indescribably spoiled; he had, as he said himself, never learned to will. Dietrich von Hildebrand, long his friend, applies to him Lessing's word, so telling of modern unrest: If God were to offer him in one hand eternal and absolute truth, and in the other the everlasting desire for it, he would grasp desire and say, Truth is for Thee alone. Scheler's philosophy at its best totally disavows this choice, and yet, deplorably, it does correspond to a trait of his character, to a deep restlessness which darkened his life.[19]

Max Scheler was born in Munich on August 22, 1874, the son of a Jewish mother and a Gentile father who, for the sake of marriage, had adopted Judaism. Thus Scheler was born a Jew, but he grew up with no religious formation. His first acquaintance with the spiritual world was through the Catholic serving-maids in his home, whose tranquil strength and simplicity seemed uniquely theirs. But not until he met at the *Gymnasium* the priest who taught religion did the Church grip Scheler's interest, for in him he met a different world, the world of the absolute. In his priestly character, his dedication to God, Scheler must have glimpsed, as through an opening door, the world of grace, and divined the phenomenon of holiness, of which in later years he was to speak so strongly. He must also have sensed the motherly arms of the Church, her peace, for he was baptized at about the age of fourteen.

After completing his work in the humanities at the *Gymnasium,* Scheler studied in Berlin, where Wilhelm Dilthey, Franz Stumpf, and Georg Simmel set the intellectual tone; from there he went to Heidelberg, and later to Jena to study under Rudolf Eucken, staying on as a University lecturer. In 1907 he returned to Munich to teach at the University, where the most significant period of his life was to begin. His constant intellectual communion with the "Munich School"—the followers of Theodor Lipps who had attached themselves to Husserl—and later in Goettingen with Husserl himself, inspired him to truly productive work, encouraging him, by temperament a teacher, to write, and so make his great and specific contribution to the history of thought.

From the time he left the *Gymnasium* until his transfer to the University of Munich, Scheler's life was under a dark shadow: he had entered a civil marriage with a woman, divorced and much older than he, who tried first to dominate then to ruin him. But back in Munich he freed himself from this bond, which had brought him pain and unhappiness from the first moment. A few years later he was to say: the more guilt grows, the more it is hidden from the guilty, but the more humility increases, the more visible becomes even the smallest trespass.[20] This had been his own experience. Once he had broken the chain of sin, his remorse grew; stronger became his sorrow for having forfeited the life of grace and greater his longing to regain the mercy of God. In those years, he often visited the Benedictine Abbey in Beuron, which he had known while still at Jena, to breathe its peace, and it was there, in 1916, that Scheler returned to the faith of his boyhood. "I have made my confession; I have come back to the bosom of the Church," he rejoiced. "I am infinitely happy, and I know I owe this to the Blessed Virgin." Nor did he remain alone in his happiness, for Maerit Furtwaengler, whom he had married a few years before and whose love had sustained him, made her profession of faith soon afterward.

Though Scheler's desire then to be a full member of the Church was genuine, nonetheless he was never more than an enthusiastic and admiring onlooker, to whom the sacramental order, for instance, was for a time an object of the greatest philosophical interest, but nothing he could live for long. His mind was stirred by the knowledge that, in the sacraments, water and oil, bread and wine, common material things, serve in the most spiritual task, the glorification of God and the sanctification of man; but his soul could not hold it fast. At Mass, his attention seemed to be all to his missal, to the rich and daily changing book, but he was at a loss before the sacred event itself, always the same. A transport like Edith Sitwell's "The universal language of the Bread"; her cry: "Our Christ is arisen, He comes to give a sign from the Dead," might have struck him forcefully, but could he have dwelt in their mystery? The theology of the Eucharist gripped his thoughts, but could he pray with Paul Claudel?

O Lord, Thou seest this world Thou hast given us to consume:
In this bread all heaven and earth for my sustenance conspire.
This man whom Thou hast fashioned do Thou, in his turn, consume!
With us, ransomed in bread and wine, do Thou eat, in an upper room,
The Pasch of Thy great desire! [21]

With his heart remaining always restless and divided, Scheler embodied the ill of modern man. And yet it was Scheler—another sign of the contradiction he was—who was the relentless critic of modern man, "groaning, walking beneath a burden of his own manufacture, his mechanisms. His limbs heavy and only the earth before his eyes, modern man has forgotten his God and his world." [22]

Unsparingly Scheler castigates him, who has lost the great confidence in *being* which is part of human wholeness; man unmanned, who is by creed a skeptic, meeting the world with *a priori* distrust. Lacking boldness and generosity, he makes achievement and usefulness the measure of persons and things, and never-ending activity the disguise of his inner void; where there ought to be love of creation and joy in its riches, there is anxiety to defeat creation as an enemy. While the integral man looks at the objective world with undisturbed and love-led devotion, knowing that the human mind, created by God, the Fount of wisdom, can grasp the essence of things, modern man doubts, as a matter of principle, the powers of his mind. Driven by his deep-seated hostility to the world as it came from the hands of God, he considers it instead a terrible "mush," out of which his activity must make sense—he uses it for purposes of his own and determines it quantitatively, never ceasing to compare, always striving to surpass. For all that his thinking seems so complex, latter-day man has in truth relapsed into the primitive, and never before have his motives been so infantile; the biggest, the fastest, the newest, the most powerful are his ideals. These are the things a child enjoys: the giant in the fairy tale, the spinning top, shoes shining and conspicuously new, the drum that beats the loudest; and these are also the things the crowd seeks after, for it is a bigger child. With modern man allowing the crowd to shape his soul, the end is a state in which all copy all.[23]

Alive to man's integral and rich humanity, Scheler was enraged by its caricature that had been rising on the historical scene since the end of the thirteenth century. At times his speech had a passion almost prophetic, and had he been true to his insight, he would have earned the title "prophet against the times." Every Christian has a prophetic vocation, he said, but the prediction of the true prophet is not absolute, because he does not lose sight of man's freedom. True, he cries: I foresee judgment; come it must, save you repent and turn to God, and He in His mercy turn His judgment from you. The prophet cries out, but it is the historic reality that preaches. In its blood and misery, he hears the warning voice of God, and refuses to predict ease, to hold out dazzling visions of paradise.

Perforce a prophet of grief, of doom, Scheler is never a man of despair. Time and again the prophets of the Old Covenant spoke of a remnant to be spared, from which would spring new life, and this promise of a remnant is rekindled whenever the days of a culture grow short. So St. Benedict, when Christian life was imperiled by the great city, went from Rome to Subiaco; while outside, ancient culture was being ground underfoot, he preserved within his monasteries its noble fragments, together with the ideal of Christian perfection.[24] In his best years it was Scheler's desire—indeed, it was his calling, though fulfilled but in part—to undeceive modern man, who thinks he has fared well in this world; to show that the day of wrath is upon him unless he change heart; and, implicitly, to call on the remnant to carry the true values over the abyss into which man is about to throw himself.

Ressentiment and Value

Oddly enough, for his dissection of the modern ethos, Scheler uses the blade Nietzsche forged: his emphasis on *ressentiment*. In his essay on *The Role of Ressentiment in Moral Systems* (1912, revised 1915), Scheler defines it as a self-poisoning of the soul caused by systematic repression, as opposed to moral conquest, of hostile emotions like hate, spite, envy, jealousy, or revenge; a self-poisoning leading to a more or less permanent deformation of the sense of values. Only there, he says, will *ressentiment* grow where a violent emotion goes hand in hand with a feeling of impotence, derived from some physical or spiritual weakness or from fear of those against whom the emotion is directed. It springs up most readily, therefore, in those in subordinate or inferior positions, in those who are dependent, who are ruled, who serve; a virus malignant and most contagious, it may, however, spread widely and infect many others.[25] But we must add that every man, being dependent on God, is tempted to kick against the goad of His authority and is thus open to the bitterness of *ressentiment*.

If the resentful man is unable to lift his oppressive feeling of inferiority by action, Scheler continues, he seeks another outlet for his painful tension in falsehood. He drags down the values that depress him in others, or else blinds himself to them; furthermore —and this, Scheler points out, is the main work of *ressentiment*— he either falsifies values as such or pretends they are illusory, for if their validity or existence be denied, there can remain no high qualities to depress him. Or he may come to say that the good is whatever he wants, that it is the offspring of desire. This depreciation of values to the level of one's desires or abilities, far from being the normal fulfillment of the sense of values, is, on the contrary, the chief cause of moral blindness, deception, and illusion. The possibility of resignation—that a man, having lost the power to obtain a good, can yet acknowledge its worth—proves the sense of values independent of ability or desire.[26]

"There is no refuge from another's excellence save love," Scheler quotes Goethe,[27] and takes care to state that it would be utter folly to think an individual ever forced to succumb to hostility and bitterness. *Ressentiment* cannot be understood without an understanding of the process of repression, for, as Scheler might have said, the further the soul departs from the realm of the spirit, which is the realm of freedom, of love, the more subject it is to laws approaching the purely biological. Strongly felt weakness, anxiety, intimidation, depression engendered by impotence: these are the repressive forces, Scheler goes on, which make hostile emotions shun the clear light of day. Having first inhibited their expression, fear and frailty push these emotions from the conscious plane into darkness, so that the individual or group stirred by them is no longer aware of their secret work. The inhibition finally spreads so far that the impulse of hate, envy, or revenge is crushed the moment it arrives at our inner perception. On the other hand, the store of buried emotions draws each fresh emotion, incorporating it into its mass, so that each repression eases the way for the next and speeds the whole process.[28]

In this process of repression, the image of the original object of hostility is blotted out. I may hate someone, and know the reason very well: the act that harmed or the feature that pains me. But in the measure that I repress my hate—which, let it be repeated, is

145

something totally different from overcoming it by moral energy, in which case my hate and its object are both fully present to my mind and any hostile emotion is checked by virtue of a clear ethical judgment—in the measure that I repress my hate, it detaches itself more and more from its specific ground, and in the end from the person hated. First my repressed hate aims at his qualities and actions, perhaps at his way of walking or laughing, or his taste in music, at anything which expresses his personality; and later on at people, even at things and situations, associated with him. Finally, the impulse may break away altogether from the person who hurt or oppressed me, and become a negative attitude toward certain qualities, no matter who bears them, or where or when, and whether he treats me well or ill. Thus I may come to hate a whole group or class or nation. I may even come to hate or torment myself.[29]

Having examined the phenomenon of *ressentiment*, Scheler asks what it can contribute to the understanding of value-judgments, whether those of individuals or periods, and toward the understanding of entire moral systems. It is evident, he declares, that from it there can never spring genuine judgments, but only false and deceived, for true morality rests on an eternal hierarchy of values. There is a moral order, Pascal's *ordre du coeur*, which moral genius uncovers in the course of time piece by piece; its grasp and gain are historic, but never the order of moral values itself. So little is *ressentiment* the source of values that one must rather call it the source of revolt against values, the explosive charge that overthrows the eternal order in man's mind. Nietzsche himself, the skeptic and relativist in ethics, implied as much, Scheler asserts, when he spoke of falsification of the tables of value through *ressentiment*, for falsified tables presuppose true ones.[30]

The Newness of Christian Love

Nietzsche introduced *ressentiment* into philosophical writing that he might denounce Christianity as the "revolt of the slaves in morals." In it, he said, the Jews sought revenge on their enemies by overthrowing the "aristocratic" morality, the prerogatives of the "fair" and noble, of the strong and aggressive, and by exalting in their place the poor and lowly as the good, the mournful and suffering as the blessed. With a contempt that was a cover for his own anxiety, he wrote: "This Jesus of Nazareth, the incarnate gospel of love, this 'Redeemer' bringing salvation and victory to the poor, the sick, the sinful," was Israel's most sublime revenge—it repudiated him before all the world and nailed him to the cross, "so that all the world, that is, all the enemies of Israel, could nibble without suspicion at this very bait." [31] Scheler repelled Nietzsche's assault on the gospel; at the same time he saw that in pointing to *ressentiment* as the root of a moral system, Nietzsche had made a veritable discovery. His error was in thinking that it was Christian ethics, whereas it was bourgeois morality, which had grown from it.[32]

Scheler proves him wrong by contrasting Christian love, which Nietzsche called "the triumphant crown of the tree of Jewish revenge and hate," [33] with the love of the Greeks, whom Nietzsche thought superior beings, overflowing with gratitude toward life.[34] For all ancient thinkers and poets, Scheler points out, love was a movement of the lower to the higher; in it the imperfect tended to the perfect, the unformed to the formed; in it appearance moved to essence, unknowing to knowing, poverty to possession. Between each pair it was the mean—hence it was no more than a *methodos,* a way. Even to Plato it remained always on the sensible plane, a form of desire, of want or need, alien to perfect Being. For Aristotle, there was in all things an urge toward the Godhead, the *Nous,* the Thinker blissful in himself, who moves the world, not as one who wills and communicates himself, rather as one who draws and lures, as does the beloved the lover.[35]

This was ancient Greece. Christ, however, Scheler rejoices, gives love a course entirely new. But this is an instance of Scheler's overemphasis, for Christ has not abolished love as desire—indeed, He gives it as desire its full meaning and true goal; it is over and above this that He adds to love a new direction. In Him and after Him, love reveals itself in the bending of the noble to the ignoble, the hale to the sick, the rich to the poor, the fair to the foul, the good and holy to the evil, the Messias to publicans and sinners. Now love moves boldly, a challenge to Greek thought, bending without the antique fear thereby of losing nobility—nay, certain of gaining, in the very losing, the highest: likeness to God. No longer is God seen only as the goal of all things' desire, a goal eternally still like a star—He is One who cares. He is not merely

147

the Prime Mover, but the Creator who made the world out of an infinity of goodness, not merely the idea of the good, nor perfect order—He is Person. What antique man could not have conceived save as a contradiction in terms, an impudence or sin, is now the joyful message: God is a loving God; and more unthinkable still: He came down to man as a Servant and died on the cross as if He had not served well.[36]

From that hour, Scheler declares, to say that one should cherish the good man and despise the bad, love the friend and hate the foe, is hollow and meaningless; all are worthy, for God's love makes them so. Love is of all good things the best, not for what it may achieve but in itself; its achievements are merely symbols and proofs of its presence. This also is truly novel: love is not part of the sense world. Acts of the senses use themselves up in reaching their desired, not so love; love waxes in loving, its deepest reward is in itself and not in what it wins.[37] Its gifts are rich: it helps us discover great things, it gives strength and fervor, it makes us see with the eyes of God—its gifts are many, there is no term to them. Still, love's greatness is not in them but in itself. Scheler's vision is confirmed by these words of St. Bernard: "Love is sufficient of itself. Of itself it pleases and for its own sake. It is itself its own merit and its own reward. It seeks no motive, no fruit beyond itself. It is its own fruit, its own enjoyment. I love because I love. I love in order that I may love." [38]

Such is the tremendous change from the Greek concept to the Christian reality of love, and it was not *ressentiment,* not the revenge of the weak on the strong, that caused it; far otherwise, it bears the mark of a superhuman strength. In true condescension, the strong bends down to the weak because inner wealth urges him, while, in its counterfeit, the hollow man flees his inner dearth. The sources of true condescension, Scheler says, are an inner stability, a strong sense of protectedness, an unconquerable abundance of life and with it the consciousness of being able to spend of one's own. He sees it as a spontaneous overflowing of strength, accompanied by joy and peace, for he thinks readiness to love and sacrifice natural to man, and all egotism, even the urge toward self-preservation, signs of obstructed and weakened life, life being essentially growth and unfolding, self-preservation a mere epiphenomenon.[39]

Here as elsewhere, Scheler is like Lot's wife, who was led out of Sodom but could not tear her thoughts away; about to be freed, she could not free her heart. Though Scheler's main thesis completely demolished Nietzsche, still he remained captivated by him, for here his Christian bears the features of a "god." No, the Christian's bending down is more than a "spontaneous overflowing of strength," for it may spring from a heart once crushed under a burden of sin or sorrow, its source being not in itself but in heaven. The Christian is driven by grace; he dwells, to use Scheler's own words, in "the castle of ultimate being, which Christ called the kingdom of God," and to abide there he must die each day; he must be crucified in order to rise—this, the quintessence of the life of perfection, is a mystery Scheler often tends to forget. Moreover, what exalts the infused virtue of supernatural love over natural love is that its acts may be summoned by the will and yet be unforced, that it is given to all who seek it, that it can be had for the asking.

If the Christian comes to the aid of the poor, the ailing, or the ugly, it is not, as Nietzsche might have thought, from a desire to plunge into the phenomenon of poverty or illness or ugliness but rather, Scheler emphasizes, for the sake of what is sane and sound in the afflicted. That St. Francis kissed the festering sores or hospitably suffered vermin to remain on his body may appear a perversion when viewed from without. It was nothing of the kind, no lack of natural sensitivity nor pleasure in the loathsome. His was a conquest of loathing by the strength of a fuller life, the complete opposite of modern realism's resentful attitude in art and literature, with its ostentatious preference for the small or its obsessed digging in the sordid. Such artists see in all that lives something buglike, is Scheler's verdict, while St. Francis saw even in a bug the sacredness of life.[40]

Love, as Jesus meant it, helps and helps energetically, which Scheler sees as a mark of true condescension. Still, love does not consist in helpfulness, he continues; good will and good deeds are but its fruits, and never can profit be its measure, only the heart of the one who loves. The world might profit greatly and yet there be little or no love, and profit little where love is great. The widow's mite was more in the sight of God not because her gift was small nor because the giver was a widow and poor, but because

149

her deed betrayed more love. Love is not one among many forces promoting the welfare of society; rather is its excellence the wealth it showers on the person who loves, for it is not a means but an end, it is no philanthropical institute—what matters is not the amount of welfare in the world, but that there be the maximum of love among men. The rich young man was bidden to give his goods to the poor not that the poor might gain nor that society might fare better through a more equitable distribution of property. He was bidden not because poverty as such is better than riches, but because the act of relinquishment, with the inner freedom and fullness of love it bespeaks, would ennoble him and make him infinitely richer than before.[41]

The primacy of love pervades also the bond between man and God, once a contractual, now a filial bond. Our love for God ought not to rest only on His works, on our gratitude for what He gives us hour by hour; all these should but guide our gaze back to their Author. He ought not to be loved for His heaven and His earth, they should be loved for Him; because they are the works of a Lover should they be cherished. Antiquity thought the amount of love in the universe limited, and therefore demanded that it be spent sparingly, on each according to his desert. But when one knows, as does the Christian, that love has its source in God the Infinite, in never-ending Bounty, then it must be lavished on every man, just and sinner, kinsman and stranger. Summing up his test of Christian condescension, Scheler exclaims: "There is in it nothing of *ressentiment,* only a blessed courtesy and the power to condescend, flowing from a superabundance of strength and grandeur." [42]

The Modern Substitute

The counterfeit of condescension comes not from "the grace of God which is in courtesy," [43] but from want, and Scheler rightly calls humanitarianism a euphemism for flight from self. In true love, a man turns away from himself in response to a positive value he has seen, but here the turning away is his original intention. Love of neighbor becomes a cloak for self-hatred. Lest he see his own wretchedness and have to face all that is within him, he devotes himself to something not himself, to another just because he is another.[44]

If one attends, Scheler remarks, not to the consonance of words but to their meaning and atmosphere, one breathes at once a different air, one enters an entirely different world, on going from Christian love to modern humanitarianism. The modern love of man is a concept born of protest and suckled on polemic. It protests against the love of God, and with it, against the oneness of the love of God, self, and neighbor the New Testament teaches; it wishes to love, not the divine in man, not man's full stature in and through Christ, but man only in so far as he is a member of his species. The mankind it dotes on is not a spiritual whole, embracing the living and the dead, ordered according to an aristocracy of personal values; its mankind is merely a biological phenomenon, something earthly, visible, and limited, living for the moment. Hence the modern love of man is without piety for the dead, without reverence for the men of the past, aggressive against tradition. The place of the person, who alone represents the spiritual depth of humanity, is now taken by man as a collective—significantly, the Christian word is not love for "mankind"; its cardinal concept is love of neighbor.[45]

With the rebel's gleeful shout, Swinburne ends his "Hymn of Man":

Thou art smitten, thou God, thou art smitten;
  thy death is upon thee, O Lord.
And the love-song of earth as thou diest
  resounds through the wind of her wings—
Glory to Man in the highest!
  for Man is the master of things.

Earlier in the poem, his delirium gushes forth:

But God, if a God there be,
  is the substance of men which is man.
Our lives are as pulses or pores
  of his manifold body and breath;
As waves of his sea on the shores
  where birth is the beacon of death.[46]

As if this were not enough to show that the modern exaltation of man as opposed to God has nothing of true love but all the marks of *ressentiment,* Swinburne went out of his way to choose for his subtitle "During the Session in Rome of the Oecumenical Council." This was the Vatican Council of 1870, which reaffirmed that man is not left to himself, that God has sought him in love, spoken to him in revelation, but also that faith and reason are not enemies, for the light of man's reason can see that God is and has spoken. The Vatican Council declared, too, that the pope's magisterium, his solemn definition of revealed truth, is infallible, because the marvel of divine assistance is promised to him, as the successor of Peter, the "Rock"-man. Indeed the Council exalted man—but first God; and so do all the teachings of the Church. Not in smug self-sufficiency is man's greatness; to her, his grandeur is to be but a vessel of the Spirit who is Truth, who is Love. Against this real but dependent dignity, *ressentiment* protests.

As the object of love has changed, from man the person to mankind the collective, so also its essence. Modern love, Scheler states, is not an act of the spirit, a movement of the soul, as independent of the *physis* as thought, but a feeling caused by the senses' perceiving in others exterior signs of pain or joy, and transmitted by "psychic contagion." With his soul prostrate before the idol of a future mankind happier merely in the sensual world, man's entire experience has changed, and so philosophical theory has reduced the phenomenon of love more and more to a mechanics of necessary deceptions. Love, it holds the outcome of sympathy, and sympathy in turn is traced back to an artificial putting oneself into the state of another; to a reproduction of one's own earlier reactions to circumstances now experienced by others; to a being tugged into the feeling of another, a kind of hallucination, as if one suffered within what one saw without; or finally, to the mere psychic accompaniment of impulses having their origin in man's primitive history. These impulses are supposed to have become fixed because of their usefulness to the species, so that in the end sympathy has become an outgrowth of a herd instinct, existing even in the animal world. So sadly has the theory of love been debased: what was once sign and symbol of the supernatural order, even the stream of power flowing through the kingdom of God, has been turned into a refined and intricate development of animal impulse, originating in the sexual sphere.

These changes of object and essence are by no means all; the esteem accorded modern "love" has changed too. No longer is its value the salvation it works in the souls of lover and beloved, rather the furtherance of the "general welfare." But none of its social implications and effects constitutes love's worth, Scheler says, and in the best world, not general welfare but love abounds; the greatness of love is not that it may be useful but that it is blessed.[47] The modern notion of the general welfare which Scheler decries is something entirely different from the Christian idea of the common good, *bonum commune*. Perhaps nowhere is the difference more striking than in their evaluation of a life dedicated wholly to the loving praise of God. Whereas the modern advocates of "general welfare" consider the cloistered life selfish and unproductive, a complete waste, St. Thomas says that it belongs to the common good that there are men who give themselves to the life of contemplation.[48]

That *ressentiment* is the hidden core of humanitarianism is betrayed by the fact that in spite of its protestations, mankind is not at all the immediate object of its affection; mankind is only played against a detested other. Above all, humanitarianism is repressed rejection of God, a mask at times even of hatred—a situation masterfully portrayed by Dostoyevski in *The Brothers Karamazov*. What is most revealing, it often insinuates itself with the plea: there is not enough love in the world to squander on a being other than man; or with the exclamation: when every man is fed and clothed, then will be the time to care for someone else. Humanitarianism's basic sentiment is always unwillingness to bear One who sees all things, rebellion against God as the source and unity of all values with their dominion over man, bitterness against the sovereign Lord; the "loving" condescension to man it parades is secondary. It condescends to him only as a being in whose many sufferings it hopes to find arguments against God's good and wise government. Since even for the unbeliever, all higher values are, through the power of tradition alone, anchored in the idea of God, his "love" inevitably seeks the lowest in man, what he has in common with the animals.[49]

The name "altruism" given to the modern substitute for love is another proof of its resentful center, Scheler proceeds, for Christian love is devotion, not to the other as other, but to the person in its spiritual essence, be it the person of another or the lover's own, which is why it is sinful for the Christian to surrender his soul's salvation for another; "Love God, and thy neighbor as thyself," [50] is his precept. To this, modern man takes exception; Auguste Comte, the champion of altruism, accused Christianity of supporting "egoistic impulses" by its commandment to have heed for one's own salvation, and wished to substitute for it a new Positivist command to love others more than oneself.[51] But it is hard to understand how the "other" merits devotion, just because he is another, for if I am not worthy of love, how should the other be, as if he were not an "I" to himself and I an "other" to him? [52]

Christian love is a formative principle which, little though it claim the advancement of life as its purpose, is nonetheless an expression of "ascending" life; modern love, the soft undiscriminating sympathy for the "other" solely because he is an "other," is, on the contrary, a leveling principle, says Scheler, disintegrating to human life, for all that it expressly claims to advance it. In degrading itself to a mere means for general welfare, in insisting that it has only technical, only pragmatic value, humanitarianism falsifies the tables of values to an unprecedented degree; it subordinates the excellence and bliss of love to each and any sensuous pleasure, and that divorced from the person who enjoys it. Hence the great men—even the holiest figures in history, those who love the most, in whom is visible the kingdom of God—are no longer the exalted models by whom mankind orients itself ever anew, who give it meaning and dignity, but servants to increase the pleasure of the masses. It is *this,* Scheler replies to Nietzsche, which is the slave revolt in morals: the lower values have overthrown the higher, those that ought to serve have usurped the places of their masters.[53]

The Slave Revolt in Morals

Having stripped humanitarianism of its fancy dress, Scheler cites, in his essay on *The Role of Ressentiment in Moral Systems,* some of its consequences, certain characteristic shiftings of value. Though his criticism is impulsive, lacking clear distinctions and moderation, what is good in it ought not be overlooked. He points out first the rule, so decisive for the bourgeois ethos, that moral value belongs only to qualities which the individual man acquires, or to actions he performs, by his own strength and labor. Consequently bourgeois ethos recognizes no innate aptitudes as having moral worth, nor does it acknowledge special gifts of grace such as vocations or infused virtues, which place one man on a level higher than another; it knows no original sin, no inherited guilt nor inherited good in any sense.[54] Ailing from the neglect, even the contempt, of the gratuitous and unearned, our time has torn from its heart any understanding for the things that are *given*. Two phenomena so disparate as the Marxist theory that labor alone produces value and the doctrine of modern Christian sects which divests baptism of its sacramental character, so that rebirth is no longer something that happens to man but something he achieves, corroborate Scheler's observation. They bespeak the same worship of effort, the same *ressentiment* against the bestowed, the communicated, and with it, against rank and hierarchy.

If intolerance rather than unenvying, ungrudging acceptance of the more highly gifted is the prevailing attitude, if the gaze at objective values is deflected to the subjective effort with which they are acquired, then moral value, Scheler points out, is accorded only to what everyone can do, and the lowest common denominator is the standard. As a further consequence, the solidarity of man in guilt and merit is denied, denied that "all sinned in Adam" and that all who have been "buried with Christ" are "risen with him," [55] that the merits of the friends of God are shared in the communion of saints, and that the souls in purgatory are helped by the suffrages and works of the living. This is the attitude which, in a common phrase, says: I don't want charity, or: I don't accept gifts. The esteem for the man-made and the self-acquired alone leads, according to Scheler, to yet another principle of modern morality, egalitarianism. Behind the demand for "equality," there often hides *ressentiment,* which cannot regard superior values cheerfully and would decapitate those who bear them.[56] Long before Scheler, Kierkegaard in *The Present Age* pointed at envy as its leveling principle.[57] And indeed, egalitarianism does more and more eliminate the many differences which give the human world color and zest, which make up its riches and beauty, though they mean struggle and sorrow as well—till it creates the robot man. Men are not "equal" before God and His grace, for God does not love all with an equal affection, but each with an infinite love.

There is another important transposition, that of the useful and the pleasant. Everything that can truly be called "useful" is so,

Scheler continues, as a means to something pleasant, or, it should be added, to something higher than the pleasant. The meaning of every civilization, in so far as it produces what is practical, is at the least the enjoyment of the agreeable, for the final worth of useful things depends on the capacity for enjoyment on the part of their users; if the work needed to produce them lessens this capacity, it is not worth the trouble. One can and ought to subordinate enjoyment to higher, above all, to religious values, but to subordinate it to the useful is an absurdity; it is to subordinate the end to the means. Yet it has become a rule of modern morality that useful work is better than the enjoyment of the pleasant. Again it is *ressentiment* against a keener sense for enjoyment, against a richer life, which drives modern man so to exalt the functional. A vastly complicated mechanism is set up for the production of the pleasant, requiring for its maintenance never-ending toil but disregarding its final enjoyment.[58]

It may be objected that there has been no other age in which pleasure and enjoyment were so much to the fore, but reflection on the uses to which some modern inventions have been put proves Scheler right. The automobile, which was to open the world to man, often makes his roads impassable. Radio, which was to bring recreation into every home, pours out a din that deafens the ear and deadens the mind. The printing press, which was to enlighten the many, has blocked their view of the world, their pursuit of truth, has become a tool delivering them into the hands of dictators. Such is the tendency of modern civilization, Scheler declares: to heap up pleasure on pleasure for the benefit, eventually, of no one.[59] But to speak in the words of Pius XII in his Christmas message of 1941, "it would be a wrong interpretation of what we have said against materialism to deduce a condemnation of technical progress. No, we do not condemn that which is a gift from God. From the first days of the creation He has hidden in the bowels of the earth treasures which the hand of man must draw forth, both for his needs and for his progress." [60]

These are but some of the shiftings of value, for modern morality has not and could not have stopped with them. The common ground of all modern theories is that values in general and moral values in particular are subjective, and that apart from man's consciousness they have neither meaning nor existence. This denial of objective values has led either to the justifying of complete anarchy in moral judgment, in which nothing is certain, nothing lasting; or to the accepting of one or the other surrogate for stable values, of, for instance, a so-called "mind of the species," which is credited with general validity and which allegedly asserts itself to the individual with a commanding "thou shalt." [61]

Behind this attitude there lies again *ressentiment,* Scheler stresses. If a man, oppressed and tormented because he does not measure up to the objective order of values, gives in to *ressentiment,* he will "devaluate" the idea of value itself. Within himself, he says to those justified by the objective order of values: your values matter no more than mine, which are my own creation; yours are no better; down with them—all values are subjective! The man who speaks thus began with the intention, natural to every man, of directing his will to the good, which he deemed objective and eternal, independent of human wit and whim, for he was as yet uncorrupted by the wish to deceive himself. However, the less successful he was in his pursuit of the good, the more he tended, if he gave way to envy, to divest good of its property, to degrade it to the mere mirror of a momentary desire. Driven by the knowledge of his sinfulness and nothingness, in vengeance against the idea of the good before which he cannot stand, he dynamites the beautifully ordered universe of values, saying that values are merely relative to man, race, people, et cetera. But soon he feels the need of having norms again, for the man of *ressentiment* is a weakling, unable to stand alone with his conviction—the complete contrast to the one who, though he may be alone in seeing an objective good, pursues it even against a world of resistance.[62]

Hence "currency" takes the place of objectivity for the man of *ressentiment* in any age and particularly in our own, when almost everyone breathes in the *ressentiment* of generations. The resentful man does not inquire into what is good, but seeks his support in the question: What do you think? What do people think? What is public opinion, what the general tendency, what the wave of the future? In what direction is evolution moving, so that I may align myself with the current? It is strange indeed, Scheler stands amazed: what no single person is able to see is suddenly seen by all; by heaping zero insights on one another, there is achieved a positive insight; what could never be good of itself becomes good because yesterday it was the accepted thing or because it is the wave leading to tomorrow. What the herd thinks, or the class, or the age, takes the place of objective good; what, at any given moment, is generally held, must substitute for truth.[63]

The Hierarchy of Values

Though the shifting of values is the work of man, the values themselves and their order are not. There is a world as spacious, mighty, rich and harmonious as that of suns and stars, the world of values—Scheler blazoned forth in his *Ordo Amoris,* an essay written in 1916 and 1917 but published only after his death—a world which is the most fundamental sphere of reality and which would continue if man ceased to be, as surely as would "two times two is four." It is fully independent of man, but it is given him, his heart being a replica, an ordered likeness, of this cosmos of goods worthy of love. Our age has come to look on the heart as mute and subjective, without meaning or direction, a chaos of blind sentiments, but this is a consequence of generations who chose to be slovenly in matters of feeling, who lacked seriousness about what is profound. *Le coeur a ses raisons,* Scheler quotes Pascal,[64] the heart has sure and evident insights not known to reason; it owns a logic in its own right, and inscribed in it are laws—the *nomos agraphos,* the unwritten law of the ancients—which derive from the plan by which God built the world.[65]

Not man's preference but God's all-love creates what is worthy of love in things; the task assigned to man is to acknowledge their objective challenge, to surrender to the hierarchy of values, through which God's sovereignty speaks. Our inclinations and disinclinations may be in harmony or discord with this hierarchy, one with or divorced from the love with which He loved the universe before He created it and with which He maintains it in every instant. But it is our perfection to love things in the order God loves them, as far as such a love is possible to man, and to know that in our act of love, divine and human love coincide. When a man overthrows this order of values, be it in thought or deed, he overthrows, therefore, at least in intention, the divine order, and in its overturn, the world as an object of his knowledge, as a field of will and work, tumbles after.[66]

158   *Max Scheler*

The scale of worth exists in itself, but it speaks to man and he is ordered to it; who has the *ordo amoris* of a man has the man. It bespeaks him as the crystalline formula tells the secret of the crystal, making him transparent, so that his soul can be read, as far as a soul can be, and its simple lines seen through all exterior manifoldness and intricacy. The *ordo amoris* of a man is the hidden source that feeds the rivers of his soul, the great determinant of his life, his moral milieu, his fate, the sum total of all that can happen to him and to him alone.[67]

The objective hierarchy of values Scheler proclaimed, a hierarchy not to be altered, is an ancient Christian heritage. Christ said to those who fretted over their material needs: "Is not life itself a greater gift than food, the body than the clothing?" [68] He warned the Twelve: "Fear not those who kill the body but cannot kill the soul. Rather fear Him who has the power to destroy body and soul in hell";[69] and when the demands of salvation clashed with the strictures of authority, the apostles replied: "We must obey God rather than men." [70]

As a herald of this hierarchical order of values, Scheler wrote his chief work, *Formalism in Ethics and Material Value-Ethics* (1913-1916), an impeachment, on the one hand, of the relativism which has morals change with mores, and on the other, a critique of Kant's moral philosophy. In order to assure ethics' purity and universal validity, Kant thought it necessary to strip it of all material content, founding it solely on a formal concept of duty, on a general "thou shalt," the categorical imperative: "Act only on that maxim whereby thou canst at the same time will that it should become a universal law." [71] Though one with him in condemning a utilitarian ethics, Scheler rejects Kant's formalism. For, he argues, every moral act realizes not merely a formal and general rule but a concrete moral value—it is an act of patience or of purity, of forgiveness or of love. And since moral values are thus determined in content, are "material," all ethics, he insists, must necessarily be "material value-ethics." [72]

To determine the place of these ethical values in the total hierarchy of goods is one of Scheler's main tasks, as is also the bringing to light of the scale of values as a whole. He fails to root his philosophy of value firmly in a philosophy of being, nor does he make clear the great difference between what is agreeable and what is significant in itself; some of his other distinctions too are not sufficiently precise and elsewhere in his writings vary. For all that, his contribution here ought not to be slighted.

Lowest in the hierarchy, Scheler states, is the large group of values relating to the senses, to man's comfort, to all that is useful and agreeable, such as wealth of the individual or of the nation. Here trade and industry, the economic and technical worlds with all they produce, have their place. Above these are the biological values: health, vitality, physical courage, all that serves the welfare of the person or of society. When life is in danger, a man of sound heart will relinquish all exterior possessions to save it, because at that moment, with nonessentials stripped away, his heart clearly knows life to be above any material good. Still higher than the realm of life is that of mind, the values proper to man's intelligence, those that specifically constitute culture: politics, pure science, fine art, philosophy; the order of justice and law, the region of the beautiful, the sphere of the true. A scientist who risks his life for the sake of a truth, an artist who prefers hunger to deserting his art, a Socrates—all these exemplify their import. And as material goods serve life, and life is subordinate to mind, so the intellectual ranks below the moral. Plato had no doubt that all ideas submit to the idea of the good, nor Kant that the categorical imperative calls for the abandonment of all inferior values; indeed, every man uncorrupted by the betrayal of the good feels and knows that it is of all these values the highest. Yet, towering above it and above all is the domain of religious values, the holy, for in the realm of values, which mounts like a pyramid, the summit is God, the infinitely holy, Love uncreated. Of all things deserving love, He is at once the goal and the source, the beginning and the end, and our hearts are restless till they rest in Him.[73]

The world of values is infinite, but people today often dwell in a narrow room. This narrowness, Scheler stresses, does not rise from any subjectivity of values but from an outlook that is merely instinctive, as well as from the competitive attitude characteristic of our civilization. The "natural" man is tempted to recognize only values that meet his physical urges. Failing to live the life of a person, he blinds himself and despoils, impoverishes the world;

he is a "slave to his belly," his vision confined to the goods which serve, and only in so far as they serve, his vital needs. The beauty of an apple, its harmony and architecture, even more its reflection of a higher beauty, he is inclined to overlook; its fragrance and color are nothing more to him than indications of use and pleasure. And not only this tyranny of instinct, also the spell of modern civilization, renders the world small. Many a man, haunted by the spirit of competition, values only the rare, only the things held by few or requiring toil for their production. He esteems, in short, goods that can be owned, particularly when they can be owned in greater quantity by one than by another, for, possessed by a need for comparison, he gives less attention to what he has than to what his neighbor has and he has not.[74]

If a man will but lift his head above the fog of our times, Scheler exclaims, he will see that values are real, independent of himself. To acknowledge this, that they are abiding, founded on truth, he must give his attention to the intrinsic worth of things; he must ask not what they mean to *him* but what they *mean*, not what they *yield* but what they *are*. He must not look for happiness, which is a free gift, something "thrown in," to be had without asking—the only way to seek it is not to seek it. Envy must be forced out of his life; his highest esteem must be rendered to the goods which are least to be possessed, and of the things which *can* be owned, to earth, air, and water, and to all things which are so abundant that to one's own joy in them is added the joy that others can rejoice in them. As this shared joy opens the soul to the realm of values, so much more, thanksgiving. The religious man gives thanks for light and sound, for movement and breath, so that where others find only indifference, he discovers significance; his world is peopled with values, replete with meaning. Indeed, says Scheler, the universe of values is unlocked in its entirety to none but those who live St. Paul's antithesis: "Beggars enriching many, paupers possessing all things." [75]

Man, A Theomorphism

Scheler was not a thinker who could be coldly indifferent to the modern mutilation of man, not one who could be taken in by the fantastic theories which make of man a machine grinding thoughts and emotions out of the raw materials fed to it, or a mixture of chemical compounds one day to be produced in the laboratory, or at the most, an educated animal—behind them all he saw *ressentiment.* Only eyes shut to reality as a whole could see nothing but nature and still regard man as its crown, observes Scheler in his *Formalism in Ethics,* for man is the most dependent of all living forms, and therefore the most vulnerable, the most menaced. Viewed biologically he is an "animal afflicted," and his intelligence, when compared with instinct, a poor device for biological progress. He requires elaborate and variegated apparatus merely to keep himself alive: what the animal achieves with its simple equipment, he must do with his complicated nervous system, thereby violating all the rules of economy. Beside an animal, he is like an Alpinist beside a mountain lad, who cuts himself a wand and walks the mountain lightly and unburdened, while the Alpinist loads himself with spikes and cleats, hooks and ladders, axes, ropes, and goggles. But for all this the lad is still the better, and so also would the beast be superior were it not that man's greater differentiation is given him that he may realize values higher than the struggle for existence.[76]

Biologically, man is inferior, and to see in him the highest beast, the apex of evolution thus far, is little more than self-infatuation. Man is in fact superior, but those who admire him as the animal-made-wise are presupposing, whether they will or no, other and higher than biological values. He is superior because he sees and embodies values not rooted on earth—the intellectual, the moral, the holy—and so transcends himself, his life and all life. This newness that bursts out in him is a superabundance of the spirit. Through him, as through a rift, there appears the personal order, whose values excel life and whose bond is justice and love; through him there shines the idea of God and His kingdom, and save in this light, he cannot be understood. Man, says Scheler, is the movement toward heaven, the tendency to the absolute, the transition to the divine, the corporeal being directed toward God;[77] and to this he adds, in his essay *On the Idea of Man* (1914), he is the one who prays, even the prayer of life, through whom the universe reaches toward its Creator; he is the one who seeks God, nay, the one whom God seeks.[78]

St. Thomas Aquinas said: *In homine quodammodo sunt omnia,*[79] calling man *quasi quidam horizon et confinium corporeorum et incorporeorum*[80]—in him are, in a way, all things; he is a limit between two worlds, as it were a horizon in which earth and heaven meet. As united with the body, his soul is measured by the flux of time, while as a spirit, in itself, its measure is eternity.[81] Definable in its relation to the body, as its form, the soul, in its relation to God, is indefinable[82]—mystery mirroring Mystery. Thus far Scheler parallels St. Thomas, but intoxicated by his vision of the mystery of man, he makes his indefinable character his be-all and end-all; seeing man *move* toward God, he almost forgets that man *is*. For Scheler, the cut is not between man and animal but between the God-seeker and the Philistine, between man reborn and the old Adam. A difference not of kind but only of degree separates *homo faber,* man, the toolmaker, from the beast, he maintains, the essential cleavage being between *homo faber* and the child of God.[83] In this Scheler contradicts his own thought: were tool-making man and the beast beings of the same sort, either man would have as little chance as the beast, or the beast as much as man, of moving closer to God. True, there is a tremendous chasm between a life confined to the lowest values and one which brings to fulfillment the highest, all the difference between the Philistine and the saint, between the self-satisfied and the man of infinite desire. But what marks man out is precisely this: that he can change and be converted, that he is the creature who repents.

Another discrepancy is found in Scheler's early thought on the person.[84] Wishing to stress that the person is not a *thing,* he defines it, in his *Formalism in Ethics,* as "the concrete unity of all its possible acts," and goes on to say that it "exists only in the accomplishment of its acts." [85] Later in the same book, however, he says that the essence of the person is the foundation of all its various acts,[86] and in its preface he states, as its most important thesis, that "the ultimate meaning of the universe is to be gauged by the pure existence—not by the achievements—of persons, by their unfolding, their highest possible goodness, their beauty and harmony; and toward them converge all the forces of the cosmos.[87]

"An epiphany of God in the stream of life"—such is man, exclaims Scheler, and adds that one of the most foolish notions of the modern mind is its calling the idea of God an anthropomorphism. He is amused that this charge is leveled by just those who recognize nothing higher than man, for whom meaningful and meaningless, true and false, good and bad are but accretions laid on in the course of natural evolution, adaptations of man's brain to his milieu. For to speak of anthropomorphism is of point only if man is *not* the measure of all things; the very thought can be conceived solely by one who has the idea of God at the back of his mind. It is not God who is an anthropomorphism—nothing could be further from the truth; it is man who is a "theomorphism," His image and likeness.[88]

The Hero, the Genius, the Saint

A philosophy awake to the dignity of man, to the person's kingly state and privilege, cannot ignore, Scheler writes in *Models and Leaders* (1911-1921), the prime role of the person in the genesis and growth of all human groups. Not Kant's law of reason nor Hegel's personless Idea, not Marx's economic tools and trends nor the dark power of blood, determine history—no such anonymous forces, but great men. What is weightiest in human affairs is the influence not of the many but of the few; it is always a minority of men, those who lead and those who inspire, who most strongly shape man's personal and social life. But while leaders merely move our wills to act, models raise our souls and mold our inner dispositions even before we come to will. To leaders we submit, but models we love, and in loving, become akin to them.[89]

Commonly, history is seen as a series of external events, but its soul is rather the ideals of its several ages, and at the center of this soul are the models, the men who embody those ideals, who draw and possess us. To them as personal exemplars, says Scheler, must be traced, ultimately, all ideals, norms and laws which men obey and disobey. Corresponding to his five ranks of values, which in this essay he gives, somewhat differently, as the agreeable, the useful, the noble, the intellectual, and the holy, he lists five kinds of models: the "artist of living," the "civilizer," the "hero," the "genius," and the "saint." There are, of course, men who can at once claim more than a single rank: there are the genius-saint, the civilizer-hero, and others. Moreover, all these types assume different hues and tints in different times and places. The ideal of the man to whom living is an art varies from the English gentleman to the French *honnête homme,* from the Japanese *samurai* to the Italian *cortegiano*. For the peasant, the townsman, and the knight, for the doctor, the engineer, and the soldier, the hero wears a different garb. Even the genius and the saint are not fully the same in the East as in the West.[90]

The lower in rank, the more dependent the model on social structure, and the higher, the freer of outer circumstance. It is highly improbable that a pauper should be a connoisseur of fine things; a slave will seldom be a civilizer or a hero and only less rarely a genius—but a saint may be slave or king. There is yet another law which shows the freedom of the *homo religiosus:* all the other models, from genius down, are directly or indirectly dependent on him. For religion is prior to science, art, and philosophy; at work before a culture is thought of, it is still at work when a culture is forgotten, preceding its birth and outlasting its dying.[91]

Unlike the genius and the hero, the "original saint," or what is commonly called the founder of a religion, is for his followers never one among others; he is, Scheler points out, always the *one.* Great minds do not necessarily dislodge one another, playing a part that is not exclusive but complementary; Homer, Sophocles, Dante, Cervantes, Shakespeare, Goethe—all may be cherished at once. Within any one group, however, an original saint can only dispossess another; he can never admit him as equal. He must say: "He who is not with me is against me," [92] for the claim of religion, by its very essence, permits no rival. And when the saint's message is his, not because it is shown him in "illumination" nor because it is given him by "revelation," when it is His by His very oneness with God, then His claim is singular no longer merely within certain historic limits, but singular on the cosmic plane, universal, catholic, absolute, true for all the future as for the present and the past. Hence Christianity, Scheler stresses, is *not* the most perfect—it is the absolute religion.[93]

The uniqueness of the original saint is manifest also in that his presence to his posterity is immediate. While the hero influences future generations through his deeds, which must be recounted, and the genius bears upon them through his individuality, embodied in his work, the saint himself stays among his descendants. He lives on in those who follow after him and reproduce his per-

165

son ever anew; he is present also through authority and tradition, an authority and tradition which receive their being from this immediate personal link. To tie the "vision" of him to the knowledge of a book means to degrade the founder of a religion to the rank of genius, for the scriptures that speak of him are rather sign and fruit of his abiding with and dwelling in his followers. He himself leaves behind no writings to make himself known to the world, nothing like the painting of the artist or the score of the composer, no work divorced from its master, which would subject his influence to the chances to which all matter is exposed. What he leaves behind is himself; what he carves is not wood nor stone but man. The human person is the matrix in which he creates, and he is therefore present in and through persons.[94]

The arm of the original saint reaches as far as love. The hero's realm is a nation or people, that of the genius the earth, but the realm of the saint extends throughout and above the world, as far as the brotherhood of those who love him, and beyond that to God, the Origin of all things. Followed after in the freedom of love, the saint is superior to fame, not admired the way a genius is nor worshiped like a hero. Rather does he give, and in his heart all have sanctuary, seeking their and the world's salvation. Still other evidence of his presence, Scheler observes, is that *not* to remember him, *not* to bear him in mind, is impossible. True, he can be "forgotten," but this "forgetting" is unwillingness—it may be, unconscious—to acknowledge a presence that is felt; it is an instinctive turning away from his challenge. One can repress the thought of him, but not to think of him at all cannot be done, so mighty is his presence.[95]

Scheler's analysis of the models of man is purely philosophical, but it is interesting to note that in discussing the religious model he can speak only in Christian terms. He speaks of the "saint," of "indwelling," "following," and "communion of love," all names of phenomena genuinely Christian (for whatever may seem to correspond to them in the non-Christian sphere is a shadow, a faint analogy), and thus shows that religions cannot be compared on an equal footing, as a modern folly would have it; they cannot be appraised without a yardstick. In applying Christian language to all religious models, Scheler instanced his own assertion that once Christ's voice is heard, it is remembered.

Faith or Idolatry

Man's choice is not between belief and unbelief, but between faith and idolatry. Scheler holds this to be an exactly demonstrable thesis of the philosophy and psychology of religion, and equally the intimate experience of every man. On examining his own heart, everyone knows himself to be so closely bound up with some good that in effect he says to it: With thee shall I stand and fall; without thee I cannot live, I will not live, I ought not live. The religious act Scheler calls a dowry of the soul so essential to it that the only meaningful question is whether it finds its adequate object, or crowns a finite and contingent good with the nimbus of the holy, the absolute, and divine. Reason and heart so naturally tend to God that when man does not believe in Him, he makes a god of that in which he does believe. Hence the agnostic deceives himself when he says there is nothing he believes in— rather does he believe in "nothing." It is not that the religious act is lacking from his soul, but that the thought of nothingness has captured it, so that tied to the quest for the One who Is, a quest natural to and innermost in every human heart, is an unnatural embrace of the surface of things, of their appearances. But if the idolator learns that his gods are dead, great things may happen in him—he may be ready for faith in the living God.[96]

Religious experience for Scheler is original and underived. Calling aseity, infinity, all-efficacy, and holiness the formal attributes of the "divine," those which constitute and demark the sphere of religious objects, he maintains, in his *Problems of Religion* (1921), that they are not won from any prereligious experience by way of abstraction, idealization, or analogy, that they are known rather by an immediate intuition. Whether its object be imaginary or real, a fetish, an Apollo, or the true God, the religious act belongs to a sphere of reality and value independent of others. No doubt there is a rich and manifold religious development, but it is a development *within* the religious realm, Scheler emphatically states, not an evolution *toward* religion. It is quite pointless, therefore, to investigate the origin of the religious object in man's soul, and there is as little sense in the search for the historic genesis of religion as in a search for the origin of reason or language. They are given with man, they are part of his nature.[97]

167

According to Scheler, the formal attributes of the divine are known immediately, but not so the positive attributes of God. Only in the measure that man lives by the spirit and not by the belly can he know that God is Spirit, that He is Creator, Omniscience, All-Goodness, Mercy; only in love enlightened by revelation can he know that He is Person. We must be guarded by humility and awe if we are to arrive at the knowledge of the Creator, all-mighty and all-good, for awe makes us see the secret of things and their depth, preserving horizon and perspective in the world of values; without it, the universe is flat. Akin to the sense of shame, to modesty, which is at once hiding and unfolding, the manifestation of beauty by its very veiling, awe—modesty become spirit—clothes our mind with dignity by confessing its imperfection. In awe we are suddenly aware that our nature is tremendously inadequate for the knowledge of the highest, and is yet called to it; we are aware that the infinite appears in the midst of our finitude and poverty. Hand in hand with awe goes humility. The proud man, bound to himself, lives in a darkened, desert world and walks toward hell, which is want of love; the humble, however, has an open soul—humility, the way of the lover, breaks the walls around the ego and readies the soul to give itself and serve.[98]

What sets the religious act off from all others is, first, that it transcends the world, all the world, including the self; and second, that it bears with it the insight that by its very essence it cannot find its fulfillment in the world or in any finite object. In the religious act, our thought turns to a being different from finite being; we tend toward a good whose place no temporal good, however lovable, can fill; we seek a bliss which, we know clearly, no progress of mankind nor increase of inner or outer good fortune can give; we experience a fear related not to some concrete danger but to the frailty of contingent being, to its dependence on a power above it; we hope for something no eye has seen nor can see, a hope, then, grounded not on calculation nor on vital confidence; and we render thanks for a gift of which the favor we have received is but a symbol, and to a Giver beyond our imagination. In all these, in love, fear, and hope, in thanksgiving and praise, marvel and worship, prayer and adoration, the spirit transcends not only this or that finite good but the very essence of the finite, and seeks an object which, though most positive, can be expressed only in such "negative" terms as incomparable, incomprehensible, indescribable, ineffable.[99]

The third distinction of the religious act is its demand for an answer, for a response on the part of the object to which it tends—which shows that religion in the strict sense exists only where the object is personal. It *receives* the truth it intends and the salvation it seeks. Hence, the religious act and, in its broadest meaning, revelation, are correlated. Neither God nor even the idea of God can be constructed, for the intellectual power of construction, which is the greater the more relative an object is to our consciousness, is null in regard to the absolute Being, who is dependent on nothing and on whom all else depends. All knowledge *of* God is necessarily knowledge *from* God; the object of the religious act is at the same time its cause. This is just what man experiences in his religious life, and it is the impossibility of accounting for man's religious disposition in any way other than admitting an absolute Being, that is for Scheler the surest warrant of God's existence. All rational proofs are to him merely verifications of God already found.[100]

Scheler's philosophy of religion says at times too much and at others too little. It is true that for men as they are, born with the light of reason darkened, the will weakened, and for modern men in particular, bred in an atmosphere of resistance to God and to objective truth, the rational proofs of God's existence may often lack force; it is true that for men reborn they are only one more evidence of God already found, possessed, and loved. But neither of these considerations detracts from their validity. Again, Scheler, wishing to emphasize the uniqueness of the religious act, claims for it such an autonomy—with categories, laws, logic, and evidence all its own—that he almost isolates it. At the inner core of the human person, at the bottom of the soul, there *is* the seed of religion, a seed often unnoticed but always wishing to grow: the soul is drawn toward heaven, desires the infinite, has an inkling of the absolute, but this seed of religion, though it needs the sun and dew of grace, will not spring up and flourish unless it is cultivated by the labor of reason and will—indeed, the whole man, with all his faculties, is at work in the assent of faith. Furthermore, were Scheler to say that the meaning of "God is Person" can be fathomed only by love, he would be right, but *that* God is Person can be known without revelation. On the other hand, the soul may long for God's mercy, but that He is Mercy seeking the sinner, must be told by Him. To let St. Thomas speak: The soul is by nature *gratiae capax*, able to receive grace, but only by grace is the soul *capax Dei*, able to receive God.[101]

What led Scheler to assign to the metaphysical proofs of God's existence no role other than that of verification were certain faults in his own theory of knowledge. Rightly he opposes the common notion that love obscures the mind, that genuine knowledge is to be gained by indifference to the value of its object, by rigid abstinence from all emotion. Quoting Leonardo da Vinci's "Each great love is daughter of a great knowledge"[102] and Goethe's "One comes to know only what one loves,"[103] he says that both assert the intimate tie of knowledge and love. Though for one, knowledge is the parent of love, and for the other, love of knowledge, both defy the bourgeois belief that love blinds, rather than opens, the eyes. Scheler is not content with affirming that love opens the eyes; for him it is love that presents values to us, makes them "flash up" in our minds; love "feels" (*erfuehlt*) them, and reason's only part is to verify what love has found. Thus he holds that "an emotional contact with God as given in the love of God, a feeling of His presence as the *Summum Bonum*, a stirring of the 'sense of the divine' . . . must, as ultimate source material, precede all proofs of His existence."[104]

Scheler is correct in that the soul must seek and hearken if it is to know truly, that it must be animated by interest and concern. His error is in taking this longing and reverence for full and true love, in giving the disposition the title and power of the fruit. Again, the experiences of a spiritual life, the loving contact with God, the feeling of His presence are, no doubt, inner evidence of His existence and nearness. But though they lead to a deep knowledge of God, they are definitely not the source material for all our knowledge of Him, as Scheler would have it.

His own approach Scheler often thought of as akin to St. Augustine's. But wrongly, for this is how the Bishop of Hippo expressed the interplay of knowledge and love: "We do not love what we do not in some way know, but when we do love what we in some way know, love works that we know it better and more perfectly." [105] The order in which the Saint beheld being, knowledge, and love is evident when he writes that the Blessed Trinity is intimate to us in every creature, and so also in the city of angels: "If we ask whence its being, God is its Creator; whence its wisdom, God is its Light; whence its happiness, God is its Bliss. As existent it is fashioned, as beholder it is illumined, as participant it is gladdened; it is, it sees, it loves. In God's eternity it lives, in God's truth it shines, in God's goodness it joys." [106]

What is tangled in Scheler is hierarchically ordered in St. Thomas, to whose theory of knowledge he shows at times an aversion, though he never knew and understood it entirely. At once humble and rich, St. Thomas's thought gives both the senses and reason their full due, but at the same time acclaims a knowledge far surpassing all that reason can attain, a wisdom fruit of love. Even the many terms he used to designate the various ways in which knowledge is acquired reveal the wealth of his thought. There is discursive knowledge, knowledge gathered by the use of reason, by rational inquiry, by study and teaching, or by argumentation; and contrasted with these are affective knowledge, experimental awareness, knowledge gained by inclination, by way of the will, by connaturality, or through love. And among the ways in which the soul is led to know God, there is knowledge arising from the innermost self; knowledge attained in the manner in which we understand first principles, that is, intuitively; through the contemplation of the soul made Godlike by grace; through her affinity with the divine; by divine instinct or sympathy with divine things; the knowledge given through the soul's union with God; and, as it were, through touch and through taste.[107] In place of Scheler's oversimplification, there is in St. Thomas the real abundance of life, natural and supernatural.

All the flaws in Scheler's theory of knowledge, and hence in his philosophy of religion, do not invalidate the judgment of Père Paul Ortegat, S.J., who called his presentation "the most remarkable contribution to the religious problem by the phenomenological school." [108] Amid the mediocrity of contemporary writers on religion, his thought stands out as a testimony to its singularity and sovereignty. Against those who would reduce it to a means for the adornment of life, for the thrill and enthusiasm of the soul, he affirms that God is the absolute end. And against those who would make it an adjunct or supplement to culture, a mere aesthetic or moral factor, an educational force or an agent of synthesis working toward the betterment of human relations, he affirms its "independence": its claim does not derive from the service it renders. The very thought of a kingdom of heaven tells that it is the ultimate expectation of the soul and that nothing can rival this kingdom and its King; compared with them, all human culture, actual and possible, is peripheral and vain.[109] To think "God," the Eternal Being and Supreme Good, existing above all contingent things, is to see that there is no measure to take of Him; He is the Judge, He cannot be judged. If a man says "God," if he utters His name and does not stifle mind and heart, he enters another world; he is, like Moses, on holy ground.

Science and Immortality

The immortality of the soul, without which the Christian's hope for everlasting life would be vain, is not a problem we need wait for death to solve—now, if ever, we are immortal. Day by day, instant by instant, the answer is offered each one of us. Constantly I feel, see, grasp, that I am a being who is master of his body, lord and king in a desert of dead things. I feel, I see, I grasp, behind the few fragments striking my senses, behind the scraps falling to eye and hand, in each of my brethren a person, center of a whole world, a something extending into depths my love and understanding can never exhaust. How then, asks Scheler, should I, should my brother, not survive death? [110]

Philosophical inquiry confirms this common experience that the person, in all his acts, goes beyond the confines imposed by his body, by the bonds of space and time and the limited content presented by his senses. Even seeing and hearing surpass the work of eyes and ears, and surely remembrance and expectation, memory and hope, transcend the hour in which the body dwells. My friend and I can feel with one another the same sorrow, the same joy, a thing impossible in merely physical pain and pleasure, which are tied to the body or even to a part of it; in feelings of the spirit, the person leaves the body, as it were, to meet another. If it is proper to the spirit, here and now, to swing out beyond the boundaries of the body, will it not be so in the act of dying? Since the spirit is independent of the body in the body's lifetime, will it not be so in the body's decay? [111] With Bergson, to whose argument Scheler's is akin, he asserts that it is the doubter who staggers under the burden of proof.[112]

Scheler was not content to assert man's immortality; in his posthumous essay on *Death and Survival*, he searched out the reasons for the modern waning of faith. Today's contention is that cerebral anatomy and physiology have shown the life of the soul so dependent on the nervous system that this conclusion is forced on us: With the death of the tissues, the life of the spirit must end. Modern psychology, it is further said, has done away with the unity and simplicity of the self, and thus immortality has become past saving. But the facts, or to be exact, the observations of scientists, compel no such conclusion, Scheler assures us. For the view which regards the soul as compounded of sensations and needs, and not, like immediate experience, as one and simple, is by no means the fruit of experiment; it is rather a bias which itself conducts the tests. And all discoveries about the brain are well accounted for if the soul is understood as an independent substance, related to the body as the pianist to the piano.[113]

The reasons for man's failing faith are not scientific, for science is powerless to harm religion, Scheler insists; it is a modern superstition to see it at the root of every spiritual change. Far from its being higher criticism which shattered the credibility of the Bible as the word of God, for example, it was lack of awe—that is to say, want of depth, a mediocrity which pulls all things to itself—which made higher criticism possible. When a religious belief dies, it is not science that has caused its death; all science does is dig its grave. The ultimate reason for modern man's changed attitude toward immortality is not the progress of science, but his changed attitude toward death. Because he no longer lives in the sight of death, because by his way of life he pushes back the inner certainty that he must die, he does not prize immortality.[114]

Scheler claims that, quite apart from external events which teach that all living comes to an end, man has an intuitive certainty of death (which must not be confused, he cautions, with its anticipation in illness, nor with longing or dread). In every moment, we feel something hastening away, something drawing near; past crowds on future, and life already lived grows at the expense of life yet to be lived. This is the phenomenon of aging, not to be found in the inanimate world. Death is no accident, he says, not wall we run into in darkness; it is part and parcel of life, an act c the living creature itself, whatever its occasion.[115] Indeed, it is— it ought to be—the supreme act of life, for all time embodied i the words: "Father, into Thy hands I commend My spirit." [116]

Whether we be impressed more by the ephemeral character c life or by its richness and breadth, the certainty of death is pre ent, vary though it may in strength from one period of history t another, ignored though it often is in a kind of metaphysical ligh ness, in a carefree unshouldering of its burden. Altogether diffe ent from this more or less normal shelving of the thought tha death is sure and grave, is its utter absence in modern man, whor Scheler never tires of describing: his labor is not an answer to h needs; it is an urge, giving him no rest. Where he rules, migh follows wealth, not wealth might, and wares are exchanged fo money, no longer money for wares. When he begets children, is not through desire, let alone love; procreation is rather linke with the economic structure. He sees life as a "borderline case, an extreme instance of chemistry, a complication of dead matte and he calls "real" what is calculable. To him the world is an ok ject of lasting dread, no longer a chance to be seized boldly an joyfully, no longer to be contemplated and loved, but merely deal with.[117]

In his unlimited urge to work and profit, Scheler sees moder man's narcotic against the remembrance of death. He no longe fears death, because he has "feared it away," because he has re pressed the very thought of it in favor of an endless going-on, an has found a surrogate for eternal life in progress, progress withou meaning or end, progress for its own sake. He cannot help reckon ing with death and insures himself against it in a thousand ways but he has lost the power to visualize it. Death is no more th youth with lowered torch, no more the grim reaper with houn glass and scythe, no more the skeleton dancing the living to th grave nor the bright angel knocking at the door. In his povert modern man has no symbol for death, for he does not experienc it, because he never dies *himself;* it is always the *other,* and whe his time comes to die, he will die as another in the eyes of others As an embroiderer lays upon her pattern silk of many colors, s the full man builds his multitude of instants into the entirety o his life, present to his mind; he lives with death before him, that death which forms and judges, outlines and orders his life. But modern man lives for the day till, suddenly, no new day arrives.[118] His repression has robbed him not of his immortality but of his faith in it.

Rue and Rebirth

Not death but sin threatens the spiritual life of the person. It is frightening indeed, says Scheler in his essay *Rue and Rebirth* (1921), that life once lost we can re-win only on a road of pain, the road of contrition, but what glory that there is a road back to life at all! Modern theories on contrition see in it something negative, superfluous, even wasteful. Some call it a fixation on the completed and unalterable past; others a trickery of the mind which deceives us into thinking that what we could now omit, or so we imagine, we could have omitted in the past. For Nietzsche it was the inward turning of aggressive impulses whose free flowing society had dammed. By others, it is thought of as a self-inflicted punishment for having acted against one's own interests, or just a conditioned reflex: having previously experienced punishment, one expects it always, but if one lacks knowledge of the when, the where, the what, the who, of the punishment, fear becomes vague remorse. And there is finally the theory that contrition is depression following on indulgence, nothing but a "hangover." [119]

So many modern theories, Scheler remarks in a pointed parenthesis, seem to be "nothing buts." God is nothing but a projection of the ego, or else nothing but the common denominator of all that lives; man nothing but a glorified beast; immortality but wishful thinking. Hope for heaven is nothing but a sign of maladjustment; morality nothing but the remnants of tribal taboos; all cultural life a mere superstructure on material production, or else nothing but a sublimation of the libido—all "nothing buts," clear evidence that these theories are the spawn of *ressentiment.*

In the eyes of moderns, contrition is at best without meaning or purpose, when it is not an actual hindrance to life and action. The very opposite is true, Scheler retorts; even if religion is left aside and contrition seen purely in the moral sphere, it is a means of restoration, the healing of the soul, the only way it can regain its lost integrity. Viewed religiously it is still more: it is a gift God

175

bestows on the soul that, having strayed, it might return to Him.[120]

The chief cause for misconstruing the nature of contrition may be, Scheler ventures, a false notion of the structure of our inner life. Were our personal existence like a stream, rushing along in the same objective time as do the events of nature, it would be quite correct to say that no part of it could turn back and affect the past, that what is done can not be undone. The time of nature is one-directioned and one-dimensioned, not permitting any reversal or bending back, no re-flection. But the human person has, marvelously, present to him at each moment of his life the whole of it; at every instant of it, he dwells in the present by perception, he can bend back to the past in recollection and stretch forward to the future in expectation. Hence at every instant the meaning and worth of his entire life (though not, of course, its events) are within the sphere of his power, and until his death, the past keeps asking him how he will use it.[121]

If something that occurs in objective time becomes our past, it is henceforth *ours*, and therefore subject to us as persons; how and how much it will affect our lives is left to us. Every event in the history of an individual, a nation or mankind, is consequently incomplete, unfinished, and in a sense redeemable. In recollection we begin to free ourselves from the dark might of the recalled, so that history known delivers us somewhat from the power of history lived. And what recollection faintly foreshadows, contrition fulfills: far from being a futile beating against the immutable, to repent an act of the past is to imprint on it a new meaning. To the confusion of the determinist, it changes the unchangeable. If he doubts his freedom, he need but repent, and he will experience that it frees him from the onward rush and sweep of guilt, that it breaks the iron link of cause and effect by which an old guilt ever begets a new. He will find that contrition makes possible a fresh start, the virginal beginning of a new sequence of events, that it works the miracle of rejuvenation.[122]

The determinist is right: we are chained to the past—but only so long as sin is unacknowledged and unmourned for. But when there is readiness for contrition, the past is a light, what would otherwise be forgotten being seen and remembered. Contrition,

176   *Max Scheler*

the chariot of candor, sweeps away the power of repression, breaks the power of pride, which admits over the threshold of memory only what satisfies or justifies vanity. Only contrite are we truthful. Unrepentant, we are imprisoned in the here and now, but rue overthrows the tyranny of our yesterdays.

If there were nothing else in all the world from which we could draw the idea of God, contrition alone would suffice, for it is an accusation, but before whom do we accuse ourselves? It is a confession, but to whom do we confess? It is an acknowledgment of guilt, but of guilt before whom? It arraigns us before a law which it senses to be holy, and absolves us from the punishment that law demands, but who is the lawgiver, and who else but he can withhold its penalty? It leads to the awareness that our guilt has been wiped out, but who has taken it away, who has forgiven it? It gives new strength of resolve and, it may be, a new heart out of the ashes of the old, but where is the well of this strength, and on what model is this new heart built? Each movement of this great moral process, if not obscured by some glib interpretation, limns before the spirit, says Scheler, the mysterious contours of an infinite Judge, an infinite Mercy, an infinite Power, a Fountain of life. Here, as so often, Scheler follows Cardinal Newman, who wrote: "I say [conscience's] very existence throws us out of ourselves, and beyond ourselves, to go and seek for Him in the height and depth, whose Voice it is. As the sunshine implies that the sun is in the heavens, though we may see it not; as a knocking at our doors at night implies the presence of one outside in the dark who asks for admittance, so this Word within us . . . necessarily raises our minds to the idea of a Teacher, an unseen Teacher." [123]

All this is the finding of philosophical inquiry, Scheler stresses, not a doctrine resting on revelation, not a specifically Christian thought; it is Christian only in the sense that the soul can be said to be Christian by nature. When these philosophical findings are compared, however, with the Christian message, it is clear, he adds, that contrition is given its deepest meaning only in Christianity, and within it, in the Catholic Church. This new meaning he sees as twofold: First, linked to and empowered by the redeeming passion of Christ, contrition leads man into a communion with God holier than the one he would have enjoyed had he not fallen and been raised, so that the Church can sing: "O truly needful sin of Adam, which by the death of Christ was blotted out! O happy fault, which merited such and so great a Redeemer!" [124] And then, Scheler finds in Christianity a new relationship between contrition and love. God's love, ever knocking at the inner door, makes the soul aware of the good life it ought to live and the wretched life it does; later, after it has repented, the soul knows that its strength came from God, so that what at first appeared to be man's love is seen to be an answer to His.[125]

Contrition's work is not with the soul alone; it has a historic task as well. By its never-ceasing tears of contrition, young Christianity renewed dying antiquity, hardened in its greed for pleasure, power, and fame, and no other remedy can help our dying age, Scheler warns. Too long have we been made fools of by the *ignis fatuus* of continual progress; too long has it hidden from us the more beautiful law, which embraces all true progress, that in order to live we must die. Too long has modern man allowed the guilt of centuries to grow, so that now he cannot muster the courage to atone for it, even to feel or face it; so that, backed up by a vast scientific apparatus, he ascribes everything to the external power of "conditions." Would he but tear from "conditions" their mumming mask, the face of guilt would appear, a new Medusa who turns stones to men.[126]

The Sacrificial Pattern

Perhaps nowhere is Scheler so fully Catholic as in his search into the mystery of mercy, in which are interlocked human contrition and divine forgiveness, for the Church has always insisted that guilt repented is not hidden but wiped out, that God is the "restorer and lover of innocence." [127] And if we follow the Talmud, that Israel is the people of compassion[128] and that whoever is merciful is of the children of Abraham,[129] then Scheler in his praise of mercy is truly of Israel.

"As rue bears within it the infant goodness," he says, "so does disappointment a ray of insight." [130] We must admit that our civilization has not brought about what it promised, that with the growth of comfort man's happiness would grow; we must allow our disappointment to unveil its idols and false values; and we must resolutely return to the very first end of all civilization, freedom from the many things for the one thing necessary. Recalling the ancient Jewish legend that before God created the world, He made—that it might not perish—the turning of the heart and a voice crying: "Return, ye sons of men," [131] Scheler sees in conversion our only hope.[132]

Modern civilization is far from a fount of happiness. To be sure, it has created and constantly creates a wealth of comforts and satisfactions, but they delight the skin rather than the soul, the fringes more than the center of our life. Our sensitive organization itself tends to frustrate our design to reach happiness, for Scheler reminds us, it is far lazier when it comes to pleasure than to pain. The range of intensity it allows discomfort is greater than that it accords enjoyment, and our sensation of pain mounts more swiftly as the irritant increases than does our sensation of pleasure with a growing stimulus. Do we not accustom ourselves more readily to comforts than to miseries? Furthermore, pain is the more stable, not normally turning into pleasure; on the other hand, there ceases to be pleasure where there is pleasure in excess, for it may become tedium and it may even become pain.[133]

Things and gadgets too, the organizations and devices man has contrived for the advance of happiness, have so entangled his soul that he has forgotten their very purpose. The world of tools he has established was to minimize chance and surprise, drudgery and danger, but he has succeeded in weeding out one set of evils only to sow a new crop. The technical world to which he has subjected himself has no regard for the person, but a logic of its own, over-riding man's direction and desires; it has pushed itself between him and his fellow, nature, God, and is in a way more demanding and unpredictable than the world before, so that at bottom he suffers more from the remedy than from the ill. Civilization, Scheler concludes, is worth its woe only if it ends in greater love.[134]

The relation of suffering and civilization is a frequent theme with him, and most specifically in his essay *On the Meaning of Suffering* (1916), in which he points out the place of pain in the organic world, never doubting that it has an objective meaning. It is commonly said that pleasure and pain are intended as inducement and warning, inviting the organism to certain activities and cautioning it from others. However sound, Scheler says, this explanation cannot give a full grasp of suffering, a grasp which can be had only in the light of sacrifice. True sacrifice is essentially personal; in it a person abandons what is truly a good for himself to attain a good more nearly perfect, more significant and sublime. But there is a suggestion and shadow of sacrifice whenever a good of higher rank is born of the death or diminution of a lower ranking good or of the sufferance of a lower ranking evil. *Rank* is in question, not *quantity*. Whoever is blind to the hierarchy of values, whoever knows only degrees of what is welcome and what adverse, can have no vision of sacrifice but merely a "calculus of pleasure and pain." When we prefer a greater pleasure to a smaller, one long lasting in the future to a brief one now, when we choose a lesser evil rather than a greater, or put a greater pleasure before a smaller pain, we are simply counting costs—*sacrifice* allows no such arithmetic. True, it is always for the sake of something, yet it seeks not amount but height, not more but the better; it is the abandonment of a good of lower dignity for one of higher.[135]

The sacrificial pattern is woven into the texture of the universe; its trace is seen in the circle of the seasons, of night and day. "Unless the grain of wheat falls into the ground and dies, it remains alone, but if it die, it brings forth much fruit." [136] To Scheler, pain is the subjective reflection of this sacrificial motif, a motif which governs the tie of the part to the whole. An organic whole is before its parts, living and working in them; the parts, however, not only live *in* but *for* the whole, as the organs for the body, the members for the group. If the group is a herd of deer or a flock of swallows, then the individual exists that there may be the kind, the species, but the human person does not find his justification in existence for a group; never can his life be absorbed entirely into the doings and dealings of society, nor is his meaning exhausted when he is defined as one of many. His personal, that is, his spiritual, existence excels the worth of all human communities, natural or man-made. It is only *qua* member that he serves the group; only as citizen, and not as person, that he is subordinate to the state.[137]

Were the world merely mechanical, were it of additive constitution—in which things are merely placed side by side—pain and suffering would be impossible; the parts, without link to the whole, knowing no solidarity, would live for themselves. But in our world, the individual dies for the preservation of the species and the organ ails that the body may be well. Death and pain—a "little death," its image and reminder—are wedded to life, the more so as the whole grows higher and the parts, with their functions, more diverse, as hierarchy supplants uniformity. The pangs of birth, of growth, of death, are inescapably bound to fellowship and, ultimately, to love. Throughout the universe, the lower is given for the higher; the part suffers and dies for the whole, that it may be saved, maintained, prospered or enhanced. The suffering of the part, all suffering, is vicarious and anticipates, as it were, the need of the whole, the common weal. All love is sacrificial.[138]

We cannot have one without the other, Scheler professes: no fellowship, no growth, without pain and death, no sweetness of love without sacrifice—an insight to be learned with the heart, an insight which, more than the thought of pain's purposefulness alone, will reconcile us to its existence. In sacrifice, life seeks a higher state, greeting the new and taking leave of the old, and in it weeping and laughter, pain and joy are wedded. This is fully evident in its most perfect form: the free sacrifice of the loving person, who experiences at once the bliss of love and the anguish of relinquishment; there, loss and gain are one. Only where our peripheral existence, our sensitive nature and nothing more, is affected, do pain and pleasure greatly diverge; but the more nearly they touch the center of the soul, the deeper do suffering and joy penetrate one another. And this spiritual experience, in which the freedom of the person comes to fulfillment, casts its light on the involuntary suffering in nature, so that the pains of all the realms beneath the spirit are pervaded with its splendor.[139]

"The philosopher and the poet are alike in this: both have to do with the wonderful," says St. Thomas,[140] and where we shrink in natural horror, they both discover marvel. So Coventry Patmore hymns:

O, Pain, Love's mystery,
Close next of kin
To joy and heart's delight,
Low Pleasure's opposite,
Choice food of sanctity
And medicine of sin,
Angel, whom even they that will pursue

Pleasure with hell's whole gust
Find that they must
Perversely woo,
My lips, thy live coal touching, speak thee true.

Thou sear'st my flesh, O Pain,
But brand'st for arduous peace my languid brain,
And bright'nest my dull view,
Till I, for blessing, blessing give again,
And my roused spirit is
Another fire of bliss,
Wherein I learn
Feelingly how the pangful, purging fire
Shall furiously burn
With joy, not only of assured desire,
But also present joy
Of seeing the life's corruption, stain by stain,
Vanish in the clear heat of Love irate,
And, fume by fume, the sick alloy
Of luxury, sloth and hate
Evaporate;
Leaving the man, so dark erewhile,
The mirror merely of God's smile.

Herein, O Pain, abides the praise
For which my song I raise. . . .[141]

Pain, Pagan and Christian

Man has met pain in many ways, and in his essay *On the Meaning of Suffering,* Scheler examines first the indifference of Buddha, for whom suffering is anchored in being itself, its cause desire. When things seem to say to us: We *are;* we are as we are, and without your leave; we exist, whether you know us or not! it is, Buddha teaches, a phantom, spawn of our craving. Desire alone invests with discreteness, with individuality, and it is desire that leads us on the road of restless wandering. The circle of our existence is shown by this equation: to desire $=$ to be $=$ to imprint with individuality $=$ to suffer. Hence the first "Noble Truth" of Buddhism is that existence, even apart from the pleasure and pain it awakens, existence itself, with its rise and fall, with all its mutations, is suffering. Closing its eyes to the splendor of being,

Buddhism, though it prompts kindliness and pity, must be blind to the dignity of suffering. "Redemption," then, is not the fulfillment of man's deepest yearning but the expulsion of all desire; not the positive bliss of the spirit nor salvation of the person, but submersion in the quiet which annihilates all thirst, all action, all individuality, all suffering.

Buddhism and the modern way of life are not so far apart as they appear, Scheler observes. True, they differ in this: modern man burns to abolish suffering wherever it can be found and whatever its cause, by hygiene, engineering, organization, in brief, by action on the world, while Buddha would annul the misery of existence by an intense interior action to end man's thirst. But whether he lives by Adam Smith or Marx, Freud or Wells, modern man agrees with Buddha on one basic attitude, opposed though their methods may be: for them, there is no difference between noble and ignoble suffering, all and any suffering is bad and should be ended.[142]

Spinoza and Goethe also teach a technique of isolation: all we need do is set suffering outside ourselves. What pains us, they claim, are our emotions (which they deemed but confused and hazy thoughts); we must therefore penetrate the world by reason, disentangling our emotions as a telescope resolves a star cloud into stars. There is some truth in this second approach: often our distress will be lessened if we look it full in the face, and reason may help us discern a scale of evils, distinguish an annoying trifle from a true grief, see our sorrow in proportion to that of others. On the other hand, Scheler points out, not only is the theoretical basis of this second way false, for emotions are *not* thoughts in a tangle, but this way cannot accomplish very much. To see one's sorrow as if it were external may even work harm, for suffering may then accumulate at the bottom of the soul, and from there diffuse throughout and poison every hope. Scheler asks whether the growing pessimism of Indian thought is not the outcome of such age-long technique.[143]

There is a third way, the flight from suffering. Its Greek prototype, Aristippus of Cyrene, says that he strives not for riches, friends, or lovers but for the pleasure they give; that only a fool seeks things, a wise man seeks satisfaction. He would not ask if his beloved

loved him in return, for when he eats fish, he does not ponder on how Aristippus tastes to the fish but only on how the fish tastes to Aristippus.[144] Aristippus is the fool, counters Scheler, for he takes away, never noticing, the soil from which springs the flower of happiness: free and loving devotion to the realm of values. He degrades the world's abundance, its content and meaning, with its gratuitous accompaniment of happiness, into a makeshift, a wretched stage on which to produce pleasures for his lonely body, unaware that true joy is given only when not the joy but that which bears it is "intended." Poor Aristippus, he does not see that the lover is happy because he turns from himself to his beloved, because he abandons the "I" for the "thou." Happiness does not come about if it is made our conscious goal, and suffering comes the surer the more it is avoided, Scheler affirms. In fact, the more we avoid it, the more sensitive we become, the more we are afflicted when it strikes us, for happiness outspeeds its huntsman, while suffering is nearer its fugitive the faster he flees.[145]

The classical attitude of ancient Greece is a fourth way, the stance of the fighter against the suffering sent by the gods and by fate, to which the gods themselves are subject. The antique hero does not flee suffering; he makes a quest for it and woos it amid adventure and peril, searches for it as for a high-born enemy, worthy to measure his strength. In combat and perseverance he overpowers his foe, asserting his value to himself and to others. Fame is his motive, to be known as a conqueror; the benefits his heroic deeds may bring to others he regards as accidental. As he lives he likes to die, with calm, composure, and firmness, with a declamatory gesture—features from which not even the death of Socrates was free. The hero's wrestling must fail before the deeper sufferings which elude the grasp of the will, Scheler contends. Too proud, then, to confess his limits, the hero maintains his brave display, pushing his grief to the hidden recesses of his soul, and so for his renown as a conqueror of external evils, all too often pays the heavy price of a hardened heart. In any event, he remains altogether dependent on the figure he cuts in the eyes of others or, at least, in his own.[146]

Where the attempt to conquer suffering does not succeed, there appears a fifth way, represented by Epictetus: the asceticism of the blunted heart. This asceticism deadens not only the sensibilities but also the capacity for joy. Moreover, the ideal of apathy aims at a shadow, for if ever realized, it would founder at once; the man who achieved it would lack that leadership and guidance which the interplay of feelings provides for the soul. Scheler cites a patient at Charcot's clinic who had lost the feelings of time and duration, of hunger and satiety, knowing neither appetite nor loathing, neither fatigue nor sympathy for her own children. She had to look at a clock to tell five minutes from two hours, to know mealtime and bedtime; not sympathy but the judgment that her children were her own moved her to maternal care. Her consciousness of existence had shrunk almost to a *cogito ergo sum,* and shuddering, she viewed her being as that of another. This unfortunate woman, dwelling like a specter among graves, needing all the powers of her reason for the simplest task, for the merest continuation of her existence, gives an approximate notion of what the ideal Stoic would be like, could there be one.[147]

Still another way known to the Stoics, the denial of suffering, has assumed various forms in the course of history. One is a metaphysical optimism, which claims that the image of evil rises from our egocentric and narrow view; we stand too near the world, like one who, too close to a painting, sees no meaning but only daubs of color. Such a metaphysics, in which evils are so blended into harmony that they appear unreal, Scheler criticizes as wicked, because it stifles the initiative to combat them. His criticism overlooks, however, that such metaphysical optimism but misreads the truth that evil ultimately serves the good. Others hold that suffering does not exist, save in and through the imagination, and that right and energetic thinking can, by suppressing this fantasy, eliminate pain. Modern Christian Science, as well as the later antiquity, wish by autosuggestion simply to throw out of the world all evils, pains, and woes. It is perhaps fear of death and unrest of social conscience that begets this delusion in Christian Science; in ancient Greece, it was deep despair. Its symbol, says Scheler, is Laocoön; in him antiquity, encircled by the cold horror of the universe, made its last and futile attempt to free itself from the coils of the serpents.[148]

In that moment of despair, Christ entered the world. The Old Testament, Scheler says, had first spoken of suffering as divine retribution, as due punishment for guilt, on the part of a man or of his fathers or of a whole generation heirs to sin. In the Psalms, however, and most movingly in the book of Job, and anew in Ecclesiasticus, the suffering just raise their voice against this dread indictment, which adds to the woe of any suffering, however guiltless, the woe over sin committed sometime, somewhere. That the Lord chastens the very ones He loves, that He chastens them not to punish but to cleanse, to lift them out of this world's fray to religious fidelity—this thought may seem harsh to a man of our day, but to unhappy Job it was the warm and gentle voice of redemption.[149] Yet it was not this solace, whose full power was not understood till Christian times, that gave Israel strength, that ripened its endurance, so often tried, so often confirmed, Scheler continues; rather was it the glow of Messianic hope, walking before God's people like a sheaf of fire. Here in the Old Testament, in the love of its saints, in the love with which Job stammered: "The Lord gave, and the Lord has taken away. As it has pleased the Lord, so is it done. Blessed be the Name of the Lord," [150] the Christian answer to suffering begins. The Christian message—the complete overturn of the antique genius that would dry the sea of suffering by interpretations, medicines, techniques, narcotics— is above all the fulfillment of Israel's wonder at the ways of God.[151]

The New Way wrought first a release of strain, which must in itself have been a redemption: now man could be truthful, simply acknowledge, artlessly express his grief. Banished was the antique haughtiness which boasted of suffering as the measure of a man; ousted was the pride that concealed suffering from the sufferer and from others beneath a façade of equanimity, beneath the rhetoric of the dying sage. On His cross, Jesus voiced unashamed the deepest suffering, and after His "Why hast Thou forsaken Me?" [152] the cry of the wounded creature, so long withheld, could sound freely through the world. No longer was there any evasion; pain was pain and joy joy. In the New Way, positive bliss, not mere surcease of sorrow, was the highest good. Now the heart was not dulled, but quickened to compassion and girded for fortitude; its new well of strength was a higher order of things, unveiled to those who know, love, and do the truth. Purification became the new meaning of endurance, God's merciful love sending suffering not necessarily as punishment but as a friend of the soul. Because it revealed this new source, Christianity could give suffering its true place in the order of the world and of redemption, neither evading its gravity nor denying its evil, and yet change it from a dreaded foe to a welcome counselor. The great paradox of the Old Testament, the suffering just, disappears before the infinitely greater paradox of the suffering Just One. Here a Man, guiltless, suffers for others' guilt—a Man who is at the same time God and who calls upon all to follow Him on His way of the cross. Through the divinity of this Sufferer, suffering has gained a wondrous dignity.[153]

The purification Christianity extols, Scheler insists, is something higher than mere moral improvement. It disperses the mist that darkens the inner eye to heavenly light; it leads the soul to its inner castle where it can welcome a higher world, to the sanctuary where it can be wedded with God. This is not to say that pain as such brings us nearer Him—which would be Greek or neo-Platonic rather than Christian—for suffering is not an end but a means; the end is love, and suffering is its cup and its overflowing. Thus the gospel demands more than patient bearing; it demands— rather, it reveals—a blessed endurance, the endurance of the blessed and blissful man, the man buried in God, and only he can endure suffering aright, can love and if need be seek it. What makes the martyrs undergo their torments with gladness is not simply a world to come but the other world *in* them, not only the expectation of a future bliss, but a present bliss in possessing a gracious God. Such tranquillity in the midst of tribulation, such peace in the midst of woe, exposes by contrast the shallowness of the hedonist, whom want of bliss, dissatisfaction at his soul's center, drives to seek a substitute for bliss in some peripheral pleasure, and so blind is he who lives for his appetites that he does not see his own despair. Conversely, happiness at the soul's foundation makes light and even sweet the burden of pain. Hence it comes to love suffering as the merciful blows of the mallet with which the divine Sculptor carves His image out of an existence lost in the maze of matter.[154]

The hedonist seeks pleasure and finds tears. The disciple of Christ has found bliss and welcomes pain that he may come the nearer to the true good. Bright and gay was the outer world of antique man, but its core was dark and sad, for behind what is called sunny antiquity yawned Moira, eyeless Fate; behind its sparkling shell lay in wait the goddess Chance. To the Christian, the outer world is a dark night full of suffering; its heart, however, is rapture, untainted bliss. And this is the ring of his gladness in sorrow, Scheler exults: from gladness to sorrow, from sorrow to greater gladness. Having renounced escape from suffering, whether through his own reason or his self-centered will, having renounced the ways of struggle, of the heroic stand and of Stoic spite, the Christian opens his soul through Christ to the power of God and commends himself to His mercy—joy comes to him, making him bear suffering with gladness as a share in the cross; and while he greets the God-sent guest, the sureness of his joy mounts higher. Thus all power of endurance wells from deep happiness, and all suffering seats happiness deeper still. It is love in Christ—not reason nor resolve nor resentment—that leads the Christian to sacrifice, and the bliss of his love is ever greater than the suffering to which it leads.[155]

The Togetherness of Men

Christ did not bring the world a new knowledge of God, Scheler stresses, a knowledge such as Buddha or Plato brought, or even Moses and the prophets, in whom God spoke. He did not simply *say* there is a loving and gracious God; this new knowledge of Him, that He is loving and gracious, is revealed by a loving *deed*, by His epiphany in Christ. Without losing sight of the differences between the thought of Scheler and St. Thomas on knowledge and love, one is nonetheless reminded here of St. Thomas's *Verbum spirans Amorem*, the Word breathing forth Love. The Son, he says, is the Word, not *any* sort of word, but One who breathes forth Love; although among the many gifts of His overflowing presence is the perfecting of the intellect, He is sent not to bring this or that perfection to the intellect but to illumine the spirit, so that it flames forth in the fire of charity.[156] Christ is Teacher and Lawgiver, the Model of man, Scheler states, because and only because He is the divine Redeemer, the Incarnation of God and of God's loving will. There is no idea, law, or reason higher than He, against which He can be measured and with which He has to conform that He may be called holy. He does not *possess* truth, He *is* the Truth; His words and works are true and good because they are His. Christianity, therefore, is not belief in an idea, such as that Christ is the Son of God—that He is the Son of God is believed because He said so. Primarily it is belief in the Person of Christ,

Pray for the peace of Jerusalem;
May they prosper that love thee.
Peace be within thy walls,
And abundance within thy towers.   PSALM 121:6–7

Henri Bergson .... *Last will and testament*

My reflections have led me closer and closer to Catholicism, in which I see the complete fulfillment of Judaism. I should have become a convert, had I not seen in preparation for years (in great part, alas, through the fault of a certain number of Jews entirely deprived of moral sense) the formidable wave of anti-Semitism which is to sweep over the world. I wanted to remain among those who tomorrow will be persecuted. But I hope that a Catholic priest will be good enough to come — if the Cardinal Archbishop of Paris authorizes it — to pray at my funeral. Should this authorization not be granted, it will be necessary to approach a rabbi, but without concealing from him, nor from anyone, my moral adherence to Catholicism, as well as my express and first desire to have the prayers of a Catholic priest.

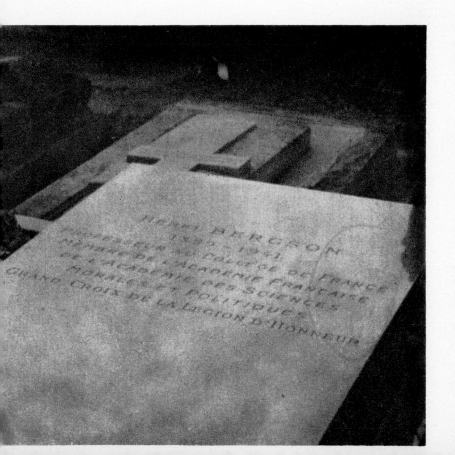

"Good Friday! What a wonderful day," was one of Huss

st words. "Yes, Christ has forgiven us everything."

Edmund Husserl

Adolf Reinach

My plan is clear before my eyes; naturally, it is very modest. I should like to start from the inner experience of God, the experience of being sheltered in Him, and shall be content to show that "objective science" cannot gainsay it. I should like to expound the full meaning of this experience, to show how far it can claim objectivity, to demonstrate why it is a genuine cognition, though of its own kind; and finally, to draw the conclusions. Of course, a presentation like this has nothing to offer to him who lives in God's sight. But it can steady the one who wavers, who lets the objections of science confuse him, and it can lead onward him whom these objections have stayed from walking to God. To do such a work with humility is most important today, far more important than to fight this war. For what is the purpose of this horror if it does not lead men closer to God?

Awe—modesty become spirit—clothes our mind with dignity by confessing its imperfections.

In awe we are suddenly aware that our nature is tremendously inadequate for the knowledge of the highest, and is yet called to it. We are aware that the infinite appears in the midst of our finitude and poverty.

Awe make us see the secret of things and their depth, preserving horizon and perspective in the world of values; without it, the universe is flat.

Max Scheler

In these altogether sinister days there remains for us only resignation to whatever looms ahead. All of us, to be sure, bear part of the guilt because of the way in which, taking all things together, we have led our lives, because of our crowding sins and our frightening omissions. "Father, I have sinned. . . ."

Carry us off, O Lord, into the far land the eye of our spirit sees, whose air breathes upon the harp of our soul. Make us strong to await and to endure Thy grace, and to walk the path it leads. Amen.

Paul Landsberg

Max Picard

On the place of earth, man is raised upright, as a question mark, as the question mark of God, who asks man: Adam, where art thou?

*Not human activity will help us, but the pas-
sion of Christ. To partake of it is my desire.*

Edith Stein

The Christ-ed beauty of her mind
Her mould of features mated well.
—GERARD MANLEY HOPKINS

who is the Way, the Truth, and the Life, and in His lasting and living presence in the world and in history.[157]

Confronted with the reproach that Christianity is bankrupt, Scheler replies—he is writing at the end of the first World War—first, that Christian ideals, norms, and measures no longer govern the soul of Western man, so that what in the anarchy of our day betrays failure is the modern mind, hostile to Christianity. In every age there has been a wide gap between the world as it is and the Christian ideal, but not only does this not condemn the Christian message, it proves its truth—Christianity has never lied, having rather pointed out, from its beginning, the discrepancy between the gospel and man's fallen nature. Yet while preaching the chasm between the Good News and the world, it has never ceased demanding that men not grow weary, that the ideal be not conformed to the "reality" but the "reality" to the ideal. It is not the gospel that must submit to man's weak and wounded nature, but his nature that must be raised to the heights of the gospel. True, to those who think Christianity has failed, it may appear old, but it is new and young to those who grasp the lasting and unchanging character of religious values. Only he can indulge in talk of bankruptcy who has not seen in faith the stature of Christ, the exalted Model of every heart.[158]

Christ lives, He lives forth in the Church. Influenced by Newman's *The Grammar of Assent*, Scheler argues in *Problems of Religion* (1921): It is in the nature of things, that is, the infinite distance between finite and infinite, that man by himself can never arrive at the knowledge of God's fullness, can never conceive the personal and spiritual God as He is unless He, in His freedom, reveals Himself. Hence the all-good God cannot—or rather, will not—leave man without revelation. But when He manifests Himself through the saint *par excellence,* the saint possesses absolute authority, and the truth he teaches is absolute, invulnerable, and open to all men, whatever their origin or blood, their education or temperament. This being so, he must also have made provision that the goods of faith be preserved, administered, and offered to all. He must have founded an institution, bearing his seal, exercising and perpetuating his authority, an institution able to formulate and dispense the knowledge he brought, so that it may be borne through the ages unharmed by the ever-changing currents of thought, by the intellectual arrogance of, for instance, the lettered and learned, or by the special interests of other groups. This authoritative ministry, that is, a universal church infallible in matters of salvation, is for Scheler inextricably linked to the idea of an all-loving God, and he concludes: "Who does not believe absolutely does not believe in an absolute Being. Who does not believe in the idea of an all-embracing institution to save men and in its lasting possession of truth does not in all earnest believe in the all-goodness of God." [159]

The Church is the trustee of salvation, not a mere sum of individual believers, Scheler affirms, and what leads men to obey her are love and confidence, a confidence based on an insight of her dignity. This dignity she possesses not because of the personal qualities of her ministers but because she and her offices are the creation of the Holy One of God. As His creation, she has an authority (essentially different from relative authorities, such as that of the state) which evokes absolute confidence, continuing the spiritual attitude which the Saint *par excellence* demands by His very nature and existence: the readiness to believe simply because it is He who speaks, Truth-made-flesh. Only because He remains the invisible Head of His visible foundation and is mystically present in her, may the Church be given such devotion, and only because of this may she demand, and none but she, the highest, most noble and perfect sacrifice a man can offer: the free sacrifice of his intellect.[160]

All that stalks about today under the guise of "autonomy of reason" or "freedom of conscience" cries out in revolt against this sacrifice as an "outrageous violation of man's integrity." But what modern man calls (with an eagerness that gives him away) "childish subservience" or "despicable slavishness," the Christian, Scheler writes, considers not in the least a grudging act wrested from him by want or fear, not a necessary evil, but quite the opposite, something kingly. This subordination of his intellect is for him a free and joyful giving up of a good he cherishes; it is a sacrifice higher than that of life or honor, one that could not be offered did he not prize his reason as the *lumen naturale,* the divine light that shines in every soul. The liberal or Nietzschean charge of immaturity and consequent submissiveness of mind, the invective "Herd instinct!" have grown no truer by repetition; on the contrary, the Catholic is aware that in reason he possesses a most precious gift, and he has confidence in its power. He does not sacrifice reason's objective principles, he does not abandon the *logos* which informs and penetrates all things; what he surrenders with gladness is the subjective, individual, fallible faculty of grasping this *logos*. Forgetting neither this fallibility nor man's fall, he knows himself inclined to error and delusion, and this the more the higher in the hierarchy of values the object of his knowledge.

True knowledge of divine things, the Christian realizes, can be won only through, with, and in the communion of the faithful, with its continuous interflow of grace; he realizes that he cannot know God and His mysteries unless he is a member of the body of love, a part of the "we," for the road to God, Scheler stresses, is not that of the isolated soul, proud in its aloofness, but that of the "togetherness" of all men in knowing, believing, loving, worshiping, and adoring Him.[161] The spiritual destiny of every man is fulfilled only within the corporate destiny of redeemed mankind; the personal, intimate bliss to which he is called is the peace of the *whole* city of God, the peace of the heavenly Jerusalem. Not as broken twigs but as living shoots of the Vine do we find life, not as torn-away sheep but as flocklings folded within the walls of love. It is not as individuals self-bound and severed from community that we walk the way to salvation, but as members of a covenant. This truth, by which the Church lives, is a Jewish legacy, just as she herself, the *ecclesia* of the New Dispensation, continues and widens and deepens the *qahal* of the Old.[162]

Christianity is the true and absolute religion, Scheler proclaims; there can be no new religion, and the man anxious for one errs, as does the heretic, not only because he asserts what is materially wrong, but necessarily, because his formal disposition toward God contradicts the nature of the divine and therefore the possibility of religious knowledge. He is at fault not only in the end, in his thesis, but in his beginnings, walking as he does not by the bridge of brotherly love but on a solitary road; and even when he appears momentarily to be right, he is and must be wrong, because he has severed himself from the community of salvation. It is hard for the modern mind to grasp, much less to accept, Scheler concludes, that in all matters of religion the Church must be heard and obeyed, that her knowledge must be preferred to what the individual thinks he knows. Her knowledge is supreme because love is supreme.[163]

Catastrophe and Confidence

For years this was Max Scheler's thought. In it essential truths were reconquered for our time; values were restored to their objectivity and hierarchical order; man was given his rightful place; contrition, suffering, and love were seen in splendor; virtue was welcomed back into philosophy—virtue, which "makes of a good deed a bird winging its way with full freedom"[164]—Christianity was paid the tribute that is its due. But Scheler's thought was frequently tainted by his temperament, so that Père Yves de Montcheuil, S.J., had to say: "If he possesses ardor and penetration, he lacks serenity. . . . Marvelously exciting, his work is never a sure guide."[165] Still, it did become a signpost to the Church.[166] Many, searching for truth, were led by him into that body of love of which he spoke so eloquently; having separated the precious metal of his philosophy from its dross, they saw reflected in it the light of the Church. And a number of German Catholic thinkers, like Dietrich von Hildebrand and Romano Guardini, Bernhard Rosenmoeller and Karl Rahner, Karl Adam and Peter Wust, in various ways inspired by his thought, remain indebted to him.

However, in 1922 Scheler completely reversed his philosophical position. Until then, he held the "Roman Church" divine, the unerring guardian of Christ's message, a communion bound by sacrifice and love, in which alone was possible a true knowledge of God and His mysteries. Of her he wrote in 1915: "She was above nations and her faith universally valid even when she was still a mustard seed. And now that the mustard seed has become a mighty tree, who dare estimate its powers of life that await the future of history?"[167] And two years later: "Only a return to Holy Church and to the Christian idea of community, which she alone fully knows and administers, can save Europe."[168] But after 1922 she was no more to him than one "of the spiritual powers still able to form and direct society . . . the most effective and wholesome in its educational influence."[169]

Before 1922 there was no doubt in Scheler's mind that nature bears the imprint of its Creator, that the heavens show forth the glory of God, that the person is His highest revelation in the natural order,[170] and that the spiritual nature of man, his freedom and immortality, are so evident that only *ressentiment* could wish to blacken them. Before, he hailed as part of "the leaven Christianity brought into the world" the truth that every soul is subsistent, substantial reality, God's immediate creation, called to the supernatural and mysterious goal of seeing Him; that every soul is responsible to its Creator and is put into this world to praise, love, and obey Him.[171] Before, he took the fall of man to be a truth not only of the theological but also of the metaphysical order;[172] with Cardinal Newman he said: "The world is out of joint with the purposes of its Creator. This is a fact, a fact as true as its existence; and thus the doctrine of what is theologically called original sin becomes to me almost as certain as that the world exists, and as the existence of God," and added: "The world needs redemption; the world sighs after redemption." [173] Before, he exclaimed: "O marvelous Christian mystery of condescension —God comes to the wife of a carpenter, descends into the dark prison of her womb! O marvelous birth of God in a stable! How greatly these mysteries of Christian faith correspond with the expectation of our reason, once God unlocks the deepest secret of His nature!" [174] All this was Scheler's conviction before 1922. But afterward he spoke of the creation of man by a personal God, of his original justice in paradise, of his fall and redemption, of his freedom and immortality, of the personal and spiritual nature of the soul, of resurrection and judgment, as "the well-known myth . . . entirely without significance to an autonomous philosophy and science." [175]

During the most productive decade of his life, from 1912 to 1922, Scheler professed, in terms not to be mistaken, his faith in God as the *Ens a Se,* the One not made, not composed, utterly independent, the One who has not *become* but *is,* whose very nature is *to be,* who revealed Himself to Moses as "I am who am." [176] "God is not potentiality," he said, "which must realize itself in time, which makes itself explicit in history, but absolute actual Being." [177] Afterward his "god" was an unfinished, a becoming god, ever rising from the *Urgrund,* from the primordial principle of the cosmos, and becoming aware of himself only in man, as man in turn assists in his begetting, to the measure that *Geist und Drang,* spirit and urge, interpenetrate one another.[178] The existence of an all-powerful personal God, who is Spirit, who made him and gave him the strength to say "yes"—this very God he denied.

What could have brought about so catastrophic a change? What made Scheler assume a "becoming god," a concept he had once called "entirely crude," "utter nonsense," and "a contradiction in terms"? [179] What could have driven him to worship a pantheistic god, of which he had said, with such felicity of expression, that "he is amenable to reason, open to advice, more than is befitting to a God; he falls in with the changing currents of history" [180]— and, we may add, to the shifting tides of personal life?

The answer is not, as Nicolai Hartmann suggested, that "the world is not without contradiction" and that Scheler but mirrored it.[181] True, the world is full of opposites hard to reconcile, full of mysteries difficult to solve, and an honest thinker will acknowledge them. But for all its riddles, the world does not tell today: God is, and tomorrow: God is not. The answer to Scheler's spectacular contradiction lies rather in his own restless soul, so unwilling to abide in contemplation, so fearful of continuity. In his younger years he expressed this trait when he said that he would like to awaken each morning with fresh images in his mind, knowing nothing of the past. And in his last years he wrote that "compared with the animal, whose existence is philistinism embodied, man is the eternal Faustus, the *bestia cupidissima rerum novarum,* the beast who lusts after new things, never contenting himself with the reality encompassing him, forever avid to break through the barriers of his *here,* his *now,* his *who,* forever striving to transcend the reality surrounding him, and with it his momentary self." [182]

In this, his new definition of man, Scheler truly analyzes himself. He decapitates his former concept, for man no longer tends toward God; now only movement counts and not the goal, dynamics are everything, avidity for new things is the mainspring of man's intellectual life, and the desire to be oneself, pure and perfect, has given way to the desire to be another. All this corresponds to an unfortunate bent in Scheler's soul. Throughout his life he was driven by a fearsome force which would not let him hold to the good he had, and made him seek ever new experiences. He found it hard to master his flesh, to withstand its urging and submit it to God's dominion. In many ways a genius, he remained in others a child, and was often so rapt in his wishes that he was almost sure facts must conform with them.

Hence, when in 1921 Scheler wished to marry one of his pupils, he imagined he could have his existing marriage declared null by the Church. When he found that he was unable to obtain an annulment, he not only ignored her teaching on the indissolubility of the conjugal bond and married civilly, but declared that in it the Church misinterpreted Christ's teaching on divorce; he then maintained that this misinterpretation had infiltrated into her thought late in her history, though giving no account of when and how it happened. This was but the beginning of his self-justification. In order to guard his delusion, he had to go further; its logic demanded that he divest of their power first the Church and then God. His new philosophy was a protest against them, against whom he had sinned, before whom he could not stand. Unwilling to endure the feeling of guilt, he tried to do away altogether with sin and repentance, with the sovereign God, with Christ and the Church, of which he had said in 1920: "I want to live and die within the Church, which I love and in which I believe." [183]

As was to be expected, Scheler's pantheism arrayed itself to his eyes as progress, not as retrogression. But at times he must have seen through this self-deception, for, only a year before he reversed his stand, he had concluded his book *On the Eternal in Man* with an emphatic "No" to the so-common search for a new religion. There can be no new religion, only a renewal of the old, he said; truth has long been found, and all that is asked of us is to seize it, ancient and ever new.[184]

It was not, as is sometimes asserted, that Scheler passed through and beyond the thought of his Catholic years; he broke with it— though it is true that he had left loopholes in his philosophy, through which he was later to slip out, such as certain of his ideas on the person, or his overstress on vitality, or his teaching that there is no obligation, in the strict sense, of faith or love, only of preparing oneself for them.[185] Here and elsewhere, he wanted, as it were, the spirit of the New Testament without that of the Old, the freedom of the children of God without the discipline of the Law. His aversion to the Law, to the just God who punishes and rewards, seems to have been all along a defensive measure, enabling him to reverse himself with a certain plausibility. However this may be, he himself had disclosed the secret of his *volte-face* when, a few years earlier, he said: "It is always our willing and doing which underlie our mistaken values; it is always, somehow, wrong practice which drags down our consciousness of values and their ranks to its own level." [186] There has hardly been another philosopher who refuted himself so effectively beforehand as did Scheler when he described the workings of *ressentiment*.

There is horror in the thought of a creature's denying its Creator, if only for an instant, yet no such denial can ever be complete. "We praise Thee, O God, for Thy glory displayed in all the creatures of the earth," T. S. Eliot's "Te Deum" sings:

> *We praise Thee, O God, for Thy glory displayed in all the creatures of the earth,*
> *In the snow, in the rain, in the wind, in the storm; in all of Thy creatures, both the hunters and the hunted.*
> *For all things exist only as seen by Thee, only as known by Thee, all things exist*
> *Only in Thy light, and Thy glory is declared even in that which denies Thee; the darkness declares the glory of light.*
> *Those who deny Thee could not deny, if Thou didst not exist; and their denial is never complete, for if it were so, they would not exist.*
> *They affirm Thee in living; all things affirm Thee in living. . . .* [187]

From the time Scheler refused to be a conscious voice in this "Te Deum," from the time he barred the strength of the Church from his life, he seems to have had few happy days. "More and more do I suffer from life," he wrote to Maerit Furtwaengler on April 30, 1926. And again, on May 10: "I live in loneliness, buried in ice." Nothing tells better his sorrow and yearning than these pitiful words of May 21: "I will never cease living in you, loving and worshiping you, as the most beautiful person fate's favor has ever sent me, as the woman who, in spite of everything, was and is the dearest to me, and to whom I owe the most fulfilled, the most tender, the most gentle hours—nay, years of my poor life." Was it his own spiritual longing that made him write on Holy Thursday, 1926, to

Maerit Furtwaengler in Rome: "I hope so much that you will take into your beloved soul, from the powerful liturgy at St. Peter's, the everlasting depth of the idea of the resurrection, and that you will rejoice in God"? [188] Was there hidden in this wish a wish for his own return to God, the joy of his youth?

In the spring of 1928 Scheler left Cologne, where he had been teaching philosophy and sociology since 1919, and went to Frankfurt to assume the chair of philosophy there. For some time his heart had been failing, under the burden and sorrow, it would seem, of the last few years, and shortly after his move, on May 19 of the same year, he died suddenly of a coronary stroke. As strange as was his life was his end. Although he had not retracted his later disbelief nor given any definite signs of change of heart, he was buried with the blessing of the Church, for the priest who imparted it did not know of his lapse. At his grave, Ernst Robert Curtius, the Romanist, spoke a word of farewell. "The concept of the person," he said, "is given a fundamental role in Scheler's philosophy, and the philosophical act is defined as a personal act of rising, in which the whole man lovingly opens himself to the whole of being. . . . Sympathy was to Scheler a key to the cosmos, and he saw in love the movement toward a higher value. . . . He knew that the essence of another man is ineffable, that it can never be exhausted in concepts, and steps forward in its purity and completeness only when seen in love. These basic theses of his metaphysics were certainties of the heart," he continued, "before they were truths of his thought. What he demonstrated as philosopher he lived as man, and applying to him his own philosophical insights, we may say that what is innermost, deepest, and truest in his nature steps forward in its purity and completeness only when seen in love. . . . It was only a few weeks ago that I last met Max Scheler, when, in a small circle of friends, he spoke of his ideal of man's activity. He called that life the highest and best which, with full effort and all at stake, devotes itself to the tasks of this world, and yet is not totally absorbed in them, but inwardly abides in the quiet of contemplation, *in der Stille der Gottesanschauung*. To the few people who heard him then, for whom this conversation was their last impression of his earthly existence, these words will remain a testament." [189] Was this "testament" a desire to live truly and forever in the tranquillity of the sight of God?

In a humble hour, years before his death, Scheler had said to Dietrich von Hildebrand: "You know, I seem to myself like a naughty child who runs again and again to a precipice, and whom God, in His infinite mercy, brings back each time just before he falls into the abyss. And still I run away from God's mercy time and again. But I have a terrible premonition that some day God's patience will be exhausted, and He will not draw me back but let me fall." Von Hildebrand, repeating these words, sorrows that his later years, as we see them now, seem to justify this premonition, but he adds that we know God's mercy to be infinitely greater than Scheler could imagine or we comprehend, and that we hope it saved him from the eternal abyss.[190] To all appearance, Scheler departed from us still entangled in the darkness of his flight, Von Hildebrand thinks. "His sudden death cut off the peaceless and shattered life of this abundantly endowed and noble mind, before, so far as we can see, he stopped in his impotent flight from Him who knows our sitting down and our rising up. But we trust that the Lord over life and death mercifully halted him, and led him into that light which, reflected in this world, he saw so often with such clarity." [191] And the late Dom Anselm Manser, O.S.B., who in 1916 received Scheler back into the Church, who used to remember him daily in his prayers, often recalled his gentleness with all; much would be forgiven him, he hoped, because he loved much.[192]

Max Scheler's judgment, like every man's, is in the hands of God and what it is we do not know, but *this* we know: though in his last years he denied his former thoughts, they remain what they were, for truth is always greater than the man who holds it.

Paul Landsberg

DEFENDER OF HOPE

"A NEW LOVE FOR THE MIDDLE AGES GOES LIKE A MIGHTY WIND through our hearts." It was an event in the history of thought when Paul Landsberg, one of Scheler's most remarkable students, thus confessed his ardent admiration for the medieval spirit, and that the very year Scheler began to move away from the Church. Landsberg was not intimidated by the "liberal dogma" that the Middle Ages were sinister and servile, priest-ridden and haunted by superstition; brushing this bias aside, he boldly contradicted the old *sine ira et studio*, without passion or part, and avowed: "Truth has always been found *cum ira et studio*, with passion and part," "Only to the eye of a lover is unlocked the deepest in things." [1] In this Landsberg is not alone; St. Augustine, for instance, indicts Stoic stupor: "What the Greeks call *apatheia* is something good and very much to be desired if we take it to mean that we ought to live without those passions which disturb the mind and militate against reason. . . . But if apathy means that no passion at all may touch the spirit, who would not judge this stupor to be worse than any vice?" [2] It was a truly spiritual passion that inspired Landsberg; his was the cry of a heart in need—when a Heidelberg professor, provoked by his seeming indifference to some everyday political event, exclaimed: "What do you want? Man wants to be active," Landsberg replied: "But I don't want to be active. I want to be redeemed." [3]

Paul Ludwig Landsberg was born in Bonn on December 3, 1901, into a family of great culture. His father, Ernst Landsberg, was a well-known scholar of the history of law, politically a liberal, personally the epitome of tolerance, equable and cheerful; his mother a woman of keen insight, of extraordinary beauty and charm, of inner fire and curbed vigor. They were of a long line of Jews settled for generations in the Rhine valley and, like most Rhenish Jews, rooted in and deeply attached to their native country. While still a *Privatdozent* in Bonn, Landsberg's father was called to a chair at the University of Koenigsberg, but declined the offer because he could not imagine living elsewhere than in his beloved Rhineland. Yet this was no provincialism; the windows of his home looked both east to Germany and west to France.

Landsberg's erudition and reading were wide—when asked: "What are you doing these days?" he was astonished: "What else would I be doing? I am reading"—but his mind was wider still, at once critical and constructive, quick at grasping situations and ideas, vivid of imagination. Enchanted and enchantingly he talked with simple people, with the little serving maid of a tavern or the artists of a traveling circus; in a thieves' den at the Place Pigalle, a pickpocket won his heart, for when someone abused the Blessed Virgin's name, the little thief defended her as a knight his lady. Landsberg loved these people and abhorred Babbitts, recoiling from the lukewarm and smug, from the Philistines who merely vegetated. "We experience more in walking down the stairs," he said, "than those people do in a whole year."

The gaiety of his student years hardly followed the usual lines. Returning from a carnival one night, he found a ragged beggar asleep on a park bench, and at once emptied his pockets into the derelict's, persuading his fellows, and even other home-goers from the ball, to do the same. Then they crept away, letting imagination paint the beggar's awakening, his bewilderment and delight. But beneath Landsberg's gaiety was a sadness that never left him. Driving once through the countryside in the late 1920s, his companions heard him murmur as they passed an I. G. Farben chemical works: "There the coming war is being prepared." Or when his friends joked about Darwin's *Descent of Man,* he brought their laughter to a sudden stop by remarking: "We live Darwinism in reverse; the evolution is from man to ape." He said it with a smile, but his heart wept, his eyes were somber.[4] It is not surprising that Schopenhauer should have been the first philosophical mentor of a man so sensitive to pain; shortly before his death, though he had long discarded that philosopher of gloom, Landsberg wrote: "In spite of the loquacious optimists, to live means to bear a cross. . . . When a man thinks he has reached the limit of human suffering, he deceives himself, for there are always moral torments still worse. We fall from abyss to abyss. In times like our own, we must be appalled by the immensity of suffering in the world; reading history, we are beside ourselves at the sufferings men have had to endure, everywhere and always—sickness, death, misery, and all sorts of perils encompass man's existence. The optimists make a mockery of us. It is no exaggeration to speak with Schopenhauer of *ruchloser Optimismus,* wicked, reckless optimism." But unlike Schopenhauer's, Landsberg's last word was not despair: "All that is left to us is Christ's example and the example of the men who have followed His, and so have proved that to go His way does not require being a God, but only God's grace—which is promised to us as well." [5]

It was a long and winding road that had led Landsberg to accept Christ with such finality. As an infant, he was baptized by a Protestant minister, for his parents, with a genuine but ill-defined desire to give him a spiritual home, turned to what was nearest in their cultural milieu. But never was he a "Protestant"; through the reading of Catholic works (which, as a matter of course, his world left unread) and through his visits to the nearby Benedictine abbey of Maria Laach, where divine worship, the hymning of God's glory, was the center of life, he first awoke to the reality of religion at about his twentieth year.

For a space his enthusiasm had been given to Stefan George, the German poet, who thought himself the conscience of his age, the tongue of heaven's wrath. "The base alone still rule, the noble perished, belief is washed away and love is wilted," he exclaimed, cursing the city as a pile "of smoke and dust and fog," and announcing the birth of a new nobility, not known by shield or crown but "by the light within their eyes." [6] Strange to say, during the same years in which Landsberg was influenced by the aristocratic George, that is, in the years immediately following the first World War, he also believed in Communism's promise to establish a classless society. Communism was young then and so was he. Hence he was blind to its horror, that it must turn people into masses and the state into a concentration camp, that its giant bureaucracy must stifle every freedom, every privacy; hence it was he thought that a new and just society would be the foundation of a new culture. But a man of his depth could not long be held by Karl Marx or Stefan George. Although he did not forget the idealistic impulse that had led him to them, he brought his dual allegiance to a sudden end when he realized that, lacking love, their voices were as sounding brass or the tinkling of a cymbal. The Church's vision had entered his life.

The Medieval Vision

Landsberg began his graduate studies under Husserl in Freiburg, and continued them under Scheler in Cologne. It was there, when he was twenty, that *The World of the Middle Ages and We* (1922) was born, a study not of the historic but of the timeless in them. His first book, it was written in a few weeks of uninterrupted labor, with no thought of publication, rather from inner urgency, in the power of his new discovery.

The key to medieval thinking, Landsberg says, is its view of the world as a cosmos, a whole meaningfully ordered and beautifully adorned, moving according to eternal laws that come from God as their first beginning and are related to Him as their last end. That this order of the world and of its causes be written into the thinking soul, *ut in anima describatur totus ordo universi et causarum ejus,* is, according to Thomas Aquinas, the goal of philosophy.[7] The confidence that a good order rules this finite world is the gigantic metaphysical optimism of the Middle Ages which, that its depth may be best appreciated, must be seen against the background of the moral pessimism that went hand in hand with it. In its train, this confidence was to bring the self-confidence of natural science, based—in its classical period, in the time of Galileo, Kepler, and Newton—on the assumption that law governed the universe. In medieval thinking, this trust was firmly rooted in the firm faith that the Creator, Preserver, and Governor of the world was personal, pure Spirit, good and just; that He cared for the world-stuff He had created: that He distinguished and adorned it. Indeed, without this foundation, the assurance of the law-full-ness of the world could not stand; without it, the concepts of law and natural science were bound to disintegrate. Whatever reverence toward the order of the universe remains in us today is a heritage from the Middle Ages we must cherish and, with open eyes, restore to its dominant role, for only the simple words of Wisdom, so dear to medieval thought: "Thou hast ordered all things in measure, number, and weight," can rebind the various spheres of life into a cosmic unity.[8]

For medieval man, Landsberg continues, the order of the world was primarily teleological, each and every thing existing for the act for which it is fitted and all things being ordered toward a highest goal. While no thing exists simply for the sake of another, nothing except God has its end within itself. Each thing serves a higher: minerals, plants, and animals serve man; and within man, the less noble organs the nobler, the lungs the heart, the senses the intellect; likewise, all urges ought to submit to reason. Among men, there is an order of government and service, an order of various estates, each working for the other and all for the common good. Finally, the whole creation, stones, plants, beasts, men, and angels, all serve the glory of the highest Being, whose goodness they mirror, in that they are, and are what they are. But those creatures who are endowed with reason have God as their ultimate goal in yet another way: in freedom they can set their course toward Him and in loving knowledge attain Him.[9]

To use a formula: In the world of St. Thomas, in the medieval world, thinking was metaphysical; in the modern, historical. We are constantly aware, Landsberg observes, of being men of a certain era, a certain place, a certain people and a certain occupation, but we forget our simple humanity, rooted in a plane of being nontemporal and nonspatial. Medieval man was the opposite: however much he felt himself bound by his national origin or his walk of life, this feeling was never basic. It was first as an everlasting part of an everlasting order that he thought of himself—as a subject of salvation, a citizen of the city of God, for he knew the relationship of God and man to be so essentially nonhistoric that it alone could give man's life center and unity.[10]

But to stress the metaphysical approach of the Middle Ages is not to imply that they had no historic consciousness, Landsberg declares. For them, history was the realization, in time, of a divine plan above time; limited, like the spatial world, history had in creation its beginning and in the day of judgment its sure end. And history had an axis as well, a center, the Incarnation of the Word in the fullness of time, when the prophecies of Israel were fulfilled and the peace of Rome rested on the world; it ushered in the sixth aeon, which will find its consummation with Christ's return at the end of ages—the great and lasting Sabbath.[11] When modern man speaks of historic development, of progress, he owes the idea, however distorted, to St. Augustine's *excursus;* [12] and all his confidence in evolution, in a meaningful movement ending in well-ordered repose, rests on Augustinian, and hence on medieval, thought. Even Hegel's philosophy of history is merely an echo, though pantheistic, of St. Augustine's "God has built the order of the ages, like a fair and perfect poem, by a series of antitheses." [13] But once faith in God faded, there vanished the metaphysical foundations of our modern confidence that the world's course is meaningful, and, as in Spengler's *Decline of the West*, history fell apart, leaving us with its broken pieces.[14]

Landsberg's observation can be carried further: Though today perverted, the idea of progress is so Christian that it was St. Augustine's answer to the pagan theory of cycles, of the *circuitus temporum*, which held that time was circular and that all persons and events were destined to be repeated throughout countless ages of the future as they had been through unnumbered ages of the past.[15] To the notion that in times past and future the same Plato would have taught and would teach the same students in the same Academy in the same Athens as he did in our age, St. Augustine's answer was: Christ died for our sins once and for all, and risen from the dead, He dies now no more.[16] No round of repeated patterns is human history, but a movement to the ultimate goal.[17]

Medieval man was not concerned with what was accidental in an outer event but with its essence, not with "the way things really were" but with the way they are eternally. The medieval writer of history was a writer of legends who in stories, perhaps "untrue," made visible the true nature of persons and events. Where, asks Landsberg, is there the more historic truth—in the *Fioretti* of St. Francis or in the modern biographies of Plato? The manner of our historic thinking has not only cheated us of the inner truth of history but leads directly to a moral vice: servility to the times, so that we take any historic development for a moral demand, and in listening to what we think the call of the hour, fail to hear the voice of eternity. For this slavishness to the trend, this seeking after history instead of being, the young Landsberg sees but one cure: the wondrous music of the liturgy. *Sicut erat in principio, et nunc, et semper, et in saecula saeculorum, Amen,* "As it was in the beginning, is now and ever shall be, and through all the ages, Amen." This simple verse, sung after every psalm, spoke for medieval man his flaming link to things eternal, the link we so bitterly need.[18]

The Ordered Soul

The medieval doctrines of history, ethics, and politics, having their root and reason in metaphysics, are part of a philosophy to which its authors, so humble in their own regard, gave the name the modern ear finds overproud: the perennial philosophy. Surely it is not hard to understand, Landsberg remarks, how ethics fits into a philosophy of order, for if the world is built according to a divine plan, man should correspond with it; if it is a great harmony, man should sing with it. Thus, when St. Thomas composed his *Summa,* he made the book on man and the conduct of life follow the book on God and His work and the order of the world.

That he himself struck a discordant note was not hidden, of course, from medieval man. He knew the divine design to embrace the idea of the ordered soul, whose core was Christ's great command to love the Lord with wholeness of heart, with wholeness of soul and mind and strength, and to love one's neighbor as oneself.[19] The ordered heart was a heart attached not primarily to things, men, or itself, rather to God; men and things, itself above all, were lovable only in Him. Toward love was the soul ordained, and its love toward God, and toward man and the world *in* God, so that St. Augustine defined virtue forever as *ordo amoris,* the order of love.[20] For unspoiled nature, order was the law of being, but in man there was the possibility of revolt; of all the orders, the order of love alone could be turned into disorder. Opposed to *amor ordinatus* was *amor inordinatus,* and contrasted with *amor complacentiae, amor concupiscentiae,* with the love that gives, the love that covets. The movement of the rational creature toward God, St. Thomas's ethical formula,[21] could be changed to a movement from God; with the "I will not serve" of the pride-thrown angel, man could turn from his Creator, like Judas, and betray his Lord and Master for the thirty shillings of a finite good. The terror of it! All creation obeys, but man can sin, and as sinner must hang his head in shame before every tree and drayhorse.[22]

But how was the cleavage sin had wrought possible in a world framed and governed by the all-loving Father, the Middle Ages asked. And the answer the Church gave from Scripture was that the first man, created whole and holy, of his free will forfeited the sanctity of his soul and its integrity, so that his heirs are fallen and wounded. But how is it that God granted him free will and thus set a "limit" to His own omnipotence? Because men are not mountains; because the world could not be complete were there in it only beings compelled to praise; because God "needed" servers whose freedom would make their service worthy, pleasing and profound. Landsberg speaks here not the stern language of theology; rather, with the mystics, does he seek a word for a "need" that is no need. Out of overflowing goodness, not out of want, God wanted man's love to be not a necessity appointed but a chosen giving, and whoever knows that there can be no true love without the freedom of the lover will see this mystery: man, made in the likeness of his Maker, reflects the Freedom that created him.

Modern man finds a difficulty in the coexistence of freedom and the laws of nature, but the medieval problem, Landsberg points out, was that of freedom and grace. The effort then was not to take human freedom out of the continuum of mechanical causality, but to hold fast to freedom in face of sin's tremendous power and grace's overwhelming might, a fidelity manifest in the saying of St. Thomas that grace does not destroy nature but perfects it.[23] As long as man lives, there stays with him the dire possibility of turning from God to an idol, and ever present too is the wondrous possibility of his contrite return to the living God; with him at all times is freedom. The sinner may repress or respond to pangs of conscience, the just may overcome temptation or succumb to it; and in the glimmer of hope left to the one as in the delight in God which prompts the other, they experience freedom to walk the road of salvation. For eternity, life's last moment is the decisive one, but every moment ought to be lived in the awareness of our responsibility and of the unsearchableness of the counsels of God —it ought to be lived as though it were the last. Man is free always, but freest when he loves God, for then is his will freed from the fetters of sin, then is he redeemed.[24]

Where the order of the universe invokes man's freedom, there that order is the moral law, *regula morum*. This bond between the natural and moral orders, so clear in the work of St. Thomas, is absent from the moral systems of our time, which are embarrassingly suspended in thin air; whatever is good in them, Landsberg declares, lives on from the Middle Ages, when metaphysics bore up morality, gave it meaning and permanence. Now that modern man has lost metaphysics, in all logic morality should also have disappeared. Indeed it is an uncanny phenomenon, yet consoling, a witness to the power of truth, that conclusions outlive their premises, and perhaps never so obviously as in our contemporary jurisprudence, the "science of law without law." Despite the denial of the natural law by the nineteenth century, despite the disintegration of the medieval concept of *jus* founded in God, whoever makes or enforces law cannot avoid a certain recourse to the natural law, much as modern jurists would prefer to do so. But ethics or jurisprudence without religion and metaphysics are as little fit to live as limbs without a body.[25]

Throughout his study, Landsberg stresses that, willy-nilly, our time owes many of its proudest possessions to the Middle Ages, that is, ultimately, to the Church. Natural science is founded on her metaphysical confidence, the idea of progress on her assurance of a divine plan in history, morality and law on her belief at once in the divine order and the freedom of man. It was not long after Landsberg discovered this dependence for himself that Gertrud von Le Fort sang to the Church she was soon to enter:

The world's compassion is your runaway daughter, and all the
*   rights of man live on your bounty,*
All the wisdom of men has been learned from you.
You are the hidden writing under all their signs. You are the hid-
*   den current in the depths of their waters.*
You are the secret power of their enduring.
The wayward are not lost, because you know the way, and because
*   you make intercession sinners are spared.*
Your judgment is the last reprieve for the hardened one.
Should you be silent for a day their light would fail, and were you
*   to cease for a night they would be no more.*
Because of you the heavens do not let the round earth fall; all your
*   slanderers draw their life from you.*[26]

The Ordered Society

For all human life the guide is the commandment to love God and neighbor, on which depend the Law and the Prophets and all the realm of virtues with their great three: faith, hope, and love. Of these, love is the greatest, the one that contains them all, for "who loves rightly cannot but rightly believe and hope," as says St. Augustine.[27] And again: *Dilige et quod vis fac,* "Love, and do what you will," [28] for if your will is moved by love, you will choose what is right. Yet it is not first a commandment, Landsberg adds, that is the rule of our life, but Christ the Model, who leads us more by the infinite certitude and goodness with which He lived every situation of His life than by any mere utterance of law, more through the power of rebirth He bestows than through teaching. The Gospels, and not some ethical treatise, are the true sources of practical moral instruction, so that for the Middle Ages, books of ethics were those which set forth the example of Jesus; and St. Thomas, having given the concepts and principles of morality, crowns his *Summa* by unfolding the mystery of Christ's Person. "First, we shall treat of God," he says in the introduction, "second, of the rational creature's movement toward God; third, of Christ, who as Man is our way to God." [29]

Nowhere is order so realized, Landsberg goes on, as in the social life of the Middle Ages, with its threefold grouping of those who teach, who protect, and who provide: the clerks and teachers; the warriors; the farmers, craftsmen, and traders. Corresponding as it does to the true hierarchy of values, the intellectual, the vital, the useful, such an order makes for the health of society, rendering it not stagnant but stable; in the Western world of today, however, the order of estates is turned upside down. Only when a new faith in the old truths and a mighty effort born of it combine for the abolition of the present frozen disorder can we hope for social recovery. Our need is for active faith, Landsberg calls out, for a radical Christianity: "Faith without works is dead." [30]

The threefold social order, Landsberg concludes, was the constitution less of single nations than of the whole of Christendom, of the city of God in the making, and no matter how they differed, they were all necessary. Protestantism has blocked the avenue to the medieval idea of Christendom, for as in its concept of God Himself, so also in its doctrine of His kingdom, it tore asunder this world and the world above. It left between them merely the thinnest thread, "God and the soul," stressing with characteristic one-sidedness this favorite motif of St. Augustine while utterly overlooking his avowal that he would not believe the gospel were he not persuaded by the authority of the Catholic Church.[31] This sundering makes the kingdom of God either so "spiritual" that it resides entirely in the other world, as for the early Lutherans, or so flat that it is confined to this, as for liberal Protestants. For the Catholic Church—no historical accident but, in God's saving design, ordained from eternity to eternity—the kingdom is at once visible and mystical, close at hand and transcending this world. In her earthly striving, as the Church in pilgrimage, she is God's kingdom acoming, which (till it realizes its fullness at the end of ages) is being realized in the Church triumphant, the heavenly fellowship of saints, so that without gap this world flows into the other. Because she knows that the world above enters and intervenes in this, the air of the Catholic Church compels even the coarse and spiritless to look upward, while the remoteness of the other world in Protestantism leads to this-worldliness, to secularization, so that for many today there is only this world remaining, and it no longer a parable, a symbol, of the other.[32]

Heaven and Hell

Is it not the particular torment of modern man that he cannot envisage life's meaning? Stripped of its significance, his existence has become a dreadful burden, and the more dreadful for the more profound. All the modern answers are but apparent, Landsberg asserts, for they relate only fractions of life to one another, such as leisure to work, or work to pleasure. Nor is the problem solved when man obliterates himself in the vastness of society—he is made for eternity, and no addition or multiplication will make the finite infinite. "God alone can fill the heart of man," says St. Thomas.[33]

The life of medieval man was determined through and through by an unwavering conviction of its meaning; that he was to see God in the beatific vision, Landsberg continues in his description of the world of the Middle Ages. Life in time is change and movement, but only that moves which does not possess its entire meaning within itself. How, then, could *we* move were our own meaning borne altogether within ourselves, were we not drawn by the presentiment of a higher good? Again, there would be no movement were there no rest, for rest is at once the efficient and the final cause of movement, that which stirs it and that toward which it tends. But rest, when it fulfills its law, is eternal rest; hence interior life necessarily moves toward everlasting peace and has there its meaning. That this eternal repose is blissful vision comes home to us in the vivid, though finite, experience that we have our happiest, most perfect and quiet moments when we gaze lovingly at something meaningful, be it thing, man, or God. It is the contemplative and not the active life that contains the highest human possibilities: on this, the Orient, antiquity, and the Middle Ages agree, as against the modern world, which, under the sway of Protestantism, tends to make movement an end in itself. One cannot but admire the depth and discretion of medieval thought, which never forgot that we move in order to rest, says Landsberg, and so struck was he by the purity and strength which ranked being before becoming, loving vision before loving works, that he exclaimed: "Here medieval Christianity discloses its most lofty and arresting sweetness." [34]

"I cannot conceive Christianity," Landsberg continues, "without its belief that heaven is blissful vision, a belief distinguished by its exalted personalism." In the Eastern religions, the soul is said to be absorbed into God, but in Christianity, while seeing Him, resting in Him as the seer in the seen, it remains distinct; ineffably near Him, it is still not one with Him. One can hardly overestimate, he says, the ethical importance of the truth, upheld by St. Thomas against Averroes, that the soul, even in its happiest vision, remains itself. Together with the belief that each soul, individual and unique, is created by God from nothing, in a new act of creation, it gives force to the ideal of selfhood, voices the imperative that the self be fulfilled, whereas the Eastern notion, which makes individual souls but manifestations of an all-soul, demands that it be dissolved.

The ideal of selfhood does not call for isolation; on the contrary, only in community can it be realized, and Christ's Mystical Body is the self's true home. So much is community the land of the self that even the blessed in heaven form a community—indeed, the ideal community. Clearly, modern individualism, making a stranger of one's brother, is unchristian, and so is any asceticism which suppresses the self rather than suppressing the ego in order to free the spiritual self. In the Middle Ages, on the other hand, "personality" did not remain an empty word, as their saints and artists are living witness.[35] Nothing but sanctity is true selfhood —this is the corollary to Landsberg's thought—the saint is the personality *par excellence* because he realizes to the fullest measure the special word God spoke over his soul at its creation, as He does over every soul.

211

If the soul lives true to its meaning, if it lives toward God, it will at last arrive at the state we call heaven, the vision of God, which is delight. How hard it is for modern man to grasp the idea of heaven! for he has lost joy, with Schopenhauer seeing it as the mere absence of pain, particularly of sensuous pain; the spiritual joy of the Christian, however, is not an absence but a presence; like love, it is "the weight of the soul." [36] Yet not every soul reaches heaven. There are two ways of dying well: first, the death of saints, the almost visible swinging of the soul into never-ending contemplation and incomprehensible rest. But this death is rare; most men do not fulfill on earth their metaphysical vocation, and for them is ordained a further purging, in purgatory, which cannot be understood without an understanding of the new splendor Christianity sees in suffering, having seen it first in the passion of Christ. It is a weapon in the struggle of self against the ego or, in the words of Meister Eckhardt, the swiftest steed to carry man to perfection. Purgatory is not only suffering, but also gladness; in all the visions of St. Catherine of Genoa, its joys as well as its torments are greater than those of earth, for as in the final stretch of a marathon, anxiety and hope burn more strongly, change more swiftly, so in purgatory, both pain and delight are deeper.[37]

There is yet another death, that of the unrepentant sinner, whose fate is hell—for all its terror a mystery no less exalted than that of heaven. Though to medieval man hell's torment was not solely spiritual, it was primarily separation from God, the knowledge of having missed life's meaning and lost the highest good; it was a hopeless void where love should be. Landsberg wrestles with the mystery of damnation, and every word he writes compels respect, for only he who believes, who is drawn to God, can be pained by the thought of hell. Whoever prefers to think that nothingness enshrouds man in this life and awaits him after it, whoever sees nought but darkness, cannot logically object to this dogma, and if he does, he gives the lie to his unbelief, for he appeals to the very values he claims do not exist. Landsberg asks if the gift of freedom God gave His children can go so far that through it they incur everlasting guilt. Assuredly it is possible, he says, to visualize God's love as so passionate that it turns to wrath when His creature seals himself off from it. But would this not mean to project into infinite love the qualities proper to finite love? Again, the difficulty is not to admit the everlasting punishment of an everlasting sin, but that God's omnipotence, all-justice, and all-love should permit a sin to last forever. And can it be that one province should irrevocably fall out of the great order of all there is? Having asked these and other questions, Landsberg concludes: "I feel myself that some of my reflections are tortuous and inadequate, but I am more concerned with the honesty than with the evenness of my thought, and there is nothing more real, more earnest, than the final destiny of our souls."

For a Christian, he says, the last word rests with Christ, who in the Gospels speaks of never-ending punishment, not once but often. Hence he refuses any explanation that would compromise with the eternity of damnation, for, he exclaims, "this is the alternative: to make or not to make the venture of faith." [38]

The Summit of Knowing

This faith medieval man had, is the jubilation of *The World of Middle Ages*. Neither a sentiment nor a theoretical conviction, neither a vague feeling nor the cool assent given to a mathematical theorem, it was for him the grateful acceptance of revelation, the free submission to divine authority. In faith, he made his soul a tablet on which God wrote His word. Landsberg thinks that reflection on the ways of knowledge could restore to many today the lost meaning of faith, and attempts his own theory on its epistemological value, a theory striking though imperfect.[39]

Faith is a kind of knowing. One of the ways in which the various kinds of knowing differ is in their degree of activity. The act of imagination, for instance, builds its content by its own power and of what it will, while the act of cognition receives its content from its object, permitting it to be prescribed; measured before the goal of objective knowledge, it is just this standing humbly before truth that gives the cognitive act greater dignity. From this criterion of creative activity or receptive passivity, Landsberg establishes a hierarchy of the kinds of knowing. Since truth, the equation of thought and thing, is the goal of all knowledge, he argues, the less an object known is the work of the knowing consciousness, the more must the knowing consciousness be the work of the object known. Further, the more passive the act of knowing, the more absolute must be its object. Thus, roughly, the hierarchy of knowing leads from hallucination and imagination as its lowest rung, yielding the least knowledge of reality; through the inner perception of one's own and others' feelings; then through normal sense knowledge; through the philosophical knowledge of essences; to the highest rung, the knowledge of God.[40]

In the normal act of cognition, the activity is with man; in the act of faith, the activity is with God revealing, addressing His word to man. Needless to say, moral activity is necessary to prepare the soul for its acceptance lest man lock the gates of his heart, lest, with God standing before them, he bolt the portals of his spirit. Painters of the school of Siena pictured the Annunciation as a ray of light springing from the mouth of the God-sent angel directly to the heart of Mary. Here, with the simplicity, candor, and beauty of medieval symbolism, the nature of faith in a revelation is portrayed: Mary had but to leave unbarred her soul, and God sent shining into it His word. She had indeed to keep, with all her mind and heart, the content of this revelation, such an active preserving of His message being essential to the state of faith, in contrast to the act of faith, which is passive receiving of it as God's. Faith is the one fully passive kind of knowing, and hence the purest and most certain.[41]

Faith, being God's gift, not man's creation, is uncontaminated by man's toil and invention; in it he does not walk by his own efforts toward God but gives His wisdom entry to his heart. Because of this emphasis on this passivity of faith, of faith as knowing, Landsberg tends to minimize man's activity, though he does not overlook his part in clearing the way for faith and in guarding it, the courage he needs and the perseverance. Man is passive when he receives revealed truth, yet he is eminently active when he assents to it. Embracing what is offered him he is at his most human, for to respond is man's high trust, and it is his noble work as theologian to expound eternal truth embraced, as apostle to tell the message once received.

Discipline and Passion

Landsberg's medieval study is no academic survey of the past; it has a personal immediacy, his problem being the Middle Ages and *we*. Of their spirit he exclaims: "More is asked of you here, O man, than inert existence, than mere earthly growth and labor. You must transcend your earthbound ego and arrive at your true self, free to see God." This spirit he sees ideally realized and luminously alive in the great religious orders, particularly in the Benedictines and the Franciscans. And that to this very day they are still moved by this same spirit is a sign to him not that they are outdated but that their faith and their way of life are suprahistorical.[42]

The Benedictine idea is the marriage of Christian passion and Roman discipline: as St. Benedict combined the "virtue" of a Roman and the charity of a Christian, so his *Rule* joins Roman justice and Christian love. In his monasteries, Roman restraint, the school of proud paganism, became Christian discipline, the seminary of sanctity, because and only because it was confronted with a new passion, the Christian idea of order and its tremendous demands. (Likewise, humility can be lived only from the great height of the Christian ideal, for man becomes proud when he asks too little of himself.) On the other hand, a great passion requires a great discipline, for in spite of its will to endure and grow, passion, like all things in our fallen state, quickly spends itself and perishes, unless it is formed by discipline and forced back ever anew to its source, thus gaining quiet beauty and irresistible power. That, in the harmony of passions which makes the truly ordered man, the love of God may fill the kingly place which is its alone, that love may become the never-tiring wing for the soul's flight to its Creator, there must be discipline. This need of all passions is particularly the need of the purest and highest, the one which has it in it to be the strongest, the love of God; and it is love's passion, ordered by discipline, seeking and yet already possessing its Lord, that is the distinction of the Christian monk.[43]

All the great religious orders, Landsberg writes, are various ways to the one goal of the Middle Ages: to run, in harmony with the order given the universe, through the love of God, to the vision of God. What sets them off from non-Catholic monasticism is, first, that their ascesis does not seek to kill the self, but rather, by overcoming the ego, to help the self live most fully; second, that for them the love of God is inseparably linked to the love of neighbor. As Landsberg sees it, Eastern monasticism tends to forget neighborly love, a fruit that should spring abundantly from the love of God, while Tolstoy falls into the opposite error, seeing and loving God only in his neighbor, an error that soon becomes love of neighbor without God and then no love at all. St. Augustine, and Western monasticism with him, loves neighbor in God: *Omnis homo, in quantum homo est, diligendus est propter Deum,* "Every man, insofar as he is man, must be loved for the sake of God." [44]

In contrast to the medieval orders which, notwithstanding their origin in time, are timeless, Protestantism is typically modern and therefore dated. If we compare the highest and most sympathetic types of Protestant minister and Catholic priest, what strikes us first, according to Landsberg, is the contemplative way of the Catholic as opposed to the ethicist way of the Protestant—not that the Catholic is less ethical, but that his ethics stands in second place, is self-understood and therefore less apparent, while the highest type of Protestant always seems a moral demand embodied—a difference that leaps to the eye in Newman and Kierkegaard.

For the great religious orders, as for timeless medieval man, ethics is the fruit of faith, love of man the offspring of love of God. Still another fruit takes shape most purely in the Franciscans: love of creation, of the *vestigia Dei,* of the mark of His strong wise hand on each, even the least, of the things He has made. There is a richness, a variety, an individuality, among the religious families, and yet they are one; common to all of them is the drunken sobriety which signs those who attain the heights of human life. *Laeti bibamus sobriam ebrietatem Spiritus,* "With joy let us drink of the sober ebriety of the Spirit," the Benedictines, in the name of the whole Church, have greeted the morning in holy delight ever since the sixth century. And this is the form the Yattendon Hymnal gives this morning song:

And Christ to us for food shall be,
From Him our drink that welleth free,
The Spirit's wine, that maketh whole,
And mocking not, exalts the soul.

Rejoicing may this day go hence,
Like virgin dawn our innocence,
Like fiery noon our faith appear,
Nor know the gloom of twilight drear.[45]

216

It is for a renewal of this timeless spirit that Landsberg pleads. In view of the false mysticism attracting many today, he exclaims that what our age needs is binding, not loosing; it staggers and needs a staff. Much is being written about the need for inner religion, for greater depth. Very true, he replies, every age has want of them, but *our* most pressing want is for definite forms, for outer worship—formal religion. Heirs of Protestantism, we have many great seers of their own souls but few of the world's order, many souls of depth but few of clarity. Heirs of the Renaissance, we have at times a nearness to things and men that borders on the mystical, but we have no vision of the cosmos as an ordered whole; passion we have often, but seldom discipline. Bitterly do our souls need molding by the scholastic and the Benedictine spirits, in their old forms and in new. And like our souls, society cries for a love-breathed order. If we are to find the new culture that beckons us, Landsberg ends *The World of the Middle Ages and We*, it will be in the power of tradition, in the true spirit of the Middle Ages. There must be a new order, resting on what is best in antiquity, resting above all on the gospel, on a new obedience toward God— or there will be chaos. Toward this culture and order, may God renew the face of the earth! [46]

The Springtime of Faith

Rare acclaim greeted Landsberg's study of the Middle Ages: "Enraptured, yet astonishingly mature . . . lighting new paths," [47] "awakening, life-giving." [48] The reviewers admired Landsberg's "sovereign freedom over the material, his profound earnestness, his vibrant courage in trying to master our misery today," [49] "his burning heart seeking the way to a new civilization." [50] "A philosophy of history . . . which no one in earnest about his own life and about truth may ignore";[51] a study "filled with the wondrously chaste breath of reverence for what is sacred and eternal in the Middle Ages";[52] "a marvelously beautiful book, written with the ingenuity of love, which soon will be the banner of many followers" [53]—these are some of their praises. "The book's message, I confess, entered my soul like a great miracle," [54] wrote another. Extravagant these expressions may sound, but they were sincere. Those who hailed Landsberg's book as a beacon of light, as the herald of a new birth, were not blurb writers who held words cheap; among them were men like the historian Alfred von Martin and the poet Hermann Hesse, nor were their tributes the voice of a few lone admirers of medieval times, but that of thousands of readers.

"It must make the representatives of scholastic science blush," Friedrich Muckermann, S.J., had to say, "that here a man, young and not even Catholic, ventures and carries out a study on the Middle Ages which, in its manner, originality, grace, and synthesis, is without parallel in Catholic literature." [55] Yes, this evaluation of the medieval spirit was the work of a Jew. In regard to things Catholic, and particularly to the Middle Ages, every Jew of today labors under a threefold burden; the Jewish, the Protestant, and the neo-pagan antipathies, none of them easy to recognize for what it is, none of them easy to throw off. More than once did suffering touch the bodies and souls of medieval Jews with searing hand, leaving scars and unhealed wounds—wounds that still ache, because they were the work of men who made religion, God's work, their disguise. Protestantism is uneasily aware that, as a whole, it is not a genuine protest against the undeniable ills of the declining Middle Ages but rather their consequence and hence a protest against the true medieval spirit. It has often pretended, therefore, in self-justification, that true Christianity began with the Reformers and that what is good in modern society is the harvest of their sowing. Likewise modern paganism, which lives by contradiction of the past and insists on its own rising as the real day of man's creation, blackens the Middle Ages and preaches that salvation lies only in a complete break with the medieval mind. Landsberg was sufficiently whole and manly enough, however, to free himself from this "medieval complex," which cripples modern man and, even more, the modern Jew.

In the writings of St. Augustine and St. Thomas, Landsberg found what the great paintings, tapestries, and cathedrals, each in their own way, tell. The medieval painters made visible the invisible, in their gold, red, and blue holding fast the air of grace. As one body, many were at weaving, spinning and dyeing, laboring in concert at the tapestries, each giving of his devotion to the whole —a replica of the cosmos that is the Church. And no advance in machines and materials can match medieval architecture; faith was the builder of cathedrals, those high darings that made matter obey the spirit and quarries sing. Gazing at their greatness, Landsberg was not dazzled, not at all blind to the shortcomings and sins of the Middle Ages, nor did he wish time to reverse its course and bring them back with all their limitations. His aspiration was not, of course, that semifascist outlook which would reestablish a society of one mind and one mood by a "benevolent dictatorship," rather than by toiling and suffering for the triumph of the good; the return he pleaded was to their lasting virtues of faith, hope, and love.

The vision which is the merit of his medieval study reappeared in Landsberg's doctoral thesis of 1923, *The Nature and Significance of the Platonic Academy*. So deep was his concern with matters of faith that, though the subject of his dissertation did not demand that he mention it at all, he voiced it at every opportunity, the fullness of his heart making its way into long footnotes, such as one on the birth of Christianity. Because Christianity is divine, depth is needed to see its true beginning, and the shallow find it easier to attribute its origin to some social or economic condition. The German sociologist Max Weber, for instance, called Christianity *eine Lehre wandernder Handwerksburschen,* a doctrine of wandering craftsmen,[56] to which Landsberg countered that journey and craft were St. Paul's *chosen* means: having abandoned the study of the Law, he voyaged far and wide, precisely in order to spread the Good News, while he used his trade of a tentmaker to proclaim the apostolate above economic systems.[57]

Again and again in his thesis Landsberg emphasizes the great difference between the philosophies, which dissolve God into a mere idea, and the newness of Christianity, which teaches that the Logos became flesh at a given moment, in a given land, and that He suffered His singular death. "No man can grasp this who is but philosopher," Landsberg writes. To the Platonic mind, the Incarnation and its fruits will always be embarrassing, "sullying the realm of the spirit." Thus the German philologist Ulrich von Wilamowitz, comparing the body's resurrection with the Platonic idea of the disembodied soul's survival, finds the Platonic concept the purer and nobler; he did so "with the instinct of the liberal Protestant," Landsberg remarks. For he himself sees clearly that the Church's teachings on the body—in particular "the mystical thought that it is not the sacramental food which is converted into the body of him who receives it, but the body which is transformed by the sacramental food . . . and that therefore ought the relics

219

of the saints be honored"—bud from the truth that, in the keen and daring words of St. Augustine, "God became man that man may become God." [58]

The honor with which the Church vests the human body is a theme Landsberg delighted in. "Brother Body," though also unreasonable "Brother Ass," was what St. Francis of Assisi named his body, he writes in his medieval study; to him it was not a prison of despair, nor was it to St. Thomas, who saw it lovingly as an instrument, and one that should become a ready instrument. There has been fabricated an all-too-easy contrast between "sense-gay" antiquity and the "body-hating" Middle Ages, for who would have said of St. Francis what his biographer said of Plotinus: that he looked as if he felt ashamed of being "stuck" in a body? Rather was the body of St. Francis flooded through and through by a soul given to the love of God. For St. Thomas, the earth-sprung body and the God-made soul, its substantial form, were servant and lord. Far from being eternal enemies, as they seem today, they were destined to live together in peace—more, in solidarity, so that man was not simply a soul but an incomprehensible unity of soul and body. This is the mind of Christ, so that a visionary heard Him say: "I am come not to deaden the senses but to illumine them." The Christian is far from the Platonic disparagement of the body as the chains of the soul, from which it longs to run away and be alone;[59] and equally far from the earlier Greek deification of man just as he is, "hide and hair," with no need of rebirth. The body is clothed in splendor, for even now it shares in the fruits of redemption; it will rise in the resurrection and be permeated by the glory of the spirit. To this dignity of the body, medieval sculptures testify—one has only to look at the angels of the Cathedral of Rheims.[60]

The cardinal difference between the Greek and the Christian concepts of deification is this, Landsberg stresses in his dissertation: The Greek, not stepping out of the wall of self, relies on his own power to be made godlike, whereas the Christian—who, awed by the greatness of his hope, prefers to speak of sanctification rather than of deification—prays to God that in grace, in the freedom of His love, He may enter his innermost being. "I live, or rather, not I; it is Christ that lives in me," St. Paul exclaimed.[61]

Consequently, there are two types of philosophy: the autonomous, patterned after Plato's, which undertakes to bring about man's redemption; and the heteronomous, which, following St. Augustine's lead, does not feign to be man's guide to his last end, but takes him to the very portals of faith and there withdraws before the one thing necessary. Landsberg concludes his paper on the Platonic Academy with the anxious question: In which footsteps will the philosophy of the future walk? [62]

The Church, Heir of Heresy

The same year that Landsberg wrote his doctoral thesis, he published, in Germany's foremost Catholic monthly, an article *Church and Paganism*. "The history of thought, regarded as the history of knowledge bearing on salvation, is in the main," he affirms, "the history of man's senses for the supernatural, of the sickness and healing of his soul's eyes and ears, with which he can see transcendent reality, hear the word of God. In the Platonism of antiquity the cure progressed as far as it could without a supernatural physician. Under the Old Covenant God tore from His people, little by little, the caul of sin, particularly through the prophets He sent them. The true healer of the blind; however, the true physician of mankind, did not come till He came in Christ." [63]

The article deals with Klages's accusation that under the influence of Christianity spirit has profaned life, strangled the whole vital sphere. To this, Landsberg answers that the life of the spirit is indeed the heart of Christian existence, that in it person is joined to Person, grace keeps tryst with prayer, God's giving love with man's responding love. It is thus to the personal center of man that Christianity speaks. Though he is born a person, the Fall has made him forget this land of his birth, and only God's revelation reopens his eyes to its beauty. To the pagan, therefore, lacking faith and blinded by things, the personal world is a land little known; the neopagan hates it, however, and would have the spirit swallowed up by life. He will come to grief, for he does not do justice to reality; he will dash himself to death, Landsberg wrote, long before Nazism's rise and fall. That the power of the spirit may not crush the neopagan, Landsberg appeals to him in the words of St. Augustine: *Tota opera nostra, fratres, in hac vita est*

221

sanare oculum cordis, per quem videtur Deus, "In this life, brethren, our whole business is to restore the eye through which the heart sees God." [64]

True, among Christians life has often been depreciated and the sense world decried, but contempt for the earth (not, however, that ruin Luther wrought when, by denouncing all that is human, he rent the medieval harmony of grace and nature) was the price the absorption of a spiritual faith exacted of mankind. In order to receive the message of Christ—infinite wine in a finite vessel, the vast heaven in a small cup—man was compelled, by his own limitations, to disregard all that was not new and specifically Christian, to disregard the universe of creation for the sake of the universe of redemption. Nonetheless, Christ held all creation higher than ever man could by himself, and it *is* Christianity's goal to render spirit and life one, by pouring the spirit into life and by quickening the spirit, by creating the ideal order in which the spirit rules and shapes life while life serves the spirit and gives it body. Hence Landsberg pleads with the Christian not to be deaf to the neopagan's complaint but to heed what is justified in it, for there is some good in his search. Has it not always been the Church's province and concern, he asks, to receive the partial truths of a given time, and by receiving them to take from them the curse of wry one-sidedness, to give them quiet part in the great whole of truth? Today, faced with the clamor for life, the Church must be what she has always been: the heir of heresy.[65]

The heir of heresy—this startling title Landsberg gives the Church is great with meaning: it tells of hope, of her youth and of her claim. Older than the heretics, still she is young, for, as St. Augustine says: "God is younger than all." [66] Heresies are doomed the instant they are born, but the Church is slain in one land to be reborn in another. Pronounced dead by clerk and tyrant, she prays at their funerals, hears the confessions of their sons and daughters, or baptizes their grandchildren. The custodian of truth on earth, she claims by right all truths as her own; even those her foes proclaim are her heirdom. In their errors she sees truths concealed and from their lopsided doctrines cuts shapely columns; for she is the eye and arm of God, and all thoughts, great and small, ancient and new, He gives her to build wisdom's dome. All things good and true must in the end serve her, daughter of eternity and mistress of the future.

Fugitive in Wasteland

With this deep understanding of the Church's true nature, Landsberg was bound to join her, for the stern summons of truth admits no cavil or compromise. Yet he fled its bidding, wandering into those wilds which spiritual nomads like to call "experience." One wonders what turned him for a time into a fugitive. Perhaps it was an excessive fear of being unable to live up to the full Christian standard; or perhaps he was kept from the Church by an estheticism which made him demand of her members and of all the facets of her life an intellectual and artistic perfection they cannot possess, for the Church is the home of all, of learned and unlearned, of the crippled as well as the straight. It may have been that Landsberg's approach was in the beginning mainly intellectual, so that his power of decision was starved, his inner resources exhausted in those endless discussions which suck the souls of so many young students. It is impossible to determine what made him shy submission to the yoke of Christ—heavy to look at, light to bear. But hardly a believer, hardly an unbeliever, hardly anyone who has not suffered the anxieties of conversion, can know how threatening the assaults of evil can be.

Years later Landsberg himself wrote in his diary about his philosophical work: "I feel I was truly born for significant intellectual achievements. What I lack is the ability to cling for long to one and the same thing. My interest is torn now this way, now that, and so my strength is splintered. To conquer this!?!?!?! . . ." This entry suggests his many efforts and his many defeats, and all that he said here of his intellectual life might also be said of his religious search. He struggled much against the inertia of heart that threatened his inner existence, but for a few years he succumbed. Lame in will, he submerged himself in many passions, and it was a miracle of grace that he did not perish in the desert of "experience," where the soul feeds on mirage, in the wasteland from which, humanly speaking, there is no way out.

If in a decisive hour, a man ignores the call of grace, he will likely try to justify himself; he will become a skeptic or a cynic; he will

223

persuade others that his sin is virtue, his failure strength, and in trying to prove it, he will only sink deeper and deeper into skepticism or cynicism. Had not inner depth, longing, and resilience been spared to him, had angels not guarded his soul and a special grace recalled him, this might easily have been Landsberg's fate: in despair of himself and in rage against his weakness, he might have put his rich talents to the use of the wreckers of faith and of man, as so many others have done. For a short period, indeed, he stood at the brink, ready to throw himself into the grave of skepticism: true knowledge seemed impossible, philosophy's function was merely to elucidate the situation of man, living without hope in darkness. "Whence I come I do not know, Whither I go I do not know, What I am I do not know, How strange that I'm so gay," was then his refrain, burying all desire to write.[67] That he wished not to pen his sick thoughts and give them permanence was a sign that sickness had not invaded the core of his personality and that, despite his notions to the contrary, hope had not entirely left him. And when his soul recovered the truth, he began to write again. *Pascal's Calling, Problems of the Doctrine of Grace, Augustine the Philosopher,* and *Introduction to Philosophical Anthropology,* written between 1928 and 1933, show again his faith and his wealth of thought, but not his former power; the youthful fire, the first love, was gone.

Darwin and Michelangelo

For many, the world is a huge factory whose gauge is efficiency, whose pulse is the assembly line; but the Creator—no engineer but an artist, yea, a lover—fashioned His world not with calculating, businesslike prudence, but with magnanimity, a magnanimity that is His alone. Thus created, the world is not an arena of chance, nor is it ruled by the "survival of the fittest," a slogan echoing more the capitalistic pattern of life, the modern clangor of competition. Landsberg has little patience with this picture of a competitive universe. In his *Introduction to Philosophical Anthropology* (printed in 1934, one year after Hitler's rise to power, and therefore never put on sale), he does not deny the principle of evolution a limited validity, for evolution and creation are by no means incompatible, but he finds it highly unlikely that animal life evolved from plant life, impossible that life as such sprang from dead matter and, above all, that man as man issued from the animal kingdom. None of the manifestations of his humanity—

neither love nor language, neither religion nor art, philosophy nor science, not even the way he uses his tools—can be identified with any vital function of animals or plants. Yet naturalistic evolutionism has sought to do precisely this, and thus started that torrent of dehumanization, that "wave of the future," which was Hitler. In the wake of Darwinism, *humanitas,* man's bond to his fellow men, becomes idiotic weakness, for it contradicts the "law of nature" which dooms the feeble, while war is hailed as the great servant of nature, working the "natural selection" of nations.[68]

With Nazism before him, the first major sign of this havoc, Landsberg could not give quarter to naturalistic evolutionism; he had to rip it apart. Were the evolutionist consistent, Landsberg argues, he would attach little importance to any human thinking, including his own; in fact, did he follow his theory to the limit, he would give himself up to an agnosticism so ruinous it would ruin his theory, along with all others. Instead, the followers of Darwin (Landsberg stresses "followers") combine their evolutionism with the most naïve confidence in the human mind and its capacity to grasp the world. But how it is possible that man, a random product of the blind play of atoms—how it is possible that reason, a mere accident of evolution, should solve the riddles of the universe, is their inscrutable secret. May one be forgiven a limerick? No other verse form seems adequate: "A life-force afflicted with doubt as to what it was bringing about, cried, 'I am blind, but I'm making a mind which may possibly puzzle it out.'" On the one hand, man is lowered to the animal; on the other, his thoughts are credited with a power of penetration impossible unless his thoughts are more than a cerebral secretion, unless there operates in his thinking a principle analogous to that which worked in creation and works still in the structure of things created. To call man's mind a discharge from his brain, and then to claim that it can and will arrive at the ultimate understanding of the world and its laws—this is indeed *die Weltanschauung der Halbgebildeten,* the philosophy of the middle-brows.[69]

Man's situation is one of extremes, miserable and great, animal and image of God, extremes which form the main motif of Pascal's theistic anthropology. The Darwinian exaggerates these extremes wildly, to the point of nonsense, for he claims for himself as scientist a power of penetration he denies to himself as man. Boasting of having broken man's "arrogance" in believing himself God's likeness, evolutionism makes the run of men instead beasts of prey, while the Darwinian professor, whose reason can master all problems, it makes a demigod. It is psychologically interesting, Landsberg says, that man is urged more strongly to self-exaltation at the price of his fellow man than to self-exaltation plain and simple: "Rather the first in a hamlet than the second in Rome." This general urge is at work particularly in the bourgeois, who always wishes to outdo others, and it is the bourgeois, Landsberg concludes, whom the Darwinian represents.[70]

Yet, there is in the Darwinian at the same time a peculiar tendency toward self-abasement. In pluming himself on having thrown man down from his privileged position, he betrays, to Landsberg, his desire for self-degradation. Farfetched though it may seem at first, atheism is the root of this desire, for, since Christ, no one of the Western world can deny God without a feeling of guilt, without oppressive anxiety—a feeling of guilt which often forces him to deny also his ability to sin, an anxiety which urges him to self-punishment. When he denies God, man slays Him, as it were, in his own heart, and to escape the bitter reproach of his crime, as well as to repress the uneasy exaltation of having made himself a god, the Darwinian degrades himself to the animal. This is the Darwinian's ultimate and unconscious motive, Landsberg asserts, in reversal of Freud: man's alleged animality is the alibi, so to speak, of the patricide, by which he tries to prove, to himself above all, that he "couldn't have done it." [71]

Man is either more than an animal or one among many, Landsberg affirms, but in no way and never can he be thought of as the highest. To an unbiased observer, with no other than zoological measurements, he shrinks to puny stature before ant and spider, for while they are born with the knowledge and abilities they need during their lifetime, he must gather his experience slowly and with pain. Even the protozoon dwarfs man. The simplest of animals, the infinitesimal amoeba, performs with its one single cell all the vital functions for which man requires billions, each contributing but one small task to the whole. True, man has certain marks in common with the animals, but in his essence he differs entirely. Hence all evolutionist theories apply at best to man the living being, but never to man the man.[72]

His birth Landsberg sees sublimely visioned in Michelangelo's "Creation of Adam," which portrays the instant that man the animal received his humanity. Michelangelo's Adam is not creature only but also image of the Creator-Spirit, for the mysterious something which flows invisibly from the finger of God to the finger of man is not the life he shares with beasts and plants but the spirit that relates him singularly to God. A moment ago Adam was an animal, in its way perfect, strong and beautiful, but now that God stretches forth His hand to him, he is man. Outwardly there would seem no change, were it not for his eyes; in them, of all the human body the most human part, a new principle awakens, giving the whole of his existence a new sense: he is chosen and set apart. The new principle which enters man and transforms him comes from God, it could not have come from Adam himself; it is bestowed, never could it evolve from his animal nature. Still lying on the ground, only half raised, he is full of marvel, yet not quite certain, like one who has just awakened but is not fully able to believe in his waking. Now that he is no longer sleeping, all things gain a new presence, the world and the "I" being truly *there* for him; before, only life and dream crowded on him, but now he sees the clear world of form and the enigma of his inner universe. And as he wonders over all that has happened to him, there awaken in Adam the prime questions of philosophy: Who am I, whence do I come, whither do I go? He discovers that he is unique, a person.[73]

Thus man was made, thus was he converted—for, so is Landsberg's thesis, man's becoming man can be understood only by analogy to religious conversion. In both, a new principle breaks in, changing man's entire existence; as grace is to nature, so is the specifically human to the prehuman principle. This conversion, which stamped the advent of the first man, also stamps the rise of the full humanity of every man: more and more must he become what he is. As Landsberg puts it: Only to man is his essence assigned as a task. From its first day to its last, a cat is in complete possession of its nature, and so is man—but only as member of his species. No one would think of saying, "Be a cat!" but we do say, "Be a man, be yourself!" for man the man must grow, and he grows little by little as in pain he becomes truly himself. The only being called upon to wrestle with himself, to mold his inner world, he is creative in the agony of growth. But since our inner being is related to the Absolute, the Wellspring of personal existence, how could we, without the Absolute's intervening, possibly have power over our inner world, Landsberg halts to ask, how could we shape it? Is not the shaping of our soul intimately linked to prayer, which seeks—and more than seeks—which opens the soul to divine assistance? That in our own age prayer and the forming of the soul are both disappearing is experiential evidence that it is in prayer alone, in communion with the Absolute, that man can win the strength to form his inner being. The inner anarchy so marked today is the sign of man's turning from God: as the art of prayer is lost, unsculptured hearts are the graceless results.[74]

Disorder in the heart of an anthropologist is not without influence on the way he experiences man. As the eye of sympathy alone reaches the deep, unsearchable singularity of a person, likewise sympathy for man himself, love for his eidos, is needed to grasp his unmatched reality. For the anthropologist who loves this reality, all modern discoveries, even if intended to belittle man, enrich his image. Indeed, more clearly than ever before, the sciences have shown that man is held by many cords and that his soul is wondrously spun: biology has brought into focus man's kinship with all that lives; sociology, his many links to his fellow men, to the body politic; history, his roots in the lives and works of past generations; psychology, the mysteriousness of his heart. Yet for all his dependence on the laws of nature, of human fellowship and of his own soul, he can rise above them, so that in the end they serve him and help bring out his fullness. He is both subject and king, king the more, the more he is bound to God.[75]

Man must be loved that he may be known, and he can be fully known only when seen with the eyes of God, who loves him and in love created him. Thus for Landsberg the philosopher it is not philosophy which says the final word about man, but theology, flowing from that revelation which lies "in the unique existence of Him who said of Himself, 'I am the Truth.' " [76] Here his *Introduction to Philosophical Anthropology* comes to a climax: "Philosophy is, consciously since Socrates, 'human wisdom,' that is, knowledge corresponding to man's situation; in other words, man's situation repeated in his consciousness and clearly grasped. Theology, however, is, since St. Paul, 'divine wisdom,' a partaking of God's wisdom in Christ. Philosophy is always the 'knowing of unknowing,' and all its clarification deepens this kind of knowledge alone; but theology is the 'knowing of knowing,' knowledge coming from the power not of man but of God. If a theologian applied to himself the philosopher's confession: 'I know that I know not'—and if he spoke not as man but as believer and theologian—it is not humble he would be, but plainly remiss, unmindful of the arduous high office of proclaiming divine truth." [77]

Resignation, Engagement, Grace

By the time his anthropological study appeared in print, Landsberg had become a man without a home. Long before he would have been forced to leave, in fact the very day Adolf Hitler seized power, he left Nazi Germany so as not to breathe its envenomed air. He went first to Switzerland, then to Paris, from there as visiting lecturer to the University of Barcelona; but soon his work was again cut short, this time by the Spanish civil war, so that he decided to return to Paris. From the day he fled Germany till the hour of his death in a German concentration camp, he knew the hardships, the sufferings, the dangers of exile. Being thrown into exile is like being dropped into a river: singularity and distinction melt away, there is no room for persons; all that seems left of them is filing cards, the one has become the one-among-many. Against this threat Landsberg saw only one safeguard: "To make the lot of exile a personal one!" he wrote in his diary, to view the uncertain existence of a refugee not as something that merely happened, that befell him, but to accept it as a challenge. He knew that the life of an expatriate, who has no one roof over his head, imperils continuity, so important to all deeper existence, intellectual and spiritual. In his diary he cites as model the unbroken spirit of Fray Luis de León, the great Augustinian friar and teacher of St. John of the Cross, who spent five long years in one of the prisons of the Inquisition; his innocence proven, he resumed his chair at the University of Salamanca and began his lecture: *Dicebam hesterno die*, "As I was saying yesterday . . ." [78]

"The situation of a refugee," reads another entry in the diary Landsberg kept from 1933 to 1939, "is that of a man who has constantly to beg for something. So his pride is slowly broken. The

229

thing to do is not to fool oneself, but to pass through this test without losing genuine self-respect. To spend many hours in corridors and offices is certainly no joy, but for people to whom nearly everything so far has been offered on a silver platter, it is a school of equality. Does not the man who learns this lesson save what is rightful in his pride? There are two elements in pride: the feeling, which ought to be abandoned, that it is warranted to be always the exception; and the sense, which ought to be preserved, of the dignity of every man and hence of one's own. If we base our self-respect on our humanity and on nothing else, as we ought, it will concur with our respect for all others. As long as we are unable to do that, we are, without knowing it, still fascists." Yet this was not all Landsberg read in the situation of the refugee shuffling from gate to gate and begging admission. One of his early diary notes, on the mystery of the beggar, sees its depth in the beggar's likeness to the Son of Man, who had "nowhere to lay His head";[79] he closes with a reference to the *Rule* of St. Benedict, in which the patriarch counsels his monks to receive with awe all who knocked at the monastery door, to receive the guest as Christ Himself, who is one day to say: "I was a stranger, and you took Me in." [80]

Landsberg left his home the day Nazism lied its way into power, not for a second doubting its true nature. Hitler, he knew, was a despicable fraud, a smalltime comedian, to whom he applied the words of Nietzsche: "Just listen to the ring a mind has when it speaks; every mind has its ring, loves its ring. That one over there, for instance, is sure to be an agitator, that is, an empty head, an empty mug: whatever goes into him, comes back from him hollow and thick, heavy with the echo of the great void." [81] Though Hitler bore all the badges of the "spieler," "the masses rightly scented in him a power of the metaphysical and religious order," for in him the devil was at work, and it was not by *aufklaererische Polemik*, the polemic fathered by Voltaire and Rousseau, that he could be downed.

On August 27, 1939, a few days before Hitler invaded Poland, when his intention to throw the world into total war had become clear, Landsberg's diary, usually undated, received this examination of conscience—a document stirring and truly Christian: "In these altogether sinister days there remains for us only resignation to whatever looms ahead. All of us, to be sure, bear part of the guilt because of the way in which, taking all things together, we have led our lives, because of our crowding sins and our frightening omissions. 'Father, I have sinned. . . .' And yet, we never willed evil nor did we ever knowingly falsify God's measures. This guilty innocence, this innocent guilt, lies bared to His eye. We implore His mercy and, together with peace, it is granted to men of good will. I am not aware of having ever harbored ill will toward my neighbor, but is this, of itself, good will? It seems to me that the slothful and self-willed paralysis of our will the very moment it sets out toward a positive good is the real vice of men like me, and that only because of His goodness can we hope to be forgiven. Should destruction be visited on us we would suffer no injustice, yet there abides with us hope in the clement hands that hold all things. . . .

"Such is our case before God. . . . Oh, that these dreadful times would serve to atone for at least our undeserved happiness. After all, who knows the laws of the great balance? No doubt, we often lost ourselves in happiness and heartlessly ignored our neighbor's misery. The terrible thing is the paralysis of the will I constantly feel, this confusion of theory and practice, which robs them of their worth and convincing power. Though it be professed with dignity, with subjective honesty, even a true cause is hurt by ingrained weariness and, so to speak, objective dishonesty in its witness—the darkness in him obscures the light of truth. True enough, in a certain sense this conflict between word and deed is common to all men. The teacher of truth, being human, is ever unworthy of truth. Yet these are hollow excuses. It is not the universal situation that matters here, but my own. . . . And the specific thing in my own case is the weakness of my struggle to bridge this chasm—that inertia of soul which is my basic fault. . . .

"That behind fate providence is at work; that the dire darkness of what appears as fate comes from the mysterious light of God, light beyond all light; that this dusk is only within our dazzled eye, blinded by overmuch brightness—this I believe. Yet faith so held should lead to resignation, and that is what I find so hard. I believe in an all-too-abstract way, but true faith in providence is to accept trials. In rebelling against our fate, we prove that we believe only in the 'God of philosophers,' who is within our range, easily understood, who rules all things 'reasonably,' for such a faith obviously and grotesquely contradicts the reality of this world and cannot survive this contradiction when things come to a crisis. . . . Were faith in God's providence deducible from the state of the world, would it be worthy of the name faith? No, like all genuine faith, this too is surrender to a mystery; the true purpose and all that governs every event are altogether hidden in the slow workings of divine providence. Therefore it is our duty and privilege to believe, and only to *believe,* that in this mystery there lies the highest oneness of justice and love; unworthy though we are, it is our duty and privilege to put our trust in this oneness. . . . Nowhere is there strength today save in abandonment to the mystery of providence . . . it is our wanton freedom that is being broken."

While the un-man Hitler with the mad glee of an incendiary was about to unlock hell, Landsberg prayed for mercy. While the apostate from Christianity, proud and covetous, marched to murder, shouting his success, the Jewish Christian knelt humbly, searching his heart, confessing his frailty and praying for a living faith in God. Little though we know of the laws of the great balance, surely Landsberg's trust, and the trust of all who pleaded with God, outweighed Hitler's malice—more than guns, their confidence helped finally to defeat him. Nor was Landsberg's sorrow over his failures without promise, "for if our heart reprehend us, God is greater than our heart and knows all things." [82]

Resignation did not mean passivity to Landsberg. "Why are we, as Christians, Hitler's unconditional opponents?" he asked, and answered: "Because Hitler is a tool of anti-Christ. For us this is no metaphor, no figure of speech. Anti-Christ is present and active wherever Christ is crucified; and Christ is crucified wherever unjust might persecutes the innocent, the least of the innocent. In this the Christian can have no part, he must be vigilant and firm. . . . You must make your choice: Christ or anti-Christ! With whom are you: with the slaughterer or with the lamb? *Agnus Dei,* Lamb of God, who takest away the sins of the world, have mercy on me!"

More and more, Christ's com-passion became Landsberg's staff: whenever a man suffers, Christ suffered first; in our sorrow, there is His; when He endured the agony of the garden, when He staggered beneath the cross, when He hung between heaven and earth, our agony and pain were present.

Slow are the years of light: and more immense •
Than the imagination. And the years return
Until the Unity is filled. And heavy are
The lengths of Time with the slow weight of tears.
Since Thou didst weep, on a remote hillside
Beneath the olive trees, fires of unnumbered stars
Have burnt the years away, until we see them now:
Since Thou didst weep, as many tears
Have flowed like hourglass sand.
Thy tears were all.
And when our secret face
Is blind because of the mysterious
Surging of tears wrung by our most profound
Presentiment of evil in man's fate,
our cruelest wounds
Become Thy stigmata. They are Thy tears
which fall.[83]

It was Hitler's inhumanity that made David Gascoyne sing, in his "Lachrymae," of Christ's tears and ours, as it made Landsberg call on the Lamb of God. We must mourn, but we must also breast the waves of falsehood and injustice, Landsberg repeats in his diary over and over. "In the storm of this age all life worth living perishes. To resist as much as possible is the only thing left us. But the inner problem is how to combine genuine grief and genuine resistance. For the devil can vanquish us either by saddening or by hardening us. Yet never can our own strength solve this problem. So the necessity of divine assistance is learned in a hard school —but was there ever any other than the school of heaven?" Then: "The lot of today's European is to be drowned in mud. When he refuses, he is called 'war-monger'. . . . We at least do not want to tarry in our testimony to truth. Shameful cowardice can never be imposed on us as an obligation. We are or we are not. There is no third choice. . . . To live means to strive for truth and to spread it." And: "Freedom is the gravest duty and the sternest taskmaster. Nothing is easier than to go chained along with the masses, but nothing will more surely make us miss life's meaning." Again: "There are poltroons who would like to reserve the one and divine truth for God to such an extent that it becomes entirely insignificant for man. They forget the duty of approximation, which is part of the prime duty of becoming man. Needless to say, God alone knows pure truth—but this can never excuse a lie. To become like God is the impossible but necessary task through which man becomes man. And what holds for truth holds for justice."

To put one's hand to the plow and not look back was for Landsberg a command of widest scope: who lays his hand to the plow and falters is not fit for the kingdom of God, neither can he be fully man. Convinced that he who does not thrill to truth and justice cripples himself, Landsberg frequently set forth this "law of humanization." In *Reflections on the Engagement of the Person* (1922),[84] one of many essays he wrote for the French Catholic periodical *Esprit* during his years of exile, he admits that, placed in this world full of contradictions, we all feel at times the desire to withdraw from action and to live, detached onlookers, apart from, if not outside, events. However unimpeachable our motives, the ivory tower does not correspond to our true human situation, which is so entwined with the several communities to which we belong that, unless we participate in their history, we can never attain the meaning of our lives. Barring those who, like monks and nuns, have special vocations, whose lives are exceptions, our existence here and now is realized only in the measure that we consciously help shape the future, for historic presence is proper to man. Unlike the animal, prey of instant succeeded by instant, we transform past into future, which is ever before our eye. At every step a perspective of things to come is open to us, a vista ranging from our own immediate possibilities to those of mankind, and our historic conscience is the more alive the greater the circle it embraces. Tempted though we be to throw off the burden of historic responsibility, we cannot, we stand under an obligation. Hence we must engage ourselves; we must accept concrete responsibility, be active in the realization of the good; we must make definite efforts in fashioning what is to be.

Engagement, Landsberg says, is the work of the entire man, of fused mind and will; it is an act at once total and free, in which the person accepts his place in history and espouses an authentic cause, ready for the sacrifice and suffering his decision may entail. Never an abdication of personhood, *engagement* is as far as can

be from that blind enlisting in which people identify themselves—
out of weakness or despair—with any movement whatsoever, provided it is powerful and can carry them as a stream a drop of water.
Such enlistment is, on the contrary, desertion from responsibility;
it is treason to freedom and betrayal of the future. *Engagement*
is no less opposed, on the other hand, to that intellectual isolation
which takes the world to be but a sum of facts and man's intelligence but an instrument for their notice and classification, which
assumes that dignity and exactitude of thought depend on the
thinker's "neutrality." Only by engaging himself in the pursuit of
the good can man arrive at a true understanding of history, while
neutrality blinds him to truth, viewing, as it does, causes just and
unjust indifferently, on the same level, the plane of facts, so that
engagement is an intellectual as well as a moral necessity. Far
from leading to unalloyed truth, neutrality—so willingly confused
with objectivity—must bring about a schizophrenia, a split of the
soul into two selves, one theoretical and neutral, the other practical
and fanatical; and above all, it must rive the world into impotent
intellectuals and irresponsible gangsters. The mendacious tolerance of evil by "isolationists," who are content merely to *explain*,
paralyzes the Western mind; their pretentious superiority, Landsberg cries out, smites the world as with a pestilence.

Paradoxical though it may appear when seen against the great
modern denial of the good in both philosophy and life, the agreement on what is good is in many ways today more general than
before. Organized deceit is the witness. That the dictators of our
day need to lie, and to lie night and day, in order to disguise their
true aims and the nature of their acts before the world and particularly before their own people, proves that in their own hearts
they know themselves monsters. Neither Attila nor Genghis Khan
required the service of the lie, today's elaborate machinery of per-
versions which turns the aggressor into the attacked and the victim into the villain.

It is the objective character of values (which Landsberg goes on
to discuss, though without doing it full justice), that demands the
engagement of the whole person and gives it import. To the sub-
jectivist for whom values have no weight, no significance, no reality beyond the span of his pleasure, this, he says, is the decisive
answer: Give your yea, engage yourself, and you will see that val-

ues are objective. (This is true, of course, only if *engagement* is taken in its widest sense, for to many values not action but contemplation—marvel, joy, gratitude, or praise—is the proper response.) Without the transsubjectivity of values, there could be no authentic *engagement*, for all our decisions would be arbitrary and all our acts morally the same. In the very experience of *engagement*, however, in the response to values, we gain inner evidence that they exist, that they are not merely words, not "coinage of the brain." This is by no means a vicious circle; no, it is the temper of values to speak only to those who are willing to hear. Because of their exalted nature, no one may truly know them unless he gives himself to them—a law the more rigorous the higher the values. Hence Christ said: "If you abide in My word . . . you shall know the truth." [85]

Man stands in time and he must redeem it, not the least reason being that he walks toward eternity. As Landsberg grew alive to man's part in history and his responsibility for the body politic, he riveted his eyes upon the end unending. "Man's general destiny is beatitude," he reflects in his diary. "All of us most certainly wish for bliss. And yet we may miss it; we may follow illusions. Without grace, fallen man seeks content in creatures. Man's specific destiny is *ad Deum*, to God, and there is his true beatitude." True action, which under God renders man maker of the future, can never dispense with grace, Landsberg says, and many of his entries refer to their hand-in-hand relationship: "In freedom man's being fulfills itself; compulsion obstructs it. Grace is a power that frees; sin is its opposite." On the form of address *Vuestra Merced*, "Your Grace," St. Teresa of Avila so often uses in her writings, he comments: "Grace is the highest attribute of the sovereign person, who, by virtue of his freedom, rises above life within the group. Nothing can excel grace." On another occasion he writes: "Happiness is a gift, is a being blessed, not because of merit, but freely. Sublime and gladsome aspect of the doctrine of grace! So St. Augustine—he does not want his happiness to come from himself. Just so St. Teresa."

Grace seeks the soul's innermost point, which is never deceived by the illusion that only clutchables have reality, the point from which wonder and trust, the powers of the child, never depart. "Only in mystery are we at home," Landsberg meditates on

Christmas Eve, 1939. "The light of the Christmas tree shines forth only in the dark winter night. The locked room before Christmas Eve is the place of mystery where the very bottom of our soul, so like a child, abides in expectation. 'Unless you be converted and become as little children, you shall not enter into the kingdom of heaven.' [86] The mystery of that great pristine home of souls is the hidden solace by which men are able to live. Everything superficial is sacrilege. . . ."

To Landsberg, unlike some facile writers of today and yesterday, the mark of the mature mind is that it keeps the soul's childhood, its thirst, its awe before mystery. "Nothing is more convincing of the dignity and truth of Christianity than a thorough knowledge of the many attacks upon it, from Celsius to Rosenberg. What a market of stupidity, what a din of sophists—only here and there a terrifying flash as of hell-fire. . . ." Landsberg longed for the soul's ultimate home; considering in his diary the lives and writings of saints and how they can be truly understood—only by those, he holds, who by a personal religious life, a life of grace, possess a certain affinity with them—he suddenly breaks forth: "Carry us off, O Lord, into the far land the eye of our spirit sees, whose air breathes upon the harp of our soul. Make us strong to await and to endure Thy grace, and to walk the path it leads. Amen."

The Presence of Death

What is death's import for man? Landsberg asks in his study *The Experience of Death,* written in Paris in the middle thirties, during the relative quiet between Hitler's ascent to power and the beginning of the war. Many tried then, all the harder as they scented danger, to lull themselves into a false security, but Landsberg was always alert, and then more than ever, to the fragility of human existence. He launched his discussion with a sentence from Voltaire, who wrote, in his article on man in the *Dictionnaire philosophique:* "Of all the species, the human species alone knows that it must die, and it knows this only by experience." [87] The usual interpretation of this dictum, Landsberg remarks, is that we gain insight into the inevitability of death the same way we come to know that the sun must rise in the east: from the observation of many instances of dying our reason infers a rule, a likelihood. However, Voltaire's "by experience" contains more than he himself recognized, Landsberg continues, for there is a distinctly human experience of death which tells man immediately that none can escape it.[88]

Before offering his own portrayal of the immediacy of death, Landsberg sets right Scheler's attempt. What Scheler really described, he comments, was the experience of aging: At every moment of our lives, the burden of the past waxes while the possibilities of the future wane; every added year shrinks our feeling of being free to shape the future and thus transform life. This is frighteningly true, Landsberg remarks, and only the highest spiritual acts can overcome this tendency of life to an ebb. Yet in human experience, death differs entirely from the extreme limit of physiological decline, to which it is likened in Scheler's analysis. There is no necessary connection between aging and death, for many die young and instances of so-called natural death are rare. But even when death is caused by old age, some added factor—a cold, inflammation, or injury which breaks down the resistance of the body—is often needed to bring life to its close. The inexorability of death which man experiences has nothing in common with the biological thesis that multicellular organisms use themselves up, that tissues wear thin.[89]

Not only do I know without a doubt, Landsberg affirms, that one day I have to die, when, that is, my strength is spent and my vitality can sink no lower. Beyond this, I know for certain that I am face to face with the real possibility of death, not at some time in the future but at each moment of my life; today and every day death is near me. My ignorance of the "when" is not a flaw in biological science; it is the not-knowing of my destiny—*mors certa, hora incerta,* death is certain, the hour uncertain. Our awareness that death is inescapable transcends by far anything biological science or the feeling of growing older can tell. And this is death's subtle dialectic: even when absent, it is present.[90]

The genuinely human experience of death is not found among children or so-called primitives, Landsberg says; they are little aware of its inner necessity, seeing it always with an external cause and a more or less incidental character. In primitive society man becomes conscious of his individuality mainly through his position in the group, through his function in a larger body. When he dies, his function and his name pass on to another, and the soul is thought to enter this heir. It is as if nothing much has happened —the group simply grows another limb, substituting a new member for the lost. Thus the law of reproduction hides the significance of individual death; as the classical image puts it, men go and come like the leaves of a tree. The full consciousness of death is linked, in Landsberg's opinion, to the emergence of men whose personalities are formed not from without but from within, so that not only are they more deeply aware of their personal singularity, but they are in actual fact more singular and distinct; the change in consciousness is rooted in a change in reality. Correspondingly, the consciousness of individual death is sharpened, because the menace which is really and always death's now looms higher. Now that the individual has found a content all his own, necessarily going beyond the confines of the group and therefore also beyond the group's power of reproduction and the possibility of being born again in another of its members, death threatens the annihilation of an existence truly unique.[91]

Since the grasp of the grimness of death mounts with the rise of men who tower above the common, epochs rich in great individuals are frightened more than others, Landsberg observes, by the thought of death. In late antiquity, for instance, whose élite displayed a new height of individuality, there appeared a new fear of death, to which the mystery cults and the philosophical sects were answers. Another such period of signal personalities and leaping fear was the Renaissance and Reformation, a time of sudden panics, of *danses macabres,* of realistic representations of Christ on the cross, and of a theology dominated by the individual's wish, at his last hour, to know himself justified. So a heightened sense for death clamored and cleared the ground for the great historic doctrines on survival. To men for whom enclosure in a ceaseless round of birth and death had become unbearable, Buddha preached liberation from both birth and death, holding out the expectation of a death that would not result in another birth and thus not in another death, while Christ promised and made possible a new birth that knows no dying. For the Brahman faith, which Buddha's doctrine presupposed, the endless concatenation of deaths and births was fastened by existence as such. But for the Israel of old, to whom Christ brought His gospel, the link of birth and death was welded by sin and hence, He announced, could be broken by a new kind of birth, by the intervention of grace. Whereas Buddhism is the negation of life for the sake of death, Christianity is the jubilant affirmation of a life that conquers death. Triumphantly therefore St. Paul exclaims "Death is swallowed up in victory. O death, where is thy victory. O death, where is thy sting?" [92]

The Sundering of the "We"

In the measure in which our own personhood is strengthened, we are aware of the singularity of our neighbor, for through love we touch it, as it were; we feel its inexpressible existence, its pulsing core, the center which for all time distinguishes him from us. And so when a friend dies, whom love has lucidly shown us unique and irreplaceable, we walk not on biological but on metaphysical ground, for the death of one close to us differs radically from that of "an other" or of men in general.[93]

To gain for philosophy the full meaning of the death of one dear to us, we must relive, inwardly repeat, the experience. The friend whose final illness we recall is at first still with us, but helpless and hiding behind his body's agony. One thing is dominant in these critical hours, that a living body is racked with pain, and sympathy makes our own flesh tremble. Once or twice our friend comes out of his retreat, speaking a few words, his last words, and for a little while he whom we love stands fully before us. Then there is quiet the strained lines of the beloved face ease, all struggle comes to an end; for a moment we feel relief, for our body suffered with the stricken, and now our pain has ceased. But very soon we are drawn into the chilly, alien country of irrevocable death. Our physical sympathy reaches into a void, and is suddenly arrested when we fully understand that the one we love is no longer here in the uniqueness of his personality nor able to return into the clay-cold body before us. We know now that he is gone, that life together is past; no more will he speak to us, no more live in our company— never again. At every instant of our life, death is present in absence, but while we stand by his deathbed, our friend is absent in presence.[94]

When love witnesses death—that love in which heart speaks to heart—we learn that death, so common, is unique, as unique as the way each person walks the earth. And though, or rather be cause, this experience is unique, the participation in the inner life of another person which true love grants offers an insight into the necessity of death. A covenant bound us to him who is now dead; together we had woven a "we," a bond we felt would last forever; but now that the "we" is breaking asunder, we follow it as it breaks, to the furthest limit. For a moment we touch the beyond, breathe the air from the land of the dead, the land that has bereft us of the one we love, and when shortly we return, we feel that the great coldness has gripped us; no longer are we what we were before, and no future will restore us or blot out the print of that cold and awful hand.[95]

The awareness that death must come, thrust upon us by this experience, is not the usual assertion that all members of the human species must die because of the finitude of their vital energy, because for them life means constant struggle against dangers and obstacles and thus the consumption of the organism's power to fight on and regenerate itself. For the general necessity of death we experience as we watch at our friend's side is not so much of a logical as of a symbolic order. The dying friend represents all men; he is Everyman, Everyman of whom Baudelaire wrote: "God is the eternal confidant in that tragedy of which everyone is the hero." [96] It is this Everyman who dies every time one close to us dies his unique death, and forced then on each of us is the certitude: I die with him. While he was yet alive I could draw near him, but now he is far; his lips will not open for me, the glazed eye will not rest on me, the stiffened hand will not seek mine. Our communion is cleft. In a measure *I* was that communion; in the same measure death now pierces the core of my existence, and without further reflection makes me feel that no one can flee it.[97]

Life is our true country, but through such an immediate experience of death, it is as if we were banished. We are alone, we feel deserted, as if the one we loved had been untrue to us. That there is in the experience of death the suffering of a tragic infidelity, that there is a link between death and disloyalty, words like "He is dead for me, he has gone out of my life forever," disclose. Theologians and mystics give us insights, stemming from revelation, which correspond to this experience (though, of course, they could never be gathered from it): they tell us that death is the fruit of a deliberate infidelity which put the entire world into a state of treason, and that God alone is true, faithful forever, for He alone will never die.[98]

Nothingness or Hope

Much of Landsberg's book is devoted to a discussion of death's ontological purpose, but, still in the toils of one of Scheler's errors, he almost defeats his purpose by speaking of "person" as *akthaftes Sicherbauen eines "Werdeseins,"* as an existence which is being constituted by its acts, a "becoming-being." [99] It is true, and a matter of great moment, that in the history of mankind and in that of each individual man, personal existence is put in relief, is brought to maturity and to an ever fuller realization, by *acts*, by men's own steps and trials (though we must at no time forget that, through Israel and the Church, God's word and work impel man's inner growth). But man's acts do not and cannot "transform him from a biological specimen into a person";[100] they do not make, rather do they express, what he *is*. Only in the sense that he becomes and ought to become more and more a person, which he is from the very first moment of his existence, can man's personhood be called "becoming-being." *Agere sequitur esse,* doing follows being; as with all that exists so in the instance of man, his nature precedes and informs his deeds. Hence there can be no ontological foundation of man's experience of death unless there is an ontological, and not merely an actualistic, foundation of the person. Yet, surprisingly, Landsberg proceeds unhampered by his inadequate definition of the person, his true philosophical sense prevailing over his error.

Seldom has a personal existence been fulfilled by the moment of death, he says. That fulfillment and death do not commonly coincide is a dissonance which proves to him that death is not immanent in personal existence; issuing from the vital sphere, death approaches specifically human existence as a stranger, entering it, as it were, from without. Every person's task and test is, indeed, to build into his life the fact that death cannot be fled, but the very effort this conquest requires shows that death is foreign to our innermost nature. Personal existence is not overpowered by fatality; rather is it challenged to answer freely and to overcome, in a certain sense, all fatality, in particular that of death—we are not born for the purpose of dying, the human person is not an "existence unto death." So Landsberg exclaims against Martin Heidegger, for whom the human person is *Sein zum Tode,* a being for death, an existence doomed from its very beginning, carrying within it the cancer of mortality.[101] And Landsberg continues: "As is every other existence in its own way, so is human existence directed toward *its* realization, towards eternity. It strives for its perfection even if it must hurdle the ancient and immovable rock of death. There is no other way for man to surmount that strange rock than to convert death, making it a means to his own fulfillment." [102]

Against Heidegger, master of frustration, Landsberg affirms with the confidence of the true philosopher, that it is not nothingness —the nothingness we become aware of when we know dread and anguish—which is the origin of metaphysics, but being; nor can the ontological character of the person be derived, as Heidegger would have it, from a negativity with which man must come to terms. It is true, sin and despair can *make* his life an "existence unto death," but it is not so by nature, for the dread besetting him at the thought of dying is more than physical fear of the pains that accompany it, and could not be understood were the fundamental structure of our existence not built toward immortality. Did we not tend by our very being toward everlastingness, death would be simply a fact, lying in the future, unpleasant perhaps, but without the brunt of an exception, not a menace of metaphysical magnitude. Our dread, however, reveals that death and nothingness are contrary to the truth of our nature, to a tendency that cannot be swerved aside. This tending of our nature is not only the urge to endure, common to all that lives, not Schopenhauer's *Wille zum Leben,* but an impulse, embedded in the very center of the human person, to say "yes" to itself, to render more and more luminous its own singularity, and in affirming and realizing this singularity, to transcend the limits of time.[103]

We who believe that the person survives death have far more than a consoling reassurance for our trembling hearts; we express what we are, we bring to light our ontological structure. The craving of our nature for immortality cannot be attributed to freak or fancy, to selfishness or atavism—to do so is to vex truth and no more; our craving voices our metaphysical constitution, for, as Landsberg says, consciousness follows being. Only a man who, in despairing unbelief, lusts after negating his own personhood can imagine

243

death the annihilation of his entire existence; who has fallen from hope thinks death the end. Hope it is that gives meaning to our lives, continuing in the realm of the person the self-affirmation proper to being; it is one of the three virtues without which man cannot be. A philosophy of existence like Heidegger's, which wishes to void the ontological foundation of these virtues, is in truth a philosophy *against* existence.[104]

The hope in which personal existence manifests itself is essentially different from the manifold stirrings of emotion which are hopes for something, Landsberg emphatically states. Not that hope lacks an intentional content, quite the contrary—precisely because it possesses its content in the most intimate manner, it cannot exchange contents at random. Both hope and hopes turn toward the future: the future of hopes is that of the world, the years in which various events are expected; the future of hope, however, is that of my own person, the time in which I am to fulfill myself. There is no necessary relationship between the reasons on which our little hopes are based and the events they look for; the direction of hope, on the other hand, is harmonious with our personhood, in which it is grounded. Thus hope aspires to its fulfillment most patiently, in a tranquil confidence, whereas hopes are rooted in an impatience which constantly doubts itself and anticipates the things to come. While hopes wander in the world of chance, drifting toward illusion, hope moves in the realm of freedom, toward truth. And it is not this or that disappointment which wars against hope, but despair. Even disillusionment, the sum of manifold disappointments, need not be opposed to hope; in fact, it may forward hope's purgation, that it may transcend the "world" and awaken to its own full meaning. In little hopes our imagination busies itself, but in the one great hope our existence advances daringly. As trees cannot put forth living leaves without the impulse of spring, hope's analogy, so man as a spiritual person cannot exist for a moment without creative hope—the earth in which supernatural hope takes root, that hope of which it is written that it will not confound us.[105]

Landsberg's thought meets in many ways that of Gabriel Marcel, whom he quotes: *L'âme n'est que par l'espérance; l'espérance est peut-être l'étoffe même dont notre âme est faite . . .* , "The soul exists only through hope; hope is perhaps the very stuff of which our soul is made. . . . To despair of a man, is it not to negate him as a soul? Is not to despair of oneself to kill oneself by anticipation?"[106] *Being* he proclaims as the place of fidelity, *l'être comme lieu de la fidélité;*[107] on the other hand, he says, we live in a world where betrayal is possible at every moment and under all forms: the betrayal of all by all, and of each man by himself. When a man despairs, he affirms that in the realm of reality there is nothing that deserves his credence, no anchorage, no security; that all things, the world and himself, are bankrupt. The structure of our world seems even to recommend such failure; to an eye asquint the spectacle of death is a perpetual incitement to denial. That on this earth despair is forever possible is linked to our freedom, whose part and price it is that it can be traitor to itself; and so the way to despair is always open, and nothing outside ourselves can close it. But always open too is the road to hope, or to use Gabriel Marcel's bolder image: death is like a springboard of absolute hope.

Hope must not be likened, he says, to a detour one takes when the road is barred, to a bypass running back into the same road at the far side of the obstacle. No, hope opens into the invisible world—an affirmation of eternity, of the everlasting goods, of transcendent order. It has a prophetic tenor; not bearing on what might have to be, or even on what shall have to be, it says simply: So it will be. Its manner is not to wish or to desire; rather, with a prophet's tongue does hope assert. It is an *élan,* a leap, not only a protestation dictated by love but an appeal, a fiery, passionate recourse to an ally, and the ally is love. Never resting on calculation or statistics, hope affirms that there is at the heart of being, beyond all appearances, beyond all inventories, a mysterious principle which is with us, siding and working with us; it wills as we will, if only we will what ought to be willed and will it with our whole being.[108]

What marks hope is that it does not, that it cannot, use techniques, for every technique is in the service of some fear or some desire. It is the weapon of the unarmed, or to be more exact, it is the opposite of a weapon, and in this, mysteriously, resides its efficacy—a marvel difficult to grasp for those who know no power but might. Yet far from being a kind of languid and lifeless waiting, hope heralds and bears up action, for it is itself the lengthening into the

245

unknown of an activity grounded in being. Child of humility, hope has for its domain all that does not depend on ourselves, all that is outside our control; it wills not only this or that, but the absolute, the infinite good. In all genuine hope, as for the recovery of a sick friend or the liberation of an oppressed country, there is confidence that a living order will be restored in its integrity; the body's or the country's integrity, however, is a prefiguration, a symbolic expression of a supreme integrity. Hence, Gabriel Marcel says, all hope is ultimately hope of salvation; hope of salvation is its archetype.[109]

Both Landsberg and Marcel distinguish between hope, the original utterance of our humanity, the movement of being, and hope, the supernatural virtue, which stamps the movement of our nature with a heavenly newness, showing it its true, transcending goal. Hope the virtue stretches out beyond the fulfillment of personality toward our rise to glory, toward rest and bliss in God. Not anchored in ourselves, in the fidelity of being—finite, however great—it is founded in Him who says: "I have redeemed thee, called thee by thy name; thou art Mine." [110] And it expects eternal life, that is, God Himself, from God's magnanimity and mercy, *sperat Deum a Deo*. All its expectation is in and through Christ: "By the hand of hope Christ is held. We hold Him and we are held. Yet greater is it that we are held by Christ than that we hold Him. For we hold only as long as we are held." [111] Natural hope is always in danger of tiring, and therefore needs supernatural hope, the strong and swift pinions of the soul, infallibly carrying it to its destiny as long as it moves in God's power. Sin and selfish anxiety may choke the virtue of hope; fear, however, that loving fear which looks not at self but, lest it lose it, at the good it loves, is hope's helper.[112]

The great poets have sung the wonder of hope. In it, for Dante, eternity and time, eternal beatitude and all that lies on the way to it, are blended.[113] In praise of "dear hope, earth's dowry, and heav'n's debt," Crashaw sings:

. . . by thee
We are not Where nor What we be,
But What and Where we would be. Thus art thou
Our absent Presence, and our future Now. . . .

True hope's a glorious hunter and her chase,
The God of nature in the fields of grace.[114]

Perhaps the most impassioned poetic expression of hope is that of
Hopkins, so full of hope that he need not call her name:

. . . the Resurrection,
A heart's-clarion! Away grief's gasping, joyless days, dejection.
*   Across my foundering deck shone*
A beacon, an eternal beam. Flesh fade, and mortal trash
Fall to the residuary worm; world's wildfire, leave but ash:
*   In a flash, at a trumpet crash,*
I am all at once what Christ is, since he was what I am, and
This Jack, joke, poor potsherd, patch, matchwood, immortal
*   diamond,*
*   Is immortal diamond.*[115]

St. Augustine's Pilgrimage

As his chief witness, Landsberg calls on St. Augustine, who tells in
his *Confessions* how the death of a friend, with whom his bond
was "sweet above all sweetness," threw him, still a Manichean,
into the pit of sadness. Among those who tell their lives, St.
Augustine is unique. Whenever he searches his thoughts and deeds
in the sight of God, he transcends the psychological plane, Landsberg observes, and rises immediately to a lucid vision of the
metaphysical and existential; he becomes Everyman, and thus
his *Confessions* is the symbolic history, the drama, of everyone. As
he candidly lays bare *his* life, he paints a true picture of the life
of *man,* and in disclosing the temper of his own soul on the death
of his friend, he gives a universal experience. "Grief utterly darkened my heart," he confesses, "and whatever I beheld was death.
My native country was a torment to me, and my father's house a
strange unhappiness; and whatever I had shared with him, wanting him, became a cruel torture. My eyes claimed him everywhere, but he was not given me; and I hated all places, for that
they had not him; nor could they tell me, 'Wait, he is coming,' as
they did when he was alive and absent. I became a great question
to myself, and more than once, I asked of my soul why she was so
sad, and why she disturbed me so sorely; but she knew not what
to answer me. And when I said, 'Hope in God,' very rightly she
obeyed me not; for that man, whom she had held most dear and

then lost, was both truer and better than that phantasm she was bid to hope in. Only weeping was sweet to me, and it succeeded my friend in being the delight of my soul." [116]

In this passage Landsberg finds all the essential elements of the experience of death. It is at work as the present absence, powerful enough to turn the entire world into death: "Whatever I beheld was death." There is the radical difference between the relative absence of the one removed in space and the definite absence of the one torn from us by death: "My eyes claimed him everywhere, but he was not given me. . . ." *Factus eram ipse mihi magna quaestio,* "I became a great question to myself"—this was the birth of truly existential philosophy, Landsberg contends, of that philosophy in which man seeks to grasp and gain his human existence, in which he moves either toward hope or, if he fails, toward despair. This "question" to which the death of a loved one leads us makes us discover that our mortal life is not our true existence. Yet it points at no alien misery, rather at one abiding with our very mortality: "Wretched I was; and wretched is every heart, chained by the friendship of mortal things; he is torn asunder when he loses them, and in this loss feels the wretchedness which in reality he had even before he lost them." [117] Brought to light only by loss, this misery is lodged in an attachment to things that gallop to an end, in a jarring love, jarring because all love wills eternity, yet here its will clashes with the short-livedness of what it loves— it is from the fleeting to the lasting that our sadness points.[118]

St. Augustine's heart tries to hope again, for the person is created with hope. "Hope in God," he counsels his soul—but it would not, since the god in whom he then believed was the god of the Manicheans, no reality but a phantasm. So his only comfort is flight, self-deception; in his own tears does he find the imaginary presence of him whom he laments: "I wept most bitterly, and found my repose in bitterness," *requiescebam in amaritudine.*[119] Conflicting emotions stir his soul: "I loathed exceedingly to live, and at the same time feared to die. I suppose the more I loved him, the more did I hate and fear, as a most cruel enemy, death which had bereaved me of him." [120] There is no way out of his misery; he and despair are knit together, till he meets the true God, whom here and elsewhere he calls *Spes mea,* "my Hope." [121]

Existential participation, the "we" woven by the communion of two persons, is not missing from St. Augustine's account, Landsberg continues. When this "we" is torn apart, he not only encounters death in general, but is thrust into the mystery of his own dying: "I wondered that others, mortals too, did live, since he whom I loved, as if he should never die, was dead; and still more did I wonder that I, his second self, could live, he being dead. It was well said when one called his friend 'Thou half of my soul,' [122] for I felt that my soul and his soul were one soul in two bodies! Thus was my very life a horror to me, because I would not live halved. And it may be that I feared to die lest he die wholly whom I had loved so much." [123] He had confided his personal existence to a communion with another human being, but now this friend, by his death unfaithful and fleeting, rips his inner life: "I stormed, sighed, wept, was tossed about, had neither rest nor counsel. I bore about a shattered and bleeding soul, impatient of being borne by me. . . . I remained to myself an unhappy place, where I could neither be nor be from thence. For whither should my heart flee from my heart? Whither should I flee from myself? Whither not follow myself?" [124]

In this whirl of anguish, antique thought could give no help, for Augustine's misery would not let him toy with the earnestness of death. The Epicurean sophism: As long as we are, death is not; when death is, we are not; therefore death is not,[125] could not dupe him. If reality consisted in nothing but sensations, death would indeed have no hold on us, for once dead, the body cannot feel it, and all that would matter would be to die as pleasantly as possible. Yet to deduce from the cessation of pain in death and from the insensibility of the corpse that death has no power over us, in fact, no existence for us, is but a trick, an attempt to deny in words what cannot be eluded in reality.[126]

Neither could Augustine find peace in the Stoic argument that death is fair, since it subjects to the same rule all without exception; that it is not to be railed at, because man is but led back whence he came; and that it is not absolute, for nothing is ever truly lost in this cosmos, a cosmos unable to fulfill its great task of expressing the richness of being unless it wrecks individuals. It is by keeping death before our eyes, the Stoics taught, that we free ourselves from its strangle hold and overcome its terror. But with his own existence halved by the death of his friend, with his love wounded, his heart plucked from him, Augustine saw no peace in an argument extolling indifference, which wished to dry tears by parching love and made personal existence the dung of cosmic life.[127]

Then, the life of a philosopher offered healing, because from the height of philosophy man sees death far below him, small and stripped of power, and by every true act of knowledge, transcends the walls of the flesh, entering a realm death cannot touch. For Plato, the philosopher takes part in the world of ideas; to philosophize is, freely and victoriously, to "die," to leave behind this world of images, to exchange this cave of shadows for another world, really existing, because existing in continuous presence.[128] But the soul cannot exist save in communion, Landsberg interjects; isolation, incompatible with the inner structure of personal existence, nears extinction—there is no spiritual "I" without a "thou." Thus, if it is to outlast death, the soul must not withdraw into isolation but must join a new reality. Plato sees this reality in the world of ideas, but after all is said in its favor, the world of which antique philosophy speaks remains still a world of things, of things intellectually seen, *eine Welt von Sehdingen,* and those who people it are not fully men; they live in public and in a way resemble things seen. For the Greek world was not one of neighbors, formed by *caritas*—the more-than-natural love of God, which shows men lovable in His sight and makes them loved for His sake —and hence the unfathomable depth of the human person was as good as undiscovered. And the transcendental world shared the character of the empirical. Hurt in the quick of his being, Augustine could not be healed by the prospect of joining a realm of ideas, but only by a hope which restores and makes whole. Never halting at partial truths, he would not stay at philosophy's defiance of death, but sought till he found the heaven where the Three-personed God is each person's Light, where He is seen and loved, face to Face.[129]

Gateway to Glory

In a way entirely new, Christ frees everyone who believes in Him from the tyranny of death, Landsberg exults at his essay's climax. The realm He reveals is one from which death is forever banned but which man may enter; open to him now is the possibility of a life so close to God, of a union so deep, that through it he shares in God's eternity. Christ came, and by His coming and example man's situation is changed, a change mirrored in the thoughts of Christian thinkers on the dialectic of death and life. "I know not whence I came hither, into this dying life or rather living death," St. Augustine declares.[130] At every instant the world tumbles as past swallows future; the instant, the only *where* and *when* allowed the present, the only place and opportunity for true existence on earth, dies as soon as it is born, gliding in time "from that which is not yet, through that which has no space, into that which is no longer." [131]

Unceasingly our unrest strains toward the future, leaves behind the past, while swiftly traversing the present. Though our perception of time is based on this unrest, this inconstancy, it injures the roots of our existence, and it is this restlessness of our souls which brings forth the uncurbed mobility of concrete time. We ourselves are this time, in so far as we have no part in eternity, in the pure present, the constant and everlasting now, which is one with God. Hence unrest, sown into our souls by sin, its witness and wages never leaving us, is the seed of our mortality. At no time of this earthly span can we exist without recalling the past, often in remorse, nor without turning to the future in ever new hope. At every moment man parts from something of this world and from something in himself, and at every moment he goes forth to meet, and to change into, something new: "We live our lives, forever taking leave." [132] Yet if death lies in wait in every atom of our lives, so does the tendency that wrestles with death. As Landsberg points out, in St. Augustine's interpretation the Christian's time is the time of the soul, which in seeking God, seeks its own existence and duration: "Thou hast made us for Thyself, and our heart shall find no rest until it rest in Thee." [133]

Through grace man has part in God's eternity: the free and boundless Love which spoke in the Incarnation transforms his transient days into one lasting morn. Since this participation is made perfect only beyond death, death is a truer birth: "Hide not Thy face from me. Lest I die, let me die so that I see Thy face." [134] Damnation is thus the only real death, because it is the irrevocable severance from the Well of life; the beatific vision, however, to which the saints are born in the hour of their dying, is eternal life, the perfect presence. Never can man as person be reduced to nothingness; he arrives at his definitive existence either in hell or in heaven, in that death or life of which death and life on earth are but shadows. Hence the Christian's fear of death becomes more and more fear of life without God, and his clinging to life more and more a clinging to the true life. Since death is, or can and ought to be made, the gateway to glory, his concern is no longer with the fact that his days are numbered; his care, growing in importance day by day, is rather: Shall I die well? This shift in gaze, this turning of things cherished and things dreaded, this conversion of fear and desire, though seldom complete, must needs be found in all who seek to grow more truly Christian.[135]

It is in the mystics of the Church, who have boldly recast their lives, that Landsberg places his entire confidence. Others may feel free to dismiss mystical utterances on death as psychological documents—"As for myself," he writes, "I do not wish to hide that I hold for certain: Here is the truth." The mystic's is not an absurd and uncanny variety of religious experience, he affirms, but a singular grace, giving unique access to the same mysteries all the faithful believe. Christian mysticism—in no way irrational, in no way against but very much above reason—is part of Christian life and not part of the genus "mysticism." For the likeness of non-Christian with Christian mysticism is at best one of forms and expressions, never one of the spirit, Landsberg asserts, and quotes Suhwardi d'Alep, an Arabian mystic of the twelfth century, who counseled: "Keep on taking the poison till you find it pleasant; love death if you wish to live." [136] With the more or less Stoic resignation of the Moslem mystic, Landsberg contrasts the eagerness of St. Bonaventure: "Seek not glittering light but fire that inflames you totally. . . . God is this fire, and His furnace is in Jerusalem. On earth it was kindled by Christ the Man in the fervor of His most ardent passion. . . . Let us die therefore . . . and with Christ crucified pass from this world to the Father." [137]

The same desire for the blessing of death, for the "Enter into thy Master's joy," was in St. Monica, St. Augustine's mother.[138] It was even stronger in St. Teresa of Avila, who, dauntless and forceful, wrote: "I found myself dying with desire to see God, and I knew no way of seeking that life save through death." The pain of her transports foreshadowed to her that last agony which leads to God's presence, so that she could say: *Señor, o morir o padecer,* "To die, Lord, or to suffer!" So strong was her sensing of God's presence that eternal life flooded her life in time, or, to speak in one of her favorite images, the butterfly was about to break open the cocoon and take to flight. Her yearning for death was not the result of weariness, Landsberg underlines. There are those who tire of life because a surfeit of pleasure has killed their zest; but St. Teresa was a contemplative, and the joys granted her could never pall. Equally alien to her was the disgust of those who find life empty because they shun responsibility, work, devotion; hers was an activity wide and fruitful such as few can call their own. Nor was she a sterile complainer of her fate. She suffered that death tarried because she had learned to love it, or rather, that highest possibility of existence death unfolds. It is not only because he believes firmly in the promise of eternal life that the mystic impatiently awaits his last hour; he has already *felt* its bliss in the mystical union.[139]

Love, which determines where we are present and have our stay, goes for the mystic beyond this world. Thus in death he walks up to the altar where the soul is forever wed to God, where her communion with Him who loves with an everlasting love is sealed. As in rapture so in death, agony is but the prelude to the limitless joy, in which our being is perfected and abundantly rendered itself, in which our ontological hope is fulfilled by something it itself could never bring forth. On earth the spiritual man dwells in hope, in what is not yet, but what is still to come; he is *in statu viae,* a pilgrim on his way. And that he may reach hope's fulfillment, he must die; all his life he must die in order to be. Such is the light, Landsberg concludes, the mystics give us who do not possess their experimental knowledge of man's destiny. With a chaste "we" veiling his own striving, he ends: "Thus we try to understand, thus we strive for our ultimate existence. *O mortis profunditas,* O deep of death!" [140]

If to be an heir of Abraham is more than to be one of many veins through which the blood of a great stream is driven, if it is freely to accept the spiritual patrimony of Israel, then Landsberg was his true son, for he is a Jew who is one inwardly.[141] In *The Experience of Death,* Landsberg lives the anguish of Job: "The days

253

of man are short, and the number of his months is with Thee. Thou hast appointed his bounds which cannot be passed." [1] Yet even more does he voice the hope of which Israel, encircled by pagan despair, was so long the sole champion. He echoes what Isaias spoke to that people of hope and to all men: "They that hope in the Lord shall renew their strength. They shall take wings as eagles; they shall run and not be weary; they shall walk and not faint." [143]

En Route

Landsberg died so young that the little book, *The Experience of Death,* was to be his greatest work. Loving the world, life and man with the heart of a Christian, he hated Hitler's attempt to turn life into a graveyard. In 1939, soon after the invasion of Poland, he entered the battle against Hitler, in obedience to what he had taught was every man's—in particular the philosopher's— duty: to do his part in building the human city that man may dwell in justice, and to engage himself in its warfare against its adversary. Though propaganda was utterly foreign to his make-up, he put himself at the service of the French government and worked on the broadcasts its Center of Information sent daily to Germany. In May 1940, however, when her defeat left France aghast and unable to tell friend from foe, all aliens were interned, men and women, Landsberg and his wife, in separate camps. Torn from her husband and from what had become their home in exile, staggering under the terror Hitler's onrolling armies cast ahead— a terror added to the many buffets of the years just past—Madeleine Landsberg suffered a breakdown and was placed in a hospital. Several weeks later, while the Germans were literally at the door of the French internment camp, Paul Landsberg, with some fellow prisoners, escaped over a wall. On a bicycle, he traveled through the Occupied Zone, seeking contact with the slowly rising Resistance and searching for his wife, till at last he found her in a sanitarium in the South of France. Friends in the United States, among them Jacques Maritain, Gouverneur Paulding and Kurt Wolff, wished to secure for him a professorship at one of our universities, but Landsberg decided that his place was by his wife and in the country of his adoption, whose sufferings he wanted to share. So he stayed, under an assumed name, in Pau in the Lower Pyrenees, not wanting to leave his wife in her illness.

254   *Paul Landsberg*

though knowing torture and death to be his only prospect were the Gestapo ever to discover his identity, while she, as a Gentile, was likely to go unharmed.

The darkness which for a time clouded the mind of Madeleine Landsberg was only a shred of the black night that then fell over one country after another. Like an enormous pall, Hitler's conquests lay heavy on all of Europe, burying forever, it seemed, true human life. Yet in this apparently complete triumph of evil, Landsberg kept hope, the anchor of the soul, sure and firm, reaching that sanctuary beyond the veil which Jesus Christ, our Escort, has already entered.[144] This anchorage, this strength, he found in prayer—he once said: "Never will I forget the old nurse of my childhood who taught me to pray." [145] Pouring his soul's suffering into a quartet of poems, "To Christ," he prayed in one of them:

With my hand in the hand of Thy goodness I have walked my life.
The sweet strength of Thy blessing hath filled my cup.
Am I to think Thy wondrous power frail illusion?
Am I to call the coming of Thy love a lie?

Unsolaced the present lies before me,
And the future's woe, adrift from hope.
Still is Thy patient love my governor,
Still over life and death the lord.

I dread to stand again before Thee unsonly, unresigned;
But begging, as I must, this single favor,
I cannot lie—still will I pray:
Lord, let the night of the world around us pass!

The quartet was written early in 1941, in the quiet winter that followed the collapse of France, when her downfall was felt in all its gloom. It is with this blackness before him, hiding Christ, as it were, that Landsberg in another of the four poems begs God's pity, begs that in death he may fully find Him, sure that "from out the mystery truth beckons, our final gladness calls." In yet another poem he cries: "Shield me in the long hours of impatient waiting, that each new turn may be turned into hope for union." And he calls on Christ, *liebstes Licht*, dearest Light of his soul:

255

Thy beauty, with its sword-sharp edge,
Hath halved me wholly, so that but with Thee,
Thou Two-in-One, I can be whole.

This, his prayer, led Landsberg to a fuller commitment to Christ —how full, he revealed in *The Moral Problem of Suicide*, his last essay, written in either 1941 or 1942. Suicide was not only a theoretical problem to him, but an existential, for knowing well the Nazi perversion, which was not content to slay its victim but sought first to dehumanize him, he was often tempted by the thought of taking poison should the Gestapo ever lay hands on him. Thus he found many of the usual arguments against suicide not entirely convincing, at least not in the hour of trial, but there was one argument that stood supreme and silenced all temptation: Christ's example. "To understand why Christianity opposes suicide, one must recall the fundamental character of the Christian life, which, in all its forms, endeavors to follow Jesus Christ. This effort demands a radical conversion of man's natural attitude, above all toward suffering, for by nature he has a horror of suffering and a yearning for happiness. If a man kills himself, it is almost always to escape the suffering of this life for an unknown happiness or calm. In his heart he says: Whatever happens, I want to go elsewhere, I do not want to endure this meaningless suffering which surpasses my strength. It is here that the Christian spirit intervenes with its extreme paradox—yes, to live *and* to suffer! You must not be astonished that you suffer. If happiness were the meaning of this life, suffering would indeed be revolting and unbearable. It appears in an altogether different light, however, if life is a purification, an advance toward a transcendent goal, and if its meaning manifests itself precisely in suffering and is realized by it." [146]

"To one who suffers and is tempted to kill himself, we can say but one thing: Recall what Christ suffered, and what the martyrs. Like them, you must carry your cross. Your suffering will not cease, but by an unknown force, coming forth from the center of divine love, the cross of suffering will become sweet. You must not kill yourself, for you must not throw off your cross. You are in need of it. Ask your conscience whether you are really innocent. You will discover that though you may be innocent of the things with which the world reproaches you, you are guilty in a thousand

256   *Paul Landsberg*

other ways. You are a sinner. If Christ, the Innocent, suffered for others, and, in the words of Pascal, shed a drop of His blood for you, even you, what could give you, a sinner, the right to refuse suffering? . . . [The way to inner freedom is] loving adherence to God's will. The Christian may prefer life to death, or, it may be, death to life, yet he must prefer absolutely God's will to his own. . . . God alone may set the measure of our suffering. . . . By labor and suffering Christ leads us to the light." [147]

With his resolve to follow Christ and to commit himself to Him wholly, Landsberg's attitude toward the Church too became more definite. Many who knew him well, even before his had ripened into a fuller Christian life, to this day find it hard to believe that he was not a member of the Church. As often as he joined in religious discussions among men of varying views, his own stand was unwaveringly orthodox; so sound was it that one of his friends of the 1930s says that he was stunned when he heard that Landsberg was not a Catholic. Through innumerable books and through the many priests he knew, the Church spoke; thus it was she who had awakened and tended his faith. Not only did Landsberg make first St. Thomas, then St. Augustine and St. Teresa his spiritual guides; for long periods he attended holy Mass regularly. In 1938, for instance, while staying in a small Savoyan village, he sang with the people on Sundays the *Kyrie* and *Gloria,* the *Credo, Sanctus,* and *Agnus Dei.* He loved the liturgy of the Church; her Latin was his spiritual mother tongue, of which one of his diary notes says: "Latin: language of imperative counsel, of prayer that strikes your innermost will and your true need." And yet, though his mind and heart had entered the Church, his will, as if paralyzed, for long remained without. In 1935, after a visit from a former colleague at the University of Bonn, the Church historian Monsignor Wilhelm Neuss, he remarked in his journal: "This noon Neuss' departure. A touch of melancholy. These dear friends are sad when bidding farewell, for one thing because they find their prayers still unanswered."

The few times in the thirties when he was confronted with the question why he was not a Catholic, Landsberg replied that he would become a Catholic when the Church became Catholic, meaning when she should reembrace all those who had separated from her. As he did to the human person, so he applied to the

Church his defective concept of *Werdesein,* "becoming-being." The Church's existence is indeed at once being and becoming; she brings, and must bring, to ever fuller realization the catholicity she manifested on the first Pentecost, when those who lived in Jerusalem and those who had their homes elsewhere, when Jews and proselytes, from Mesopotamia and Cappadocia, from Egypt and Rome, from every country under the sun—when all who opened their hearts to love heard the apostles tell the *magnalia Dei,* the great works of God, each in his native tongue.[148] But whoever understands "being-and-becoming" in this way is immediately aware of his own obligation to enter the Church. The moment he grasps that she is the spiritual universe, where all men and the wealth God gave them are to be gathered together; that she is the great chorus whose song is always perfect, because it is Christ's, but which, to be complete, calls for every voice—he cannot keep himself aloof. On her way to God, growing toward "the mature measure of the fullness of Christ," [149] to perfect manhood, her body must be nourished with all the elements of human nature, with many men of many ages and nations and cultures. All of us are called to be both stones and masons of the Church; "the workmen of God we are, and to this day, the temple of God is being built." [150] Who remains outside the Church, be it for what seems the best of motives, leaves his share of the work undone, just as he who knows schism, heresy, and sin to be the wounds of the Church widens them, instead of nursing them, when because of them he shuns her.

To be a Catholic is, according to St. Augustine, to stand *in communione orbis terrarum,* to be in communion with the globe of the earth, with all the peoples blessed in the Seed of Abraham, who is Christ.[151] For the Church was all peoples when she was but a little flock, the sphere when still a seed; even when, as today, the Church is a minority, she is the majority still—spiritually, she is the whole. But the Landsberg of the thirties, in his concept of *Werdesein,* stressed becoming at the expense of being, and so thought the Church Catholic only in the making. Yet this was not his final, settled conviction; it did but translate his own unrest. As one friend saw it, the dissonance between Landsberg's enormous frame, his rosy face, like that of a happy child, and his restless, hunted glance, his pinched lips, the uneasy set of his shoulders, betrayed an inner tension, at once a sturdy mind and a tender, anguished heart.[152]

There came a time when Landsberg moved ever closer to the Church, seeing himself as a Catholic in the making. Madeleine Landsberg tells that he understood his own spiritual existence as *Werdesein* toward the Church, as being *en route* toward her, as an advance toward the great "We" of faith and love; and that in 1941, after the religious experience which is crystallized in the four poems "To Christ," he determined to knock at her door. As soon as the war was over and his mind free, so that he could prepare himself with the care and warmth his earnestness demanded, he planned to take extensive instructions with the French thinker Père Gaston Fessard, S.J., and with the German theologian Romano Guardini. At the Benedictine abbey of Hautecombe, he hoped to be washed by the saving waters, in conditional baptism, and there become a member of Christ's Mystical Body.

But Landsberg was not to know the end of the war. Although as early as 1941 many people in Pau had learned his identity, a miracle seemed to disguise him from the enemy. At the beginning of 1943, however, what was bound to happen happened. Warned that the Gestapo was about to seize him, he left his lodgings that evening to take the last train, but arrived at the station too late. He was imprudent enough to return to his hotel, and the next day at dawn, February 23, as he was leaving again for the railroad station, he was arrested. Contrary to all expectation, his true name remained unknown to his jailors; it was as an Alsatian suspected of hostility to Nazism that he was imprisoned, first in France, and finally, that autumn, at Oranienburg in Germany.

In this notorious concentration camp, Landsberg was a center of fortitude. *Jamais il ne douta,* Emmanuel Mounier could write, having listened to survivors of Oranienburg; never did he doubt nor lose hope. Or as another friend summed up the witness of Landsberg's fellow prisoners: "Not for a moment did he abandon determination, goodness, faith." [153] Yet life was harder for him, with his tall, untrained body, than it was for many others; and when his comrades, realizing his high spiritual gifts and poor health, affectionately arranged to do his assigned labor for him and thus free him for intellectual work, his candor could not conceal his "idleness" from the guards. Nor could he feign submission when he felt revolt; hence he was beaten, taunted, chased from place to place, till one day he was taken to the infirmary emaciated and exhausted. Though his inner courage never failed his body broke, and he died on April 2, 1944.[154]

April 2, 1944, was Palm Sunday, when the Church prays: "O God to love Thee and hold Thee dear is the just life; multiply in us the gifts of Thine ineffable grace. By Thy Son's death Thou has given us hope for the things in which we believe; through Him risen grant us to reach our journey's end." On Palm Sunday she greets Him in whom we are "victorious over the empire of death": "O King of Israel, hosanna in high heaven." [155]

Four years later, at a memorial celebration for Paul Landsberg held by the University of Bonn at the burial place of his family Monsignor Wilhelm Neuss said: "The first to speak here, I speak above all as a priest. For there is no doubt that if Paul Landsberg had been saved through the dread-filled years of persecution, if he had been able to rebuild his life on firm ground, that then, one day—many years from now, we may assume—at the hour of his going home, there is no doubt that a Catholic priest would have stood by his grave and accompanied him to everlasting rest with the prayers of the Church." [156] And these prayers of hers resound with the Voice of hope: "I am the Resurrection and the Life. He who believes in Me, even if he die, shall live, and whoever lives and believes in Me, shall never die." [157]

Max Picard

POET OF THE HUMAN FACE

"I AM AN ARCHREACTIONARY, AND ALWAYS HAVE BEEN," MAX Picard closed a letter which began: "I'm glad you liked Graham Greene's *The Labyrinthine Ways,* the novel about the whiskey priest—I didn't expect that you'd approve of it. The marvelous thing about it is that in spite of his sins, the priest remains a priest. . . . Nowadays, when nothing is valid that transcends calculation, how important it is to show people that amid all downfall and decay, even their own, the priest remains. . . . But what scares me is this: Today, the religious substance of people has shrunk so small that every least action of a priest leaps to the eye. In the Middle Ages, when, it is said, the priests sometimes led loose lives, men's religious substance was so great, so weighty, that a priest's single actions were not so visible. That is not to say that they were concealed, rather that the universal religious reality was so strong that the sins of priests were drowned and dissolved in it. . . . It is nonsense to reproach the Church for the abuses of the Middle Ages, for it is only to us miserable wretches, with our almost withered religious substance, that these 'immoral' petrifactions are visible—no proof that the medieval Church was in a bad way, but that we are in a bad way." [1]

"I am an archreactionary"—this is the challenge of an angry man, of a "prophet turned fool." [2] For must not a man of the spirit be wrathful when he sees man wasting his substance, existing at his self's periphery, living as if his flesh were the carriage of a zero and not of a soul? Max Picard is angry because he knows that today man is at stake, because he cherishes man's substance and self, the soul which makes him kin to God. His is no abstract, impersonal sympathy for abstract man, but reverence and gratitude for real men, wherever he finds them. He speaks with admiration of a village confectioner whom he likes to watch at work and whose sherbets' praise is likely to be among his first words to a guest— "He uses nothing but natural ingredients, he has respect for his God-given material," he may say. And with warmth he tells of his parish priest that he is always good and gentle, so that in his presence unbearable people become easily bearable, evil men sympathetic: "One can pluck his smile, as an apple from a tree."

There is nothing academic about Picard, nor about his criticism which can be sharp and vehement when he finds men of intellect leading other men astray. Karl Barth, he maintains, is "a pope without love," his theology is neither divine nor human, invoking God's tremendousness only to make Him remote, so that man is under pressure and strain and feels His existence no longer, or rather, feels it only as pressure—and this makes Barth's theology like Nazism. Of Thomas Mann, Picard says that he bears more responsibility for softening of the brain and hardening of the heart than those writers who came out for Hitler, for to explain Joseph psychoanalytically is more miserable than to explain the Jews racially. And Hilaire Belloc, who explains them sociologically, he accuses of serving anti-Semitism by his book on the Jews, though he reiterates that Belloc himself is no anti-Semite. Nevertheless, his demand that the Jews single themselves out as a nation within the nations asks of them, and of them only, that they take a clear position while public life as a whole remains unclear—a position sure to provoke antagonism. But the Jews are not a nation within the nations; it is their singularity that they cannot be encompassed within the usual categories. To ignore this, never once in the whole book to say that what is called the Jewish question is really a question asked of the Jews, a plea for their faith in Christ, and a question asked of the Christians, a plea that they love His kinsmen, is worse than anti-Semitism.[3]

"I am an archreactionary." Picard keeps the old hours of wake and sleep, rising before dawn for a long walk by the lake and seeking his bed not long after sunset. Clock and calendar disturb him little; indeed, "clock time is for him a ghost time," his friend Monsignor Karl Pfleger wrote on his sixtieth birthday, "a time false, external, empty, inorganic, inhuman. Hence he finds so many people inhuman, unreal and ghostlike, for their lives are a race with hour hand and minute hand. The element in which he lives is Bergson's *durée:* the duration the Creator gives His creatures that in it they may grow and ripen; time, but not as chase and haste, rather as a perfect whole, making possible man's unfolding; the drop of God's creative rest that is allotted to every being. That is how Picard's time looks—like rest, like quiet. 'I need quiet. That is my luxury. One I cannot give up,' he says. 'Food, even sleep, I could forego, but not quiet. I need quiet from the din of men and radios.' "[4]

Picard's own books are notable for this quiet and leisurely temper; in a meditative stroll, he walks around their topics, looking at them from every side. The history of the world in three hundred pages, with the rise of Christianity in five lines, is a horror to him. "One can put the philosophy of Plato into a pamphlet, but it will not be the philosophy of Plato, because every important thought needs time and space for its display. One can compress the life of a man, its significant events, into two days—yes, two days—but a man's few significant situations want around them many years, the full space of a whole life. One can reduce water to H_2O, but water is rain, mist over a lake, the hands of children paddling in a brook, the talk of women at a village well, and many, many things more." [5]

"I am an archreactionary," Picard says in the teeth of "progressive philosophers" and newspaper witlings, who prate of the "independent intellect" and the "fearless, unfettered, versatile, and critical mind." It is not by these that the world will be saved, he pleads, but by the rooted mind, by the traditional values, by the fetters of goodness, by truth—not a gadget to be reinvented in each decade—by faith—not a fashion to be doffed and donned at the beck of the tyrant opinion. At home in the world of the God who is Beginning and End, he is a stranger in that of modern man for whom God is at best a working hypothesis, of the man who graciously admits: "Perhaps He is," when all the while he himself exists and is held in being by God's "Be!" Of Picard, there holds what the German poet Matthias Claudius said of the fathers of old, Abraham, Isaac, Jacob and Joseph: "For them, the fear of God was not a footman on the rear of the carriage, but at once coachman and lord." [6]

It holds too of the men of whom Picard wrote in his *Expressionistic Peasant Painting* (1919), a book bearing as motto these same words of Matthias Claudius and containing twenty-four reproductions of primitive paintings on the back of glass, among them of the Blessed Trinity, the Madonna and Child, the Magi, the Flight into Egypt, the Baptism of Christ, the Last Supper, Abraham's Sacrifice, St. Martin, St. George and the Dragon. In his few pages of comment, Picard tells how their artists differ from the modern expressionist who, weighed down by today's chaotic mass of knowledge, by a vastness of bits and ends, calls God in (if at all) as a last resort, that he may store it with Him; God must come to relieve him of his burden, and man would be glad if He disappeared with it at once. This is our misery: We know everything, we conjecture everything, we are everywhere, we have been everywhere, but our hearts are empty, God is not in them; the most He can be is a counterweight to knowledge. Lacking the immediate experience of God, the modern artist may indeed arrive at Him, but the old peasant painter takes from Him his start.

These peasant artists are unaware of the connections of things with one another, Picard continues; they see each as if it had just been made by God and had not yet met any other, as if it did not yet fit into the current of things, as if it could not yet move or react. In all their paintings, limbs are distorted and fingers miss their mark, for the world in which they will be able to move is yet to be created. Hence the space around things is still, with a stillness in which God is heard louder when He speaks loudly and lower when He speaks low. Things are connected with God and with God only, and they can find their way to one another only through Him—without Him, this world of isolations would fall apart. So these primitive artists give God no rest, but never was a world so peaceful as this, in which God is given no peace. They put Him everywhere, like lamps in the night, so that the eye can leap from light to light through the darkness; no harm can befall one, because everywhere is the divine; the novel is not needed, because always there is the same divine.[7] Where there is this joyful sameness of God, there is no need for the novel—this, Picard's avowal in 1919, is one with his confession of thirty years later: "I am an archreactionary," a oneness bespeaking the continuity of his inner life.

Max Picard was born on June 5, 1888, in Schopfheim in Germany's Black Forest, a few miles from his ancestral Switzerland, where his family had dwelt since the early seventeenth century, when they migrated to Canton Aargau from France. Happy to be of one of the few old Jewish families in Switzerland, Picard has in his home a portrait of his maternal great-grandfather, Abraham Ris, who had been Chief Rabbi of Lengnau. And he speaks with pride of his great-uncle, who was the first Swiss Jew to study the humanities and to teach Latin in a *Gymnasium*. Picard himself studied medicine, and for a year after receiving his degree was assistant at the University Hospital at Heidelberg. Though his intuitive gifts made him a diagnostician of unusual promise, he abandoned his medical career because he found the mechanistic approach of his day utterly alien, and for a short time he attended philosophical courses. It was thus that he was freed for the greater task: to diagnose the present ailment and point to its only cure.

Picard's first book was a small collection of aphorisms, *The Bourgeois* (1914), and his second a study in art, *The End of Impressionism* (1916). His work on old peasant painting appeared in 1919, and a year later *The Last Man,* a nightmarish vision of man, appendix to the machine. At about this time, Picard moved to Lake Lugano, in the hope of bettering his wife's health, and he has lived there ever since, at the moment in the little village of Caslano, with its warm sun and transparent skies. Though he is now long a widower, the guest in his home feels both the absence and the presence of his wife. One of his books, *The Human Face,* is dedicated to Margarethe Picard, the same book that bears the motto:

> *The Wain still travels heaven,*
> *But there is one wheel broken,*
> *And in the night's sadness there is one star put out.*

> *Your words your voice brings through to me no longer*
> *So that my heart was lost in the anguish of the world.*

> *And now the sea-wind sighs over the islands*
> *Whence my lonely soul looks for the Morning Star*
> *That He may come to it.*[8]

Does this tell of Picard's grief for his wife, or does it tell also his sorrow at being almost alone in a lost humanity? This sorrow has been great, but a heart of grace can never be without the radiance of the Alleluia. In a letter to André Gide on December 10, 1921, Rainer Maria Rilke described Picard as "the simplest of men, the most candid I know, the complete opposite of a *littérateur;* perhaps one ought not even call him a writer. He is a man who suffers, and whose suffering is of a terrifying precision. He has the saintly timidity of those whose whole courage is forever engaged in a great inner combat." [9] When, years later, Picard saw these lines in print, he said: "That's very beautiful, but it's completely wrong, for in it suffering is extolled as the highest, but there is something higher than suffering—mirth, the one reaped in the Fall, the other sown in paradise." [10]

The Human Face

Picard's visions are not of high heaven, but of heaven and of hell on earth. What every man could see, if only he dared, if he were not afraid of the wonders and demands of love, Picard sees, because his eyes rest lovingly on the things Love created, looked on and found good, and in finding them good, filled them afresh with goodness. In every eye innocent and undulled there is something of the power of this gaze, luminously manifest in Picard's *The Human Face*. "Since Dante there is hell, since Bernanos there is Satan—well, since Picard there is the human face," said one of the critics.[11]

Before Picard, physiognomy was a doubtful science, but when his book appeared in 1929, it gave physiognomy a philosophical, even theological dignity: "The little field of the human countenance becomes for him the arena of a divine comedy." [12] Those who dismiss as fairy tales all that is not "scientific," who smile to hear that "the Lord God walked in the garden in the cool of the day," [13] belittling with witless obstinacy the tremendous reality of God's meeting man, which must garb itself in metaphor—these will not understand him or his language, with its Hebrew rhythm, simple, slow-paced, grave. When Abraham was bid sever every tie to the oldness of idolatry and go forth to the newness of life, he was told to leave his country, and his kinsmen, and his father's house; here and elsewhere Scripture heaps expressions one on the other, its liberality a sign of God's liberality, its "wastefulness" a sign of unhurried contemplation, of the breath of eternity. Picard's language has this Scriptural quality: in every chapter finding new reasons to praise the staggering truth that the littleness of man can mirror God's majesty, like a lover never weary of repeating his one theme, he hymns the Sculptor of the human face. His book is a poetic commentary on the 27th verse in the first chapter of Genesis: "God created man in His image; in the image of God He created him." [14]

When we look at a human face, Picard says, our whole being is struck, for it is an appeal calling and holding the soul together.

Therein lies the joy, that before a human face we ourselves become one and entire again, and the double delight is that we feel our wholeness before God's image, the face of man; in the inscrutable human countenance, the Unsearchable shows Himself. If God, whose voice spoke in the thunder, whose eyes flashed from the burning bush, were to pursue man as eternal thunder, as everlasting flame, terror would long ago have driven man to hide in the bowels of the earth. But God gentled His approach, left behind His power, made mild His image and entered man's figure and face, entered it humanly, so to speak, as a friend enters the house of a friend, without stir, hardly knocking at the door. It is a tempered image, says Picard, it is the mildness of God, that appears in the face of man.[15]

As the planets circle about the sun and in circling are formed, so there are human faces which, ever circling around God, are formed after His eternal Archetype. And as there are moons around the planets, so there are about the great human faces lesser faces, molded after them. But in all their midst there is always God. Thus God is in every face, and He looks out of one on His image in another, so that it is the glance of the Creator that unites the two faces, filling the space between them, filling it with love. Today God is expelled from the space between His creatures; there is a gap between them, for God is no longer between them. Where God had dwelt, now man has intruded, thrusting himself everywhere, driving creatures apart, condemning them to loneliness. With man always between them, they are separated, and they corrupt.[16]

These are the marks of God's likeness: highness, confidence, reserve, peace, and clarity. The human face that knows itself created in God's image is humble, for it cannot comprehend the privilege that it alone among all creatures should bear this likeness. But because it is given this privilege, it has dignity as well—highness, not haughtiness, augustness, not arrogance. So it was, at least formerly. Not that there was never pride in the faces of men, Picard continues, but it was a dangerous and daring thing to put one's own haughtiness in the place of God's highness. Today, however when the grandeur of likeness is often banished, what daring is needed to put conceit in its empty place? A face must be loud today to be noticed at all.[17]

268 *Max Picard*

Confidence there is in a face that has kept the firstness of the day it was made. When in death, such a face returns for the last time to its Creator, it grows great, greater even than it was in life; it seeks to expand, that eternity may have room to build into it the last, the ultimate image. But in our age, faces sometimes fall apart at the touch of eternity, as does a specter when touched by holy reality. Again, what marks the true face is *ein schoene Scheu*, beautiful reserve, and at the same time, openness. With eyelids cast down, the likeness of God hesitates to let the eyes' light flood over it; suddenly it realizes that it, God's likeness, must shine more brightly than all other creatures—then the eye dares raise itself. Because there is shyness there is also silence, as if all the words had already been spoken by Another, a Greater; and the face listens into the silence for their echoes. It is for the sake of this silence that man again and again represents the human face in stone, for there, in the stillness of stone, it is shrouded by the air of God's silence. Peace dwells in the human face, and movement too; but the movement does not break the quiet—it is the quiet that breathes. Like God, whom it mirrors, the human face owns clarity and mystery; there is no fog to hold back the rays that leap forth from it into the world. Today, however, Picard laments, mystery has vanished from the face; where there was mystery there is now cloudiness, and what was once clear is now indiscreet.[18]

High, noble, quiet, silent, clear—that the human face is thus, that it is a likeness, we have God to thank.

Ich danke Gott, und freue mich
Wie's Kind zur Weihnachtgabe,
Dass ich bin, bin! Und dass ich dich,
Schoen Menschlich Antlitz! habe.[19]

With a tongue sublimely simple, Matthias Claudius opens his "Daily to Sing": "I give thanks to God and I delight, like a child on Christmas Day, that I am, am! And that I have thee, human face so beautiful!" The great Godhead was humble enough to rest there, to make Itself small for the sake of the small. When the human saw before it the godly so small, it smiled, and its smile grew into a tear, and seeing itself in the mirror of this tear, the human grew. So also grew the divine, until it was as great as it was before. Then the divine smiled, the divine and the human together in the human face, and humor was born. Humor is nothing else than this: that the small in the face of man does not remain alone and become furtive and malevolent, but joins with the great. Today, when one finds greatness in a face, it seldom shares its place with the small, leaving the great like a textbook, pedantic, humorless.[20]

When God's image is in ruins, when it falls apart in a face, the demons move in. Still, all men are God's property and God is the possession of all men; His likeness belongs to every countenance and not only to those in which it can be seen. Those in whom it is resplendent bear it not for themselves alone but also for the others; like a holy banner in procession, they carry God's image. But no face stands as a mere reminder of what was once in all faces; even the last human face is a sign of what is and always will be. No matter how much effaced from the face of man God's likeness is, He claims him; "On the plane of earth," says Picard, "man is raised upright, as a question mark, as the question mark of God, who asks man: Adam, where art thou?" [21]

Because man's face is God's image, it is not just a single plane, stuck up on the front of a skull; not just a plane anybody could stick up in passing and which anyone could just as easily pull down again. God's image is to be with man forever and securely. Man's face, therefore, has an architecture; it is a body, Picard says, built up of three planes—the brow, the fore planes of the cheeks, and their side planes. Being so ordered, terraced, as it were, the face does not receive its impressions all at once, as a shock, but spreads them slowly and evenly, sifts them. Thus all things, being so received, are happy to be ordered once more in the face and to be watched over. The three planes are at once distinct and united: when a word is spoken, it is as if a pebble were tossed into a lake, forming ripples which grow wider and wider until they encounter the waves that move downward from the cheeks toward the mouth. These two waves flow toward one another, not hitting but gently meeting; just so, in all its parts, the human face is marked by give-and-take.[22]

Man has a front face and a profile. Seen from the front, his face is static, at rest; in profile it is dynamic and at work. Perhaps it was on the front of man's face that the eye of God rested when man, just created, stood before Him. God's glance resting there filled it with rest; hence in the front face, the world of man is simply there, without commission to go forth into the world outside; in the profile, the world of man bursts forth, moves, is on the march—in the saint, for one, the profile strains toward eternity, moves toward God. And since, for all the saints, the road into the world is the same, the road to God, their profiles seem alike. In the Church of San Zeno in Verona, twelve apostles stand on the balustrade of the choir; so strikingly do they differ, when seen from the front, that here, as never before, the spectator realizes that each one is unique, that they are *twelve*. But when viewing them from the side, he is startled and glad, for in profile they resemble one another, all traveling in the same direction, toward God, the One, the Self-Same. Their profiles are like strips laid side by side, to make a highway on which they, and also we, journey to the divine End. In the paintings of the old masters, we see the saints so clearly separated that we shudder and ask how they can reach one another, until all at once we see the gilded background, burned ruddy in the divine fire, and know that the saints all came out of this one golden curtain which veils the throne of God, while behind it God waits. The saints, Picard declares, are God's ambassadors to earth, *die Kundschafter der Ewigkeit,* the harbingers of eternity.[23]

The human face is one, it lives by its whole being, it is more than its parts; therefore it is impossible, Picard stresses, to judge a single element by itself. A hooked nose, for instance, on the face of a miser, may well mark his avarice, but the same nose may be on another face and its owner not be covetous at all, for each feature receives its meaning not only from its own form but from the whole of the face. As God, everywhere present, is visible nowhere, so the soul is everywhere in the face but cannot be fixed to any one feature. One may think: There, right there! at the corner of the mouth, resides loveliness. One looks closer and it has slipped away to the corner of the eye; one looks again and loveliness has fled to a dimple in the cheek. Sometimes there is a face so perfect as a whole and, at the same time, in all its parts—the mouth, the nose, the eyes—that each part is like an entire world and the whole face the world's abundance. What fullness! he exults. What happy abundance! [24]

For it is not only God whom the human face proclaims—the whole creation is written into it, not carved into it with a chisel but breathed upon it like dew. So much is the design of the world in every face, Picard thinks, that from it one could rebuild the world were the world destroyed. The human face is its inventory. The sky is in man; as the vault of heaven arches over the earth, so man's skull crowns his figure. Beautifully arched is the firmament of man's frame, as if the great firmament above had learned to arch from this model. Sometimes when one sees from afar a man in the fields under the sky, it is as if the greater vault lowered itself upon the lesser, to rest there; but then, when the man moves, the sky rises again and spreads, a mighty bow, more lofty than before. And the sun is in the human face. There are foreheads so clear that the sun seems to have touched them, at each rising, with the curve of its going. There are eyes filled with the light of day, as if they shone with the sun together in a common sky; at times they stand still together for a moment—it is the noon of eternity. And evening may come over the face, with its moon of melancholy. The stars too may trace their course in the human face, the stars of which Picard says with Matthias Claudius that a clear night tells us that they "cannot be cold and idle spectators, but are kinsmen of the earth, friends of the house." [25] The earth is pictured in man, whose body is a piece of wandering earth, a little hill; flowers may blossom in his countenance, and the flowers of the earth look up to the flowers of the face. The forest's solitude, the repose of trees, the flow of rivers, the sea—all the wide universe is there, having there its encounter with the wideness of God. Thus creation exists twofold: once outside and once within man, as an image, and so the Lord is twice with His handiwork, twice with His world. [26]

Only because in the days of creation God Himself was near to a human face can one human face be neighbor to another. When they truly bow to each other, it seems as if it were the first of bows, as if God sent down again His first bow to man. And this bow is passed from one face to another till all men bow to one another and all together bow to God. Again, when two faces look upon each other, there is a silence, rising not from earth but from eternity. For an instant time stands still, and all the hours that are hidden away in time begin to strike together. Then marvelously, their tones add up to silence, and in this loud silence of the hours, eternity enters in. This is the way time beckons to eternity. Hence when two human faces look upon each other, eternity is between them and looks on both.[27]

With the eyes of a seer, a poet, Picard looks on the faces of Julius Caesar, Hoelderlin, Dostoyevski, Eleonora Duse, and many others, whose pictures are included in *The Human Face;* he looks on the faces of young and old, of man and woman, of the captain of industry, the laborer, the man who is poor; and he discourses on the influence of landscape, race, and profession. Every face, he says, can change, from good to bad and, astonishingly, from bad to good. Today, however, we have given up hope for this transformation; hence scientists dare to imprison men in types, and people take kindly to it, for they wish to be guarded from surprise. But surprise can break even through the iron bars of typology, surprise from God or from the human heart. For the heart is near God, and therefore can it change, suddenly and all at once, itself and others. A man may be evil, confirmed in evil, but one beat of a heart may shake his very bones and transform him. So man need never despair. "No one can go so far astray," Picard quotes Kierkegaard, "that he cannot find again his way to Thee—Thou, who art not only like a spring which lets itself be found; Thou, who art like a spring which seeks the thirsty, the erring. Never was there heard of such a spring." [28]

Reproach of the present age for its emptiness runs through *The Human Face,* but at the end, in the spirit of the mercy-daring Abraham, who pleaded for Sodom and Gomorrha, Picard touches on the mystery of pity. He tells the Jewish legend that the world rests, as on pillars, on thirty-six just men, who are unknown, even to one another, even to themselves; and he adds his own belief that the faces of men rest on thirty-six just faces. No one sees them, they do not see one another, they do not see themselves—but God sees them. Yet there need not be thirty-six, he says; one may be enough. When God's eye moves from the other faces to this one, all the faces are re-bound to the eternal order by the arc of His gaze. And even if it could happen, Picard continues, that God's gaze no longer found the one but found emptiness in his place, even if God's gaze had to return to Himself, then this and just this, that God sees Himself, would be the salvation of all the faces of men.[29]

273

When Picard wrote this epilogue, he was not yet a Christian, but a true Jew is a Christian unborn and thus his words may at times tell more than he himself knows. No one man—merely man, however just—could ransom his fellows; Abraham stopped his pleading with: "What if ten should be found there?" [30] But at the same time, Picard's words were truer than he knew, for we are indeed saved by the loving regard of the Lord resting on the face of the One who is just, who, as His perfect Image, could say: "Philip, who sees Me sees the Father." [31] In seeing Him God sees Himself, and looking up to Him, we see the face of Love—*Ta face est ma seule patrie*, "Thy face is my only home," said St. Thérèse[32] —the face which restores our own.

The Flight from God

With the divine likeness vanished, the dominant face today is the cinema face, and the motion picture the symbol of the world we live in. Picard's *The Flight from God* (1934) is given to a description of the screen of unreality, of racing shadows, that the world has become. The world of faith in ruins, a hostile world has set itself up, the world of escape, and in it all things exist in terms of flight. At all times has man fled from God, Picard tells us, but formerly, when the very air was faith, whatever flight there was took place within man; it was by an act of choice that the individual loosed himself from the all-surrounding world of faith, and if he would flee, he himself had to initiate his flight. Today, however, faith is the exception, flight the rule, and the individual above all a fugitive. He who believes must daily make the decision of faith against the world outside, severing himself from the universal flight, for to live and to flee now seem to be the same. So normal, so independent has the flight become that we no longer ask: Why do we flee? that we forget we flee from God.[33]

The strife, the inner hither-and-thither, the dilemma: Should I flee or should I not? which in an age of faith racks one or the other man, or even a thousand men, has become an outer hither-and-thither, engulfing everyone. Because it is so general, it is no longer seen as flight from God. Flight has become a thing, having its own laws, a state knowing no respite, no alternation between flight and nonflight, a monster, and man is its employee. Like an avalanche, it drags with it every human sphere; like the air, it is ever-present, so that the scripture of this world can say: In the begin-

274   *Max Picard*

ning there was the flight. When faith is sovereign, a man is born to realize himself in and by faith, and his birth is the beginning of fulfillment; but when flight has ousted faith, birth marks the end of realization—it is but the push-off into flight; man is born not to be man but to be a movie star. The screen actor is the hero, and nowhere is flight so explicit, so unashamed, as in the motion picture. The figures on the screen exist only for the flight. As a man in haste casts away his baggage, they have cast away their bodies. If ever they seem to stand still for an instant, anxiously looking back as though they were followed, it is but an act, for who could catch such phantoms? [34]

In the world of faith, the world of permanence, man need not be prepared for the many things that might be, but only for the One who is. Nowadays, with man in flight and so not knowing what he may meet, man and things are fitted not only for the places where they are, Picard grieves, but for every place and every occasion; a thing is not a real thing but a bundle of possibilities wrapped up to look like a thing, and a man is not where he is seen to be—what is there is merely the place from which he flees. In this world of possibility, one thing produces another, not for the sake of that other thing but for the sake of a new possibility. Indeed, it produces that other thing with a deliberate flaw, in order that yet a third thing, not possessing that flaw, will have to follow; but it in turn will have its own deficiency, and hence there will always be a reason for letting one thing follow on another. The defective, the unfinished, is no longer an incentive for man to complete and perfect a thing, serving him instead as a mere starting point for a new variation, for an infinite series of possibilities. He will not even try which of the possibilities is the best: the mere state of possibility is enough. In fact, he shuns certitude, for were there even one thing certain, the sureness of that one thing would explode the whole world of possibility. So the world of flight has to be filled up with possibilities, that there may be no room for certitude.[35]

"Impossible" has been expunged from today's dictionary; all that it admits is the "not-yet-possible." To create life, to abolish all misery and even to do away with death, are no longer out of man's reach—"all in the world of tomorrow"—that is the byword. Always escaping, clinging to nothing, the man of flight is frivolous,

Picard accuses, an opportunist and eclectic, without a stable measure. The tenses are no longer ordered for him, for in each possibility are mingled past, present, and future. Hence there can be no guilt or contrition in his world, no truth, no lie, no faith, no death. Faith, for instance, is certitude, and where everything is only possible, one cannot believe. Nothing is unexpected, therefore the poetry of things is absent. In the world of flight, God too is degraded to a possibility—and this is less than an impossibility. When, in the world of faith, a man says: God is not, his negation fades away before the affirmation, so much stronger, that God is, so that to be heard at all, a man has to shout: God is not, to shout stubbornly and without ceasing, like one in despair. Together with his *not*, he is often absorbed by the *is*, and it may even happen that his saying *not* is his death. But a man in flight lives on saying *possible*; he risks nothing, for his god, being but a possibility, cannot draw him into an abyss of majesty. When flight is the exception, everything would be impossible were God merely possible; but when all flees, all is possible by the very fact that God is no more than possible.[36]

All things have been made movable, adapted to the flight; they would be useless to the flight in the unyielding state of being, and so being has been exchanged for becoming. Now things count not because they are but because they have become. Religion, for instance, cannot be endured as a phenomenon unique and lasting, legitimate by its very existence; it has to be made the first stage of the evolution from religion to metaphysics, from metaphysics to positivism. For the man of the flight, religion is a primitive attempt to explain the secrets of the universe, which is followed by a philosophical interpretation and this in turn by science. But in all this, it does not matter to him what follows; it suffices that something follows, that there is change. Sociology too makes man limber for the flight, for it makes the sovereign spirit dependent on the places of its manifestation, on social strata. The one spirit is broken into bits, so that each social group can have its own special "spiritlet." And so the flight can go on, with motorized rapidity. On the flight, man likes to be radical, but his radicalism is of form, not of content; it is not to promote a cause but to serve a man, to make him visible amid the general murkiness. It propels him toward the margin, toward a "border situation," which gives him the illusion of adventure. But he forgets that he dares nothing, he risks nothing, for having already cast the great things aside, he has nothing to lose.[37]

Strange though it seems, Picard observes, the flight—which is a flight from God—tries to take on His attributes. So great has the flight become that it seems to have neither beginning nor end, nor any pause in which man could stand still and ask: Where did it come from? It is as if, with it, cause and existence are one. As the flight apes God's infinity, so also His omnipresence. In the world of faith, a man can only be either here or there, and any movement from one to the other is an event, because he encounters God's omnipresence in a new place; in the world of flight, a man is, of course, now here, now there, yet he is also neither here nor there but everywhere. He is both man, who is here, and ghost, who is everywhere, this man of flight, who copies God's omnipresence. And further, God is inscrutable, incalculable, and in this the flight seeks to mimic Him by suddenness. Unexpected inventions appear, new illnesses arise, sects spring up, new ideas explode, new schools of art burst forth—they come suddenly and disappear, and it is their suddenness, their jerk, that is sought after. God is incalculable because the moment of His choice, the moment in which He manifest Himself, is not of time but of eternity. In the world of fugitives, however, time is not and therefore eternity is not. Instead of the eternal instant, there is a mechanical jerk; instead of eternity, boredom.[38]

But in every man and in every thing, Picard continues, something remains that does not sell itself to the flight and so threatens it, because from this immovable something there can rise, at any moment, a halt, recollection, return. To make this immovable movable, to do away with its threat, ever new contrivances are invented—the passion of an inward man, for instance, which is the passion for the eternal, is used like a mechanical force: many men of flight observe the tremendous dynamism in Pascal, Kierkegaard, Dostoyevski, but they change the inner movement of these inward men to an outer, hooking themselves on to it as if it were a locomotive. While Dostoyevski, Kierkegaard, and Pascal let their passion move them toward God and were aglow only because of Him, the men of the flight make of this passion a mechanism to hurl them from one place to another. Those *died* of their passion; these *maneuver* with it. The apparatus of psychoanalysis

277

serves the same end: all phenomena are reduced to one source, Picard says, not because they spring from it, rather because they do *not* spring from it and hence recoil from it into a vortex—it is exactly this whirlpool, this turmoil, that is willed.[39]

Love above all else keeps man from making himself mobile for the flight. Who loves another looks at his beloved clearly and unhurriedly; he seeks to see if there be some spot he does not yet love. And love is patient, waiting until the beloved grows into love. But all this takes too much time in flight, too long for one on the wing. So, systematically, the world must be made loveless and all relationships be destroyed in which love can dwell. People are together only to flee together. The man of the flight empties marriage, friendship, and family till they are nothing but outward relations, till nothing can detain him there because there is no love. All he accepts of love is its jolt, the suddenness with which it bursts through, and this for the sake of mobility not toward the beloved but away from him, away in all directions. Primarily, love is expelled because the man of the flight fears that, were he to meet it, he might be reminded of the greatest Love, of God. His eyes might fall on Him and in His vastness find a spot he does not yet love, and so his flight would be not only hindered but impossible.[40]

Who flees from God, and knows that it is God from whom he flees, is ridden by anxiety. Never can he understand how the blast that tore him from God and flung him into the flight did not rip him asunder; he does not trust himself, cannot believe that he is still a complete being, one that holds together—in brief, he has anxiety. This anxiety is circumscribed and definite, because in the face of God's clarity, even anxiety becomes clear. Such a man carries anxiety always with him; having fled from God, he clings to it instead; it is for it that he has bartered away God. When he looks at something, he is not alone, for anxiety is with him; indeed, he must give it a part in everything, because he can no longer give God His part. As a traveler leaving his own country takes with him a clod of earth, so the fugitive wears anxiety, a constant reminder, says Picard, that he has fled from God.[41]

A man who has forgotten, however, that he fled from God, one who flees and does not know that he flees, much less from whom—

278   *Max Picard*

such a man does not have anxiety, anxiety has him, Picard exclaims; he is merely its appendage. This sort of anxiety orders man to stake out the whole space of night with lamps red, green, and blue, and where he cannot reach with his lamps, to stir up the darkness with searchlights. Like watchfires in the wilderness are these lamps and lights, like watchfires of anxiety, around which men keep themselves awake with noise and singing. Day and night are no longer the halves of waking and sleeping; they are one single plane, so that the day is no longer given to men that things may be in it, but only that they may be investigated; at night, the soul is no longer permitted to rest and in dreams to play with its images; even sleep is spied upon, and the dream is sent out as anxiety's spy.[42]

There is more anxiety today than man can contain; it smothers him, so that when God calls: Where is man? the only answer is the sullen silence of anxiety. Of course, Picard grants, anxiety is by no means unknown to the man of faith, but it does not stay with him; it arises when he is in danger, when unawares he has strayed a little from God. It serves him, a messenger calling him back to the Lord; on the flight, man is the slave of his anxiety, and hysteria his illness. Unable to endure waiting in the vast space of anxiety for the terrible to pounce, man often anticipates the attack and himself creates grief in his body and soul. Now, he thinks, I suffer; what more can happen to me? So he is happy and clings to his illness. He splits his personality, and is this not the most terrifying cause for anxiety: one man split into two, two personalities confronting one another—to whom do they belong? Whither can this lead but to madness? Indeed, many of the insane are like confidants of anxiety: they hear the words, they see the pictures it sends, they speak, and only anxiety understands them.[43]

Flight's End

When man does not escape into insanity, he often flees into evil in order to fill up the emptiness of his anxiety; he sins that anxiety be no longer a blank, that at least there be evil in it. The great peril is that even an outrage seems small compared with it, and man is content that sin is as nonexistent beside the hugeness of anxiety. But perhaps sin has waxed so great, Picard ventures, only to bring about God's own intervention, that He Himself may come to destroy anxiety and evil together. Perhaps anxiety has grown to such an immense mass so that man, if he would only be conscious of his freedom, could seize anxiety and throw it away from himself and from the whole world; or rather, that he be humble and that anxiety wither and fall away of itself. For the mere awareness that within him is a world of freedom which can conquer the world of anxiety may make him proud, but if he holds this awareness in humility, his anguish will become smaller and smaller, and die. Then the lights of the city will no longer be lamps of fear but lamps of expectation that God may come. The noise and singing of the night will no longer keep man awake frightened, but will remind him that God loves to appear suddenly and unnoticed, in the midst of unrest.[44]

But since the flight has not yet come to this standstill, Picard must return to its danger. His images of the flight chill the heart. Factories are built not to manufacture wares but for the sake of new factories; war demands and takes all things, so that it seems war came first, and man and front lines and war materials afterward. The word is unsouled, the word is dead, its place taken by the whistle, the signal, and all speech is monologue, for the eternal Listener is not there. Because He seems to be no longer among them, people crowd into the big city, the headquarters of flight. There the streets are like tubes into which men are sucked, and with them a few trees which stand frightened at the edges of the sidewalks and do not know their way back into the country. As gypsies gather once a year at their meeting place, so the fugitives convene in the big city, to demonstrate that they belong to one single tribe, the tribe of flight.[45]

Even nature, man has pulled into his agitation: spring, summer, autumn, and winter, day and night, even these lasting things of the earth are restless. How gladly the seasons of the years used to come, how patiently did they wait their turns! But now they are unsure, as beasts are before an earthquake or a storm. What man has done to nature, he has done to his own endeavors; he has dragged economy, for instance, into his flight. He does not want to control economic life, for its very instability makes it liable to crises; knowing that no matter how upsetting they are, they are more easily endured than the crises he would meet on his way to God, he prefers to be shaken by economy rather than by Him;

economic convulsion tosses him about, like a new motor for the flight—but God might bring him home.[46]

However wildly the monster flight rages, it cannot corrupt and destroy at will, Picard pledges in his closing chapter, "The Pursuer." Though many things are on flight, all that flees is God's possession, and wherever the fugitives run, God is there. They flee from every place, because God is in every place, and wherever they arrive, God is there before them; there is no spot where God cannot be, and hence none to which they cannot run. The flight is great because God is great. It is because He never ceases going after the torn-aways that they can run so violently; they are hunted by God, and only because He pursues them can they hasten. Of these strong Feet that follow, follow after, Francis Thompson says in "The Hound of Heaven":

> . . . *with unhurrying chase,*
> *And unperturbèd pace,*
> *Deliberate speed, majestic instancy,*
> *They beat—and a Voice beat*
> *More instant than the Feet—*
> *"All things betray thee, who betrayest Me."* [47]

This is His love: that He, and no other, is so fleet that He is always near them, that He is so fleet that the pursued trail behind— "Fear wist not to evade, as Love wist to pursue." This is the end of the flight.

What makes one shudder is the presumption of the fugitives, who risk fleeing only because they know that God is faster than they and that at any instant they can stop and let themselves be captured. It may happen, however, that God the Pursuer wishes to halt the chase sooner than the pursued. Perhaps someday He will pursue no more; then the fugitives will fall, and as dead moons revolve around a living star, they will circle around Him, still drawn by Him but no longer aware of Him. This too, Picard warns, could be the end of the flight.

Still do men flee, still does God go after them, and the faster they flee the more visible does He become. Never before has He been so clear, because all that is not He, all that is uncertain and unsure, has been picked up and dragged along by the flight; those who wanted to be lords of flight are now sweepers and pack carriers in the service of God. No longer can anyone say that God is only a possibility; it is futile to doubt Him, ridiculous to fall away, for all individual apostasy is but a clumsy copy of the tremendous machinery of flight, and all doubts, all uncertainties, all anxiety are herded there together. Now there are only these two: the flight, in which all unclearness crowds together, and the wholly clear One, God.[48]

Though the name of Christ is nowhere mentioned in *The Flight from God,* it is a Christian book nonetheless. "Where will he go, the fugitive from the face of God? He turns this way and that, as if he sought space for his flight. . . . Where will you go? Where flee? If you wish to flee from Him, flee to Him. Flee to Him confessing, not from Him hiding, for hide you cannot but confess you can." [49] These words of St. Augustine are the book's motto, for Picard does not count his duty done in a description, much less a satire, of the flight, but in voicing God's appeal to man's freedom, that he break loose from the mechanical apparatus of the flight. Though the very sparrows tell that the age flies to ruin, no man is inextricably caught in it, every man can be redeemed.

Picard's book is Christian because in it the flight is overshadowed by Love's pursuit, the great theme of the Old and New Testaments. From the first "Adam, where art thou?" and "Cain, where is thy brother Abel?" to the final "Behold, I stand at the gate and knock," God goes after man.[50] "All the day long I stretched out My hand to a people unbelieving and contradicting" [51]—so in His name cry out both Isaias and Paul, for prophets and apostles are His huntsmen, the ambassadors of His suit, and His quest for Israel is an image of His quest for every man. In Christ, who came to seek what was lost,[52] God's wooing was made flesh.

The Flight from God is a Catholic book, though Picard hardly knew it when he wrote. In Protestantism are rent apart God and the world, Christ and His Mother, Scripture and tradition, grace and freedom, the sacrifice of the cross and of the altar, marriage and virginity, all the elements of the spiritual life, each extolled at the cost of another; all this, which seems irreconcilable to the Protestant mind, in the Catholic Church is in harmony and without the fear that dignity requires isolation, that communion degrades. Of Karl Barth's dialectical theology, which looks on God only as the totally Other and so abhors the "analogy of being," denies that man is the likeness, however distant, of God, Picard says that it is in truth a means to keep man in a continual state of alarm. *There* it sees God, infinitely great, *here* man, infinitely small; but in speaking of the infinitely great and the infinitely small, dialectical theology speaks less of the natures of God and man than of boundary lines, one very high, the other very low; day and night it has man under surveillance, whether he adheres to his boundary line or shifts himself upward. This whole theology, Picard says, is distrust, hurry, breathlessness. Did this tension between God the Creator and man His creature really exist, all creation would then be tensed one part against the other, each measuring itself by another; there would be no rest, no duration, no assurance, no certainty, only constant explosions and wakefulness—there would be no sleep in the world. Picard's startling argument is akin to Péguy's praise, so Catholic through and through:

I don't like the man who doesn't sleep, says God.
Sleep is the friend of man.
Sleep is the friend of God.
Sleep is perhaps the most beautiful thing I have created.
And I myself rested on the seventh day.
He whose heart is pure, sleeps. And he who sleeps has a pure
    heart. . . .
He who doesn't sleep is unfaithful to Hope.
And it is the greatest infidelity.
Because it is infidelity to the greatest faith.
. . . Blessed is he who hopes. And who sleeps.[53]

Beyond the Human Face

Still veiled in *The Flight from God*, Picard's faith in Christ is clearly manifest in *The Limits of Physiognomy* (1937), the book he considers his best. Seeing in the human face the prints of the loving Fingers which formed it, always seeing behind it the face of the Fairest of the sons of men, Picard cannot withdraw his eyes from it. But he looks at it trembling—how could he otherwise, since it is made to be seen by God? It takes long looking, he says, till a face is fully known; it takes something of the patience God has with His creature. The slowness with which one man comes to know another honors man, and any physiognomy which pretends to furnish a short-cut knowledge of the human face, Baedeckerwise, is not only false but without dignity.[54]

For the knowledge of most things, reason is enough, because reason orders them, and by this order they are made remote and their weight is partly taken from us. But a human being, Picard accents, must not be made remote; rather must he be brought near, and it is only love that can work this nearness. Only in love's atmosphere can the face preserve itself as the likeness it was created; if it be not surrounded by it, the face stiffens, and what is seen is not a face but unliving matter. Thus he alone who holds love in readiness may seek to know a man, but such knowledge must never be the goal, rather the means of showing where love is needed. If a man seeks to know another merely for the sake of knowledge and not for the sake of love, he degrades the other, he degrades knowledge, he degrades himself—for what he does, the registration of qualities, could be done by a machine. It may happen, though, that a face provokes this degradation if, having lost the divine likeness and become a collection of loose parts, it seems to call for analysis rather than love.[55]

That his love may fail to rise to the level of his knowledge is man's danger, for in God alone are knowledge and love always and assuredly one—man's distinction is that in him they *may* be one. Sometimes, when the love to which a face has a claim is denied it, the face becomes burningly clear, as if to admonish: I am present. Van Gogh's face was like that, as violent as if it were the only real face, and all the others ghosts. Physiognomists, who at every moment refuse what man at every moment demands, are inhuman, Picard declares, and no less inhuman does he find graphologists, astrologers, and psychoanalysts, who pretend to know man by his handwriting, his stars, or his dreams. Handwriting, for instance, is a peripheral phenomenon, as it were, a secretion on the surface; but to know man the periphery never suffices, the fullness is needed, for on the margin man never shows himself as he really is but only as the border situation, the transition, seems to demand. That there, at man's borderline, a science, graphology, has been erected, indicates that there is something which wishes to lure man to the edge, perhaps that he is at the edge already. And what the psychoanalyst digs out of the wreckage of dreams are no longer living images but images become stone; they petrify themselves rather than fall alive into his hands.[56]

There is a chaos in man, the dark abyss into which he leaped by sin, and constantly this chaos threatens to force its way upward; constantly, therefore, must it be thrown back. To hold down this rebellious chaos, man has been given a weapon: the likeness, *die Ebenbildschaft,* Picard exclaims, the likeness in which he was created and re-created, the soul remade in grace. Not even at night, he continues, when in sleep the mind ceases to watch against the assault of the abyss, can it harm him; although it tries to steal into him under the enticing guise of dreams, it cannot ruin him, so safely is he protected by the likeness. But it is this very abyss psychoanalysis invites, urges, up into the brightness of creation; this is its crime, this is its treason, that it wishes to change the triumph of the likeness over the abyss into the triumph of the abyss over the likeness. Were man not God's likeness, psychoanalysis would be right: the chaos in him would be an autonomous world and the bright realm of creation its offal; not a step could be walked up in the brightness without its echo in the caves of chaos. But what psychoanalysis decrees is wrong: man does not depend on, nor can he be explained by, chaos. On the contrary, Picard exults, the chaos must accept the law of man; it must let itself be judged and convicted by the likeness of God.[57]

Picard's verdict on psychoanalysis may seem extreme; and indeed he is intense, for he is not concerned with this or that psychoanalytical concept or with any facts psychoanalysis has uncovered or with the variety of its schools, but with the spirit (not to say the un-spirit) that animates so much of its work, coloring so many of its concepts and findings. With prophetic anger he cries out against this or any other degradation of man, against all the modern attempts to read the whole of man by some fraction of him. Man is not a sort of embroidered chaos, nor is he an eighteen-billion-neuron calculating machine, nor is he the most advanced product of nature's laboratory. There is a fundamental difference, Picard holds most firmly, between man and beast, a gulf revealed by their relationship to time.

Beasts do not stand before time, because they do not stand before eternity, nor does it come to them as it comes to man; they have it with them as they have their bodies, living on it as on a store and using it up. It is *their* time, and there is nothing in it which can burst on them; it is as if they knew all it contained in advance, so that their lives are without surprise. They are wrapped up in time as they are in their fur; hence they are lonely and imprisoned in time, meeting each other only in space. And since they use time up, they become less with its passing, while man becomes more. Not only that: time in turn becomes fuller through man, in fact, it only *becomes* through him. Man arrives at the end of his life with time replete, but beasts arrive with time emptied, they fall over, because they are truly at their end; hence a beast dead looks so much deader than a man.[58]

In the beast the outside corresponds entirely to the inside, Picard notes; all that is within passes on to its appearance. Hence the beast is as it looks; it has nothing to express that is not expressed already in its exterior, in its image. But while man can be as he looks, he need not be: word and deed are given him to reveal what his face does not manifest. Moreover, what is within need not appear without; sovereign, not compelled to give account of itself, creative and free, the inward being can come to the fore when and how it wills. Above all, there is love's power—if it be present in a face, no difference, no discrepancy, matters between inner and outer.[59]

Man can, but the beast must, look like what he is. Locked up in its image, the beast cannot evolve into man; there is no transition between them. All other living creatures are like swellings of the earth, waves from below, hills raised from the ground—man alone is put on the earth from above, he is like the axis of heaven. Or to change the image: Man was brought from the darkness of the earth into the light of day, and this, God's work, is engraved in man. His face springs forth from the skull, as from a background remote and dark; like something unawakened, like earth, covered with hair as with a forest, so is this background, the roof and back of the head. All at once, in one leap, violently, the face springs forth from it; only in a single, sudden and undivided act, in one instant, could it have been born, of which the unexpected that is in every face, the surprise it is, give witness. Had the human face come into existence little by little, in the course of evolution, it would be spongy, shapeless, as if it had crawled up from the body, the mere continuation of something, and not, as it really is, without past, pure beginning.[60]

Though there is no transition from beast to man, nature outside of man presses toward him, Picard thinks, that it may be liberated through him. Man, who at the beginning of his history fell, would probably have fallen deeper still had he not been given the task of receiving and redeeming matter, which strives upward from corruption to redemption. Man's face is the site where his spiritual nature, falling, is borne up by matter, mounting, where spirit. and matter meet—the mean of meeting. It is as if matter awaited its elevation, its redemption, in the human countenance; therefore does it seek to come near the face, to penetrate and have part in it—a promise is extended from the human face to the whole of unliberated matter. Lower nature ventures even into woman's womb: the human embryo looks at one stage like a fish, at another like an amphibian, so that many scientists think it necessary for the embryo to pass through these forms in order to reach its own. But quite the contrary, Picard retorts, it is not that the human embryo depends on these animal forms, but that they depend on it; and if other embryos pass through similar stages, they but imitate and confirm what occurs in man primarily and to its proper end. Everything seeks man, the mediator, the redeemer.[61]

Picard can call man, himself so greatly in need of a Redeemer, the redeemer of matter, because man, the likeness, is created in the image of Christ. Rejoicing that man has the Son of God for his exemplar, Picard is at the same time terrified by the almost unbelievable: In Jesus, God was made flesh and still the world exists. As Man, Christ was nailed to the cross, and thus the figure of man is forever outlawed and wounded and flayed. From that moment, Picard stammers, man should have ceased to look like a man, for it is audacious to look like Him who dared to look like a man and for His daring died; it is incomprehensible that a man should bear the human form, since in it the Son of God suffered death. In the paintings of Matthias Gruenewald there happens what should have happened: human frames seem to break apart, because having been present at the death of Christ, they cannot endure to be with man. And faces, too, would have been rent, like the curtain of the Temple, had they not been held together by God. Having been bidden then to abide with man when they would have fled, man's face and figure were created anew, and so through Christ the shape of man is forever secured; from now on he can wear no other.[62]

Man can be other than he looks, now not only by that freedom wherein he differs from the beasts, but, since the coming of Christ, by heavenly franchise. *Christus, aussen ein Knecht und innen ein Gott;* Christ, outwardly ministering but inwardly reigning, a servant to look at but truly God—before *this* rift, any rift between what a man is and what his body tells of him is as nothing. Yet his face does tell whether or not he has made his decision for God: goodness, not beauty, is its mark. A face looks good if a man has chosen Him, the supreme Good, for He communicates Himself not only to the soul but to the body: *bonum diffusivum sui,* it is the way of the good to spread itself. Hence who looks on a face that bears the mark of decision feels the call to goodness, but he who is looked on by Christ and who looks at Him takes fire. Were a man able to let no moment pass without the great decision, without choosing God, were he wholly with Him at every instant, he would be so *present* that, Picard says, he cannot conceive how such a saint could die, the spirits of heaven would have to carry him off from time to eternity.[63] There *was* such a saint, full of grace, wholly with God at every instant, her life an uninterrupted "yes" to the eternal Yes—she *did* die, but was assumed, body and soul, into heaven, into the timeless realm of love, and forever her face is lighted by the face of God.

In early Greek sculpture, the face was little distinguished from the rest of the body; head and torso, arms and legs, had almost the same importance, Picard points out. Only when Socrates and Plato saw in man a being who decides was the head raised above the members and the face given the mark of decision. Socrates and Plato summoned man to decide for the good, but since Christ appeared in time, man has been bidden to decide not for abstract good but for the concrete Good, for God, who has come, and holds Himself out to him in order that he receive Him. Now man cannot scatter himself and hide in the abstract, for he is confronted immediately with the Concrete of the concrete, with God, before whom he must collect himself for the decision, a decision which makes him a center of recollection and his face the true center of his body. In deciding to become Man, God prepared and made easy man's decision for God; no longer is the man who decides for the good the exception, as with the Greeks—from now on, in Christianity, the exception is God, who has come to man.[64]

This tribute to Christ, in whom he sees fulfilled Isaias' prophecy of the Servant of Jahve, crowns Picard's book. And these are the "limits of physiognomy": man cannot be explained in terms of his own world, upheld by his own strength, healed by his own remedies; he cannot be cured, sustained or understood, without the cross. For there, on the cross, is shown irresistibly what in the Old Testament is but said in words—the meaning of man: he is spoken to, he is the *addressed* of God. Questioned by the Crucified as to whether he loves, he must answer. But even if he fails in his answer, even if he has gone to the very edge of the world that the voice of love may not reach him (as have the figures of Daumier, which are, says Picard, more insects than men), still, divine love can reach him. Where human love is powerless, the love of the Servant-Lord can still recall a face to true human presence.[65] The beams that bore Him in His death bear man's life; without them man cannot be wholly man.

The Unconquerable Marriage

After this confession, an angry silence fell upon Picard; it was the face of Hitler that for a time left him speechless. To him it was infinitely less than the face of a confidence man who preys on women, or of a street photographer who, uninvited, takes snapshots, or pretends to take them, and then demands money but never delivers the picture. Their faces, at least, seem to apologize for being as they are and would be different if they could; Hitler's face, however, Picard felt, was the obtrusion of vacuum, of the null. There have been kings who looked like murderers or madmen, but in Hitler not even crime or insanity was visible—only the totally nondescript. For the first time in history nothingness invaded a ruler's face and there squatted brazenly.[66]

In Picard's stricken silence there sounded, in 1939, this prayer of the Church: "God of Abraham, God of Isaac, God of Jacob, God who didst appear to Moses Thy servant on Mount Sinai! Thou didst lead the sons of Israel out of the land of Egypt, giving them as Thy deputy an angel of Thy faithful love, that he guard them by day and by night. In like manner, we pray Thee, Lord, to send

289

Thy holy angel from heaven to guard this servant of Thine and to lead him to the grace of Thy baptism." Picard broke his silence when he answered her question: "Wilt thou be baptized?" with: "I will." [67]

Having experienced the power of the sacrament, he fought the invasion of nothingness with an unexpected weapon: praise of the sacramental order. Hitler's name never occurs in *The Unshakable Marriage* (1942); yet against Hitler's expansion of an empty ego, Picard proclaims the simplicity of marriage, the selflessness of its life, the objectivity of its bond; against pride in nothing, he extols the humility of wedlock; and against the reign of terror, impotently seeking to terrorize forever,[68] the reign of love, which husbands every hour and conquers the fleetingness of time. Hitler, a monstrous picture of rootless man, undertook to make a "new start" with everything,[68] to shake the world from its foundations; but the world's foundations cannot be shaken, for there is always God, and there is always marriage.

> . . . *Equal and entire,*
> *Therein benevolence, desire,*
> *Elsewhere ill-join'd or found apart,*
> *Become the pulses of one heart,*
> *Which now contracts, and now dilates,*
> *And, both to the height exalting, mates*
> *Self-seeking to self-sacrifice.*
> *Nay, in its subtle paradise*
> *(When purest) this one love unites*
> *All modes of these two opposites,*
> *All balanced in accord so rich*
> *Who may determine which is which?*
> *Chiefly God's Love does in it live.*[69]

"This is in marriage," Picard begins his book, "not more: a man, a wife, a few children, some household goods for eating and sleeping, and perhaps a few animals. It is as at the beginning of creation. And from the beginning of creation till today there is always present: a man, a wife, with a few children and a few things in the house of marriage. Empires were founded and destroyed; multitudes of men peopled the earth and disappeared beneath it; the Flood came and again a new earth—yet always there stood together in the same way a man and a wife, with their children and the few things in the house of marriage. To this we can return again and again, here we can always begin." [70]

In the world outside of marriage, a man takes his existence as ready-made, as a finished product fresh from the factory; but in the house of marriage, Picard delights, it is not so. Here his existence trembles, thrills, as at the beginning; things are not taken for granted—they have their pristine freshness, the beautiful uncertainty of the original. When a man and wife plant a tree in their garden, it is as if it happened for the first time, and they marvel that the earth holds the tree up, that the weight of heaven does not press it down. Their meal is not a combination of calories and vitamins, the meat on the noonday table is not dead; it is, as it were, the very life of the animal, the whatness of meat, sizzling gaily because it is near man, because it is taken in by a man and not by a consumer of calories and vitamins. In the house of marriage, water is not like an industrial product, serving other industrial products; it serves indeed, but keeps its elemental nature. Having been forced into an iron pipe, to take its way into the house of marriage, it leaps out, shining and singing, glad to be free. It is like a fountain, reminding man and wife of springs and origins. And the air is not an empty avenue on which airplanes travel, but a beloved element, caressed by the breath of the wife and struck by the breath of the man, a still sign that the other is there. Language too is not stereotyped but newborn in the house of marriage. "Good morning," says the husband to his wife on awakening, and it is as if it were morning for the first time—after the night the morning. In marriage things are brought before man that he may name them: "The stove, ah, the stove," says the wife, and it begins to be warm under the warmth of her word. Here names are not mere identity tags or signs for classification; name and thing are one. [71]

"A man, a wife, a few children and a few things in the house of marriage—this is more than the sum of man, wife, children, and things. It is a picture, *ein Bild.*" In a picture the parts are not there for their own sake, but in order to express a meaning by their togetherness; so man, wife, children, and things are in marriage not only for themselves but for the sake of meaning. Every picture is a symbol, and the picture that is marriage is the symbol of the encounter of the higher with the lower, the hallowed with the profane. Only a picture joins parts to one another as if they had been a unity from the beginning, and hence husband, wife, and children are with one another as if they had always been. Because the picture is more than its parts, marriage is more than the husband, the wife, and the children; just as one sees first the whole picture and not its parts, so one sees first the picture that is marriage before seeing the separate individuals who compose it. And since the soul loves to have and to keep things as pictures, neither husband nor wife needs to search memory for past events in order to think of the other. Marriage is always with them and, as a picture in their souls, follows them wherever they are and whether they will it or not.[72]

The state of marriage is not created by husband and wife; on the contrary, husband and wife are created by it. It is objectively given —Picard never tires of calling it *eine objective Gegebenheit*— and need not wait for man to bring love to it; love is there already and is added to the love of husband and wife, so that within marriage they can love more than they could outside. The married state has a store of knowledge and wisdom, on which husband and wife can draw, so that their judgments on things and people have more substance and less of the accidental, coming as they do from the wide and ordered world of marriage. In it subjectivity must be given up, or rather subordinated. Thus the concern of man and wife is not what they might lose, not whether marriage will be sufficient for them, rather whether they will be sufficient for marriage. Likewise, conjugal happiness is not the subjective happiness of husband and wife, not their sum, but just the happiness of marriage, and that they can participate in it is their greatest joy. So great is the power of wedlock that even so aberrant a thing as "companionate marriage" assumes outwardly the form of objective marriage, and probably the truth influences the error inwardly as well; it is as if a cathedral were turned into a cinema— the moving picture is played, but by themselves the holy prayers pray on.[73]

In the course of history there have been two movements of the mind, one ancient and lasting, the other novel and born to die. Man's mind today does not like to wait passively for something else and be its goal; it itself moves toward a goal, toward the "higher," so that the chart of its "upward" view of the world is: without matter no life, without life no consciousness, without consciousness no world of the spirit. In so constructing the universe from the lower to the higher, he denies the higher an existence of its own, always dissolving it into the lower from which it is said to spring. The result, says Picard, is a reduced world, with values but locations, points in the world's topography; sex and spirit, for example, are merely stages in the movement of sublimation.

Entirely different is the mind's movement from the higher to the lower. It does not hasten toward a goal nor need it perfect itself by its movement; the mind *has* its perfection and carries it to the less perfect, and this is the significance of its journey—to spread the perfect to the things below. Since the mind does not depend on the things it meets—rather the things on it—it does not have to push them out of its way; since it has everything, it does not abuse things for the sake of a "purpose," and its errand is one not of "purpose" but of love, traveling to things much as grace does to man. What matters to the mind is the *being* of a thing, that it *is*, and thus the mind's journey is a quiet one. Still, in the world of the mind, things are not frozen but alive, alive in expectation, for through the mind's descending to them, the love that is in them meets the love from above.[74]

All that happens in Scripture, Picard continues, is marked by this movement of the high to the low, and its holiest example is God's coming down as Man to men. Throughout the Middle Ages, man's view was patterned after this movement which has its beginning above; since then, his mind no longer starts above but below, and climbs little by little from one thing to another. Not always does he arrive, and seldom does the higher at which he does arrive mean much to him. However, in matrimony there is still preserved this sacramental movement, in which the higher bends down to kiss the lower, in which God bends down toward the husband and wife and toward the little things in the house of marriage.[75]

The presence of the divine among the things of earth—this is for Picard the sacramental heart of marriage. And as there is a divine movement which brings it about, so there is a divine structure which is its prototype. Today, the structure of science, of economy, and of life, is such, he says, that they, with all their parts, are directed toward a goal in one straight line. The modern method of production is one unbending road, with detours barred, from raw material to finished product, so that it seems as though the product mattered less than the straightness of the road. Our thought and inner experience too move along one straight line, and what cannot be pushed forward on it is discarded. Hence the poverty of our perceptions and our withered spiritual life. Totally different from the linear is the centered structure, mirroring the flow of life and love in the bosom of the Trinity, a structure found in the narratives of Scripture. They are not lined up one after the other in a logical row; they rise from a common center and return at their end whence they began, and it is through this center that all the stories are related. Marriage too is ordered around its sacramental center; in it, as in a circle, every event radiates from its focus and to its focus every event returns. In marriage, movements are not toward a far-away goal, as are those outside, where often the several parts do not know their destiny. Here journey and goal are one: the doings of husband and wife are not movements toward marriage, but the movements of marriage itself.[76]

Consequently, argues Picard, man and wife do not live first for one another, but for the sacrament; only because they both belong to it do they belong to one another. The sacrament so widens the otherwise narrow house of marriage that they can live together in it, without the husband's tiring his wife or the wife's tiring her husband. When the sacramental power is expelled, man and wife meet ill-temperedly, under a constant strain, in the narrow house. But when they rely on the strength that is not their own, their lives become effortless, as it were; their souls acquire a spiritual instinct, for the sacrament leads them. The children too do not belong to the man and wife but to the sacramental heart; they are the growing space for the ever-expanding power of the heart, as were in former times also the sisters and brothers of the husband and wife, living with them in the house of marriage. Possessions also are drawn into that sacred province, so that everything receives a new meaning from the sacrament: the slice of bread the wife gives the beggar at the door is not merely food shared but part of the sacramental blessing.[77]

A man, a wife, a few children, and a few humble things—this is so simple that one can hardly believe it is a sacrament. And yet this is its secret, it loves to be inconspicuous, almost unrecognized on earth; and if the anxieties in the house of marriage, the complications of little things, become involved, it is as if to protect what Picard happily calls the *incognito* of the sacrament. As Christ was not recognized when He came to man in the simplicity of a Man, so the divine is hard to see in the simplicity of marriage. But it is just this simplicity which makes it possible for the sacrament to be everywhere. So firm is its structure that God was born into a marriage, that Christ, the absolute and sacrosanct, was born into the house of marriage—and it did not break asunder. Every other way of human existence—His village of Nazareth, the kingly city of Jerusalem, the Synagogue and the Empire—had no room for Him, but marriage, used to the holy, stood Him when He came.[78]

To think that a man and his wife need not invent marriage, that marriage is there before them, makes Picard rejoice, because the objective character of wedlock gives love the freedom to be wholly and only love. This is love: the lover wings his way from the finitude of earth to the infinity of love. Love detaches him from the earth, making light him and the things around him, otherwise ponderous and unwieldy. This winging from the finite to the infinite shows love's divine origin but makes it perilous too. Nowhere else than in the shelter of marriage, where it is guarded by the safe finiteness of cups and plates and knives and forks, of chairs and tables and fire tongs, of the chores and events of every day, can love safely trust itself to the great uncertainty of infinity. Outside the changeless house of marriage, that which is love's beauty, its soaring, receives an ugly independence; instead of being centripetal and intensive, it becomes centrifugal, extensive. This sort of love depends entirely on feelings and moods, always requiring new things, more outer world, to prove to itself it exists. While it uses up things and world, the other, conjugal love, creates—not in need of daily demonstration, not dependent on the moods of husband and wife, this great love is hidden in the great phenomenon of marriage, but it is seen in the little things.[79]

In marriage man is safe. Sex has this danger, that only the moment counts; and since it is opposed to duration, it dynamites the unity of a life, its history, so that a man totally given to it would be historyless. For this reason alone the psychoanalysis of Freud and Reich, which attempts to make sex the history of man, is false, Picard contends. Because in sex, man delivers himself to the moment, he ceases to be linked with his fellows. It imprisons him—not in a solitude in which he finds himself, in which he finds God—in an isolation in which his own being falls to pieces. The Fiend, therefore, often tempts man through sex, wanting to tear him out of his context, out of his history, for if his life becomes unordered, his being disjointed, God's image in him is shattered; grace has no hold in him. But in marriage, where everything has a place, the abyss of sex too finds its great role. Where form abounds, the chaotic of sex can do no harm; the abyss rebels no longer, but serves. The world of marriage might become stiff with security were it not, from time to time, shaken by the volcanic and irrational abyss of sexuality, and what outside of marriage engenders isolation, within it begets continuity, the family, the line of generations. Never would man have dared turn an agent of isolation into an agent of perpetuity—never he, but God alone. Hence, as God was there when the first man rose from dust, so is He by when every man is begotten. Above all, His almighty care is clear when the cherished line of Jesus' ancestors is recorded: the tables of generations are told and retold in Scripture not only to set forth the history of salvation, how the world was made ready for the coming of the Christ, but also to show the splendor of all the families of earth, that their generations, their continuity, are protected by God's holiness.[80]

In Picard's *The Unshakable Marriage,* the house of Tobias is alive, gentle as water, strong as rock. "Lord God of our fathers . . . When Adam was made of earth's clay, it was by Thy hand; when Eve was sent to cheer him, it was of Thy gift. Thou, Lord, art my witness that I wed this sister of mine not for fleshly lust; only in the dear hope of leaving offspring behind me, offspring in whom, Lord, may Thy name be ever blessed!"[81] As long as the God of Abraham, Isaac, and Jacob joins two in one, so long does He fulfill His merciful purpose in us,[82] so long does man know that he is loved and not left alone. While many of man's creations speak of ruin, the sacrament, God's work, spells hope, is Picard's message. The oneness of two in the flesh, image and mirror of the oneness of Christ with His Church, is a sign that in spite of man's resistance through the ages, in spite of the satanic attacks of the dictators of our age, He is the Saviour.

The Discontinuous Man

That marriage is a never-failing well of hope, which will outlast all those who try to choke it, that marriage is unconquerable because God is unconquerable, was Picard's answer to Hitler while Hitler was still alive. After the Lord's wrath had felled him, Picard wrote again, not, however, to judge the already judged, but to strip us of our imagined innocence. It is the thesis of *Hitler in Our Selves* (1947) that only in a world of total discontinuity could such a *nothing* be a leader. To see a miniature of this discontinuous world, one need but look at a popular magazine, Picard says: page one shows a half-naked dancer; page two a battalion of soldiers at machine-gun practice, and further down, a scientist in his laboratory; the next page features the evolution of the bicycle from the middle of the nineteenth century to the present day, as well as a Chinese poem; after that comes the calisthenics of factory workers during their rest period, and the knotted string writing of a South American Indian tribe; opposite these, Senator X in his summer retreat. Yet the discontinuity of such a magazine is old-fashioned beside the radio: 6:00 A.M., morning exercises; 6:10, recorded music; 7:00, news; 8:00, Morse code lesson; 9:00, sermon; 9:30, "In a Lake Dwellers' Village"; 10:00, a Beethoven sonata for flute and piano; 10:30, farm hints; 10:45, chronicle of the world; 11:00, Overture to "Rienzi"—and so on, till the Spanish course at 10:00 P.M. and the Jazz Hour at 10:30.[83]

Not content with being chaotic, this world of the radio produces chaos, presenting things without context or connection, so that they are forgotten as soon as they are presented. Right from the beginning they appear in a fog of oblivion; there is no longer any outer world to be grasped, only a jumble, and no longer any mind to grasp it, for the mind is a jumble too. In this radio traffic, man neither chooses nor examines his objects—a disjointed, fluid world moves past disjointed man, and it does not matter *what* goes by, only that *something* goes by. Into this procession anything could worm its way and not be noticed, even an Adolf Hitler. But once inside the confusion that is the soul of modern man, whether or not he hangs on depends not on the victim but on Hitler's skill.

297

The visage of Nazism, as Picard sees it, is this: Out of an enormous void something bellows, one knows not whether the commanders or the commanded; arms are flung up, and one does not know whether in assault or in defense, whether by the hangmen or the hanged. The yells of the Hitlers and the Goebbelses are meant not for the people alone but above all for themselves; it is as if a scrap of tin, in order to prove to itself that it still existed, were to rattle forever: I am a piece of broken tin. In Nazism the void itself cries out, well aware that it really is *not* and trying by its shouts to prove that it *is*. No, this is not a phenomenon of the political or socio-logical or psychological orders; it is the offspring of demons.[84]

The horror of Nazism is not torture or murder, but that murder and torture are so quickly forgotten. The Nazi who yesterday was gassing Jews may today sell stamps at a post-office window or greet you as the manager of a hotel, wholly unconscious of the killer he was yesterday, just as yesterday he was oblivious of the *petit bour-geois* he was the day before. Tomorrow he might slay again, although today he would run after you, even for a mile, if you overpaid him fifty pfennigs. Held back by nothing, he can adapt himself to any situation, for, as the man of discontinuity, he is de-termined by nothing but by his action of the moment; what is worse, he comes into existence only through the moment. His in-ner being contains nothing of the past; he commits the most evil deeds, and they all fall into an abyss where there is no memory. A human life counts for nothing; where nothing *is,* where every-thing blinks up only to vanish again, there a human life is easily pushed aside, easily annihilated. What marks the Nazi is not that he kills—he forgets that he kills.[85]

In the world of Nazidom, Bolshevism can now be called world enemy number one, shortly afterward the great ally, and after a while world enemy number one all over again. Of course, this can happen and has happened elsewhere, but elsewhere it happens consciously and deliberately, here unconsciously, with the extinc-tion of memory, with "doublethink," as George Orwell calls it.[86] It is useless, therefore, to demand repentance of a Nazi. Con-trition can exist only where there is an inner life, where past deeds are remembered, examined, and seen in their sinfulness. But as it is, the atrocities of Buchenwald, Maideneck, and Belsen will soon be forgotten, forgotten not through greatness of heart but through the greatness of the void into which everything is sucked.[87]

Of time, of true duration, all that is left is the moment; the rest is destroyed in the world of discontinuity. If a thing, then, lasts for but an instant, its true nature remains hidden behind the flash of its arrival and departure. So the mechanism of the momentary renders all things alike and hence meaningless, blotting out, along with all other distinctions, the difference between good and evil. Here is no longer Nietzsche's "beyond good and evil," which required an effort of the mind and an effort to sin: morality has been done away with mechanically, good and evil are only labels to attract and deter. Where the moment alone reigns, there is no time for organic growth, only for increase in quantity; there is no unfolding, no transformation, nothing but an ever-enlarging mass. What is oppressive about such a world, with its big cities, its factories, is that the enlargement can go on without limit. This was also the oppression of Nazism (and, one might add, it is no less of Communism), that it kept mushrooming till it came close to filling all space. It mushroomed, but it did not develop; it did not adapt itself, nor could anything change it. Unalterably Nazism stood, which gave it the look of something superhuman, but it was inhuman. Inhuman too was its bulking there as if there had been nothing before it came, and this very effrontery, says Picard, captivated people.[88]

Modern man, of whom the Nazi is the oversized portrait, has no inner inventory; therefore he tries to make an inventory of the outside world. With automobile, railroad, and airplane, he seeks to bring all things together mechanically; he abbreviates space, so that at least in space things may be near one another, that in a mechanical cohesion of things he may find a substitute for his lost memory. Behind railroad, car, and airplane, man can still be seen as he hurriedly herds together the world outside. In the case of radio, however, there is only a humanless apparatus, which lines the world up incoherently—again what counts, Picard stresses, is that something be lined up, *what* does not matter. All things are torn within and without, the blare of the radio alone endures; man no longer bothers to connect this with that, for the continuity of sheer noise does it for him. Such an apparatus made it easy for Hitler to shape man after his own—Hitler's—image.[89]

There was, of course, discontinuity before Nazism, but Nazism made it visible, established it as a world in itself. Evil, which in God's creation is momentary, Hitler made lasting, and what should be lasting became momentary, discontinuous; the good he pierced, so that discontinuity, the sign of dissolution, the sign that the end of a world is near, became the normal state. The fractured moment, the moment that destroys, is the exact opposite of the sacramental moment, the instant in which good is done. Because the moments of the good, the moments of man's inner life, are lifted out of clock time and offered to eternity, they endure. It is love which creates this continuity, for through love, things gone by are ordered and locked into an inner unity.[90]

Since love has altogether left the Nazi, Picard calls him the man of atrocities, unlike any before him. There have indeed been other men of violence, like the Huns, but their cruelty was the cruelty of nature turned savage: when their hordes swarmed over Asia and Europe, they were like a thunderstorm or a tidal wave. Similarly, crimes gush forth from human passion, as in the French Revolution: they were evil passion become flesh. The crimes of the Nazis, however, are calculated, tried out in the test tube of laboratories; they were committed with scientific rigor, with the exactness of an engineer. Neither nature nor passion, rather the production of factories, in magnitude they are industrial. It is totally false, Picard insists, to think of their wickedness as a sexual disorder, as an extreme form of sadism. They are in no way tied to sex, to any perversion; they are not tied to anything human at all, and therefore are they monstrous. Even the cruelties of a Nero or a Caligula were bound to them as men, to their debauched flesh and corrupted senses, but the Nazi cruelty originates from a laboratory apparatus, from men who have become total apparatus.

When Tamerlane built his walls with the bodies of living men as rocks, and together with rocks, and the heads of living men as stones, and together with stones, his crime was clear and unmistakable, and it remains: to this day one hears the crashing of bodies and the crushing of skulls. The atrocities of the Nazis, on the other hand, were incidental, by-products of a machine adjusted at one moment to crime, at another to public welfare or child education. In this disjointed, mechanical world, one need not wonder that Himmler, the head of the Gestapo, was a good interpreter of Bach, nor that Heydrich, the hangman of Czechoslovakia, wept in concert halls to hear Mozart. Murder and music, the gas chamber and the concert hall, are side by side; it is the same hall, at one moment rigged up for art, the next for torture. Mozart before or after the gassing of human beings, Hoelderlin in the knapsack of an SS man, Goethe in the guards' library at a concentration camp—this is possible only in a world in which things exist no longer in their essence but piecemeal. Here even murder is degraded, for it is a matter of indifference what fills the moment, whether it be killing or Bach, gassing or Hoelderlin.

Where the hand that now caresses a child can in a second move the lever that releases death into the gas chamber; where the togetherness of murder and music is not *against* the structure of the world, but rather *is* its structure, conversion is impossible. In such a world, no persecutor can become an apostle; never can another Leo the Great change the heart of Attila, so that he desists from spoiling Italy and spares Rome. After Kierkegaard had suffered for years from the slanders of the journalist Goldschmidt, he stopped him one day in the streets of Copenhagen, made him listen while he held his sin before him, and moved him to tears, so that he ceased his calumnies. But the Nazi cannot be made to listen, cannot be moved.[91]

The Great Degradation

"They that have despised the Word of God, from them shall the word of man also be taken away." [92] The discontinuous man has lost the word. In language, Picard states in *Hitler in Our Selves,* there is a binding force that ties the doer to his deed and the deed to the target of his doing: the subject to the verb, the verb to the object. The same tie unites the less important to the more important, the subordinate to the principal clause, so that all that belong together stand together. Truth needs this firmness, this law-fullness, of language if it is to express itself, and man too needs this welding power, the logic of language, to keep together what would otherwise disintegrate. The world is one for him because it is one in the word, word in its fullest sense. Though the spoken word vanishes even as it is spoken, the truth it conveys remains, and round it as their enduring center gather people and things, a world. Because truth is not only lasting but bestows lastingness, because it makes the order of the universe intelligible, language, truth's vehicle, helps man to be continuous and bears him in his humanity.

But when man is inwardly shattered, as he is today, language shatters too: it loses its texture and hierarchical order, and what was the sign of integration turns into a signature of dissolution, the curse of Babel, a sound without content, emptied of creative power, merely commanding, like a whistle or a bark. With Hitler the process of dissolution came to a climax and so in him the word was utterly deprived of meaning—meaning requires permanence and continuity—it was only the shriek of the moment. What he established was not merely a political dictatorship but the tyranny of the slogan, which ruled in the place of the word. When the word, which is given measure by truth and which therefore confers measure upon things, ceases to order them, everything happens and grows outside the word, outside measure; all things grow into the monstrous. Since these monstrosities have not risen from the *logos,* since they have not grown from the word, they cannot be described by words; language cannot receive them. How impossible it is for the human word to depict the inhumanity of factories in which men are exterminated by gas, torture factories with a special department for the tanning of human skin to serve for lamp shades. The human word cannot take it in—Picard sums up the destruction Nazism wrought.[93]

Since words can no longer convey, convince, convert, God permitted the monstrosities of Nazism that their sight and stench might turn us from our discontinuity. Hence Picard interrupts himself to pray with Hoelderlin "for the incurable":

Hasten, O hesitant time, to lead them into absurdity,
That they may see how utterly senseless they are.
Hasten, ruin them utterly, into frightful nothingness lead them,
Else they will never believe how rotten they are.
These fools are never converted if they be not confounded,
These never, if putrefaction they see not.[94]

In Hitler's discontinuous world, a world without love as it is without truth, there can be no conversation between men, no word that flows from one to another. A man speaks only to himself, because he knows nothing of an other; he does not even acknowledge his existence. There was much monologue, long before Hitler—when scientists or artists gathered, when representatives spoke in Parliament, they spoke to and for themselves—but with him it became absolute. Never did his speeches call for an answer; they were merely heaped-up cries. But in the world of continuity, the one spoken to is always present; indeed, the conversation goes on silently even after the talk is mute. It seems as if the words do not begin with their speaker, as if he but continues what was bequeathed him by others, like bricklayers who pass bricks from the ground to the very roof, whose hands are a pathway for bricks to travel.[95]

Hitler's world, the disjointed world at its worst, supplants truth by statements of fact, Picard continues. Day in and day out, a thousand facts are stated, by science, psychology, graphology. Even the arts, poetry, music, and philosophy, constantly fall into stating the momentary, though their care should be for the things that do not perish. Hitler gained his followers by chasing after facts and delivering them like spoils to an eager people: statistics on the populations of Germany and of the countries to be overrun, export figures, the birth rate, the count of the unemployed. When Hitler assumed power, there were seven million unemployed in Germany, and by 1939 only a few were left—this is a statement of fact, but not a truth. Indeed, it is a lie, exact though it is, for Hitler did not reduce the number of the unemployed by bringing order into a disordered world, rather by making a world out of joint more so, by using, even using up, the unemployed in war.

Once the world is chopped up, some one splinter, some one notion, some one person or thing is made absolute. There is, for example, the physician who has the fragment of an idea that at the bottom of the soul there lie repressed sexual urges. This fragmentary idea about the soul is then declared its center, even the center of all human existence; all discussion and research, not only in psychology but in literature as well, in art, religion, sociology, ethnology, politics, revolves around it. Though it is not certain that it is a splinter of the soul, only that it is a splinter of an idea, this mere chip of the soul, repressed sexuality, is made the world, even the creator of the world. It is demoniacal that man, after having destroyed the wholeness of God's given world, wants to create another from one of its particles, be it from sex or, as in the case of the Nazis, from race.[96]

The Nazi is the man without reality. He can grab some reality, a country or a human being, club it down, overpower it, but, being disjointed, he cannot possess it. And because he cannot possess reality, he likes to destroy it. Though he invaded country after country, he was unable to own any of them and so no amount of expansion could ever satisfy him. In his world of ghosts, there was no proportion between the outlay of energy or the hugeness of the undertaking, and the result: soon after a conquest, it was as if Germany had gained nothing at all. It is not the Nazi alone, however, not only the German, but almost all of Europe and America that is severed from reality. We no longer trust our own eyes and ears; when a parade marches through the town or a streetcar collides with an automobile, our retina still registers and the labyrinth of our ear receives it, but it does not count. The reality we see is accepted only if it is confirmed on the air or printed the next day in the paper. This is the reality of the discontinuous man, of the Nazi in the making, Picard mourns: not the event itself and its immediate experience, rather its report on the radio.[97]

One thing in particular shows for Picard the decline of humanity in the last centuries: the rationalization of anti-Semitism has grown shabbier and shabbier. Two hundred and fifty years ago in Bossuet, the Jews were denounced because they had denounced Christ. At the turn of this century, Carl Lueger, the mayor of Vienna, and Friedrich Stoecker, the Lutheran chaplain at the Kaiser's court, fought the Jews because of their economic power. Racial anti-Semitism, however, demanded the annihilation of the Jews because of their inferior race. How the sense of value has fallen, how lowered the way man is looked upon! Bossuet tested the Jews by what is essential to man, by the spirit and the truth. Lueger and Stoecker no longer saw man in his full nature but as reduced to the sociological level, a lesser but still human standard. Two hundred and fifty years, even fifty years ago, the anti-Semite and the Jew lived in the same world, they met as man meets man. But the modern anti-Semite does not see a man, only racial marks: the cephalic index, the dark hair, the hooked nose—and if it isn't hooked, he hooks it for himself—he does not see a living being, merely an abstract conglomerate which he measures, labels, and catalogs. Now the Jew is reduced to a wax figure in a shop, but while the tailor's dummy is draped with clothes, the racial dummy is covered with index numbers. Man reduced to a dead number— this is the ultimate degradation. If one dares to confine man within a few narrow numbers, it will not be long before one cages him in a concentration camp.

As if racism, the veneration of skin, skull, and nose, were not enough, Nazi anti-Semitism sank even lower; it was not even real anti-Semitism but merely a psychological device. A blurred and messy ego can notice its own existence only when confronted with something distinct and definite, and the Jew happens to be more conspicuous than others. Hence the Nazi sought out in the Jew all that contradicted himself, construing him as the totally opposite; he wished to collide with the Jew because only in collision did he become aware of himself. To him the Jew was like the Fuehrer: both were landmarks for orientation in his nothingness. The Fuehrer's watchword was awaited that its shout might tell the Nazi that in the void he inhabited there was *something,* and that he himself was *there* where he heard the shout. Just so the Jew was to him nothing but a means to disguise his own fearful emptiness. He murdered, tried to wipe out the Jew, and the more he murdered the more he thought he concealed his need of him. Picard sees a horrid relationship between the total void of the Nazi, who needs the Jew if he is to be aware of himself, and his murder of the Jew to cover up this use he makes of him—not a relationship of the human world but the mechanism of chaos.[98]

Pioneers of Degradation

That the expansion of emptiness, the total discontinuity of Nazism, did not appear overnight is the emphasis of *Hitler in Our Selves.* For a long time termites were at work to bring down the house man lived in, the solid frame built through Greece and Israel by human wisdom and divine. There had grown up in Greece a language, a philosophy, a cast of mind, ready to receive and serve the message of Christ, not that it did not need baptism —like Naaman, it had to be washed seven times in the Jordan, wholly buried in the waters of Christ—then it gave a tongue to the full idea of man. With a wondrous continuity, the antique world was brought into the Christian.

Today's education, however, Picard decries, has smashed the Greco-Christian image of man, of man soul and body, hierarchically ordered in all their faculties, aiming instead at preparing man for the discontinuous life. Hence a disjointed course of studies is poured into the students; the most disparate subjects, literature, flying, history, home economics, chemistry, appreciation of art, and whatnot are piled up in their minds, the Greco-Christian ideal of man being just one subject among the rest, brought down to their level. In the world of continuity, where all threads weave one perfect fabric, the manifoldness and disparity of subjects serves to make man harmonious; they converge, complementing and balancing one another. But in the fragmented world, each subject remains a fragment. The students never grasp that the various subjects are parts of one world—each is made a world by itself, each conflicting with the others, each asserting itself only in competition. So the school is a school of discontinuity and raises youth for a Hitler, for a master mechanic of disjointedness.[99]

Painting and literature too have helped undermine the world in which things are friends and not enemies, in which they meet in order and beauty, because led by love. Pablo Picasso and Paul Klee and, in general, the painters of the cubist and abstract schools, wade in chaos. Their painted objects, Picard says, are not only disjointed; they are deformed and in pieces, as if they were broken and strewn all over, as if they had been drifting in chaos. In a crashing world, the futurist stands on one fragment and tries to lasso as many other bits as he possibly can, and in his paintings his catch is lined up for inventory. Man is no more, nature no more, God no more; all that remains is the machinery of disjointedness, and the artist shows how it functions. The novels of James Joyce and John Dos Passos suit this discontinuity of today. No one thread holds them together, each thought is pushed aside by the next, scene chases after scene; indeed, thoughts and scenes seem hardly able to wait to be displaced. Even in those modern novels which show no such fits and spasms, true continuity is often lacking, for though they have a content, they are without a real context. In the world of true, hierarchical context, one man or one thing can represent the whole order, and whatever other man or thing is added is a sign of fullness and superabundance. The writer has no need to construct context and continuity: they are

306 *Max Picard*

the world in which he writes and lives. Most modern novels, however, portray the wrecked world, and in turn wreck it still further, particularly the novels of Jean-Paul Sartre, which out-Hitler Hitler.[100]

Another pioneer of degradation is Heidegger, in whose philosophy man is but a little exclamation point between two empty dashes; tossed from nothingness to nothingness, he follows on nothing and nothing follows him, and anguish alone proves to him that he is. Heidegger's anguish is taken from Kierkegaard; but in Kierkegaard anguish is the result of man's having lost continuity with God, it is the sign of death, like dark flowers on a grave. What Kierkegaard knows to indicate the defeat of truly human existence, Heidegger makes its sum total; what spells death to the one, the other calls life. No wonder that the Heidegger-man, anguished and lost in the Heidegger-nothingness, was ready for allurement and sharp orders, eager for the Hitler-nothingness to drown out his own.[101]

Nor is Heidegger alone; by their divorce from the hierarchy of values, Fichte, Hegel, and Nietzsche were among the forerunners of the dictator. In Fichte's and Hegel's thought, the state is taken out of context, severed from the true order of the universe, made absolute, and so it was in Hitler's speeches and acts. But while they still acted out of esteem, however mistaken, for the political realm, Hitler's only motive was to use the absolute state for the destruction of order. To uproot was all that counted with him. This was also why Nietzsche's superman, the uprooted man *par excellence,* fascinated him, for in the superman he found confirmation that it was possible to be torn away from oneself and still exist. But even without Nietzsche, Hitler would have arrived at the situation of the superman, for where else can the totally uprooted man go if not "above" or "below" man, to crime or to madness or to both? Summing up, Picard states that all thinkers who uproot and destroy, who hate order and measure, are, no matter how unlike Hitler they seem, akin to him.[102]

It is frightening to think how ready society was for the total state. Justice was ready, and so was science. Picard gives as an instance the trial in the thirties of Kuerten, "the monster of Duesseldorf," the slayer of many women. Psychiatric and psychological experts made so many speeches, he recalls, that the court ceased to be a court and became a seminar in criminology. The point was no longer murder, no longer the value of human life, rather the validity of certain psychological hypotheses. Murder, life, court, justice were all brushed aside, and enthroned upon the seat of justice was psychology, so that little effort was needed for the total state to do away with justice entirely. And long before Hitler, one half of the I. G. Farben laboratories was producing the most complicated drugs for the prolongation of life, the other half the most elaborate tools of destruction, such as poison gas. Hence chemistry too was ripe to be taken over; with its help the total state could establish side by side the killing machinery of total war and the machinery of total life control.[103]

Not only philosophers and writers, artists and scientists, but the high-strung, nervous mood of our age prepared for Hitler's power. Living in and for the moment, the discontinuous man has no time to grow, and since everything has to be done in haste, he becomes restless and nervous. Also, because the moment of experience is not joined with the past, it must bear its full burden alone, with no other moments to share the weight. So souls are overburdened, weighed down, worn out, and they scream; when Hitler came and screamed the loudest, Picard shudders, they let him cry for them.

What is worse, some souls are so isolated in this world of discontinuity that they fear to move from one mental impression to another, because they fear that in moving they would leave behind the first and not attain the second. They cling therefore to the one impression, fastening themselves to it, so that their idea becomes a fixed idea or their action a compulsive action. So cut off is the obsessed soul that nothing seems to exist of it or of the whole wide world but the one idea or the one action. The neurosis of such a man, who no longer jumps from moment to moment as the age demands but is paralyzed by the compulsion of just one moment, is really an attempt to get well, to escape from the rush of momentariness, Picard explains. But finding it impossible to free himself from the race of moments by stopping in one moment, he falls sick—it may well be that God's eyes rest on him with more friendliness than on the sort of analyst who would prefer to push him back into the discontinuous world. Psychoanalysis tries to make mobile again such a soul fixed in one instant by establishing a connection between the fixed idea and some former experience; having made this one step, the soul is expected to be able to go on and make others. Yet even if this device succeeds, the patient is not cured; he is merely enabled to manipulate, to function in the world of the momentary again. Agile once more, he finds himself returned to the race of moments, again exhausted, again wishing to scream and glad to find someone to do the screaming for him. If, on the other hand, the neurotic is not set in motion, if he stays stuck in his fixed idea, he may be glad to exchange his little obsession for a big, for Hitler.[104]

As a horrendous climax, schizophrenia and cancer show how well suited the world was for the Fuehrer, the captain of discontinuity. In schizophrenia, *the* mental disease of the day, the person is as if broken off from himself; even the "normal" person today is split in two, the difference being only that the "well" man takes this rupture for granted and lives with it undisturbed, while the victim of schizophrenia can no longer maneuver—in his case, the machinery of discontinuity has come to a stop. The "normal" man operates with discontinuity as if it were legitimate; the split man, however, feels discontinuity as a sin, and still having the power for catastrophe, refuses to be a profiteer of disjointedness, which makes him more human than the "well." Schizophrenia was a preparation for the rule of Hitler, and at the same time it is a warning to those who would have man and the world run on discontinuity.

Cancer, too, corresponds in its structure to the structure of the world. Bursting apart the pattern of cells, growing rank and parasitically, worming its way in all directions, it is as if it were all by itself and not at all in a body, which can live only by cooperation. *It* is there, the cancer, and nothing else. Again is man warned—the peril his mind failed to detect is demonstrated in his flesh: man dies of discontinuity.[105]

Judgment and Rescue

Ordinarily punishment is deferred, a generation or two passing between sin and its penalty, but our day, like Jeremias', is extraordinary: the punishment is instant, Picard trembles to see. In 1934 Mussolini had King Alexander of Yugoslavia and the French Foreign Minister, Louis Barthou, assassinated with a sub-machine gun; a few years later, he himself was slain with a sub-machine gun. When Germany stole the Sudetenland from Czechoslovakia in 1938, Poland grabbed for a share of the spoils; it did not take long before Poland herself was despoiled and divided. The Nazi government expelled the Lorrainers and Poles from their homes and gave their land to Germans; not long afterward, Germans were driven from their villages in East Germany, Czechoslovakia, and Yugoslavia, and had no place to go. The Nazis turned the Jews out of their homes with fifteen kilos of baggage, packed them into boxcars and sent them into the wide spaces of death; very soon, the Germans had to order their own people out of their houses with fifteen kilos of baggage, into cattle trucks, to flee from the Russians, and the only shelter they found were the craters in bombed-out cities. Only the mass-production tortures in concentration camps, the factorylike vivisection of human beings, the routine gassing of millions, have so far gone unpunished —probably because these crimes are so unhuman that the only fit penalty would be to wipe out not only the criminals but all men, and with them, all the world.[106]

Would one not have expected that a crime machinery as vast as that of National Socialism, which employed a hundred million people and used the whole space of Europe, would run for centuries, and that it would take hundreds of years more for it to wear out and crumble? The uncanny thing is that it lasted only a few years and took only a few months to break apart. That sin and punishment are pressed into so short a space corresponds to this world of the momentary. Today crime does not stand alone, punishment is right at its side—and this is a sign. "Word came to me from the Lord," said the prophet Ezechiel, "Strange, that a proverb should be current in Israel, The fathers have eaten sour grapes, and the children's teeth are being set on edge! As I am a living God, the Lord says, this proverb shall be current in Israel no more. . . . It is the guilty soul that must die." [107] Punishment no longer tarries; whoever does evil will himself bear the penalty, and not only his sons. Since our age no longer trusts the teaching that violence and hatred and crime must not be given recognition, must not be given a home among men, the events of the day have to demonstrate it to us. There were violence and hatred and crime in former days, but there was also true doctrine, and when someone acted against it, his crime was a falling away from doctrine. Today, however, in the Nazi age, with doctrine despised, the crime itself must do the teaching.[108]

This swift succession of crime and punishment is apocalyptic; it seems as if time were running out, as if the Last Judgment had begun, Picard declares—but he hopes that it is rather the painful process of healing. In Nazism, all that is disjointed, decayed, and evil was drawn together as poison is drawn together from the members of the body into one organ, there to be diagnosed, there to be eliminated. In many of their crimes, the Germans acted as proxies for the rest of mankind, but they cannot excuse themselves on that account, nor can the other nations claim not to have been infected. Nazism was a monument of evil—like the tower of Babel, where no one sorrowed when a workman fell to his death but all grieved over a fallen stone—a monument erected in Germany with contributions from all the world, a reminder for all the world to look at. That Germany gave it room and lent hands to its building, that the evil work went on without halt, is her terrible guilt. Then when the tower broke down, it was not only to punish Germany but also to warn all nations; it broke down that the power of evil might be broken not only in that one country but in all.[109]

Dare we expect that the power of evil will be broken? Among the tokens of hope Picard mentions are the individuals, the exceptions, as he calls them, who have remained unsoiled amid the general decay; to whom goodness, truth, and beauty, once with the whole people, have fled, as to shelters chosen and guarded by God. Then there are the primal phenomena of human life, with their healing power: In the midst of disintegration and ruin, still is a child born and loved by its mother, man and wife love one another, and death comes and brings sorrow, as if no man had died before. Yes, these are the primal phenomena, and in their presence it is as if the world of dissolution were not. Whenever a child is born, whenever two love each other, whenever a man dies, a chance is given for a wholly new man and a wholly new world. Perhaps, Picard muses, it is more than a chance, perhaps it is a sign God gives Himself to be mindful of the new man and the new world. Then it would be more than a mere human expectation; it would be a divine promise. There is another token of hope, the poverty that has come over Germany and Europe. Despite the devastation and suffering it brings, poverty can awaken in man his primal powers, for in it he has nothing save that he is, and so comes close to God, who Is. And if the help we give to this elemental poverty possesses elemental strength, new life can spring from their union.[110]

Man's ultimate hope is in Christ, Picard rejoices; only in Him are these tokens redeemed, only through Him can man regain the continuity he has lost. Before His coming, there was an abyss of discontinuity between God and man, between the Infinite and the finite, between the Eternal and the mortal, between the unceasing Lover and him whose love is broken. But Christ is the Bridge. By God's becoming Man and man's faith in the God-Man, by God's love and man's response, not only is discontinuity abolished but the greatest continuity is created. So much does man need God-made-Man that only through Him is his humanity held together. As man is held together by Christ, so all human events. All history before Him pushed toward the spot where He entered the world; the history of the Old Covenant moved together and all at once found itself the prelude to Christ's coming. So great was the might of His coming that all the past entered into continuity with its haloed presence, and that from it there radiates continuity to the end of time.[111]

Christ is man's ultimate hope, the hand of the Lord outstretched, the love of heaven proffered. He is God leaping to the side of man, and this is what the world needs most: divine intervention, the intervention we knew, Picard exclaims, when, against human expectation, Hitler was annihilated. For years he stood on the verge of total victory, but he never quite reached it. He was about to invade England, with every chance of success, but he let the the moment slip by. He saw the very towers of Moscow, but he could not march into Moscow. He raised the banner of the hooked cross over the highest peak of the Caucasus, but he never conquered the desperately needed Caucasion oilfields. His scientists came very close to the atom bomb but, as Churchill said, God's providence did not let him have it; it did not permit the most terrible of weapons to be put in the hands of the most terrible of men. So great were the prospects of his power that he should have succeeded in everything. But success deserted him. It was not that he was without skill and shrewdness; for a time the whole of Europe was at his feet and did not dare breathe except with his breath. But one day his breath stopped. When his colossal power collapsed, his fall was so total, so beyond human dimensions, that the superiority in arms of America, England, and Russia does not account for it.

Not often has man been allowed to see so clearly God's intervention in his history. Everything happened as in a great drama. There was a criminal beginning, but it was a beginning of small crimes, as if the beginner in crime was to be given time to reflect and amend. There was the second act, of growing crimes and growing victories; and after that, the third, in which crime and victory at their most swollen seemed to absorb the world of the good. Then came the peripeteia, the sudden reverse: victories ceased but crimes grew more furiously than before. And at the end: destruction, death, and the bodies removed from the stage. The strange thing is that Hitler did not have the makings of a dramatic hero: he was a wrought-up, evil *nothing*, whose malice was pedantic, bought in the "malice department" of a department store. He was a shabby villain, not a Richard III, not even a court jester to a Richard III, for he was without humor, and such a thing does not happen in Shakespeare's world, not even in his underworld. Yet Hitler had to act like a man of destiny, with a dramatic rise and downfall, as if he had been forced to demonstrate, clearly and on a gigantic scale, that when it threatens the world, evil is annihilated.

It would have been just, Picard reflects, had Hitler won the final victory; it would have suited the condition of Germany and of other nations, for he was so empty that he was nothing but the representation of an empty world, that he matched the structure of the age, its disjointedness. But he was not victorious; the world was spared. There was a love for the earth and for men which would not suffer that the whole earth and all men should be sucked into chaos. There was an intervention, although men did not deserve it. And "this is a sign," Picard ends his *Hitler in Our Selves,* "that men and earth do not belong to themselves, but to One who loves them and gives them, again and again, a chance. . . ." No darkness can dismay Max Picard's hope: he calls his most recent book, published in 1951, *Destroyed and Inde-structible World*. A diary of an Italian journey, its last words are: "Over all the doings of man, there is mercy beforehand, a great fore-forgiving. How many dreadful things pass through man's soul, through his mind, between 6:00 o'clock in the morning when he awakens and 10:00 o'clock in the evening when he falls asleep! But man is not able to do all these dreadful things, he is protected against himself. We are rescued—more than we know." [112]

The World of Silence

The thunder of judgment is in Picard's ears, the blast of the last day, he hears the cracking of the structure of the world—and yet his soul and senses are close to the world's beginnings. Soil and seeds, the curling sea and the shy first leaves of spring, the lordly wind, all creatures look at him and he at them as they must have when Adam was young. "Picard is like a man from before the Fall," said the Dominican writer Momme Nissen after visiting him—not meaning, of course, that he was without sin, rather that he was a man of immediacy, in communion with the things of creation, with their *logos*, the word God speaks through them.[113] He has reverent eyes and ears for the virgin phenomena of love, of fidelity and marriage, of life and death, for all the realities primally given, irreducible, indefinable, irreplaceable. They cannot be traced to anything else, they cannot be exchanged for anything else, he says of them; nothing stands behind them to which they can be related, save their Creator. And of these first phenomena the firstborn is silence.[114]

Before all the other elemental phenomena, there was silence, and so it envelops and pervades them, and there is more silence than speech in them; there is more of the voiceless than the voiced in love, fidelity, death, Picard writes in *The World of Silence* (1948). Present in every moment, it is always there, in readiness for it is not an absence, not nonspeech, but in itself an abundant world. Hailing from the hour when what was to be the universe was still at rest, hailing even from the bosom of God, silence's greatness is simply its existence. It does not develop, does not increase in time, but time in it, as though time were sown into it and silence were the soil in which time grows to fullness. Invisible yet manifest, intangible yet felt, extending far off yet intimate, silence is built into the very structure of man.[115]

Silence is the only phenomenon left today that is "without use-fulness," that cannot be fitted into the world of utility, that can-not be exploited for profit, for it has no other purpose than to be, Picard declares. All the other great phenomena, life and love, even death, have been drawn into economy and made "useful"; water and fire have been annexed by the world of profit, and so also the space between heaven and earth—a tunnel for transporta-tion. But silence resists all such efforts: one can "do nothing with it," nothing is to be "gained" from it, it is "unproductive." Hence it is priced as nothing, but still, more helping and healing come forth from silence than from all utility. An alien in the world of "purpose," it stands suddenly next to the all-too-purposeful, *das allzu Zweckhafte*, interrupting the race of this world, frightening by its very purposelessness. It strengthens the intangible in things, it mitigates the harm exploitation has worked, it makes things whole again, taking them out of the splintering world of profit back into the world of integral being. It bestows on things a holy uselessness, for this is another name for silence—holy useless-ness.[116]

Not only does silence restore things to their beginnings, out of it comes something new; sired by the spirit, out of its fullness comes the word. There is something silent in every word, a token of its birth, and when two people speak with one another, a third is always present—silence listens, and this gives breadth to conversa-tion, so that the words no longer have to move in the narrow space of two speakers. It may even join the two as a third: at the end of the Platonic dialogues, it is always as though silence itself were speaking and those who had been speakers had become disciples of silence. But never is silence so audible, Picard continues, as when the last sound of music has died away—music is silence sing-ing in a dream. Its sound is not opposed, like the sound of words, but parallel, to silence. Words are indeed opposed to silence, he avers, but not in hostility; they face each other as world faces world. There could be silence without the word, but never the word without silence; it would be without depth had it not silence for its background. Still, silence is not greater than the word; on the contrary, the world of silence, less the word, is unfinished, un-ordered creation. It is even menacing, but when the word rises out of silence, silence steps forth out of nature, which still lacks the final seal of the spirit; steps forth into history, the world of man, through him taking rightful part in the word.[117]

Since the word is so totally different from silence, man himself could never have made the leap from silence to speech, and that in language two things so disparate are allied is also beyond his doing. In these "impossibles" we see the hand of God, as we do in the superabundance of language. Is it not rich beyond man's need, Picard asks, has it not more in it than is necessary for mere communication? Yes, it surpasses the immediate purpose, the job at hand; in it there is more pain and joy and sadness than man can draw out of it, as if language itself, independently of man, sorrowed and joyed. At times it even makes poetry for itself: "the summer bird," for instance, flies through the summertime of language, but its wings may carry it into deadly winter, and behold, language hastens to plant "frost flowers" for it, which lead it to the "lilies of the valley"—and see, it is spring again in language. This beauty of the word, its wealth and freedom, tell its origin is God.[118]

It could not have been otherwise than that out of silence the word should come, reflects Picard, for when in Jesus Christ the Word came down to men from the silent fullness of the Father, He traced out for all time the road from silence into speech. From the beginning the Word was on His way, and so from the very beginning there was a forthbringing from silence into speech. So tremendous was the event of two thousand years ago that all silence from time immemorial was torn open by speech, it trembled beforehand and broke apart.[119]

Silence is woven through and through the texture of man, but it is never more than the ground for the higher to build on. What is higher than silence is the human word, for only in the word does truth take shape, and it is the word that makes man man. Indeed, language exalts man, for in a way it is more than man himself, Picard rejoices. By its very structure it brings him truth; in it truth presses toward him even before he seeks it—again a sign that man could not have won speech by his own efforts, that it was given him, with its logic, by a Being who is Truth itself. This logic of language points to something outside of man, to objective reality, and when he speaks, he is reminded that truth *is*.

316   *Max Picard*

Because of this objectivity of language, he often expresses more than he intends, and so often learns more from language than his own thoughts put into it. But man is not able to pour words full of truth: to fill the space of language that is thus left empty, he pours in sadness instead, which may link words to the silence in which they long to sink. Christ alone, Picard again rejoices, was able to fill speech brimful with truth. Hence His words are never melancholy; the space of the word being filled with truth, no room is left in it for melancholy.[120]

There is a radiance about truth, the glow of its yearning to expand, and this glow is beauty. Pathfinder of truth, beauty makes its way ready, quietly occupies all space in the name of truth, so that even where it is not acknowledged truth is there, ruling through beauty *in partibus infidelium*. But this radiance which is with the word of truth rests first on silence, so that Keats can speak of beauty as

Thou still unravish'd bride of quietness,
Thou foster-child of silence and slow time.[121]

Were beauty not with silence, silence would sink back into the abyss, into its own darkness, pulling down with it much that belongs to the bright earth. As it is, beauty makes silence light, tender, airy, luminous. In the God-Man, Picard exclaims, these three, word, truth, and beauty, do not simply meet, do not follow one another nor stand by one another; in Him alone are they perfectly one.[122]

"Holy uselessness" is the role of silence in the life of man, and it is just this that makes it his guardian. So needful is it that only in words wed to the greatest silence is there the greatest goodness; so needful that only in its wide spaces is happiness at home, the immensurable descending from mystery; so needful that only if there is silence in a man can grief find its poise, not holding him back from but bearing him toward peace. And it is easier to love when silent, for love's modesty abhors loudness. Indeed, lovers are conspirators of silence, and in it their love can reach out without stop, "over the hills and far away." But that love can reach out into the remotest corners is also its danger, for there it may take in things that should have no part in it. This is why the word is so important to love: to assure that it has only what belongs to it, to found it on truth, to render it clear and concrete, to make it human.[123]

Silence is needed that man may be whole. If a man has within himself the substance of silence, he need not be always watching the movements of his heart or ordering them by his will, Picard remarks; the substance of silence does it for him. And if he possesses qualities that are incompatible, still no crisis will occur, for in the substance of silence there is room enough for the contradictory. Nor do outside things which could be harmful, things which use him up, such as machines, injure the man of silence—he is protected; but today, with the substance of silence lacking, all things are naggingly present all the time. Lifting the oppression of the all-too-many requires the strength of stillness; instead, the task is assigned to typology—one determines a person's type, and from then on he is brought in touch only with things that suit his psychological constitution. But in a world where silence is at work, a man does not end where his psychological structure ends; he is allowed to stretch himself into a world beyond his "aptitudes." A child, for instance, is allowed to learn Greek and Latin, even if he has no talent for them: the silent substance takes in the alien, making it one with his personality and so widening his mental frontiers. The teaching of the ancient languages, with their blending of shyness and might, is important, for in them is manifest the advent of the word from silence and silence's power over the word, how it heals the word. Their teaching is important because they are "useless," not pragmatic, and so take man out of the world of expedience, utility, targets, matter of fact. True teaching is founded on silence.[124]

To be rescued from the many things that besiege him, that crowd in on him today, man must be made silent again—not loud, as psychoanalysis would like. Psychoanalysis belongs to the world of verbal noise, *die Welt des Wortgeraeusches,* in which the word rises not from silence but from the noise of another word; in which events lack a face of their own, for the noise levels everything down, makes them all the same; in which experiment chases after experiment, till man seems to be merely the laboratory assistant who is allowed to note down what they choose to tell him. In this world of verbal noise there rules a machinery of explanation, which seeks not explanations for phenomena but phenomena as material for ready-made explanations. This is exactly what psychoanalysis does, Picard claims. The phenomena of father, mother, and son, for example, perish in its explanations: Oedipus murdered his father and became husband to his mother—psychoanalysis reduces these monstrous facts, as well as father, mother, son, to a mere appendage of an erotic complex. But for Sophocles the tragedy, the murder of the father, makes fatherhood clear: a *father* has been slain, a father! It is true, the incest of the son with his mother destroys for the moment the image of the mother, but it rises clearer than before in the son's expiation; it becomes the primal phenomenon *mother*. Not Oedipus but fate itself seems to blind itself with tears so as not to see how, in the mightiest suffering (and not in the mightiest explanations!), father, mother, and son perish and rise again. When the tragedy is finished, the primal phenomena of father and mother stand erect, in their primal vigor, and the earth seems created more securely than before. The world psychoanalysis dissolves, tragedy restores.[125]

In the world of noise man is ill, for today noise is not simply part of the world; it has established a world all its own, the world of the radio. For the radio there is no longer silence, no longer the word; it is a stamp mill which pounds words into an amorphous mass, which makes modern man amorphous too, shapeless, undecided. Because man has apostatized from the spiritual, the never-ending radio noise, the matter-of-course radio noise, seems to him like the continuous murmuring of water or wind—un-nature like part of nature, *Unnatur erscheint ihm als Natur*. Man ought to be sad that he has lost the word and that radio noise has taken its place, but he is unaware of his loss. Something within him, however, is aware of it, without his knowing, and this makes him restless and nervous. It seems to Picard that the unlimited mass of words thrown at us by the radio is the cause of many modern psychoses, for they demand an answer, but there are too many of them and they come too fast—no answer is possible, no answer is even expected. "The present state of the world and the whole of life is diseased," Picard holds with Kierkegaard. "Were I a physician and were I asked, What do you advise? I should answer: Create silence! Bring men to silence. In today's noise, the word of God cannot be heard. And were it yelled with all the tools of noise, it would no longer be His word. Therefore create silence." [126]

319

Formerly, silence covered all things, and to reach them man had to break through it; it stood even before his own thoughts. Before things and thoughts it was stationed, encamped, and so man and things were protected. Today, the heaven of silence is withdrawn from things; there is but a little here and there, "a minute of silence" in remembrance, "an hour of silence" in a sanitarium, little chinks in time. Only in monastic communities, only among monks and nuns, is there still true silence; what was once in all the world is now cloistered. But perhaps it has not completely withdrawn from man; perhaps it is just asleep in him. Sometimes Picard wonders whether silence and noise are not arming for battle, whether silence is not preparing in secret for an ambush. Perhaps noise increases today, gathers ever new things into itself, that all the noise may be destroyed the more easily when silence launches its surprise attack. Or perhaps the monstrous machinery of noise will explode, and its blast be a loud cry to silence that its time has come.[127]

As yet noise is heavy upon us, mingling the extraordinary with the ordinary, everlasting marvels with the news of the day, so that man can no longer recognize mystery. Thus noise breeds unbelief just as silence is ordered to faith; indeed, Picard says, silence is, as it were, the natural basis on which supernatural faith builds. It is a sign of God's love that there is silence about the mysteries of faith, a reminder to man to hold ready silence of his own in which to come near them. "A God became Man for the sake of men"—this is so unheard-of, so strange to the eye, so new to reason's experience, that man's words cannot meet it. Hence a cloud of silence descends between this mystery and man, in which man approaches the silence that mantles God. When at long last man begins to speak, the word that comes out of the silence is as fresh, as young, as the first word before it was uttered. That is why it can speak of the mystery.[128]

The silence of God is other than the silence of man; it is not opposed to the word, for in Him silence and word are one. If a man has heard, like Paul, "secret words which it is not granted to man to utter," [129] then the ineffable falls heavily into his silence, and whatever words he may speak thenceforth, words coming forth from the deep where the ineffable rests, bear a trace of the ineffable, of heaven.

Within that heaven which most receives His light
I have been, and seen things past the knowledge
Or power of any who comes back to tell—
Because, as it approaches its desire,
Our intellect so deepens as it seeks,
That memory has not the power to follow.[130]

In prayer both word and silence find fulfillment: man's word is poured into God's silence, while man's silence rests there. When man is not praying, his silence receives its meaning in the word; when he prays, it receives its meaning in meeting with the silence of God. When man is not praying, the silence in him serves his word; when he prays, the words of his prayer serve his silence, leading it to the silence of God. Thus Picard ends *The World of Silence* with a praise of prayer.[131]

Return to Beginnings

A few critics have found fault with Picard, and it cannot be said that he has made their work difficult. His book on silence, they maintain, is "unfunctional," not concrete enough in its proposals; his indictment of psychoanalysis ignores its positive findings; his characterization of Hitlerism as the height of discontinuity does not take into account the complexity of National Socialism. Nothing is easier than such carping, for Picard does not want to be "functional," "practical," "complex." Indeed, so deep is his simplicity that his pastor calls him "a rock and a child." "He is spontaneity, life itself," writes Gabriel Marcel, and adds that his thought is not a system; in him all is intuition, or rather, more exactly, lightning.[132]

There is simplicity in his works but no stinting; in them is the lavishness of the elements, of the solid unhurried earth, the free wide waters, the air, all the air, the crimson unfettered fire. And more than these—grace is in his writings, and thanksgiving for it; they reveal his joy in the things that are given, that come from above. He once wrote to the son of his Swiss publisher that he, the son, was certainly more intelligent than his father, but that that was not what mattered; his father had fortune, good fortune, and on this depends everything. Merit, he said, that's a thing that comes from man, but fortune is God-sent, so that he himself would rather be with people who have fortune than with those who have

321

merit. Most beautiful, of course, he concluded, is the attempt to justify fortune from above by merit from below. And that is just what his father did.[133] To his American publisher, Henry Regnery, Picard wrote: "Though I know you are still young, I have always had the impression that you are a man who has already gone the right road for fifty years. Thank God that you are not a 'seeker' (alas, in Germany they are all 'seekers'), but one who knows the right or who is held in the right by a special grace. The latter is even better, and that is what I wish for you: that you be held in the right, not by yourself but by grace." [134]

The works of Picard are "wasteful" because they are the works of a poet, who does not tire of telling the great tales over and over; the works of a seer, for whom truths do not stale; the works of a prophet with one single cry, for a return to firsts, to the things made when in the beginning God created heaven and earth, and beyond them to Him who *was* when they were made, the uncreated Beginning. But Picard does more than call; he has answered the call by his faith. A convert to the Church, he feels as if he had been Catholic all his life—and indeed, she is the guardian of beginnings, of the first phenomena.

In the summer of 1948, my war-interrupted correspondence with Picard was resumed: "I have thought of you often, in prayer and outside of prayer," his first letter to me says. "Some saint must have prayed for both of us, for each of us and once again for both of us together; else we would not be alive. . . . Do you know that my son and I entered Holy Church about ten years ago?" Without waiting for my reply, he wrote again: "Do you know that ten years ago my son and I were baptized, were received into Holy Church?" When I visited him a few weeks later at his home in Caslano and asked him to tell me a little of his way to Christ and to the Church, "I can't do it," was all his reserve let him answer. And he continued: "Do you remember how in 1938 you said of my first books that they could not be fully understood without Christ, that they led to the Church? Then you spoke to me of baptism and you said that I should notify you, that you would come from wherever you were. And I answered you— Baptism? That is out of the question! But less than a year later, at Easter, 1939, I was baptized." Then he told the story of a young friend of his, a girl who did not want to marry her suitor, because her love was music. And he advised: "That's all right. Let her love her music, and then love itself will overwhelm her."

It was this power of love, it was the power of truth, that conquered Picard. For a long time he was held back—"What hindered us from receiving baptism was that we were ashamed to leave the persecuted Jews," he admitted in a later letter. "My son and I knew full well that baptism would not save us from the gas chambers nor bring us any favor with the Nazis. Still, though for them we should have remained Jews just as much as before, and so could not be suspected of cowardice, we felt we would be cut off from those who were beaten the most. So for a long time, we denied ourselves baptism. Suddenly I saw that, in regard to baptism, my feelings, my likes and dislikes, mattered not at all; that I simply had to be where truth was. So we were baptized." When a Jew is baptized, he is nearer the fathers, nearer the prophets; the marvel of Jacob's ladder is worked again, the wonders of the Red Sea are wrought anew, and the new covenant of which Jeremias speaks is engraved in his heart.[135]

On the last day of my visit in 1948, Max Picard walked with me from his lakeside cottage part way to my lodgings on the hill of Neggio. Without prelude he stopped, there in the meadow beside the brook his walks so often followed, and said: "I must leave you now. But before I say goodbye, please give me your blessing." And knowing so well that what makes the human figure sure is the passion of Christ, that what makes the human face radiant is His love, he bowed his head and asked that I put on his brow the sign of the cross.

Edith Stein

WITNESS OF LOVE

An unmotherly woman—which is not at all the same as a woman who has no children—is a specter, almost all the world admits. Only a feminist, in the fever of the extreme, will deny that woman's calling differs from man's, that for all their common human nature, the souls of men and women have each their own design, declared Edith Stein, who herself had known this fever. Small and insignificant in stature, when she spoke she seemed to grow, as if she would take all things into her arms, the while her marvelous eyes looked into a far reality. So it was in Salzburg in 1930, when she lectured before the Catholic Association of University Men and Women, a lecture which all at once made her known far beyond philosophical circles. The clear and irrefutable word of Scripture utters, she said, what from the very beginning of the world daily experience teaches: Woman is made to be the helpmeet of man and his mother. For this her body is fitted and this is the endowment of her soul, tending more toward people than toward things and affairs, more toward the concrete than toward the abstract, tending always toward the living, the personal, the whole. It is the whole she wishes to foster—not, for instance, the mind at the expense of the heart, nor mind and heart at the expense of the body. This same motherly bent toward wholeness marks woman's cognitive life. What speak to her first and are her joy are image and encounter, not concept and law, so that she does not go out after fixed and solid systems but rather opens herself to contents, wide, flowing, and colorful. Her knowing, much like the artist's, is a waiting on and listening to truth rather than its pursuit.

There is nothing in women of the narrowness of the specialist; theirs is a universality not easily found in men, Chesterton remarks. "Woman," he says, "is generally shut up in a house with a human being at the time when he asks all the questions that there are, and some that there aren't." [1] To nurse and keep and shield and help grow—this is every woman's natural, motherly desire and skill, and to them are joined her desire and skill as companion. Her gift and happiness are in sharing in another person's life, and sharing means to her, Edith Stein continues in her lecture *The Ethos of Womanly Callings,* sharing in everything that concerns the person she loves, in the great things and the small, in his joys and sorrows, in his work and his problems. A man is likely to be wrapped up in his affairs, and even more so in a cause, expecting from others interest and ready service; but more often than not, he finds it hard to bring them and their concerns into focus. For a woman, who is more nearly timeless, who is never so much a "contemporary" as a man, this adjustment is natural; with the ease and flexibility that are her talent, she can enter sympathetically into, and understand, fields otherwise remote from her, in which she would have no concern were it not for her interest in a person. And it is her overflowing wealth of heart, her almost limitless ability to devote herself, her patience—while man may be able to do more, she can endure more; while he has greater thrusting power, she has more energy in store—that help her partake in man's life, a partaking which awakens his strength and multiplies his achievements. So important in his life is this hidden care, this rearing and mothering, that the mature man still needs it—even he and precisely he. Not for nothing does man call his beloved his "tender, sweet heart."

Because man serves his cause more directly and woman more for his sake, it is appropriate that she do so under his guidance. Scripture's demand for her obedience to him as her head is not a caprice, is not against the logic of things. On the contrary, the biblical command gives word to the metaphysic of the sexes. If their partnership is seen under the image of a tree, man is the tuft, woman the root, the whole hidden root bearing even the highest tuft and the sunlit tuft bearing even the furthest root, the root filling the top with its strength, the top governing the root by its encompassing power.[2] Nor is woman's destiny to obedience degrading, for it corresponds to her own inclination. "Obedient, I always felt my soul most beautifully free," Edith Stein quotes Goethe's Iphigenie; and the Countess Apollonia von Frangipani sent to her imprisoned husband in Venice a golden ring as pledge of her fidelity, engraved with the proud, submissive words: *Myt wyllen dyn eygen,* "By my will thine own." [3]

The perfect embodiment of woman, mother and spouse, is Mary, the blessed among women. Womanhood's perfect symbol, she is far more, for her every instant was grace, her whole life Godborne. The surrender out of strength, out of love, which is woman's, is transcendently magnified in Mary's humble and queenly answer to the angel: "Be it done unto me!" In the center of her life, Edith Stein continues, stands her Son: blissfully she awaits

His birth; provident and wakeful, she guards His childhood; faithfully she follows Him in His journeys, or not, as He desires; in her arms she holds His dead body, taken from the cross; then goes to do His last will. And all this is not her own undertaking; in all this she obeys a call, she is the handmaid of the Lord. Her child she does not count her own possession; into the hands from which she received Him she puts Him back, first in the Temple, then beneath the cross. As perfectly as she is mother is she wife. Because of her unlimited confidence in her spouse, she relies on an unlimited confidence on his part in her, so that as a matter of course they stand together in trial and hardship; at all times, she looks with quiet obedience toward him who had been given her as an earthly protector and head.[4]

Woman's talents, perfect in Mary, are in all other women tied to a wounded nature, and hence are always in peril of being distorted, Edith Stein warns. Her gift for the personal, if not guarded, may become preoccupation with herself and a desire for others' preoccupation with her; it may become vanity, an inordinate wish for praise or an uncontrolled need for communication. On the other hand, it may turn into an excessive, indiscreet interest in others, into curiosity, gossip, intrusion. Her sense for the whole may easily lead to a scattering of her forces, to an aversion to the disciplining of her powers, to a shallow sampling of many fields, and to a possessiveness that goes far beyond genuine motherly care. From flexibility to slavishness; from the power of bringing things together, of seeing *both* this *and* that, to ambiguity; from kinship with pain to whining; from the genius for friendship and alliance to narrowness, partisanship, and fanaticism—such are the penalties for an unhealthy exaggeration of woman's virtues. The sympathetic companion becomes an intruder, who does not allow persons and things to ripen in peace and silence, and there is petty domineering where there ought to be the joy and strength of service.[5]

As a remedy against these infirmities Edith Stein counsels the thoroughness of intellectual work, which acts as antidote to the overpersonal, does away with superficiality and, in its calling for subordination to objective laws, is a school of obedience. Provided that she avoids the cult of specialization, intellectual discipline leads a woman to maturity and harmony; it gives her true culture, a real *humanitas*. But however helpful culture's government of the soul, grace is required if fallen nature is to be purged of foreign matter and radically reshaped. Hence a womanly life must be a liturgical life, for in praying the prayer of the Church, a woman (and indeed, a man) enters a communion wide and widening, the "We" of the body of the faithful. More than that, the participation in the divine life which the liturgy grants has a liberating power, lessening the weight of earthly affairs and giving to us in time a bit of eternity, to us on pilgrimage a foretaste of the goal.[6]

Of course, the home is woman's special province, but there are many walks outside the home in which she can fulfill her womanly calling—medicine, teaching, social work, any of the sciences that deal with the living and the personal, or work that demands sympathetic penetration into another's thought, like editing or translating. Even if she is forced into a field not well fitted to her nature, such as a factory, an office, or a laboratory, a woman can play a part that is uniquely hers. In these fields, fields characteristically men's, in which they in particular can easily lose their full humanity, woman's concern for persons and for wholeness can be a counterweight.

But over and above all these, Edith Stein stresses, the Lord calls women out of the family and the world to the service of religion. Though this summons goes to man and woman alike, it has special significance for her. For to abandon oneself in self-forgetting love, to let one's own life end that there may be room for the divine life—this is the motive, the beginning and the end, of convents and monasteries. The divine life is love, overflowing, needing nothing, spending freely of itself; it is love bending down to the one in need, healing that which is sick, awakening that which is dead, protecting, nursing, teaching, shaping, mourning with the mourners, rejoicing with the joyful, serving every creature that it may come to the end God made it for. But to abandon herself lovingly, to become another person's possession and to possess him entirely—is not this what woman desires?

Love is . . . a better thing to own
Than all of the wide impossible stars
    over the heavens blown.[7]

329

If she surrenders herself thus utterly to another human being, however, her abandonment is perverted, she herself enslaved, and she claims of him what no man can give. Only God can receive such surrender entirely, and so receive it that the giver does not lose his soul but wins it. And only God can give Himself till He fills His creature's being, and yet lose nothing. This absolute surrender, the principle of the religious life, is also the absolute fulfillment of woman's want.[8]

Are we to infer from this, Edith Stein asks, that in order to fulfill her womanly vocation, every woman must become a nun? By no means. What we must conclude is that to restore woman's nature to its metaphysical purity, its authentic estate, to raise it to the height of its ethos, a bridal surrender to God is needed. If she gives the dawn of her day to Him rather than letting her cares and activities crowd on her, if she makes her will the prisoner of His will and puts her heart into His hands to be shaped, she will become what she ought to be: wide, still, empty of herself, warm and clear, filled with joy and courage and love "till others catch the living flame." [9] No matter whether she is a mother and home-maker, or a member of a profession standing in the public eye, or a religious in a cloister, a true woman must always be the hand-maid of the Lord. And what is said here of woman must be said analogously of man. Neither can live his proper part, neither can fulfill the idea of womanhood or manhood, without a life of the spirit; as she is womanly, so he is manly, only when close to God. And each is but half of humanity, for God created man male and female, and each according to His likeness. That He may be fully mirrored in mankind and that His government over it may be perfect, woman must be woman and man man.[10]

When speaking thus of woman's calling, Edith Stein, in her modesty, was hardly aware that she drew a picture of herself. Dom Damasus Zaehringer, of the Benedictine abbey of Beuron, describes his first encounter with her: "As I met her in the portry for the first time, her figure and bearing made an impression on me which I can compare only to the Orant, the paintings in the passageways and vaults of the catacombs, which picture the Church under the image of a woman with arms raised in prayer. Apart from the posture of lifted arms," he tells, "everything about her recalled that early Christian symbol. And this was not a fanciful flash. Truly a symbol of the Church standing in time and yet lifted out of it, Edith Stein, in her union with Christ, knew little else than His words: 'For them I dedicate Myself, that they also may be dedicated in truth.' " [11]

Christ, Holder of the Heart

Edith Stein was born in Breslau on October 12, 1891, that year the Day of Atonement, on which the Jews pray: "Our God and God of our fathers, let our prayer come before Thy face, nor hide Thyself from our supplication. We are not so shameless and stiff-necked as to say before Thee, O Lord our God and God of our fathers, that we are just and have not sinned. Indeed, we have sinned." [12] The Day of Atonement is one of forgiveness, and hence, it has been said, a day of great joy to God. On that day, in biblical times, the high priest placed his hands on a goat that it might be laden with the sins of the people and carry them away into the desert void, and another he slew, that its blood, sprinkled on the altar, might call down God's cleansing mercy, the whole ritual pointing toward the One who would bear man's iniquities and blot out his sins by His blood.[13] Looking back on Edith Stein's life, the date of her birth seems to set its theme.

The youngest of a large and loving family, she took eagerly to her eldest brother's tutelage. Carrying her about in his arms, he lectured to her on Goethe, Schiller, and other German poets and playwrights, showed her their pictures and told her of their works, and her exceptional memory retained it all. When her older sisters and their friends played "Authors," the four-year-old knew all the answers at once, while they had to reflect. This was not the false promise of many a precocious child, for throughout her schooldays she distinguished herself among her classmates. So unusual were her attainments that the oral examinations ordinarily required for graduation from the *Gymnasium* were waived in her case, and its director, who included in his farewell address an epigram about each graduate, characterized her: *Schlag an den Stein und Weisheit springt heraus,* "Strike the stone and wisdom springs forth." [14]

For two years Edith Stein studied German philology at the University of Breslau, and it was there, in 1912—to be exact, during a seminar on the psychology of thought—that her attention was drawn to Husserl's *Logical Investigations.* Not only did she read its two volumes, a labor Husserl was to describe at their first meeting as a "heroic feat," but she recognized at once that he was "the philosopher of our day." Soon afterward she made up her mind to study at Goettingen—a friend had told her: "There, philosophy is talked day and night, at table and on the street, everywhere." Her joy at the thought of working under Husserl was written on her face, so unmistakably that at a New Year's Eve party her friends made a little jingle: "While other girls dream of kisses, Husserl is what Edith wishes." At Easter, 1913, she moved to Goettingen and immersed herself in psychology, history, and philology, but the great experience of her years there was its philosophical world: the men and their thought.

It was the custom in university towns to pay calls on one's professors, and in Goettingen one went first to Adolf Reinach, who looked after new arrivals. Telling of her first visit to his study, which was dominated by a large reproduction of Michelangelo's "Creation of Adam," she says that never before had anyone met her with such pure goodness of heart. "Love from close relatives and from friends who had known me for years seemed a matter of course, but here there was something different. It was like a first look into an entirely new world." After the outbreak of World War I, Edith Stein left for a time the books that were her passion in order to serve as a Red Cross aide. But in 1916 she returned and received her doctor's degree *summa cum laude* at Freiburg im Breisgau, her dissertation being *On the Problem of Empathy.* This was shortly after Husserl had accepted the chair of philosophy there, and now he asked her, his outstanding student, to stay with him as his personal assistant.[15]

In the many literary and philosophical discussions with fellow students that mark university life, as well as in private conversations, Edith Stein's opinion was often looked to as a measure. But in spite of the authority lent her by her unfailing logic and wide knowledge, she never wore an air of superiority, nor did she ever fit into the frame expected of a woman who puts her mind to learning. No pedant, "grind," or killjoy, she loved to hike through the mountains with friends, and relished their simple meals in the forest—dark bread with a few slices of sausage, a little fruit and chocolate. Years later her description of the Goettingen countryside was still filled with her joy in the ruin-crowned hills, in the green slopes, tilled fields and trim villages, wreathed about with woods, in the beech trees and their autumn glow of red and gold. To this day her friends remember how enchanted she was by the many-colored butterflies and bright flowers, and how pleased she was one night they spent in a mountaintop inn, for from her bed she could look down the Rhine valley to the far lights of Basel, while the stars hung overhead. And they remember that even when plans went awry, she was equable and always happy.

What also stand out in the written recollections of her friends, and later, of her students, are her unassuming ways. One friend recalls her saying: "The translator must be like a windowpane, which admits the light but is itself unseen." Though inadequate to the labor of a true translator, whose work is re-creation, this simile tells much of Edith Stein herself, of her remarkable modesty. Again, as Husserl's assistant, she realized that many of his new students came to Freiburg unprepared for his thought and method, and so undertook to teach an introductory course. When asked: "Well, you hold a pro-seminar in philosophy in Freiburg?" she made little of her own work: "Oh no, I conduct a philosophical kindergarten." [16]

Edith Stein grew up when the twentieth century was young and presumptuous; when it thought that without the burden of belief, without a Master and Judge, without sin and forgiveness, it could run to perfection more swiftly; when it laughed at the assurance of the psalmist that without God as Builder, the builder's toil comes to nothing, that without the Lord as the city's Guardian, our vigil is vain.[17] It was an age so infatuated with the many marvelous details it had discovered as to ignore the whole, and so absorbed by the little things of creation as to have no mind for their Creator. Small wonder that in such an intellectual climate she lost the faith of her childhood, for though she had before her eyes the piety of an exemplary mother, it could not withstand what she must then have considered the "demands of reason."

Life in Goettingen, however, proved a new departure. "The study of philosophy," she once remarked, "is a continuous walking along the brink of the abyss." [18] Those who, in fearful preference for

333

mediocrity, deafen themselves to the great questions and shun alike the anguish and the joy of thought, live in an illusory comfort, while the philosopher, who has taken upon himself the search for truth, cannot plead ignorance or unawareness—every moment of his is a moment of responsibility. And in his search he may come terribly close to the untrue, for only a knife's edge divides it from the true. But though he may fall into error, darkness and despair, he may come, on the other hand, to know philosophy's insufficiency and his own, and thus be ready to be captured by the living God.

Christianity first came within Edith Stein's horizon when her Germanistic studies led her to read the Lord's Prayer in Gothic. It must have suggested to her that man's end is not man, that his goal is not within him but above and beyond, in a vision and love greater than he, the kingdom of God. She was even more impressed on hearing the same words spoken *to* God. One night she and a friend were given a bed at a mountain farm. In the morning, they were greatly struck when the Catholic head of the house joined in morning prayers with his laborers, and having begged God's blessing, shook hands with them as they set out for the day's mowing. Her first intellectual encounter, however, with the world of faith was the lectures Max Scheler gave in the summer of 1913 for the Philosophical Society in Goettingen, in which "he poured forth Catholic ideas with the whole splendor of his mind and the whole power of his language," as Edith Stein herself remarks. As he spoke of absolute being, before which the thinker knows himself a creature and dependent; of the holy, that irreducible and highest value, which is prior to all metaphysical knowledge of God and even to faith in Him; of modern humanitarianism, which isolates man from God, ridiculing even the thought of salvation; and of Christ, who bids man love God above all things, and in whose love he is saved—as he spoke of all these, pronouncing the key words with a tenderness and devotion all his own, there opened to Edith Stein a world till then unknown to her. His words "did not lead me to faith," she writes, "but they unlocked to me a province of 'phenomena' which I could no longer pass by blindly. It was not for nothing that it had been driven into us that we should look at all things without prejudice, that we should throw off our blinders. Without knowing it, I had grown up in the narrow rationalistic prejudice; now it fell away, and suddenly there stood before me the world of faith. People with whom I went about daily, to whom I looked up with admiration, lived in this world, and so it must merit, at the least, ardent reflection." Still, she tells, too busy with other things, she did not give it systematic attention, but her resistance was gone.[19]

Edith Stein might never have walked further on the road to faith had she not been urged by the secret of the cross. Her first vivid confrontation with it was in the house of Anna Reinach, whose husband was killed in action in November 1917. For a little while, Anna Reinach tells, she was beside herself with the searing, crushing pain; then came the streaming light: He is in God's peace, he is at the goal, a thing so great and important that compared with it nothing else matters. Suffering had wounded and opened her soul, as only suffering can, and then the strength of the cross, a peace not of this world, entered. So clearly was her life placed on a new plane that when friends came to comfort her, they themselves left comforted, with a solace they had never known. Among them was Edith Stein, who came from Freiburg to attend the funeral, weeks after Adolf Reinach's death, and who later gave up her position as Husserl's assistant in order to live for a time with Reinach's widow and edit his papers. The faith they revealed, together with its existential proof in Anna Reinach, prepared her to believe. Prostration beneath grief, resignation with teeth clenched, or rebellion, she might have understood, but the conquest of death, its joyful acceptance, staggered her. Many years later, not long before her own death, she told a priest: "There I encountered for the first time the cross and the divine power it communicates to those who bear it. It was my first glimpse of the Church, born of Christ's redeeming passion, in her victory over the sting of death. And that was the moment in which my unbelief crumbled, in which Judaism paled before the dawn of Christ, Christ in the mystery of the cross." [20]

She felt herself the blessing of the cross in 1921, when she freely surrendered to God something dear and beautiful, lest hers be a divided heart. So tender an event is it that one feels remiss in not telling it, but one must respect her reserve about her inner life. Once, asked about the steps that led to her conversion, she replied: *Secretum meum mihi*, "Heart, keep thy secret, heart keep thy secret." [21] Because of this reticence, it is difficult to recon-

335

struct her spiritual development. She was living at the time with her friend and fellow philosopher, Hedwig Conrad-Martius, who together with her husband worked a large orchard in Bergzabern in der Rheinpfalz. The days she spent tending to the trees or in housework, and the evenings in study—"My yearning for the truth," she was to relate of this period, "was one single prayer." One day, her biographer recounts, when her host and hostess were away, she went to the bookshelves; "quite at random," Edith Stein is quoted, "I chose a bulky volume: *The Life of St. Teresa of Avila, Written by Herself.* I began to read, was immediately captured, and never stopped reading till the end. As I closed the book, I said to myself: 'This is the truth.'" All the night till morning grayed she had read this life marked by the cross, by total love and tireless courage. And that very morning was the poet's prayer fulfilled:

Live in these conquering leaves; live all the same;
And walk through all tongues one triumphant Flame.
Live here, great Heart; and love and die and kill;
And bleed and wound; and yield and conquer still.
Let this immortal life where'er it comes
Walk in a crowd of loves and Martyrdoms.
Let mystic Deaths wait on't; and wise souls be
The love-slain witnesses of this life of thee.[22]

That same day Edith Stein went into the town to buy a catechism and a missal, which she studied till she mastered them. Only then did she go to the parish church to be present at holy Mass; "None of it was strange to me. Thanks to my previous reading, I understood every little ceremony," she is again quoted. "I waited for the priest to finish his thanksgiving, then followed him into the rectory, and without preliminaries, asked to be baptized. He looked at me astonished, and told me that preparation was needed. 'For how long have you been instructed, and by whom?' he asked. And all I could answer was, 'Please ask me some questions, Father.'" [23]

Hedwig Conrad-Martius, whose home Edith Stein shared at the time her faith was maturing, gives—though not certain about her memories—a slightly different account, but the two versions do not contradict, rather supplement one another. As she remembers

336 *Edith Stein*

it, Edith Stein, like many phenomenologists, read most intensively the writings of St. Teresa,

Those rare Works, where thou shalt leave writ,
Love's noble history, with wit
Taught thee by none but Him.[24]

Deep as was Edith Stein's veneration for the Saint, Dr. Conrad-Martius nonetheless doubts that the reading of her *Life* was the cause of her conversion. But though not the main weight, may it not have been the last ounce that turned the scales, the final impetus that persuaded her to action? Christ had stirred and seized her soul, her friend testifies; she had come to know Him as the Way, as uncreated Grace made manifest, and found in the Church God's Love-Will at work. Once, having attended, with Dr. Conrad-Martius, the Sunday service in the Protestant church in Bergzabern, she remarked: "In Protestantism heaven is closed, in Catholicism it is open." Even before her baptism, Dr. Conrad-Martius thinks, Edith Stein had risen each morning to attend holy Mass, nor could the darkness of winter deter her, for even then she knew the Eucharist the center of spiritual life;[25] she knew it so ineffable a mystery that our inadequacy compels us to say, as if this were possible: Here God's generosity outdoes itself: Here Love feeds man; here the Body of Christ, like a live coal permeated, gleaming, afire with the Divinity, enkindles man's soul and draws him into the divine life.

On the first day of 1922, the feast of Christ's Circumcision, when He bequeathed to His Father "the first fruits of His growing death,"[26] Edith Stein was baptized. The renunciation of Satan and his works, the profession of faith in the Father, Son, and Holy Ghost, the request for baptism, made by all catechumens, she pronounced in Latin, with ardor and determination, but at the same time, Hedwig Conrad-Martius relates, "she had the happiness of a child, and this was most beautiful."[27] Now, in the company of Jesus, all the wonders of Judaism paled, as do the wonders of infancy and youth when we come to our full stature. Yet illumined by their Fulfillment, they shone the more. Abraham, Isaac and Jacob, Moses and Josue, Elias and Eliseus, David and all the saints of the Old Covenant were no longer merely her kinsmen in the flesh but her fathers in the spirit. The Menorah, the seven-

337

branched light, spoke of Him who set alight the earth, for one of the several Jewish interpretations of the sevenfold lamp is the seven words that in Hebrew make the psalm verse: "From the rising to the setting of the sun, let the Name of the Lord be praised." [28] The Passover lamb hailed Him, the Lion of Judah, who was slain like a lamb. And the great exodus from Egypt foreshadowed the greater exodus of which Christ is the Leader.

From Husserl to Thomas

Early in Edith Stein's Catholic life, there appeared in the *Yearbook for Philosophy and Phenomenological Research* three of her philosophical essays, of particular interest for the light they cast on her inner development, conceived and written as they were before her conversion. In the very year of her baptism, the first two were published, one on *Psychic Causality*, the other on *Individual and Community*, and in 1925, the third, on *The State*, which culminates in a discussion of its relationship to religion. There she stresses the absolute primacy of the religious realm, that every man is subject, first and above all, to the Lord of lords and that no earthly ruler can alter this absolute dependence. "Whenever the believer receives a command from God, be it in the immediacy of prayer or through the mediacy of His vicars on earth, he must obey, no matter whether he acts against the will of the state or not," she declares. Small wonder, she continues, that the state often meets with distrust, even open hostility, the individual believer and, above all, the visible and lasting embodiment of that absolute claim that cuts through its own sovereignty, the Church. Small wonder, too, that the faithful sometimes take the state for Antichrist. The conflict can be settled only if the Lord's saying is accepted: "Render unto Caesar the things that are Caesar's, and to God the things that are God's." [29]

But by the time these three studies appeared, Edith Stein had gone far beyond mere philosophical query. Having discussed, in *Psychic Causality*, the role played in our inner life, in our response to values, by the body's vitality, on the one hand, and by the mind's freshness, the soul's vigor, on the other, she speaks of "rest in God," a state in which all the mind's activity comes to repose, in which no plans are made, no decisions taken, in which we do not act but leave the future to the divine Will. Outwardly, this rest resembles the inactivity following an experience which surpasses our strength, depletes our inner resources, but such exhaustion is like the stillness of death, while the surrender that goes with rest in God brings about a sureness of shelter, delivering the soul from dread and solicitude. When we yield to this sureness, fresh life fills us more and more and drives us, without efforts of our will, to new labors, for in this influx of new vigor, which re-creates our inner life, a power is at work that is not our own. The one thing asked of us for this little rebirth is, she writes, that willingness to receive which marks the person freed from psychic mechanism.[30]

Edith Stein had found this peace. From the moment of her baptism, her life was one of prayer: daily she said the Breviary, God's perennial praise, the psalms of Israel that have become the psalms of the Church, and as often as she could, she took part when the divine Office was chanted or recited in common.

There David standes with harpe in hand
  as maister of the Queere
tenne thousand times that man were blest
  that might this musique heare

Our Ladie singes magnificat
  with tune surpassinge sweete
and all the virginns beare their partes
  sitinge about her feet [31]

To this day, those who knew her then remember the silent sermon of her prayer. For hours they saw her kneel, never moving, her attention unswayed. Indeed, for a time she took literally the Apostle's counsel to live in joy and incessant prayer,[32] and gave herself almost uninterruptedly to the joys of God's presence. "Immediately before and for quite some time after my baptism," she was to write in 1928, "I thought that to lead a religious life meant to give up everything earthly and to live only in the thought of divine things. Gradually I learned to see that on this earth something else is demanded of us, and that even in the contemplative life the bond to the world must not be completely cut. Not till I got to know St. Thomas did I fully understand that scientific studies could be pursued as service to God, and only then could I bring myself to undertake scientific work in earnest. In fact, I believe

339

the more deeply someone is drawn into God, the more he must go out of himself, that is, go into the world, in order to carry into it the divine life." [33]

The first fruit of her study of St. Thomas was a comparison of his thought with that of the intellectual world that had formed her: *Husserl's Phenomenology and the Philosophy of St. Thomas Aquinas,* a study dedicated to Edmund Husserl for his seventieth birthday in 1929. The real harvest, however, was her unique translation of St. Thomas's *Investigations on Truth* (1931–1932). Without obscuring the special character of his terminology, she clothes his thought in a living idiom, in a German through which shines the simple clarity of St. Thomas's Latin; from her pen the perennial wisdom flows a present-day philosophy. "On every page it is Thomas and only Thomas," Father Erich Przywara, S.J., wrote, "but in such a way that he stands face to face with Husserl, Scheler, and Heidegger. The phenomenological vocabulary which Edith Stein, as creative philosopher, can call her own has nowhere taken the place of St. Thomas's language; and yet, doors open effortlessly between the two worlds." [34]

The several investigations (or in the language of St. Thomas, the questions with their articles) Edith Stein links by summaries and comments, which show her, the apprentice, entered into her mastership. Truth, to St. Thomas and to her, is the face of being, being as it meets the mind, manifests itself to it. Hence our knowledge has its measure in things, things their measure in the divine Mind—and *there* is the one, first, lasting truth, of which the many truths are but the reflections in minds created. Though being exists apart from and, as it were, unconcerned with our minds, they are in tune with one another, and it is thus that the mind's assent, its "yes," to being is possible. The theory of knowledge given in the first question of St. Thomas's *On Truth* differs essentially, Edith Stein remarks, from modern epistemologies, making no claim to be the foundation of all the other philosophical disciplines nor pretending to be a "presuppositionless science"; rather is it part and parcel of a great metaphysics. Here cognition is a real process, presupposing a triple world of realities: the divine Mind, uncreated and infinite, and the two worlds created by It, that of things and that of finite minds. Hence there is no "knowing in general"; knowing is either God's or creatures': His is an original *Innehaben*, a "having within Him," and is of all that is; ours an *Innewerden*, a "taking into us" of some one thing.[35]

Since human knowledge, together with all being, has its origin in the divine Mind, the second question of St. Thomas's *Investigations* is devoted to the divine knowing, the ideal of perfect knowledge. It is perfect in compass, comprising as it does God Himself, His infinite existence and essence, and in and through His essence, as their primal image, as their *similitudo*, all things made, all things possible, and even the negative of what is, things that are not. Perfect too in manner, the divine knowing is intuitive, in a single glance spanning all things knowable, and each wholly, with its kind and singularity and place in the entire order of being; and so clear is His knowledge that it admits of no growth or decline, nor the least change. In God all is one: the manifoldness of creation He knows in and through the Oneness of His nature. The ideas, the virgin images according to which He forms His creatures, that is, the archetypes, to which the third investigation is devoted, are, though many in regard to creatures, one in regard to Him, one in His mind.[36]

With St. Thomas, Edith Stein goes on to discuss, in the fourth to seventh investigations, the Word, Providence, Predestination, and the Book of Life—which modern thinkers deem little relevant to truth. But is it not the dignity of man's knowledge that both the things he knows and he himself, the knower, are first known to God? Since God knows in Himself all that is, He knows them in His inner Word, the Word of the heart, in which His Being is eternally uttered. Made manifest many times and in many ways in creation, which in It has its "life," this Word of the heart was, once and uniquely, made flesh in Jesus the Christ. Of this we have, though in infinitesimal miniature, a true likeness when our own inner word is made sound, is spoken and rendered public. The mystery of divine knowing encloses Providence, God's practical vision which sees the goal of every creature, that productive vision which orders and leads each, by the right means, to its true end; Predestination, the will-ing knowledge with which God brings the just to their glory, springing not from dark tyranny but from the luminous freedom of love; and the Book of Life, the Scriptural phrase for the approving gaze with which

God embraces the good, those whose "names are enrolled in heaven." [37] Leaving the realm of divine knowledge, Edith Stein walks, in the hand of her guide, through the province of creatures, exploring, in the ninth to thirteenth investigations, Angelic Knowledge; Man's Mind; the Role of the Teacher; and of the extraordinary teacher, the Prophet; then Ecstasy, the knowledge given man when he is rapt out of the darkness of the senses into the light.[38]

Needless to say, no investigations on truth can be complete unless they include one on faith, a way first of knowing, then of life. It is a way of knowing, for it has truth, indeed, eternal Truth, God Himself, for its object. Though it shares with man's natural cognition sureness of assent, it is unlike it in that it is not the fruit of reason reflecting and deducing, however great its work in preparing for faith. No, what moves the mind here is the will, with its trust in God as the infallible Witness. Thus knowing becomes virtue. In coming to believe, mind and will constantly interlock with one another. The mind takes hold of God, faith's first object; the will seizes on Him, in faith unformed, as a desire for the promised Good, and then in faith formed, as love; so in the end the will wins the mind's consent to Him and to all that speaks in His Name, as the prophet in the Old Covenant, the Church in the New. And as the powers of the soul interlock in the act of faith, so do man and God, weakness and strength, nature and grace.[39]

On this, the fourteenth investigation, there follows one on Reason and Intellect; another on Synderesis, the mind's general and inextinguishable understanding of and inclination toward the good, that is, the moral principles; and one on Conscience, the practical judgment which applies the moral principles to particular instances. How wide in range, how powerful is St. Thomas, and how unvirile those moderns who would not think of including in their theories of knowledge the light of conscience. It is "idle empty verbiage to the great world of philosophy now," wrote Cardinal Newman. "All through my day there has been a resolute warfare, I had almost said conspiracy, against the rights of conscience. . . ." [40] And elsewhere: "Whether a man be born in pagan darkness, or in some corruption of revealed religion; whether he has heard the name of the Saviour of the world or not;

whether he be the slave of some superstition, or is in possession of some portions of Scripture, and treats the inspired word as a sort of philosophical book, which he interprets for himself, and comes to certain conclusions about its teaching—in any case, he has within his breast a certain commanding dictate, not a mere sentiment, not a mere opinion, or impression, or view of things, but a law, an authoritative voice, bidding him do certain things and avoid others. I do not say that its particular injunctions are always clear, or that they are always consistent with each other; but what I am insisting on here is this, that it *commands*—that it praises, it blames, it promises, it threatens, it implies a future, and it witnesses the unseen. It is more than a man's own self. The man himself has not power over it, or only with extreme difficulty; he did not make it, he cannot destroy it. He may silence it in particular cases or directions; he may distort its enunciations; but he cannot —or it is quite the exception if he can—he cannot emancipate himself from it. He can disobey it, he may refuse to use it; but it remains." [41]

Again, how shrunken our resources! How many are they today who would inquire (as do the eighteen to twentieth investigations) into the mind of the first man, in the state of innocence; into the soul's knowledge after death, when it is no longer bodybound; and into how and what the soul of Christ knows? Where now is that high courage which, in writing on truth, wrote on goodness? Ours is a world of divorce: God and man, men and things, being and knowledge, truth and goodness, goodness and beauty are severed; all is atomized and nothing seems real. The world St. Thomas and his pupil live in is spacious and manifold, but borne and arched by the Love that built it: God cares for man, man lives for God, and all creation for its great Lord and for man, His vicar. Being, truth, goodness are one, or as Edith Stein renders it, equivalent: What is, is true and good, insofar as it *is*. To say it once more: "In the same measure as a creature participates in being, it participates in goodness," and though evil is rampant, there is nothing so evil that it is entirely without some good. Hence, even "in every sinful act, there is a remnant of goodness," St. Thomas can exclaim. *Bonum est diffusivum sui,* goodness' way is to overflow, to share, to give itself, to spread, and so God's goodness covers the world. All creatures are good through the first Goodness, not as if uncreated Goodness dwelt in them, but in that they are all patterned after It as their exemplary and final cause.[42]

For man, as a creature who is lifted above the world of matter and the senses, goodness means his willing harmony with God's will. Fittingly, then, the twenty-first investigation, on Goodness, is succeeded by those on Man's Will, the power by which his spirit strives; on God's Will, wise and mighty; on the Gift of Free Choice; on the Striving of the Senses; and on the Passions of the Soul. Here, as always, is St. Thomas's vision of oneness: by nature, that is by the will of the Creator, the powers of man's soul are friends, they work together, and so here they are seen together. And though sin has disturbed this friendship, grace is the remedy, of which the twenty-seventh investigation treats. With sin blotted out, sanctity enters the soul, a higher life, and a new man arises, modeled after Christ. Once more there is union: nature and supernature are betrothed. Having brought her masterly rendering of St. Thomas's work to a close with the twenty-eighth and twenty-ninth questions, on the Justification of the Sinner and on the Grace in Christ, Edith Stein asks: "Is it surprising that the *Investigations on Truth* have these for their finale? Hardly, if one bears in mind the spirit of the whole book. It began with the first, the eternal Truth, from whom wells all creaturely being, all creaturely knowing, and it ends with the Way, who leads creaturely being and knowing back to their union with eternal Truth," [43] He leads them back by the cross, which is an "I" crossed out, which is an "and," the "and" of reconciliation.

Throughout her studies and work of translation, the Crucified was before her eyes. One of her friends tells that while she and Edith Stein were reading the proofs of the *Investigations on Truth*, there was on the desk before them an old carved crucifix, to which her eyes were ever drawn, "or," she continues, "were they guided there by the loving glance that Edith Stein gave it from time to time?" [44]

Thou that, on the Cross of Love,
  wast crowned of lovers king,
Melt this iron Winter, Lord,
  to Love's eternal Spring;

Hold and fold us all
beneath the shadow of Thy wing.[45]

The Goal and Way of human existence is the theme of much of Edith Stein's writing. "Whereas the infant is given into the hands of his molders, the growing man, awakened to his inner freedom, is given into his own hands," she says in an essay on *The Formation of Woman's Personality* (1931). His freedom allows him to work on the culture of his soul, he can use his faculties freely and make their growth his concern, he can open or bar himself to forming influences—but at all times he is subject to the material given him: no one can make himself into that which he is not by nature. One power only is not bound by nature's limits, grace. And it is grace that brings us to the ultimate goal of our forming: to be perfect as our Father in heaven is perfect,[46] a goal standing visibly before us in the Person of Jesus Christ. "To become His likeness is the goal of us all. And by Him to be fashioned into this likeness, having been grafted as members into the Body of which He is the Head, is the road of us all. . . . Who yields without reservation to this forming is the richer for receiving his own nature purified—more, he grows beyond it and becomes an *alter Christus,* another Christ." [47]

From Thomas to Carmel

"Very strange! She could join with us in prayer, finding everything in her own book," Frau Stein exclaimed. Eager to show her affection, the daughter traveled to Breslau whenever she could to be with her mother, to whom the news of Edith's Catholic faith had brought the first tears her children had seen in her. A few times, the convert accompanied her aged mother to the synagogue, hoping to convince her, as words could not do, that baptism had not severed her from the God of Israel. "Her own book" was the prayerbook of the Church, and in a special way, the prayerbook of those consecrated to God, the Breviary; from it she read the psalms in Latin as they were intoned in Hebrew. "The sermon was beautiful, Edith, was it not?" her mother asked on one such occasion. "Yes indeed, mother," she answered. "So one *can* be devout as a Jew?" "Certainly—if one has never met anything else." Despairingly, then, her mother begged: *"Why* did you meet it? I don't want to say anything against him, he may have been a very good man, but why did he make himself God?" [48]

Once Edith Stein had grasped that in "him" Godhead and Manhood dwelt, her soul cleaved to Him and her whole life bore the indelible mark of His love. Ever after, monastic air was the breath she needed, and she sought to live in or near a convent, as she did from 1922 to 1932, while she taught at the Dominican Academy and Teachers' College of St. Magdalene in Speyer, and again from 1932 to 1933, when she was with the German Institute for Scientific Pedagogy in Muenster. Much of her time there was given to a plan for far-reaching reforms of higher education, a plan which had won the keen interest of the authorities, when Hitler's rise to power brought her work to a sudden end. But there was good in this evil, and there was no grudge in her, to whom, from the first, Nazism had been synonym to infamy. All these years, her friends and counselors had restrained her from entering Carmel by pointing out that hers was an intellectual mission in the world. Now she was free, and on October 14, 1933, she crossed the threshold of the Discalced Carmelite convent of Cologne.

To enter Carmel is to be stripped of oneself, and for Edith Stein this was so in a marked way. She was forty-two years old; had given her life to learning, to the thrill of the intellect, to the joys of philosophy; had been in the public eye—and was cast into insignificance. None of the Sisters had heard her name before, much less of her achievements; few would have been able to understand her intellectual language. Instead, the only remark of an older Sister was: "Does she sew well?" "*Ach*, Edith sewed very poorly," her biographer recollects, "moreover, at all household tasks she was so slow and inept that it was misery to watch her." There is always much housework in a community, and part of the testing of a newcomer is the goodly share assigned to her. Not in the unfamiliar domestic labor, but in the testing, did she do well, bearing the embarrassments it caused her with inner valor and outer humor.[49]

*

With valor and joy she accepted too the austerity of her new life. The first time she entered her cell, her gladness was visible as she gazed at its poor furnishings. Between two whitewashed walls, but nine feet apart, was a single window overlooking the peace of the convent garden. In one corner was a cot, made of a plank resting on four horses, on it a straw pallet and pillow, with blankets of coarse brown wool. There was a small table, a low bench, on the floor an earthen bowl and pitcher. On the bare wall, prints of the founders of the order, a holy-water font, and dominating the room, a wooden cross with three pegs but no figure of Christ—it is for the Carmelite to be fastened to it in spirit. Thus, soon after her arrival, Edith Stein was reminded by the novice mistress that in the convent she could not hope to continue her philosophical work. With dreadful foresight of what Nazism would bring, she replied simply: "Not human activity will help us, but the passion of Christ. To partake in it is my desire." [50]

The visible poverty of her cell but intimated the inner poverty she was to win there, the tearing from her soul of all that was its own till it was naked before the face of God. Her own strength she would see as nothing, and so live on faith, on divine strength.

Lost to myself I stayed
My face upon my lover having laid
From all endeavor ceasing:
And all my cares releasing
Threw them amongst the lilies there to fade.[51]

Those for whom such detachment, such forgetting—nay, shedding —of self, is an unknown country often think it dreary and melancholy, but a glimpse of Edith Stein after a few weeks in Carmel would have shown them wrong. Her face grew fresh and young, as if the past years, with their labors and achievements, had been blotted out. All the burdens of her mental work, all the bodily mortifications she had taken upon herself, the fasts and vigils, gave way to the one great mortification of the will, to obedience, whose fruit is a carefree, cheerful spirit.[52]

Two words in the language of Carmel express its mystery: the Nothing and the All. "Nothing" stands for solitude and silence, in which thought, will, desire are extinguished, in which the soul is emptied of itself so that God may enter with unhindered Omnipotence, that He may become All-in-All. Vividly is this spirit expressed when the brown habit of the Order is given to a candidate. On April 15, 1934, Edith Stein, bride-clad in whiteness, first assisted at Solemn High Mass and then proclaimed before all the people in church her longing for Carmel and her determination to persevere in it till death. Having been blessed with the words: "May the Lord who has led thee to us strip thee of the old self and of all its ways," she went, burning light in hand, to the door of the cloister. Gladly it opened to her, gladly she stepped through. There she put aside her gleaming satin and worldly ornaments, receiving in their stead the penitential habit: "May the Lord garb thee with the new self, patterned after God in justice and holiness of truth." Then the leathern belt was given her, a reminder of Peter's obedience and martyrdom: "When thou wast young, thou didst gird theyself and walk where thou wouldst. But when thou art old, another will gird thee." The scapular was thrown over her shoulders: "Take upon thyself Christ's sweet yoke and light burden." Receiving last the mantle and white veil, she embraced her new Sisters while the cantors sang: "Behold, how good and beautiful it is for brethren to dwell together in unity."[53]

Four years later, on April 21, 1938—the very day Edmund Husserl, her first master, died—she vowed herself perpetually to penance and praise. On the following Sunday, the first of May, she was given the black veil, symbol of sacrifice, symbol of modesty and awe. First the Sisters sang: *Amo Christum,* "Christ I love. . . . In loving Him I am chaste, in touching Him I am pure, in receiving Him I am virgin. With His own ring, my Lord Jesus Christ has wed me, and He has adorned me with jewels above price." Then the bishop summoned her: "Come, bride of Christ, receive the crown the Lord has prepared for thee from all eternity." And she replied: "Uphold me, O Lord, as Thou hast promised, that I may live, and let my hope not be confounded." Then he veiled her and crowned her with white roses: "His seal He has placed upon me," Edith Stein rejoiced, and the community took up the chant, "that I may admit no other lover." Then, as she lay prone on the floor, stretched out in the shape of a cross, bells and voices exulted: *Te Deum laudamus,* "We praise Thee, O God."[54]

Carmel is a solitude and a silence, like in many ways to the wilderness where the desert fathers used to dwell, a desert where the winds of joy are ever blowing. St. John of the Cross once said, and Edith Stein could now say with him: "Mine are the heavens and mine is the earth; mine are the people, the righteous are mine and mine are the sinners; the angels are mine and the Mother of

God, and all things are mine; and God Himself is mine and for me, for Christ is mine and all for me. What, then, dost thou ask for and seek, my soul? Thine is all this, and it is all for thee. Despise not thyself nor give thou heed to the crumbs which fall from thy Father's table. Go thou forth and do thou glory in thy glory. Hide thee therein and rejoice and thou shalt have the desires of thy heart." [55]

All these riches were given her ever anew in prayer, and it is on prayer that she wrote, after but a year or two in Carmel, one of her most beautiful essays. When a group of well-known priests and laymen in Germany, eager to restate the faith in the face of the Nazi heresies, published two volumes, one *I Believe,* the other *I Live and You Live,* they asked Edith Stein to write on *The Prayer of the Church*—a sign both of their esteem for her and of their courage, for even as early as 1936 Hitler's rage against the Jews had already made it dangerous to companion with her. The Church's prayer is honor paid and glory given to the Triune God, through, with and in Christ, she says: *through,* because Christ is our Access to the Father; *with,* because every true prayer is a flowering and a deepening of our union with Him; *in,* because the praying Church is Christ continued and each praying Christian is a limb of Him, a cell in His Mystical Body.[56]

Fully catholic, never inclined to vaunt community as against person or person as against community, Edith Stein stresses that not only the liturgy, not only the majestic worship, ordained, corporate and audible, is the Church's prayer; hers too is the heart's still speech with God. So truly hers is it that the devotion of her great lovers to the God who is Love, that the stream of mysticism flowing through the centuries—a swelling song of many voices—is part of her innermost life. In every true prayer she prays, for in it moves the Spirit, who abides in her and speaks in us; wordless and ineffable are His groanings. Whenever a man prays truly, something happens within the Church and within the world—and who knows how many tyrants have been overthrown, how many invaders halted, by praying hearts, she asks. For they are the invisible, incalculable powers official history does not record. When the Reformation rent Europe and threatened to engulf France, Spain, the Netherlands and Germany, were they not spared, at least in part, by the prayer of Teresa and her daughters? "The world is in flames," the saint of Avila said. "If they could, they would condemn Christ again . . . they would raze His Church to the ground. . . . No, my sisters, this is no time to treat with God about things of little importance." [57]

That all the Church's prayer, whether it be of a single member or of the whole body, issues from and continues the prayer of Christ on earth, and that it is this worship which the praying Israel of old foreshadowed, is the central theme of Edith Stein's essay. The Gospels speak of His solitary prayer in the desert and in the mountains, that hidden colloquy of which we have swift sight, as of lightning, in the Garden of Olives, and a long look at the Last Supper. And it is in the Old Covenant that His high-priestly prayer on the eve of the passion and His pleading on the cross have their type. Once a year, on the Day of Atonement, the high priest entered the inner sanctuary and all alone stood before the presence of God to intercede for himself, his household and the whole people of Israel. As he stood there, he burned incense, that its clouds might veil his eyes, a token of the mysterious solitude of his prayer.[58]

As Christ fulfilled the silence of the Old Testament, so its song. Edith Stein sees Him from His boyhood pilgriming to Jerusalem at the seasons laid down by the Law, to worship in the Temple; singing with His family, with His disciples, the psalm of anticipation: "Welcome sound, when I heard them saying, We will go into the house of the Lord!" [59] The ancient blessings over bread and wine were on His lips: "Blessed art Thou, Lord our God, King of the universe, who bringest forth bread from the earth, who createst the fruit of the vine." So the account of His Last Supper tells. But when there He blessed bread and broke it and gave it to His disciples, saying: "Take and eat, this is My Body"; when He took the cup in thanksgiving: "All of you drink of this, for this is My Blood of the New Covenant," [60] the Passover rite of blessing, giving and eating bread and wine received a new, infinitely higher meaning. There the ancient benedictions, which before had been the creature's gratitude and praise, became the Creator's grace, words of life-giving. Now that the fruits of the earth have become Christ's Flesh and Blood, creation is wed to Him anew in mystery. Changed the elements that serve to build man's body, changed then man too—through them the man of faith is made a new creature, another Christ.[61]

Through the whole of Edith Stein's essay there runs the theme of newness and oldness, and of her new link with the Israel of old. For baptism and Eucharist, faith and prayer, had made her a true Israelite, and Carmel in particular, which has Elias for its spiritual ancestor and for its motto his words: "With zeal to be zealous for the Lord, God of hosts." [62]

Being, Bounded and Unbounded

The lover of God is the true philosopher, the friend of wisdom, St. Augustine, great in both, declares;[63] and it was this love, it was prayer and not study, not writing, Edith Stein sought in Carmel. Forgetting what was behind, she strained forward to what was before.[64] Her renunciation was unreserved, but she had not been a year in the convent when she was freed from other tasks and bidden to continue a manuscript she had begun in 1931. Completed in 1936 as *Bounded and Unbounded Being*, it was to be her main philosophical work. A publisher was found, the type was set, proofs were actually struck off, but the book was never printed. Hitler's anti-Jewish laws forbade the publication of anything by a Jew—since, he reasoned, a Jew was so un-German that every word he said in German was a lie—nor would Edith Stein permit the appearance of her study under the name of someone eligible for the *Reichsschriftstumskammer,* the guild of Aryan writers.

Long afterwards, in 1950, the book was finally published as the second volume of her collected works. *An Ascent to the Meaning of Being* is its sub-title, and its starting point our own existence. God and the angels, with whom St. Thomas begins his inquiry into being, seem to many today unreachably remote, but this—our own existence—is inescapably near us, she writes. We know that we live, and this knowledge we do not have through the eye of our flesh, and therefore cannot in this be deceived by our senses. Indeed, as St. Augustine says, "the knowledge by which we know that we live is the most inward of all knowledge, of which not even the skeptic can insinuate: Perhaps you are asleep and do not know it. . . . He who is certain of the knowledge of his own life does not therein say, I know I am awake, but, I know I am alive—whether he be asleep or awake, he is alive." [65] Even if I am undecided as to whether the things I perceive really exist, as to whether the conclusions I draw are correct, I cannot doubt that I perceive, that I conclude. Undoubtable too are my wishing and willing, my dreaming and hoping, my rejoicing and mourning, in brief, everything in which I live and am. Hence the certainty of my being is, in a way, the most original knowledge—not that it is the first in time, for man's natural orientation is outward, and it takes long till he finds himself; nor that it is the foundation from which all other knowledge is derived—but it is the nearest, and inseparable from me. A beginning, behind which it is impossible to go, this sureness—that I am—is unreflected, lying before all thinking "bent back." When the mind bends back to look at the simple fact of its being, the fact becomes a question: What is this being I am aware of? At once it shows two faces, being and not-being, for the being in which I am changes with time; it is a "now" between a "no longer" and a "not yet." And as soon as this fleeting splits before our eyes into being and not-being, it unveils the idea of pure being, being unbounded and eternal, to which the "no longer" and the "not yet" are strangers. Thus unchanging being, whose existence is eternity, and changing being, which is in time, are ideas on which the mind hits by itself; they are not borrowed from elsewhere.[66]

So singularly important is this truth to Edith Stein that she inquires into it many times over. We all experience our lives, she says, as a constant movement from the past into the future, whereby things potential become actual and things actual sink back into potentiality—in other words, what is not yet fully alive reaches the height of aliveness, and full life becomes life lived. This, our being, is a becoming, is ever-perishing and mortal, and so the very opposite of ever-present and changeless being. Nevertheless, becoming cannot be divorced from being, true and full; though it is only transition to being, it cannot be determined or known as such, save through and with being. Were we to deny the possibility of being distinct from becoming, we should have to deny the possibility of becoming as well, and end in nothingness. But as it is, the becoming and un-becoming we experience within us point beyond ourselves. Though touching it only from instant to instant, becoming tends toward being; though it waxes and wanes, though it is never more than on the road to true being, our own being unlocks to us the idea of true being, with which "there is no change nor shadow of alteration." [67]

Again, the "I" lives now in joy, then in longing, a little later in reflection, or in all at once; they fade away or come to a sudden stop, but the "I" remains, at each moment welling up anew. Though the "I" would be empty without these and other experiences, though it receives its fullness from them, it is from the "I" that they receive their life. Compared to them, which owe to the "I" their very being, the "I" is being in a preeminent sense; it the carrier, they the carried. They belong to it, as does the whole stream of its experiences, so that the "I" can, as it were, walk back, run its eye over the past, and let one or the other experience live again. But this mastery and freedom are not unlimited: The "I" brings the experiences, the contents, of its life from potentiality to actuality; it brings them, as Edith Stein puts it, from the pre-stages of being to the height, but only for a while, it cannot keep them alive lastingly. And there are lacunae in the stream of its experiences, gaps in our memory. Moreover, in going back, the "I" cannot arrive at its own beginning. Others can testify to the start of its corporeal being, but its immediate experience gives no answer as to what its beginning was nor as to what its end may be. Did it spring from nothingness? Does it go into nothingness? Might the abyss of nothingness open beneath it at any moment? Not that these limitations, these questions, shake the preeminence of the "I" as that which carries experience, as that which is alive—but they make visible its impotence and frailty. The riddle of its whence and whither shows it the extreme opposite of the sovereign *being-of-itself;* put into existence and sustained there from moment to moment, the being of the "I" is *received.*[68]

My being, as I find it and find myself in it, Edith Stein continues, is a "nothinged being," *ein nichtiges Sein:* I do not exist of myself, and of myself I am nothing. Every moment I stand before nothingness, so that every moment I must be dowered anew with being. And yet this nothinged being of mine, this frail, received being, *is* being; it is closer to being than to nothingness, because it reaches the height of being not only for one instant, but is sustained there in every instant. Recoiling from nothingness, it thirsts not only for endless continuation of its being but for the full possession of being, being which in changeless presence encompasses its total content. Crossing out in its own being what it knows to be deficiency, the "I" arrives at the idea of everlasting being, of ultimate fullness. Once grasped, this idea becomes the measure of contingent being, but how does it happen that the "I" sees it also as the source, the author, of its being? Unquestionably, the "I" is brought face to face with nothingness not only by reflective thought but also by the anxiety which walks with unredeemed man in many disguises—as fear of this or that—but which is at bottom dread of one's own not-being. Unquestionably, our usual feeling of security, as if our being were a firm possession, is sometimes the result of a shallow and unthinking heart, or of the daily worries which obscure the sight of nothingness. Is our surety of being therefore unfounded and unreasonable? Is Heidegger's "passionate, self-assured and anxious freedom toward death" [69] therefore the rational attitude toward life? Edith Stein asks, and answers with vigor: "By no means!" For just as undeniable as my *fleeting* life, is that I *am*, that I am sustained in being, and that in the midst of my fleetingness I hold fast to a being which endures. I know myself borne up, and in this have quiet and sureness—not the unperturbed assurance of the man who stands on his own feet, but the gentle and blessed sureness of the child who is held by a strong arm. Objectively seen, this sureness is certainly no less reasonable than Heidegger's—or would the child be reasonable who lived in constant dread that its mother might let it fall?

The being I "encounter" within me, the being not my own but stay and ground of my unstayed and ungrounded being, is eternal Being. The roads are two by which I come to know this, Edith Stein writes: one, that of reason, of syllogistic thinking, of philosophy. To true thought, the ultimate author of my own and of all finite being can be no other than infinite being, being which is not received but is of itself, being which could not *not be* but necessarily *is*. Hence there is in it no separation, no distinction, between what it is and that it is: it is being itself and therefore one. All this is true, but as long as reasoning is our only road to the first Being, He, the incomparably Near, in whom we live and move and are,[70] remains remote. But there is the second way, that of faith, which is an answer from another world, telling us of the God of personal nearness, of the loving and pitying God, and giving such a certitude as can no natural knowledge. This road too is dark. God Himself, Edith Stein quotes St. Augustine, had to temper His words, shape them to human ears, when He sent Moses to the children of Israel, saying first what is difficult to understand: "Thus shalt thou say, He who is has sent me to you," but then adding what is sweetly apprehended: "Go, tell the children of Israel, the God of Abraham, the God of Isaac, the God of Jacob, has sent me to you." "That I am who am belongs to Me; that I am the God of Abraham, the God of Isaac, the God of Jacob, belongs to thee. And if thou art unable to see what I am to Myself, understand what I am to thee." [71]

Dark is the way of faith, and yet light. When Christ says: "He who believes in the Son has everlasting life," [72] it is a clear answer to the riddle of my being, Edith Stein professes. And when, through the mouths of prophet and apostle, He reveals that He will stand by me more faithfully than father and mother, that He is Love Itself,[73] I know that it is "reasonable" to trust in the Arm that bears up my being, that it is foolish to dread a fall into nothingness—unless I myself run away from the cradling Arm. Once this is seen, seen too is that a philosophy which makes nothingness the beginning and the end is a "philosophy of bad conscience." [74]

Edith Stein does not weary of leading us on the ascent to unbounded being, this time by the route of an enquiry into what phenomenologists call *Wesenheiten,* essences. For instance, the beautiful, by which all things beautiful are beautiful; the just, by which all just deeds are just; or joy—but not my joy or yours, not joy in work accomplished, not innermost, not exuberant, not tranquil joy, but joy as such, the essence "joy." The essence "joy" does not come and go as they do, it is not now or later, it is neither brief nor long lasting, for it has no being in space or time. But wherever, whenever, joy is experienced, the essence "joy" is realized; through it all joys are what they are, to it they owe their name. The essence "joy" is not the concept "joy," because concepts we form but essences we find. Theirs is a special kind of being, beyond time and change—differing vastly, on the one hand, from the first being, author of all there is, infinite fullness and perfect life, in that the essences are rigid and dead; differing, on the other hand, from real experiences in that they persevere unaltered, without increase or decrease. Special is their being, for it is not productive, not real: it is not the essence "joy" that makes me rejoice, nor is it owed to the essence "I" that I live. When we speak of the "realization" of the essence "joy," for example, it is not the essence which becomes real but something which corresponds to it. Yet essences are conditions for all real being; its possibility is rooted in them, so that it would be wrong to think of their "not real being" as "not being." Hence Edith Stein proposes that their being be called "essential being," *wesenhaftes Sein*.[75]

Essential being—this means that there can be no thing in time without a timeless form, *Gestalt;* there can be no knowledge in time without a timeless meaning. Were it not that essences govern the life of the "I," its life would be an unravelable chaos. But they do govern it, rendering it one and manifold, making it structured, meaningful, intelligible. Obedient to abiding laws, all the essences together are a realm of meaning, and it is in this realm that my fleeting life is grounded. Yet not meaning gives me being; rather is meaning given me together with being, shaping it. Hence, who endows me with being and fills it with significance must be lord of both. Indeed, it is in unbounded being that all fullness of meaning is contained—"In the beginning was the Logos." [76]

"In the beginning was the Logos," the eternal Word, the eternal Meaning—this, Edith Stein declares, is Wisdom's answer to the riddles of philosophy. The Logos is God's ever-living Grasp of Himself, His perfect Comprehension of His Being, His Meaning, as He alone knows and speaks It. "Without the Logos, nothing was made. All that was made, in Him was life," she quotes from an ancient reading of the prologue to St. John's Gospel,[77] and likewise St. Paul's: "In Him who is before all things, all things subsist and hold together." [78] To say it again: The "essential being" of each thing has its home in the Logos. What in time is communicated to, and realized in, creatures as their meaning, from eternity lives as part of the *ars divina,* as St. Thomas calls it, as part of the Creator's plan.[79] Thus the ascent from the finite to the Infinite, from bounded to unbounded Being, is made again. No, the maw of nothingness will not swallow us; Heidegger and Sartre notwithstanding, in the midst of our fleeting life there dwells eternal significance. This was the joy of a philosopher who was a Carmelite, of a Jew who was a Christian.

Man the Triune

Has not man's treatment as livestock or as a collection of wheels brought about results that are burned into our flesh? Who can now doubt that man is abandoned if he, in whom the above and the below clasp hands, is read from below; that only from above, in the light of the spirit, can his meaning be won? But to seek "the realm of the spirit" is to seek the Three-personed God, for in Him alone is manifest spirit at its truest—so Edith Stein in her *Bounded and Unbounded Being*. God is utter generosity—the Father stripping Himself of His Nature, as it were, for the sake of His Son, and yet losing nothing; the Father and the Son giving Themselves to the Holy Ghost, and yet retaining the fullness of divine Nature; each Person being in Himself and yet wholly in the Others. A thing so inward is spirit—an inwardness entirely nonspatial—that in going out of itself it remains within itself. And this going out of itself is of its very nature, for spirit is selfless, not in that it has no self, rather in that it gives its self completely, without losing it, becoming manifest in this very generosity. Insofar as he is spirit, the image of the Triune God, man goes outside of himself to enter an opening world, without, however, leaving himself—for this is the way of spirit.[80]

Though sunk into matter, man can rise; from a dim ground, the life of his spirit mounts like a candle flame, luminous but fed by the unglowing wax, shining but not all shining. The candle is alight, but not fully light; so man's spirit sees itself, but not wholly; so man's spirit illumines others, but does not see them entire. Though the "soil" (the body and the sense-soul) in which the spirit is planted remains "dark," yet it is given man as material to be shaped, to be illumined, to be drawn upward by the spirit—that is, by the soul at its innermost—and this ascent is his life-long task. Never can his spirit be forever quit of the body, a body assured of resurrection, and even in this life it is never mere "stuff"; it is always "my" body, as nothing external is mine. I live in it, as in my native abode, and therefore the shiver that runs down my back, the pressure in my head, the pain in my tooth, are just as truly part of my life as my thought and my joy. True, they are entirely different from the voluntary act of thinking or from

357

the joy that rises from my inner depth; still, I am in them. What concerns my body concerns me. Yet some of the things that take place in my body, like digestion and growth, are often not so much as sensed, much less do they reach my "I"; on the other hand, a bodily movement can be drawn into my personal life—a step freely taken, a meaningful gesture, are personal acts. As the instrument of my deeds, my body belongs to the unity of my person.[81]

It is in the soul that the spiritual and the sensual meet and are woven one into the other. For it is man's to be neither beast nor angel, because he is both in one, "conscious clay"; hence his sensuality is other than the beast's and his spirituality other than the angel's. The ways of the soul, in which our whole being is centered, are three. As sense-soul, it dwells in the body, in all its members and parts, being dependent on it and in turn sustaining and shaping it. As spirit-soul, it mounts above itself, looking into a world beyond itself, into a world of things, events, persons, and entering into conversation with it. As soul in the strict sense, it dwells in itself—there the personal "I" is at home, there is gathered together everything that comes from the world beyond it, there we are confronted with that world and take a stand, there we win from it what becomes our personal possession.[82]

Using philosophically the image of St. Teresa's mystical theology, Edith Stein sees the soul as a castle of many mansions, where the "I" is free to live in the outer halls or to withdraw to the inner chambers. If the "I" observes and works on itself as though it were not itself but something external, it stays in the outer halls, indeed, it seems almost to desert the castle altogether. Having thus forsaken its native place, having abandoned its original orientation, the "I" no longer possesses full and unbroken force of life. Only if the "I" lives within, is its life entire, does it mount to the height of its being, does it sense its own significance; and because it is at home, at its disposal are the soul's undivided power and full freedom. Not infrequently a man is driven into the depths of the inner castle by some great and shaking event, but it is rare, alas, that a man lives recollectedly at all times. Yet he who does sees even small things, and sees them not as trifles but in their grand context, weighing them truly since he gauges all things by ultimate measures. And not only does he receive all things at their richest, rich also is his giving; from the innermost room of his soul, from the very home of his "I," there go forth, without his willing it, the strong rays of his being, which draw others into his spell. The more profound his recollection, the more clearly do his free movements carry the mark of his personality, the more clearly does even his body bear the stamp of the spirit. While the roamer in the castle's halls and passages hears nothing, the dweller in the most inward room hears a threefold appeal to the person: a summons to reason, that he may grasp what happens to him; a summons to meditation, that he may search for its meaning; a summons to freedom, that he may respond, that he may act, as this meaning demands. But there is Someone who, more surely than created things, speaks to him who dwells within. "Stretch forth thy right hand . . . recall me from my strayings," prays St. Augustine. "Be Thou the guide—and I shall return within myself and within Thee." [83]

With the Saint, Edith Stein repeats that it is the trinity of the inward man to comprehend things eternal by faith, to keep them in memory, and to cleave to them with a loving will. She gives also his other attempts to show the trinitarian character of man's life: mind, knowledge and love; memory, understanding and will. Even love displays the three-and-one: there is always the lover, the beloved, and love itself.[84] She asks then whether St. Augustine's suggestions exclude one another, and her answer is No, for triunity is to her a basic law of the life of the spirit—and not only of spirit but of the whole of creation. Each thing that *is,* self-stands, has meaning, has power to unfold. In the realm of matter, there is the solid, the liquid, the gaseous, mirroring the Trinity; and life on earth is divided into plant, animal and man. But of the living things on earth only man has personhood, a spiritual fruitfulness which recalls the processions within the Godhead, "those Three," to use Hopkins's lines, whose melody makes good their theological imperfection,

. . . *those Three,*
The Immortals of the eternal ring,
The Utterer, Utterèd, Uttering.

For when man's knowledge perfects itself in word, then, as it were, like a ripe fruit, something looses itself from the creative mind; and when the mind looks at this, its image, there springs up that glad "yes" which is of the sort of love.[85]

By nature, man is the likeness of the Triune God—his soul is one and its forming might threewise, uniting in the oneness of his being the variety of creation. Threewise: shaping the body as does the soul of a plant, and yet in a manner altogether human, for it is a human body it shapes, instrument and arena of a free spirit; living in its body and shaping itself, after the manner of an animal soul, and yet altogether differently, because its whole sense-life is linked to the spirit and fashioned by it; rising to an intellectual life, which puts it into the company of the pure spirits— still, because of its roots in body and sense, its intellectual life is altogether singular. Triple is this power, as is what it shapes, and if this human trinity is brought into relationship with the divine Trinity, Edith Stein continues, the soul, like a fountain drawing from itself, flowing into and shaping the life of the body and of the spirit, appears as the image of the Father; the body, as the sharply defined expression of man's being, is then the image of the eternal Word; and in the spirit is seen the image of the Spirit.[86]

All these are analogies, however, rays, imprints and images, faint because finite. Far otherwise is the wondrous indwelling of the Triune God in a soul loving because loved. Here is more than a portrait; here is more than a junction as of wine which has been poured into a cup, for wine and cup, though close in space, remain apart. Here is a union more intimate than that of the soul with the body; the two have become one, but spirit and matter are still of two kinds, so that what the soul dwells in and informs is a foreign medium. But in spite of the infinite distance between the Uncreated and the created, God and the soul are spirit both; they penetrate one another as only spirit and spirit can. Never losing their identities, by their free, mutual giving they enter into the unique communion—all grace!—of God in the soul, the soul in God.[87]

Can man truly love God? Edith Stein asks, and her answer is: Indeed, since God has loved man first. Having become manifest in Christ, His love unfolds in him who surrenders. He surrenders to the Father-will of God, that He may beget in him anew His

360   *Edith Stein*

Son; he unites with the Son, that the Father may see in him none other but Him; and his life is rendered one with the Holy Ghost, becomes one great loving. So great is this transformation of man that Christ can say: "From within him there shall flow rivers of living water." [88] Yielding to the overpowering might of the Lord, he becomes strong to act as never by nature; he rises to the heroism of love, loving not only his friends and his brethren, but his enemies, everyone who comes his way. No longer the plaything of likes and dislikes, he is free.[89]

The Dark Night

"A pupil reverent and willing"—so Edith Stein characterizes herself in relation to St. Thomas, but adds that, when first she came to know him, her mind was by no means a blank slate, for, as she says, she had had the language of phenomenology for her philosophical mother-tongue and her intellectual home in the school of Edmund Husserl. From there she "made her way to the great cathedral of scholasticism," and her *Bounded and Unbounded Being* is evidence of the fruitfulness of their meeting in her. And though St. Thomas is her acknowledged master, she stresses that to her there is no "either-or" between Thomas and Augustine, between Aristotle and Plato; for the solution of a few problems she leans on Duns Scotus, and at times, with gentle daring, even proposes her own. Beginning with a sober inquiry into man's existence, her book ends with a powerful hail to the risen Christ, King of glory. Mankind's Archetype and Head, the "Firstborn," He is the Figure toward whom all human existence is ordained and from whom it receives its meaning. For this is its significance, that in it be wedded heaven and earth, God and creation: made from the elements of the earth, the human body is united with the soul, which by nature is closer to God than all creatures not personal, and by grace is capable of wedlock with Him, or, as Donne acclaims: "I shall be Thy music," "I am Thy son, made with Thyself to shine." [90]

This, the soul's bridal union with God, was won through the cross, achieved on the cross, and for all eternity is sealed with the cross, for on the tree was repaired what at the tree was broken, the union forfeited in Eden, restored on Calvary. Such is the core of Edith Stein's last work, *Science of the Cross* (1941-1942), an interpretation of St. John's mystical theology. Through the Fall,

361

human nature lost its honor, its original perfection and grace-given highness, but it is lifted anew and made high in every man reborn to the sonship of God, and crowned in those who come to the mystical union. Therefore St. John of the Cross sings in his "Spiritual Canticle":

Beneath the apple tree,
You came to swear your troth and to be mated,
Gave there your hand to me,
And have been new-created
There where your mother first was violated.[91]

How is it, Edith Stein asks, that this union is reached beneath the tree, that the places of falling and lifting are the same, that the tree of Paradise and the tree of Golgotha are one? The tree forbidden to the first man was the tree of the knowledge of good and evil, of the experimental knowledge of evil with its radical opposition to the good—forbidden, for man could gain it only by doing evil. Hence the tree of Paradise is the cipher of his vulnerability to sin, and its fruit the sign of sin committed and of all its consequences. The most dreadful work of sin, however, unveiling its horror, is the passion and death of Christ. Thus "the tree of prohibition, root of all our woe," [92] became the root of our saving: it was sin that moved Christ to take upon Himself suffering and death; it was sin, in all its many forms, that nailed Him to the cross; it was sin, then, that was made the instrument of our redemption. Now man's inner world has changed: suffering with the Crucified, redeemed man arrives at a new "knowledge of good and evil," comes to know more deeply the good, all-holy God, sees more keenly his own sinfulness; now, through Christ, the sharp and bitter pain of knowing himself is a redeeming force. But not only the soul uncovered makes pain mount; even more, God always hidden, "for pains acquired so dearly from Love, cannot recover save only through the presence of the lover." [93] And the closer the soul moves toward Him, whom she cannot see, the more flaming her desire—in these flames too is she cleansed.[94]

The metaphor for this long cleansing best liked by St. John of the Cross is the night, the dark and fearsome night, the hushed and gracious night, the night he used to watch from the window of his cell or wander through in vineyard and garden. Night swallows up the visible, deprives it of shape, makes things uncertain, makes them shadows. No less does it threaten us; an anticipation of death, it robs us of a sense, hinders our movements, cripples our faculties, banishes us into solitude, turns us to shadows and ghosts. But night is not dark-visaged only, for it can be lighted by the mild and magic moon. Then things are not swallowed up; rather is the hard, sharp and shrill subdued and chastened, so that features which bright daylight hides are revealed, and voices which noon-clamor drowns are heard. It is in such a night that our souls are given a night-mild clarity; in which, freed from the serfdom of daily business, we are loosed, collected, drawn into our own depths, aware of the ties between this world and the other. All this and more lies behind St. John's image of the night:

Oh night that was my guide!
Oh darkness dearer than the morning's pride,
Oh night that joined the lover
To the beloved bride
Transfiguring them each into the other.[95]

The first step the soul takes in the dark night is to put away from her her unquestioning delight in all the things of the senses, to learn to see and hear as if she saw and heard not, Edith Stein continues her interpretation of St. John's theology of the cross. Natural man faces the world as a coveter, a "doer," one led by his urges and appetites, and he is content if only he does not come across extraordinary obstacles. But when the dark night begins, his cozy at-homeness in a world of his "own" is done away with; all that to the natural man is the brightness of life—its pleasures, the wanting of them and the matter-of-course consent to this wanting —becomes darkness, incompatible with the divine light, must be cast out to make room for God. Having subjected his senses to the spirit, fought his nature, taken up the cross, a man is ready for passive purgation at the hand of God, who weans him from the milk of consolation so that spiritual delight may be no longer his motive. In his spiritual dryness, in his inability to use his faculties, to turn his imagination and thought whither he would, he is nailed to the cross. Now supple, humble, patient, strong and free, his soul is set on fire, "flushed to loving ardors." As she is flooded with divine light, all her higher faculties prove themselves insufficient, dark, so that the soul lives by pure faith. In this, the night of the spirit, the blessed night, the soul confesses: "I went without discerning and with no other light except for that which in my heart was burning." All purification, that of the senses and that of the spirit, has but one goal: that the soul may drink of God's "deep-cellared heart." [96]

The problems Edith Stein discusses in her study of St. John of the Cross are many, her explanations of his poetic symbols exquisite; again and again one is aware of her philosophical mastery, but throughout one feels that here speaks more than learning —mystical insight; here speaks a daughter of St. John, one who has mounted the "secret stair." [97] Mystical union—God and the soul two in one flesh—is to her the goal of man, the Christ-given goal. It was precisely Christ's wooing of the soul, His demand for an utter following, that brought Him the cross, and precisely this cross it was that opened the sluices of mercy. Thus, into those who are brave to embrace the cross, divine life, divine light, streams, but because it uproots everything that blocks its path, they experience it first as death and night. The dark night is the darker, the death of the old creature the more anguished, the more the divine suit conquers, the more the soul yields. So also is the rising of the new creature the more glorious, with its natural powers transfigured. And like the risen Christ, the new creature bears the passion's wounds: the memory of the wretchedness from which he rose and of the ransom paid for his rising, the pain of longing for the fullness of life, for the shadowless light he cannot see except he die.[98]

Blessed of the Cross

Edith Stein's *Science of the Cross,* which has been called "her most mature work," [99] was never to be finished. To her it had always been more than a book, always something to be lived, and she was to live it more fully; for the marks of the passion, which grace the new creature, she was to bear not only in her soul but also on her body. From the first moment of her believing, she saw the cross—to the Jews a discouragement, a stumbling block, to the Gentiles mere foolishness—as power, wisdom, that could not be but God's;[100] saw the wood of woe as the cradle of joy, as the "tall Tree of Life." [101] Too, during her early Catholic years, as often as she went to the abbey church of Beuron, she stayed for hours before the painting of Our Lady of Sorrows: "Beneath the cross you were made our mother," sings one of her poems. What led her to enter Carmel was first to share in the passion, for her keen, pure mind could not be deceived. She knew what loomed ahead for the Jews and was ready to bear her appointed portion of the cross, and to bear it in the spirit and strength of Christ, for her people, for their salvation. So it came that when she was clothed in the Carmelite habit, she asked for and received the name Teresia Benedicta a Cruce—Teresia Blessed of the Cross.[102]

To be sprung from the people which has always worshiped Him who is, and who wishes to be known till the end of time as, the God of Abraham, Isaac and Jacob, was Edith Stein's great joy, her prioress tells, and whenever she spoke of the Old Testament, this joy was like a still light in her beautiful eyes, a radiance which must have illumined the road to her Golgotha. Though ready to suffer, the gentlest of souls, there was strength in her anger—when the Jews were blackened, she did not hesitate to call calumny calumny. Another religious, Sister Pia, recalls her vigorous rebuke: "Just as the most fantastic things are imputed to the Jesuits, so to the Jews." She was stricken with pain when, during November 1938, the news reached the cloister that the synagogues had been set on fire, Jewish homes pillaged and Jewish men sent to concentration camps: "Oh, that my people understood!" She knew that in denying Christ, it was denying itself peace, "but woe when, for all that is done to the Jews today, the vengeance of God is visited upon this city and this country." Speaking of their devotion to the Jews, Sister Pia likens Edith Stein and Rosa (one of her sisters, who had followed her into the faith and as a tertiary into Carmel) to the great women of the Old Dispensation: "As of old their mothers, Judith and Esther, by prayer and penance rescued the people of Israel, they cast themselves into the arms of divine justice to obtain salvation and mercy for both the oppressed and their oppressors." [103]

Her praying thus was love, not weakness, for compromise was alien to her. During one of the many plebiscites under the Nazi regime, posters screamed at every corner: "Give your Yes to the Fuehrer!" Edith Stein did not appear at the polls, for it was "forbidden for Jews to vote," but since not all Jews had been struck off the permanent registration lists, two Party members arrived at the convent, offering to drive Frau Dr. Stein to the voting place, for she was surely not well, they said, and it would be their pleasure to bring her to and fro. She was told of this and, not wishing just then to reveal her Jewish origin, lest she imperil the convent, declared: "Well, if the gentlemen attach such importance to my 'No' vote—I can oblige." Some time later, when another plebiscite was just ahead, a discussion arose, most members of the community holding that it did not matter morally whether one voted for or against Hitler, since the result was determined beforehand anyhow, and a negative vote—the ballots not being truly secret—would mean the closing of the convent and of their Carmelite life. But Edith Stein adjured the sisters not to give their votes to Hitler, whatever the consequences, for he was the enemy of God and would pull Germany down to perdition with him. Two years passed, and Edith Stein, then in Holland, was summoned to the office of the Gestapo in Maastricht. Her whole future was at stake; still, she entered the office with the greeting: *Gelobt sei Jesus Christus,* "Praised be Jesus Christ." For the Nazis, it was as if a bomb had fallen in their midst. On returning to the convent, she admitted to her prioress that, humanly speaking, her profession of faith was indeed imprudent, but that she had had to make it, for here was no battle of politics but the age-old war between Jesus and Lucifer.[104]

The convent she returned to was in Echt, where she had been transferred at her own request, for she feared that her staying in the Carmel of Cologne would jeopardize its existence. When she left Cologne on the last day of 1938, her heart knew that the parting was forever, but, as she later said: "We must be grateful for our bond in the kingdom that knows no frontiers, no fences, no separation, no distance." It was in Echt that she wrote, together with a number of short essays, the work that was to be her last will and testament, her *Science of the Cross.* To it she gave every free moment of the day and part of the night, laboring with urgency, for she must have felt the time short. With the supreme good sense Bergson found so marked in the genuine mystic, she saw the Nazi tyranny in Holland growing worse every day and sought admission to Switzerland and to the Carmel of Le Paquier near Fribourg. But there was a great deal of red tape, so that when all the other permissions had been granted, still missing was that of the German occupation authorities—till time ran out and Edith Stein was in the grip of the Gestapo. Yet while that grip was closing in and bureaucratic slowness delayed and delayed, she was at peace, and wrote, in June 1942: "For months I have carried next to my heart a little piece of paper with the words of Christ: 'When they persecute you in one town, flee to another.' [105] Negotiations continue with Le Paquier, but I am so deeply absorbed in St. John of the Cross that everything else leaves me indifferent." [106]

For some time, the relationship between the Dutch bishops and Hitler's deputy, the *Reichskommissar,* had been tense. First he ordered that Jewish children should be taught only by Jewish teachers, which meant that Catholic children of Jewish origin would be expelled from Catholic schools. To this the Archbishop of Utrecht, Johan de Jong, in the name of all the bishops, replied: Never! Never will Catholic educators exclude children from their schools because of blood. Later it was decreed that all public buildings had to bear a sign, "Forbidden to Jews," but the bishops forbade its being posted on Catholic buildings. Finally, in 1942, the mass deportations of Jews, of men, women and children, began. In a wire to the *Reichskommissar* on July 11, the Catholic bishops, together with the leaders of other Christian communities, declared that, deeply shaken by the previous measures against the Jews, they were horrified by this. It warred against God's bidding of justice and mercy, they protested, and earnestly demanded its withdrawal. The only concession granted was that Jewish Christians would not be included in the deportation orders.

On July 26, then, the bishops, not satisfied with a mere exception from inhumanity, had a pastoral letter read in all the churches. Ours is a time of great miseries, they began, of which two are foremost: the plight of the Jews and the plight of the forced laborers. It is imperative that all be deeply aware of these grave woes, they continued, and therefore they made known their wire of protest of two weeks before. Before their minds the ruin with which the whole world had been threatened for almost three years, they could not but think of the gospel of the day: Christ weeping over Jerusalem's blindness and announcing the Lord's judgment on her. His tears, His forecast of doom, were equally meant for all today, the bishops went on, and asked the faithful to look into their own hearts, to do penance and to pray. "Let us implore, then, beloved, through the intercession of the Mother of Mercy, that God may soon give to the world a just peace. That He may strengthen the people of Israel, so bitterly tried in these days, and that He may bring it to true salvation in Christ Jesus. That He may shield those whose lot it is to work in a strange land, to live far from their loved ones at home. That He may shield them body and soul. That He may protect them from bitterness and loss of heart. That He may keep them faithful in their faith; may He also protect their families. Let us implore Him for all those afflicted and oppressed, for prisoners and hostages, for so many over whose heads hang threatening clouds, peril of life. Open, O Lord, the ears of Thy mercy to the prayers of those who beseech Thee." [107]

In the eyes of the *Reichskommissar,* the bishops' letter was treason, "blasphemy"; their attempt to halt Hitler's bloody despotism, their appeal from his mercilessness to divine mercy, was a "crime" that could not go unpunished, nor was the penalty long delayed. On Sunday, August 2, all Jewish Catholics, all religious of Jewish blood in Dutch monasteries, were seized by the Gestapo—a "countermeasure against the pastoral letter of July 26," the lieutenant of the *Reichskommissar* boasted. When Archbishop de Jong saw that these laymen and nuns, brothers and priests, had become the victims of the bishops' daring, at once he made grieved remonstrance, but it was not thought worthy of an answer. Jewish and Catholic, the prisoners represented what Nazism hated most, the flesh and the spirit of Jesus Christ. Of this the lieutenant made no secret: "Catholic full-Jews we must consider our worst enemies," he ranted in a public speech, "and for this reason we must see that, as soon as possible, they are deported to the East"—"east" being a euphemism for concentration camp, gas chamber or salt mine, in short, for death. "The declaration of the lieutenant of the *Reichskommissar* makes quite clear that these religious women and men truly died "in witness to the faith," wrote Father Hopster, S.V.D., of Venlo, "for their arrest was an act of vengeance against the pastoral letter. In the imprisonment of these Catholic religious of Jewish origin, it was the bishops and the Church that were struck at." [108]

Among the many prisoners were five of the seven children of Professor Lutz Loeb and Jenny van Gelder, all of them Trappists

—two priests, Father Ignatius and Father Nivardus, a brother, Brother Linus, and two nuns, Sister Hedwig and Sister Maria Teresa. At the moment of the summons, the three men felt the clutch of fear, but soon regaining their strength, they celebrated the divine Mysteries as serene as ever. They could have escaped, but this would have put the community in hazard. "Pray, pray well," were their parting words, "we are going the way of the cross, toward martyrdom." When the patrol wagon drew up at the monastery, the two Sisters already in it, Sister Hedwig sprang out with that liveliness that was her own, and with outstretched hands walked to the Abbot. Kneeling before him in her white habit and black mantle, she exclaimed: "Reverend Father, we are on our way to heaven." [109] Another victim of the *Reichskommissar* was Lisemaria Meirowsky, a physician and Dominican Sister, who, four days later, on the feast of the Transfiguration, penciled a hasty note to her confessor: "I send you a last greeting and should like to tell you that I am full of trust, entirely given over to God's holy will. Indeed, I consider it a grace and election that I had to leave under such circumstances and thus to answer for the words of our fathers and shepherds in Christ. . . . We are privileged to bear witness for Jesus and, with our bishops, for the truth," she said in the name of all. "We go as children of our mother, holy Church, uniting our suffering with that of our King, Redeemer and Bridegroom." For another priest-friend she included this message: that his heart should not be heavy and sorrowful, that, on the contrary, he should thank God with her and sing a jubilant *Magnificat*. She added too a message for Archbishop de Jong: "We are so glad to be able to help him with our sacrifice. He should be at rest and never think that we have the least regret." [109]

I will sing Thy praises on the three shores of Thy One Light.
I will plunge with my song into the sea of Thy glory: with shouts
of joy into the waves of Thy power.[110]

It was at five in the afternoon of that bitter and bright August 2 that Edith Stein was taken prisoner. The community was assembled in choir and she was reading aloud what they would meditate on the next morning, when two SS-men rang the bell. "In ten minutes Sister Stein has to leave the house," was their command. While the prioress protested, to no avail, Sister Benedicta returned to the choir, prayed for some moments and then went to her cell, where several Sisters helped her pack her few belongings—a blanket, cup, spoon, and food for three days, were all the SS-men thought she needed! First she begged the Sisters to pray for her, then that they notify the Swiss consul; and for the rest, she was silent, the Sisters from Echt recall, as if her spirit were not in the cell but elsewhere. Meanwhile crowds had gathered in the street, so that she and her sister Rosa were led to the patrol wagon amid clamor against the Nazi tyranny. They and all the other prisoners were taken first to the camp of Amersfoort, then to the camp of Westerbork, both in Holland; at one point they were driven across open country under curses and the blows of rifle butts. There were about twelve hundred Catholic Jews at Westerbork, of whom about fifteen were religious. "The distress in the camp and the confusion among the newcomers cannot be described. But Sister Benedicta stood out by her calm and composure, going among the women, comforting, helping, bringing peace, like an angel," a Jewish prisoner who escaped deportation, and so survived, remembers. "Many of the mothers, nearly insane with grief, for days had neglected their children and now sat around brooding in dull despair. At once Sister Benedicta took care of the poor little ones, washed and combed them, saw that they were fed and provided for. All the while she remained in the camp she showed such a vigilant love that everyone marveled." [111]

Knowing the countersign of sorrow, Edith Stein could forget herself and raise the downcast. "I am content with everything," reads one of the little notes she was able to write to her prioress from the camp. "A 'Science of the Cross' can be gained only if one is made to feel the cross to the depths of one's being. Of this I was convinced from the first moment, and I have said, *Ave crux, spes unica,* Hail, cross, thou only hope." [112] Yet even as she was ready to die, she was ready to live. In another note she asked for blankets, woolen stockings, warm underclothing, towels and washcloths, as well as for a toothbrush, a rosary and a cross for her sister, and for herself the autumn volume of the Breviary. And she added: "Have been able to pray wonderfully thus far." She was to have no need for the things she requested, for, having arrived at Westerbork on the morning of August 5, she and many others left "for the East" on the night of the sixth. Three times on their way across Germany she was able to send a short message, through a former pupil, through a station master, through a stranger: "Greetings. I am on the journey to Poland. Sister Teresia Benedicta." [113]

No other last words than these were ever heard from her. But there is a great deal to indicate, though not with absolute certainty, that she was gassed in Auschwitz on August 9, the vigil of St. Lawrence, when the Church repeatedly remembers the words of Christ: "If any man has a mind to come My way, let him renounce self, and take up his cross, and follow Me." [114]

There in Auschwitz a creature who had never willingly injured a fellow creature was tossed into torment; a woman pure as morning air—"like her eyes her whole being, crystal-clear" [115]—was smothered as are vermin; a thinker of truth and lover of the word was made to die a wordless death; fearlessly Christian she was, and yet her witness had to go unwitnessed, the blood of her testimony speak in silence. Is it not harrowing? Harrowing! Still, her rich life was not wasted but fulfilled.

Evil does not rest today at denying God, at crucifying God-made-Man; man too it hates. Hence the slaughter of Christ's disciples does not sate it, to take their lives is not enough, for what it really covets is their humanity. With gas to choke their words and drugs to cripple their wills, it seeks to kill their very manhood and in them to slay man the image of God. Yet in this, evil undoes itself, for it "calls forth" a sacrifice, a love, stronger than itself, and it is no others who shield man today than these brothers and sisters of the Son of Man. In Auschwitz Edith Stein's life was not wasted but fulfilled.

Fulfilled was her life, not wasted, if we measure it by the old measures. As the Bible sees man, his life is a dialogue: addressed, spoken to by God, he answers. "Go forth," the Lord bid Abram; "Moses, Moses," He called from the burning bush, and "Samuel, Samuel," in the stillness of the temple.[116] "The word of the Lord came unto them," is said of the prophets, and the Word came to man, to every man, eminently, superabundantly, substantially, in

Jesus Christ. Man, every man, is the "thou" of Him who alone can say "I am," and his dignity is to be response-ive and response-ible. Edith Stein's life and death had this biblical mark: they were a speaking to and fro. And having answered, having said her "Yes" to the end, she longed that others say theirs. After her arrest, found by chance in her convent cell in Echt was a little paper on which she had written her oblation of her life for her people, praying that many might come to know the Glory of Israel, the Light of the nations; that, as she had, her kinsmen might discover Christ.

Notes

PREFACE

1. *Bab. Shabbath* 116a; *Tos. Shabbath* 13, 5. Cf. R. Travers Herford, *Christianity in Talmud and Midrash* (London: Williams & Norgate, 1903), p. 155; *The Babylonian Talmud: Seder Mo'ed* (London: Soncino Press, 1938), Vol. II, p. 569.

2. *Bab. Shabbath* 116a. Cf. Herford, *ibid.*, p. 162; *The Babylonian Talmud: Seder Mo'ed*, Vol. II, p. 571, note 3.

3. G. K. Chesterton, *Heretics* (New York: Devin-Adair, 1950), pp. 3-4.

4. Chesterton, *Orthodoxy* (New York: John Lane Co., 1909), p. 18.

5. Rom. 10:2.

6. Annie Kraus, *Ueber die Dummheit* (Frankfurt am Main: Verlag Joseph Knecht, Carolusdruckerei, 1948), pp. 7-21. Cf. St. Thomas, *Summa Theol.* II-II, q. 46; Ps. 13:1; Ecclus. 1:16.

7. Raïssa Maritain, *Le Prince de ce Monde* (Bruges: Desclée de Brouwer, 1932), pp. 20-23; *The Prince of This World*, translated by Gerald B. Phelan (Ditchling, Hassocks, Sussex: St. Dominic's Press, 1936), pp. 10-13.

HENRI BERGSON, PHILOSOPHER OF EXPERIENCE

1. Irwin Edman, Foreword to Henri Bergson's *Creative Evolution*, translated by A. Mitchell (New York: Modern Library, 1944), p. xv.

2. Bergson, *Les Deux sources de la morale et de la religion* (7th ed.; Paris: Félix Alcan, 1932), p. 343; *The Two Sources of Morality and Religion*, translated by R. A. Audra and C. Brereton (New York: Henry Holt & Co., 1935), p. 306.

3. *Ibid.*, pp. 273-274; *ibid.*, pp. 243-245.

4. Bergson, *L'Évolution créatrice* (52nd ed.; Paris: Presses Universitaires de France, 1940), p. 239; *Creative Evolution*, p. 260.

5. Ernest Renan, *L'Avenir de la science* (Paris: Michel Lévy Frères, 1890), pp. 37, 501; *The Future of Science* (Boston: Roberts Bros., 1891), pp. 30, 468.

6. Bergson, *L'Évolution créatrice*, p. 249; *Creative Evolution*, p. 271.

7. Letter from Bergson to Père de Tonquédec (June 12, 1911) in *Études*, February 20, 1912, pp. 515-516.

8. Letter from Bergson to Harald Høffding in *La Philosophie de Bergson* by Høffding, translated by J. de Coussange (Paris: Félix Alcan, 1916), p. 159.

9. Bergson, *Deux Sources*, p. 270; *Two Sources*, pp. 240-241.

10. St. Thomas, *Summa Theol.* I, q. 13, a. 1 ad 1.

11. Bergson, *Deux Sources*, p. 270; *Two Sources*, p. 241.

12. St. Thomas, *De Pot.* VIII, 4.

13. St. Thomas, *Summa Theol.* I, q. 29, a. 3.

14. Bergson, *La Pensée et le mouvant* (12th ed.; Paris: Presses Universitaires de France, 1941), p. 159; *The Creative Mind*, translated by M. L. Andison (New York: Philosophical Library, 1946), p. 169.

15. *Ibid.*, p. 176; *ibid.*, p. 186.

16. St. Augustine, *Conf.* I, 4 (PL 32:662).

17. Bergson, *La Pensée*, pp. 101, 167, 116; *The Creative Mind*, pp. 109, 177, 124.

18. Bergson, *L'Évolution créatrice*, p. 276; *Creative Evolution*, p. 300.

19. Bergson's letter to Père de Tonquédec, *Études*, February 20, 1912, pp. 515-516.

20. Bergson, *L'Évolution créatrice*, p. 276; *Creative Evolution*, p. 300.

21. Bergson's letter to Père de Tonquédec, *Études*, February 20, 1912, pp. 515-516.

22. Bergson, *La Pensée*, p. 196; *The Creative Mind*, p. 206.

23. Bergson, *Deux Sources*, p. 265; *Two Sources*, p. 236.

24. St. John of the Cross, "Songs between the Soul and the Bridegroom," *The Poems of St John of the Cross*, translated by Roy Campbell (New York: Pantheon, 1951), p. 17.

25. Bergson, *Deux Sources*, pp. 253, 249; *Two Sources*, pp. 225, 222.

26. *Ibid.*, p. 274; *ibid.*, 244.

27. Antonin D. Sertillanges, O.P., *Henri Bergson et le catholicisme* (Paris: Flammarion, 1941), p. 7.

28. Édouard Le Roy, *Discours prononcés dans la séance publique tenue par l'Académie Française pour la réception de M. Edouard Le Roy, Oct. 18, 1945* (Paris: Firmin-Didot, 1945), p. 7.

29. Jacques Chevalier, *Bergson* (Paris: Librairie Plon, 1926), pp. 37-38; *Henri Bergson*, translated by L. A. Clare (New York: Macmillan Co., 1928), pp. 40-41.

30. *Ibid.*, pp. 41-42; *ibid.*, pp. 44-45. Cf. Pascal's letter to Fermat, July 29, 1654, *Oeuvres de Blaise Pascal* ("Grands écrivains de la France"), Vol. III, p. 391.

31. *Ibid.*, p. 44; *ibid.*, p. 47.

32. Sertillanges, *Avec Henri Bergson* (Paris: Gallimard, 1941), p. 10.

33. Bergson, *La Pensée*, p. 22; *The Creative Mind*, p. 31.

34. Cf. Chevalier, *Bergson*, p. 48, note 1; *Henri Bergson*, p. 52, note 1.

35. Bergson, *Essai sur les données immédiates de la conscience* (10th ed.; Paris: Félix Alcan, 1912), p. 140; *Time and Free Will*, translated by F. L. Pogson (New York: Macmillan Co., 1910), p. 183.

36. Bergson, *Durée et simultanéité* (5th ed.; Paris: Félix Alcan, 1929), p. 63.

37. Bergson, *Les Données immédiates*, p. 182; *Time and Free Will*, p. 236.

38. *Ibid.*, pp. 132, 128-129; *ibid.*, pp. 172, 168.

39. *Ibid.*, pp. 126, 132; *ibid.*, pp. 165, 172-173.

40. Sertillanges, "Le Libre arbitre chez saint Thomas et chez Henri Bergson," *La Vie Intellectuelle* (April 25, 1937), pp. 252-267.

41. Aristotle, *Nic. Eth.* VI, 2, 1139^b.

42. Sertillanges, "Le Libre arbitre," *La Vie Intellectuelle* (April 25, 1937), pp. 268-269.

43. Raïssa Maritain, *Les Grandes amitiés* (New York: Éditions de la Maison Française, 1941), pp. 130-131; *We Have Been Friends Together*, translated by J. Kernan (New York: Longmans, Green and Co., 1942), p. 90.

44. Bergson, *Les Données immédiates*, p. 129; *Time and Free Will*, p. 168.

45. Bergson, *La Pensée*, p. 102; *The Creative Mind*, p. 110.

46. Bergson, *Deux Sources*, pp. 334-335; *Two Sources*, pp. 298-299.

47. St. Augustine, *Sermo CLXXIV*, 2 (PL 38:940).

48. Bergson, *La Pensée*, p. 116; *The Creative Mind*, pp. 124-125.

49. Bergson, *Deux Sources*, p. 336; *Two Sources*, p. 300.

50. Os. 14:2.

51. Cant. 3:4.

52. Bergson, *Matière et mémoire* (Geneva: Albert Skira, 1946), pp. 14, 15; *Matter and Memory*, translated by N. M. Paul and W. S. Palmer (New York: Macmillan Co., 1911), pp. xi, xiii. Cf. Bergson, *L'Énergie spirituelle*

(Paris: Félix Alcan, 1919), p. 39; *Mind-Energy*, translated by H. W. Carr (New York: Henry Holt and Co., 1920), pp. 45-46.

53. Bergson, *Matière et mémoire*, p. 32; *Matter and Memory*, p. 19.

54. *Ibid.*, pp. 241, 246; *ibid.*, pp. 313, 320.

55. Chevalier, *Bergson*, pp. 153-156; *Henri Bergson*, pp. 166-170.

56. Bergson, *Matière et mémoire*, pp. 182-183; *Matter and Memory*, pp. 231-232.

57. Sertillanges, *Avec Henri Bergson*, p. 15.

58. Bergson, *La Pensée*, p. 46; *The Creative Mind*, p. 53.

59. St. Augustine, *Conf.* X, 8, 17 (PL 32:785, 790).

60. *Ibid.*, X, 25 (PL 32:795).

61. St. Augustine, *De Trin.* X, 11, 18 (PL 42:983-984).

62. 1 Cor. 2:9.

63. Bergson, *L'Évolution créatrice*, p. 271; *Creative Evolution*, p. 295.

64. Bergson, *Deux Sources*, pp. 283-284; *Two Sources*, pp. 252-253.

65. St. Thomas, *Summa Theol.* I-II, q. 69, a. 2.

66. Bernard of Morlaix, *Hora novissima*, translated by J. M. Neale. Cf. Matthew Britt, O.S.B., *The Hymns of the Breviary and Missal* (New York: Benziger Bros., 1924), p. 352.

67. Bergson, *L'Évolution créatrice*, pp. 264-265; *Creative Evolution*, pp. 287-289.

68. *Ibid.*, p. 265; *ibid.*, pp. 288-289.

69. *Ibid.*, p. 270; *ibid.*, p. 294.

70. Aristotle, *De gener. anim.* II, 3, 736ᵇ, 27. Cf. Franz C. Brentano, *Lehre vom Ursprung des menschlichen Geistes* (Leipzig: Veit & Co., 1911), pp. 18-21 and *passim*.

71. St. Thomas, *Summa Theol.* I, q. 90, a. 3.

72. Sertillanges, *Avec Henri Bergson*, pp. 39-40.

73. Bergson, *L'Évolution créatrice*, p. 245; *Creative Evolution*, p. 267.

74. *Ibid.*, pp. 53, 56-57; *ibid.*, pp. 60, 63-64.

75. Charles Darwin, *The Origin of Species and The Descent of Man* (New York: Modern Library, 1936), pp. 14, 367.

76. Bergson, *L'Évolution créatrice*, pp. 102-103; *Creative Evolution*, p. 113.

77. *Ibid.*, p. 100; *ibid.*, p. 110.

78. Friedrich Nietzsche, *Thus Spake Zarathustra*, I, "Zarathustra's Prologue," 3. Ludwig Klages, "Mensch und Erde—1913," *Der Mensch und das Leben* (Jena: Eugen Diederichs Verlag, 1937), pp. 34, 32; *Der Geist als Widersacher der Seele*, Vol. I, *Leben und Denkvermoegen* (Leipzig: Johann Ambrosius Barth, 1929), p. 253.

79. Bergson, *L'Évolution créatrice*, pp. 313-322; *Creative Evolution*, pp. 340-350.

80. *Ibid.*, pp. 129; *ibid.*, p. 142.

81. *Ibid.*, pp. 254, 248, 105-106, 89-90, 225, 106; *ibid.*, pp. 277, 270, 116, 99, 245, 116. Cf. Sertillanges, *Avec Henri Bergson*, pp. 16-17, 35-37; *Henri Bergson et le catholicisme*, pp. 29-31.

82. Bergson, "La vie et les oeuvres de M. Félix Ravaisson-Mollien," *Comptes rendus de l'Académie des Sciences morales et politiques* (1904), Vol. I, p. 686. Cf. *La Pensée*, pp. 279-280; *The Creative Mind*, pp. 288-289. Leonardo da Vinci, *Thoughts On Art and Life*, translated by Maurice Baring (Boston: Merrymount Press, 1906), p. 87.

83. Jacques Maritain, *De Bergson à Thomas d'Aquin* (New York: Éditions de la Maison Française, 1944), p. 53; *Ransoming the Time*, translated by H. L. Binsse (New York: Scribner's Sons, 1941), p. 86.

84. Bergson, *Deux Sources*, pp. 5, 85, 87, 83; *Two Sources*, pp. 4, 76, 78, 74.

85. *Ibid.*, pp. 110, 4-8, 32-33; *ibid.*, pp. 96, 3-7, 29-30.

86. Bergson, pp. 29, 47, 101, 50, 96-100; *ibid.*, pp. 26, 42, 90, 45, 86-90.

87. Sertillanges, *Henri Bergson et le catholicisme*, p. 44.

88. Floris Delattre, "Les Dernières années de Henri Bergson," *Revue Philosophique*, Nos. 3-8 (March-August, 1941), p. 138.

89. Bergson, *Deux Sources*, p. 50; *Two Sources*, p. 45.

90. Sertillanges, *Henri Bergson et le catholicisme*, p. 55.

91. Bergson, *Deux Sources*, pp. 97, 56; *Two Sources*, pp. 87, 50.

92. St. Thomas, *Summa Theol.* I-II, q. 68, a. 2.

93. Sertillanges, *Henri Bergson et le catholicisme*, p. 57.

94. Bergson, *Deux Sources*, pp. 75-76; *Two Sources*, pp. 67-68.

95. *Ibid.*, p. 76; *ibid.*, p. 68.

96. Aristotle, *Pol.* I, II, 23, 1255ᵇ, 37; and I, II, 3-4, 1253ᵇ, 20-33.

97. Marcus Aurelius, *Med.* II, 1; VII, 31; IV, 4. Cf. VII, 9, and Seneca, *Ep.* XCV, 52.

98. Marcus Aurelius, *Med.* II, 5.

99. Seneca, *Ep. LXVII*, 1.

100. St. Augustine, *Epist.* CXVIII (PL 33:437-438). Cf. C. N. Cochrane, *Christianity and Classical Culture* (New York: Oxford University Press, 1944), pp. 165-167.

101. Bergson, *Deux Sources*, p. 77; *Two Sources*, p. 69.

102. *Ibid.*, pp. 77-78; *ibid.*, pp. 69-70.

103. T. S. Eliot, "Ash Wednesday," *Collected Poems 1909-1935* (New York: Harcourt, Brace and Co., 1936), p. 118.

104. Jean Wahl, "Au sujet des relations de Bergson avec l'église catholique," *La Nouvelle Relève* IV, 1 (April, 1945), p. 5; cf. *Review of Religion* IX, 1 (November, 1944), p. 47.

105. Bergson, *Deux Sources*, pp. 105, 187; *Two Sources*, pp. 92, 166.

106. *Ibid.*, pp. 125-135, 135-144, 137, note 1; *ibid.*, pp. 110-118, 118-127, 121, note 1.

107. *Ibid.*, pp. 144-160, 161; *ibid.*, pp. 128-141, 142.

108. Jacques Maritain, *De Bergson à Thomas d'Aquin*, pp. 67-68; *Ransoming the Time*, pp. 98-99.

109. Bergson, *Deux Sources*, pp. 225-226, 235; *Two Sources*, pp. 199-201, 209.

110. Delattre, "Les Dernières années de Henri Bergson," *Revue Philosophique*, Nos. 3-8 (March-August, 1941), p. 135.

111. Matt. 5:4.

112. Bergson, *Deux Sources*, p. 243; *Two Sources*, p. 216.

113. *Ibid.*, pp. 244-245; *ibid.*, p. 218.

114. *Ibid.*, pp. 245-248; *ibid.*, pp. 218-221.

115. *Ibid.*, pp. 248-251; *ibid.*, pp. 222-223.

116. 1 John 4:16.

117. 1 Cor. 13:13.

118. Cant. 8:6,7.

119. Thomas à Kempis, *The Imitation of Christ*, III, 5 (New York: Harper & Bros., 1941), pp. 102-103; "From the First Edition of an English Translation Made c. 1530 by Richard Whitford."

120. Blaise Romeyer, S.J., "Caractéristiques religieuses du spiritualisme de Bergson," *Archives de Philosophie* XVII, 1 (January, 1947), pp. 54-55.

121. Sertillanges, "Bergson apologiste," *Henri Bergson: Essais et témoignages recueillis*, edited by A. Béguin and P. Thévenaz (Neuchâtel: de la Baconnière, 1943), p. 59.

122. Bergson, *Deux Sources*, pp. 270, 273, 253, 276; *Two Sources*, pp. 240, 243, 225, 246.

123. Raïssa Maritain, "Souvenirs," *Essais et témoignages*, p. 356.

124. Private communication from Jacques Maritain. Raïssa Maritain, *Les Grandes amitiés*, p. 116; *We Have Been Friends Together*, p. 79.

125. Chevalier, "Comment Bergson a trouvé Dieu," *Essais et témoignages*, p. 96.

126. Bergson, *Deux Sources*, pp. 236, 241; *Two Sources*, pp. 210, 214.

127. *Ibid.*, pp. 268, 256; *ibid.*, pp. 239, 228.

128. *Ibid.*, p. 256; *ibid.*, p. 228.

129. Georges Cattaui, "Témoignage," *Essais et témoignages*, p. 123.

375

130. Sertillanges, *Avec Henri Bergson*, pp. 21-22.
131. Letter by Bergson to Daniel Halévy, published in *Le Temps* (Paris), January 26, 1939.
132. Wahl, "Au sujet des relations de Bergson avec l'église catholique," *La Nouvelle Relève* IV, 1 (April, 1945), p. 8; cf. *Review of Religion* IX, 1 (November, 1944), p. 48.
133. Wahl, "Présence de Bergson," *Essais et témoignages*, p. 27.
134. Wahl, "Au sujet . . ."
135. Delattre, "Les Dernières années de Henri Bergson," *Revue Philosophique*, Nos. 3-8 (March-August, 1941), p. 136.
136. Le Roy, "Une Enquête sur quelques traits majeurs de la philosophie bergsonienne," *Archives de Philosophie* XVII, 1 (January, 1947), pp. 20-21.
137. Sertillanges, *Avec Henri Bergson*, pp. 22, 48, 23.
138. Romeyer, "Caractéristiques religieuses du spiritualisme de Bergson," *Archives de Philosophie* XVII, 1 (January, 1947), pp. 31-32.
139. Sertillanges, *Avec Henri Bergson*, pp. 22, 20-21.
140. *Ibid.*, p. 57.
141. Private communication from Mademoiselle Jeanne Bergson. Cf. Foreword to *Essais et témoignages*, p. 12.
142. Chevalier, *Bergson*, pp. 49-51; *Henri Bergson*, pp. 53-55.
143. Le Roy, *Discours*, p. 6.
144. *William James: Extraits de sa correspondence*, translated by F. Delattre and M. Le Breton, preface by Henri Bergson (Paris: Payot, 1924), p. 9.
145. Romeyer, "Caractéristiques religieuses du spiritualisme de Bergson," *Archives de Philosophie* XVII, 1 (January, 1947), p. 46.
146. Sertillanges, *Avec Henri Bergson*, pp. 57-58.
147. *Ibid.*, pp. 27-28.
148. Ps. 129.
149. *Roman Ritual*, The Burial Service.
150. Delattre, "Les Dernières années de Henri Bergson," *Revue Philosophique*, Nos. 3-8 (March-August, 1941), p. 136.
151. *La Documentation Catholique* XLIV, 994 (July 6, 1947), col. 858-859.
152. Cattaui, "Témoignage," *Essais et témoignages*, pp. 122-124.
153. Romeyer, "Caractéristiques religieuses du spiritualisme de Bergson," *Archives de Philosophie* XVII, 1 (January, 1947), p. 45.
154. Private Communication from Mademoiselle Bergson.
155. St. Ambrose, *De obitu Valent.* 53 (PL 16:1375).
156. Sertillanges, *Avec Henri Bergson*, p. 59.
157. Charles Journet in *Nova et Vetera* XVI, 2 (April-June, 1941), p. 224.
158. Pius XII, *Mystici Corporis Christi*, A.A.S. XXXV, 7 (July 20, 1943), p. 243.
159. Gabriel Marcel, "Grandeur de Bergson," *Essais et témoignages*, p. 30.
160. Paul Valéry, "Henri Bergson," *Essais et témoignages*, p. 20.
161. Bergson, *Le Rire* (24th ed.; Paris: Félix Alcan, 1925), p. 157; *Laughter*, translated by C. Brereton and F. Rothwell (New York: Macmillan Co., 1913), p. 154.
162. Sertillanges, *Avec Henri Bergson*, p. 24.
163. Romeyer, "Caractéristiques religieuses du spiritualisme de Bergson," *Archives de Philosophie* XVII, 1 (January, 1947), p. 26.
164. Foreword to *Essais et témoignages*, p. 11.
165. St. Thomas, *De Pot.* V, 5, 7; *Summa contra Gent.* III, 19, 21, 22; Dionysius, *De cael. hier.* III, 2 (PG 3:165). Cf. Maurice Blondel, "De l'assimilation," in his *Exigences philosophiques du Christianisme* (Paris: Presses Universitaires de France, 1950), pp. 217 ff.
166. Cattaui, "Témoignage," *Essais et témoignages*, p. 122.

1. Private communications from Dr. Hedwig Conrad-Martius, Munich, and Soror Adelgundis Jaegerschmidt, O.S.B., St. Lioba-Kloster, Freiburg im Breisgau.
2. Thomas G. Masaryk, "Náboženství A Spolecnost Lidská," *Americké Přednášky* (Prague: Cin, 1929), p. 40; *V Boji O Náboženství* (Prague: Cin, 1932), p. 25; *The Making of a State*, translated by H. W. Steed (New York: Frederick A. Stokes Co., 1928), p. 452.
3. "Briefe Franz Brentanos an Hugo Bergmann," edited by Hugo Bergmann, *Philosophy and Phenomenological Research*, VII, 1 (September, 1946), pp. 129, 132, 130, 104.
4. Robert Browning, "Christmas-Eve and Easter-Day," *The Poetical Works of Robert Browning* (London: Chapman and Hall, 1863), III, 193-195, 200-201.
5. Ernest Renan, *Vie de Jésus* (Paris: Calmann-Lévy, 1925), pp. xv-xvi; *Life of Jesus* (Boston: Robert Bros., 1896), pp. 21-22.
6. *Ibid.*, p. vi, p. iv note 1; *ibid.*, p. 13, p. 12 note 1.
7. Ernest Psichari, *Les Voix qui crient dans le désert* (Paris: Louis Conard, 1920), pp. 90-91, 166.
8. David Friedrich Strauss, *The Life of Jesus* (London: Chapman Bros., 1846), III, 446.
9. Martin Heidegger, *Was ist Metaphysik?* (Frankfurt a. M.: Vittorio Klostermann, 1949), pp. 30-38.
10. Alfred Loisy, *Mémoires*, 1908-1927 (Paris: Émile Nourry, 1931), III, 237-238.
11. Leo Tolstoy, *The Gospel in Brief*, XI, 302, 263; *What I Believe*, XI, 320-327, 531; *On Life*, XII, 132; *Reply to the Synod's Edict of Excommunication*, XII, 223, 225. "Centenary Edition for the Tolstoy Society," translated by A. Maude (London: Oxford University Press, 1933). Also *The Pathway of Life*, translated by A. J. Wolfe (New York: International Book Publishing Co., 1919), I, 121.
12. Vladimir Soloviev, *War, Progress, and the End of History* (London: University of London Press, 1915), pp. xx-xxi.
13. *Ibid.*, pp. 165-166; *War and Christianity* (London: Constable and Co., 1915), pp. 131-132.
14. John 8:58. Søren Kierkegaard, *Efterladte Papirer (1854-55)*, edited by H. Gottsched (Copenhagen: C. A. Reitzels Forlag, 1881), pp. 19, 119, 398; *Papirer*, edited by P. A. Heiberg, V. Kuhr and E. Torstuig (Copenhagen: Gyldendalske Boghandel, Nordisk Forlag, 1929), X, 113, 442; *Samlede Vaerker*, edited by A. B. Drachmann, J. L. Heiberg and H. O. Lange (Copenhagen: Gyldendalske Boghandel, Nordisk Forlag, 1920-36), VII, 193-194, 196; XIV, 243. Cf. Walter Lowrie, *Kierkegaard* (London: Oxford University Press, 1938), pp. 319, 523-524, 539, 580.
15. Private communication from Rev. Frederick Neumann, New York City.
16. Dan. 3:57.
17. St. Augustine, *In Psalmum CXLIX*, 7 (PL 37:1953).
18. Private communication from Professor Goetz Briefs, Catholic University of America, Washington, D. C.
19. Edmund Husserl, "Erinnerungen an Franz Brentano," *Franz Brentano*, edited by Oskar Kraus (Munich: C. H. Beck, 1919), p. 154.
20. Franz Brentano, *Psychologie vom empirischen Standpunkt* (Leipzig: Felix Meiner, 1924), I, 125.
21. St. Thomas, *Summa Theol.* I, q. 84, a. 1; q. 85, a. 1 and 4.
22. *Summa Theol.* I, q. 14, a. 1; cf. Aristotle, *De Anima* III, 8, 431ᵇ, 21.
23. St. Thomas, *De Ver.* II, 2.
24. Matt. 13:12.
25. Husserl, "Nachwort zu meinen 'Ideen zu einer reinen Phaenomenologie und phaeno-

menologischen Philosophie,'" *Jahrbuch fuer Philosophie und phaenomenologische Forschung* XI (1930), p. 564. Cf. Herbert Spiegelberg, "Der Begriff der Intentionalitaet in der Scholastik bei Brentano und bei Husserl," *Philosophische Hefte* V, 1/2 (1936), pp. 75-91.

26. Bernard Bolzano, *Wissenschaftslehre* (Sulzbach, 1837), IV, para. 718, as cited by Friedrich Ueberweg, *Grundriss der Geschichte der Philosophie* (Berlin: E. S. Mittler und Sohn, 1923), Vol. IV, p. 177.

27. *Bolzano und seine Gegner. Ein Beitrag zur neuesten Literaturgeschichte* (Sulzbach: Seidel, 1839), p. 131. Quoted by H. Fels, "Bernard Bolzano," *Philosophisches Jahrbuch* XXXIX (1926), p. 386 note 3.

28. Johann E. Erdmann, *Grundriss der Geschichte der Philosophie* (1846), p. 415. Quoted by Fels, *op. cit.*, p. 403 note 2.

29. Bolzano, *Was ist Philosophie?* (Vienna, 1849), p. 27. Quoted by Fels, *op. cit.*, p. 386 note 2.

30. Bolzano, *Wissenschaftslehre* I, para. 112.

31. Husserl, *Logische Untersuchungen* (3rd ed.; Halle: Max Niemeyer, 1922), I, 225-227.

32. Husserl, *Philosophie der Arithmetik* (Halle: C. E. M. Pfeffer [Robert Stricker], 1891), p. 11.

33. G. Frege, in *Zeitschrift fuer Philosophie und philosophische Kritik* CIII (1894), p. 318.

34. Husserl, *Logische Untersuchungen*, I, 38-39.

35. *Ibid.*, p. 4.

36. *Ibid.*, p. viii.

37. *Ibid.*, pp. 110-112.

38. Plato, *Theaetetus*, 152a.

39. Husserl, *Logische Untersuchungen*, I, 114-116.

40. *Ibid.*, pp. 117-122.

41. Dan. 10:11.

42. Husserl, *Logische Untersuchungen*, I, 154-167.

43. *Ibid.*, pp. 167-173.

44. *Ibid.*, pp. 180-191.

45. *Ibid.*, p. 139.

46. *Ibid.*, p. 151.

47. *Ibid.*, p. 141.

48. *Ibid.*, p. 148.

49. *Ibid.*, p. 142.

50. *Ibid.*, p. 150.

51. Plato, *Theaetetus*, 170c-171a.

52. Aristotle, *Metaphys.* IV, 4, 1009ᵃ, 10-14; IV, 8, 1012ᵇ, 13-17.

53. St. Augustine, *De Vera Relig.* 39, 73 (PL 34:154-155).

54. St. Thomas, *Summa Theol.* I, q. 2, a. 1, obj. 3.

55. Husserl, *Logische Untersuchungen*, I, 117.

56. *Ibid.*, p. 128.

57. *Ibid.*, p. 130

58. *Ibid.*, p. 132.

59. *Ibid.*, p. 228.

60. Husserl, *Logische Untersuchungen*, II/2, 122, 118.

61. St. Thomas, *De Ver.* I, 2.

62. *De Ver.* II, 14.

63. A.-D. Sertillanges, *La Philosophie de St. Thomas d'Aquin* (Paris: Aubier, 1940), II, 138; *Foundations of Thomistic Philosophy*, translated by Godfrey Anstruther, O.P. (London: Sands & Co., 1931), p. 231.

64. St. Thomas, *De Ver.* XI, 1.

65. *De Ver.* X, 6.

66. *De Ver.* XI, 3.

67. Sertillanges, *La Philosophie de St Thomas d'Aquin*, II, 172; *Foundations of Thomistic Philosophy*, p. 253.

68. St. Thomas, *Summa contra Gent.* I, 7.

69. Sertillanges, *La Philosophie de St Thomas d'Aquin*, II, 172; *Foundations of Thomistic Philosophy*, pp. 254-255.

70. St. Augustine, *Epist. CXX*, iii, 13 (PL 33:459).

71. St. Augustine, *In Lib. LXXXIII*, xlvi, 1 (PL 40:29).

72. St. Thomas, *Summa Theol.* I, q. 15, a. 2 ad 1.

73. *Summa Theol.* I, q. 15, a. 3.

74. Sertillanges, *S. Thomas d'Aquin* (Paris: Félix Alcan, 1910), I, 43-44; *Foundations of Thomistic Philosophy*, p. 3.

75. St. Thomas, *Summa Theol.* I, q. 15, a. 2.

76. *Summa Theol.* I, q. 16, a. 6.

77. *Summa Theol.* I, q. 16, a. 7 ad 1.

78. *Summa Theol.* I, q. 16, a. 7 ad 2.

79. *Summa Theol.* I, q. 16, a. 7 ad 3.

80. *Summa Theol.* I, q. 16, a. 3.

81. St. Thomas, *De Symbolo Apostolorum; The Catechetical Instructions of St. Thomas Aquinas*, translated by J. B. Collins (New York: Jos. F. Wagner, 1939), p. 5.

82. Ps. 25:3.

83. Eph. 4:15.

84. St. Thomas' Eucharistic hymn *Adoro Te;* Gerard Manley Hopkins, "Rhythmus ad SS. Sacramentum," *Poems of Gerard Manley Hopkins* (New York: Oxford University Press, 1948), p. 186; Richard Crashaw, "Adoro Te," *The Verse in English of Richard Crashaw* (New York: Grove Press, 1949), p. 185.

85. Aristotle, *Metaphys.* IV, 5, 1010ᵃ, 11-14.

86. Husserl, *Logische Untersuchungen*, II/1, 339.

87. Marvin Farber, *The Foundation of Phenomenology* (Cambridge: Harvard University Press, 1943), pp. 202-203.

88. St. Thomas, *Summa contra Gent.* III, 53.

89. St. Thomas, *De Ver.* I, 12.

90. Husserl, *Ideen zu einer reinen Phaenomenologie und phaenomenologischen Philosophie* (Halle: Max Niemeyer, 1922), pp. 43-44; *Ideas: General Introduction to Pure Phenomenology*, translated by W. R. Boyce Gibson (New York: Macmillan Co., 1931), p. 92.

91. *Ibid.*, p. 221; *ibid.*, p. 306.

92. Friedrich Nietzsche, *The Antichrist*, aphorism 52. Cf. Otto Gruendler, "Die Bedeutung der Phaenomenologie fuer das Geistesleben." *Hochland* XIX, 1 (1921), p. 74.

93. Husserl, "Adolf Reinach," *Kant-Studien* XXIII (1919), pp. 147-148.

94. St. Augustine, *Conf.* XI, 14 (PL 32: 816). Adolf Reinach, "Ueber Phaenomenologie," *Gesammelte Schriften* (Halle: Max Niemeyer, 1921), pp. 379-381.

95. Reinach, *op. cit.*, pp. 381-384.

96. *Ibid.*, pp. 384-385.

97. *Ibid.*, pp. 393-395.

98. *Ibid.*, pp. 396-398.

99. *Ibid.*, pp. 395-396, 401-403.

100. *Ibid.*, pp. 403-404.

101. *Ibid.*, pp. 404-405; Plato, *Phaedrus*, 246-248.

102. *La Phénoménologie: Journées d'Études de la Société Thomiste* (Juvisy, S. et O. : Les Éditions du Cerf, 1932), p. 91.

103. Alfons Hufnagel, *Intuition und Erkenntnis nach Thomas von Aquin* (Muenster in Westfalen: Verlag der Aschendorffschen Verlagsbuchhandlung, 1932), p. 195.

104. *Ibid.*, pp. 200-204. Cf. St. Thomas, *De Ver.* XI, 3; *In Boet. de Trin.* VI, 4; *Summa Theol.* I-II, q. 94, a. 2; *De ente et ess.* prooem.

105. Hufnagel, *op. cit.*, p. 205. Cf St. Thomas, *Summa Theol.* I, q. 85, a. 5; q. 88, a. 3.

106. Hufnagel, *op. cit.*, p. 205. Cf. St. Thomas, *Summa contra Gent.* I, 57; III, 41.

107. Ps. 50:3.

108. Recollections of Soror Adelgundis Jaegerschmidt, O.S.B. (unpublished manuscript).

109. Ps. 138:8-10.

110. Daniel Feuling, O.S.B., in *La Phénoménologie*, p. 29.

111. Edith Stein in *La Phénoménologie*, pp. 44, 102.

112. John Wild, "Husserl's Critique of Psychologism," *Essays in Memory of Edmund Husserl*, edited by M. Farber (Cambridge: Harvard University Press, 1940), pp. 41-42.

113. Private communication from Professor

Dietrich von Hildebrand, Fordham University, New York City.

114. 2 Kings 7:28.

115. St. Augustine, *Conf.* X, 23 (PL 32: 793).

116. Julian of Norwich, *Revelations of Divine Love*, chap. 22.

117. Luke 5:1-7.

118. St. Thomas, *Summa Theol.* II-II, q. 2, a. 8 ad 2.

119. James 2:19.

120. St. Thomas, *Summa Theol.* II-II, q. 5, a. 2.

121. Ruth 1:16. Cf. John Henry Newman, *Discourses Addressed to Mixed Congregations* (London: Longmans, Green and Co., 1906), pp. 207-208.

122. John Donne, No. XIV of the "Holy Sonnets," *The Poems of John Donne* (London: Oxford University Press, 1938), p. 328.

123. Eph. 5:8.

ADOLF REINACH, SEEKER OF THE ABSOLUTE

1. Private communication from Johannes S. Hamburger, New York City.

2. Recollections of Soror Adelgundis Jaegerschmidt, O.S.B. (unpublished manuscript).

3. Wis. 4:13.

4. Prov. 17:17.

5. Adolf Reinach, *Gesammelte Schriften* (Halle: Max Niemeyer, 1921), p. xxvii.

6. *Ibid.*, p. xix.

7. Reinach, "Die apriorischen Grundlagen des buergerlichen Rechtes," *ibid.*, pp. 166-167.

8. *Ibid.*, pp. 169-170.

9. *Ibid.*, pp. 170-172.

10. *Ibid.*, pp. 174-175.

11. *Ibid.*, pp. 175-176.

12. Cf. Dietrich von Hildebrand, "Die rechtliche und sittlichte Sphaere in ihrem Eigenwert und in ihrem Zusammenhang," *Zeitliches in Lichte des Ewigen* (Regensburg: Josef Habel, 1932), pp. 159-186.

13. Reinach, "Die apriorischen Grundlagen," *Gesammelte Schriften*, pp. 190-191.

14. *Ibid.*, pp. 192-193.

15. John Donne, No. XVII of "Devotions upon Emergent Occasions," *Complete Poetry and Selected Prose* (Bloomsbury; Nonesuch Press, 1929), p. 538.

16. Reinach, "Die apriorischen Grundlagen," *Gesammelte Schriften*, pp. 341-350.

17. Sophocles, *Antigone*, vv. 452-457.

18. Matt. 6:27.

19. Rom. 2:14.

20. Ps. 4:7.

21. St. Thomas, *Summa Theol.* I-II, q. 91, a. 2.

22. Jacques Maritain, *Man and the State* (Chicago: University Press, 1951), p. 90.

23. Jean-Paul Sartre, "Les Mouches," *Théâtre* (Paris: Gallimard, 1947), pp. 101, 102; "The Flies," *No Exit and The Flies*, translated by S. Gilbert (New York: Alfred A. Knopf, 1947), pp. 158, 159.

24. Exod. 19:4.

25. Exod. 20:2.

26. Ps. 18:9.

27. Ps. 118:14.

28. Gal. 3:24.

29. Matt. 24:43.

30. Reinach, "Die apriorischen Grundlagen," *Gesammelte Schriften*, p. 193.

31. St. Augustine, *De Musica* VI, xvii, 57-59 (PL 32:1191-1194).

32. John Dryden, "Song for St. Cecilia's Day," *The Poems of John Dryden* (London: Oxford University Press, 1925), p. 196; Richard Crashaw, "To the Name above Every Name, The Name of Jesus," *The Verse in English of Richard Crashaw* (New York: Grove Press, 1949), p. 149.

33. Prov. 8:22-30.

34. Private communication from Mrs. Anna Reinach.

35. Von Hildebrand, "Der Geist Ludwig van Beethoven," *Zeitliches im Lichte des Ewigen*, pp. 313-314.

36. Ludwig van Beethoven, *Das Heiligenstaedter Testament* (Weimar: Verlag Boehlau, 1947), p. 4.

37. Luke 12:49.

38. Phil. 4:13.

39. Rom. 5:5.

40. Luke 12:6.

41. *Beethoven im eigenen Wort von Friedrich Kerst* (Berlin: Schuster & Loeffler, 1904), pp. 23, 24; *Beethoven—the Man and the Artist, as Revealed in His Own Words*, edited by Friedrich Kerst, translated by H. E. Krehbiel (New York: B. W. Huebsch, 1905), pp. 16, 17.

42. Cf. Schiller, "An die Freude," *Saemmtliche Werke* (Stuttgart: J. G. Cotta, 1835), Vol. I, pp. 95-96.

43. 1 Cor. 13:1.

44. 1 Cor. 13:7.

45. Von Hildebrand, "Der Geist Ludwig van Beethoven," *Zeitliches im Lichte des Ewigen*, pp. 313-314.

46. *Ibid.*, p. 314; Exod. 12:11.

47. Max Auer, *Anton Bruckner* (Vienna: Amalthea-Verlag, 1947), p. 9.

48. St. Augustine, *Confessions* X, 6 (PL 32:782-783); Carl J. Perl, *Christliche Musik und Anton Bruckner* (Strassburg: Hertz und Co., 1907), p. 24 1/2.

49. Cf. *Roman Missal*, Postcommunion of the Votive Mass for Peace.

50. Cf. Auer, *Anton Bruckner*, pp. 421-422, 364-367.

51. Luke 1:46.

52. Luke 2:14.

53. Matt 26:30. The Egyptian Hallel, chanted in the Passover, is composed of Psalms (in the Vulgate numbering) 113:8-18, and 114 through 117.

54. Eph. 5:19; Col. 3:16. Cf. James 5:13.

55. *Plinii Secundi Epistolarum*, translated by W. Melmoth and W. M. L. Hutchison (London: Wm. Heinemann, 1915), X, 96.

56. John Dryden, "Song for St. Cecilia's Day," *The Poems of John Dryden*, p. 196.

57. Columba Marmion, O.S.B., *Christ the Ideal of the Monk* (St. Louis: Herder, 1926), pp. 294-295.

58. Matt. 3:17; 12:18; 17:5.

59. All these remarks are from unpublished recollections of Dietrich von Hildebrand.

60. St. Thomas, *Summa Theol.* II-II, q. 1, a. 2 ad 2. See Jacques Maritain, "The Ways of Faith," *The Commonweal* (November 19, 1949).

61. Blaise Pascal, *The Pensées in an English Translation*, translated by H. F. Stewart (London: Routledge & Kegan Paul, 1950), pp. 6-9, 362-363.

62. Reinach, *Gesammelte Schriften*, p. xxxvii.

63. *Ibid.*, p. xxxi.

64. *Ibid.*, p. xxxii.

65. *Ibid.*, p. xxxii-xxxiii.

66. *Ibid.*, p. xxxiii.

67. *Ibid.*, pp. xxxiii-xxxiv.

68. *Ibid.*, pp. xxxiv-xxxv.

69. *Ibid.*, pp. xxxiv-xxxvi.

70. *Ibid.*, p. xxxvi.

71. Rom. 3:28-29.

72. *Roman Missal*, Collect after Fourth Prophecy on Holy Saturday.

73. Ps. 22:1.

74. John 10:11.

75. Deut. 32:11.

76. Matt. 23:37.

77. Rom. 8:22; Ps. 90:4.

78. Richard Verstegan (also known as Rowlands), "We Praise Thee, O God!" *Recusant Poets*, edited by L. I. Guiney (New York: Sheed & Ward, 1939), I, 220.

79. Matt. 6:33. Cf. Romano Guardini, *Vorschule des Betens* (Einsiedeln-Zuerich: Benziger Verlag, 1948), pp. 188-190.

80. Georg Simmel, *Die Religion* (Frankfurt a. M. : Ruetten & Loening, 1906), p. 36.

81. See, for instance, St. Augustine, *Enarr.*

in Psalm. XXXVIII, 2; LXXXV, 7 (PL 36: 413-414; 37:1086).
82. Thomas à Kempis, *The Imitation of Christ*, I, 5.
83. Matt. 6:24.
84. Matt. 16:26.
85. John 8:56.
86. Matt. 22:42-45; 12:41,42.
87. Léon Bloy, *Le Salut par les Juifs* (Paris: François Bernouard, 1947), p. 20; cf. *Léon Bloy: Pilgrim of the Absolute*, edited by Raïssa Maritain, translated by J. Coleman and H. L. Binsse (New York: Pantheon, 1947), p. 267.
88. Luke 2:49.
89. Reinach, *Gesammelte Schriften*, p. xxviii.
90. "The Wonder," from *Richard Hill's Common-place Book*, Balliol Ms. (c. 1520), in *Love Songs of Sion*, edited by Nevile Watts (New York: Benziger Bros., 1924), p. 141.
91. Reinach, *Gesammelte Schriften*, p. xxviii.
92. Ps. 118:105.
93. From the Nicene Creed.
94. Acts 8:36-37.

MAX SCHELER, CRITIC OF MODERN MAN

1. Max Scheler, "Vom Wesen der Philosophie und der moralischen Bedingung des philosophischen Erkennens," *Vom Ewigen im Menschen* (3rd ed.; Berlin: Der Neue Geist Verlag, 1933), pp. 66-79.
2. *Ibid.*, pp. 74-77; Matt. 5:3.
3. *Ibid.*, pp. 78-79
4. *Ibid.*, pp. 66, 88-89.
5. *Ibid.*, pp. 102-108.
6. *Ibid.*, pp. 99, 108.
7. St. Thomas, *Summa Theol.* II-II, q. 162, a. 3 ad 1.
8. St. Augustine, *De Mor. Eccl. Cath.* XVII, 31 (PL 32:1324); *In Ps. LXXIX*, 2 (PL 36:1022). Cf. Matt. 7:7; 10:26.
9. Ps. 118:98-100.
10. Dietrich von Hildebrand, "Max Scheler als Persoenlichkeit," *Zeitliches im Lichte des Ewigen* (Regensburg: Josef Habbel, 1932), pp. 368-402).
11. Ernst Kamnitzer, *Erinnerung an Max Scheler* (unpublished memoir).
12. *Ibid.*
13. 2 Cor. 6:10.
14. Scheler, *Der Formalismus in der Ethik und die materiale Wertethik* (2nd ed.; Halle: Max Niemeyer, 1921), p. 278.
15. *Ibid.*, p. 608.
16. Scheler, "Soziologische-Neuorientierung und die Aufgabe der deutschen Katholiken nach dem Krieg," *Schriften zur Soziologie und Weltanschauungslehre* (Leipzig: Der Neue Geist Verlag, 1924), III/1, 204.
17. Scheler, *Wesen und Formen der Sympathie* (2nd ed.; Bonn: Friedrich Cohen, 1923), p. 106.
18. Father Cuthbert, O.S.F.C., *Life of St. Francis of Assisi* (London: Longmans, Green and Co., 1912), pp. 294, 154.
19. Von Hildebrand, "Max Schelers Stellung zur katholischen Gedankenwelt," *Zeitliches im Lichte des Ewigen*, p. 352.
20. Scheler, "Reue und Wiedergeburt," *Vom Ewigen im Menschen*, p. 40.
21. Edith Sitwell, "An Old Woman: Harvest," *The Canticle of the Rose* (New York: Vanguard Press, 1949), pp. 161-162. Paul Claudel, "Hymn of the Blessed Sacrament," *Coronal*, translated by Sister Mary David, S.S.N.D. (New York: Pantheon, 1943), pp. 77, 79.
22. Scheler, "Versuche einer Philosophie des Lebens," *Vom Umsturz der Werte* (2nd ed.; Leipzig: Der Neue Geist Verlag, 1923), II, 181.
23. Scheler, "Die christliche Liebesidee und die gegenwaertige Welt," *Vom Ewigen im*

Menschen, pp. 180-181; "Der Bourgeois," *Vom Umsturz der Werte*, II, 260, 264-265.
24. Scheler, "Prophetischer oder marxistischer Sozialismus?" *Schriften zur Soziologie und Weltanschauungslehre*, III/2, 17-18, 23-24.
25. Scheler, "Das Ressentiment im Aufbau der Moralen," *Vom Umsturz der Werte*, I, 55-60.
26. *Ibid.*, I, 73-76.
27. Goethe, *Wahlverwandschaften*, II, 5.
28. Scheler, "Das Ressentiment im Aufbau der Moralen," *Vom Umsturz der Werte*, I, 66, 89-91.
29. *Ibid.*, I, 91-94.
30. *Ibid.*, I, 95-96.
31. Friedrich Nietzsche, *The Genealogy of Morals*, I, 7, 8, 10.
32. Scheler, "Das Ressentiment im Aufbau der Moralen," *Vom Umsturz der Werte*, I, 107. Cf. Yves de Montcheuil, S.J., "Le Ressentiment dans la Vie Morale et Religieuse d'après Max Scheler," *Mélanges Théologiques* (Paris: Aubier, 1946), pp. 187-225.
33. Nietzsche, *The Genealogy of Morals*, I, 8.
34. Nietzsche, *Beyond Good and Evil*, III, 49.
35. Plato, *Symposium*, 202-204; Aristotle, *Phys.* VIII; *Metaphys.* XII. Scheler, "Das Ressentiment im Aufbau der Moralen," *Vom Umsturz der Werte*, I, 108-111.
36. Scheler, *ibid.*, I, 111-113.
37. *Ibid.*, I, 112-114.
38. St. Bernard, *Serm. in Cant.* LXXXIII, 4 (PL 183:1183).
39. Scheler, "Das Ressentiment im Aufbau der Moralen," *Vom Umsturz der Werte*, I, 114-118.
40. *Ibid.*, I, 118-120.
41. *Ibid.*, I, 121-123.
42. *Ibid.*, I, 123-125.
43. Hilaire Belloc, "Courtesy," *Sonnets and Verse* (New York: Robert McBride & Co., 1924), p. 51.
44. Scheler, "Das Ressentiment im Aufbau der Moralen," *Vom Umsturz der Werte*, I, 125-157.
45. *Ibid.*, I, 150-152.
46. Algernon Charles Swinburne, "Hymn of Man," *Collected Poetical Works* (London: Wm. Heinemann Ltd., 1927), Vol. I, pp. 764, 755.
47. Scheler, "Das Ressentiment im Aufbau der Moralen," *Vom Umsturz der Werte*, I, 152-156.
48. St. Thomas, IV *Sent.*, xxvi, 1, 2; *Summa Theol.* II-II, q. 88, a. 8 ad 3.
49. Scheler, "Das Ressentiment im Aufbau der Moralen," *Vom Umsturz der Werte*, I, 161-163.
50. Cf. Luke 10:27.
51. Auguste Comte, *Catéchisme Positiviste* (Paris: Carilian-Goeury et Vor Dalmont, 1852), p. 369; *The Catechism of Positive Religion*, translated by R. Congreve (London: John Chapman, 1858), p. 312.
52. Scheler, "Das Ressentiment im Aufbau der Moralen," *Vom Umsturz der Werte*, I, 164-167.
53. *Ibid.*, I, 167-168.
54. *Ibid.*, I, 183-185.
55. Col. 2:12.
56. Scheler, "Das Ressentiment im Aufbau der Moralen," *Vom Umsturz der Werte*, I, 185-192.
57. Søren Kierkegaard, *The Present Age*, translated by A. Dru (New York: Oxford University Press, 1940), pp. 15, 26-47 *passim*.
58. Scheler, "Das Ressentiment im Aufbau der Moralen," *Vom Umsturz der Werte*, I, 203-206.
59. *Ibid.*, I, 207.
60. Pius XII, *Future World Peace*, official English translation in *The Catholic Mind* (January 8, 1942), pp. 8-9.
61. Scheler, "Das Ressentiment im Aufbau der Moralen," *Vom Umsturz der Werte*, I, 192-194.

62. *Ibid.*, I, 194-195.
63. *Ibid.*, I, 195-196.
64. Blaise Pascal, *The Pensées in an English Translation*, translated by H. F. Stewart (London: Routledge & Kegan Paul, 1950), pp. 342-343.
65. Scheler, "Ordo Amoris," *Schriften aus dem Nachlass* (Berlin: Der Neue Geist Verlag, 1933), I, 244.
66. *Ibid.*, I, 228, 239.
67. *Ibid.*, I, 228-229.
68. Matt. 6:25.
69. Matt. 10:28.
70. Acts 5:29.
71. Immanuel Kant, *Grundlegung zur Metaphysik der Sitten*, Vol. VIII of *Saemmtliche Werke*, edited by K. Rosenkranz and F. W. Schubert (Leipzig: Leopold Voss, 1838), p. 47; *Fundamental Principles of the Metaphysics of Morals*, translated by T. K. Abbott (New York: Liberal Arts Press, 1949), p. 38.
72. Scheler, *Der Formalismus in der Ethik und die materiale Wertethik*, pp. 1-40.
73. *Ibid.*, pp. 103-109; "Ordo Amoris," *Schriften aus dem Nachlass*, I, 242.
74. Scheler, *Der Formalismus in der Ethik und die materiale Wertethik*, pp. 275-276.
75. *Ibid.*, pp. 259-260, 276-278. Cf. 2 Cor. 6:10.
76. *Ibid.*, pp. 294-296.
77. *Ibid.*, pp. 298-299.
78. Scheler, "Zur Idee des Menschen," *Vom Umsturz der Werte*, I, 292-298.
79. St. Thomas, *Summa Theol.* I, q. 96, a. 2 c.
80. St. Thomas, *Summa contra Gent.* II, 68.
81. St. Thomas, *De Pot.*, III, 10 ad 8.
82. St. Thomas, *De Anima*, 7 ad 16.
83. Scheler, "Zur Idee des Menschen," *Vom Umsturz der Werte*, I, 298-300.
84. Cf. Eckhard J. Koehle, O.S.B., *Personality: A Study according to the Philosophies of Value and Spirit of Max Scheler and Nicolai Hartmann* (Newton, N. J.: Catholic Protectory Press, 1941).
85. Scheler, *Der Formalismus in der Ethik und die materiale Wertethik*, p. 24.
86. *Ibid.*, p. 398.
87. *Ibid.*, pp. xii-xiii.
88. Scheler, "Zur Idee des Menschen," *Vom Umsturz der Werte*, I, 293-297.
89. Scheler, "Vorbilder und Fuehrer," *Schriften aus dem Nachlass*, I, 158-163.
90. *Ibid.*, I, 163-169.
91. *Ibid.*, I, 174.
92. Matt. 12:30.
93. Scheler, "Vorbilder und Fuehrer," *Schriften aus dem Nachlass*, I, 176.
94. *Ibid.*, I, 178-183.
95. *Ibid.*, I, 184.
96. Scheler, "Die christliche Liebesidee und die gegenwaertige Welt," *Vom Ewigen im Menschen*, pp. 197-198; "Probleme der Religion," *ibid.*, pp. 559, 563-564.
97. Scheler, "Probleme der Religion," *Vom Ewigen im Menschen*, pp. 396-400.
98. *Ibid.*, pp. 401, 415, 681-682, 421-422; "Zur Rehabilitierung der Tugend," *Vom Umsturz der Werte*, I, 23-37, 37-46.
99. Scheler, "Probleme der Religion," *Vom Ewigen im Menschen*, pp. 529-535.
100. *Ibid.*, pp. 535-537, 545-547.
101. St. Thomas, *Summa Theol.* I-II, q. 113, a. 10; cf. St. Augustine, *De Trin.* XIV, 8, 11 (PL 42:1044).
102. Leonardo da Vinci, *Thoughts on Art and Life*, translated by Maurice Baring (Boston: Merrymount Press, 1906). p. 17.
103. Here Scheler does not seem to be quoting exactly, although this thought appears frequently in Goethe's writings.
104. Scheler, "Liebe und Erkenntnis," *Schriften zur Soziologie und Weltanschauungslehre*, I, 110; *Wesen und Formen der Sympathie*, pp. 176-177; "Vom Wesen der Philosophie und der moralischen Bedingung des philosophischen Erkennens," *Vom Ewigen im Menschen*, p. 93.
105. St. Augustine, *In Joann.* 96, 4 (PL 35:1876).
106. St. Augustine, *De Civit. Dei* XI, 24 (PL 41:338).
107. Victor White, O.P., "Thomism and 'Affective Knowledge,'" *Blackfriars*, XXIV, 274 (January, 1943), pp. 8-16. Cf. *Blackfriars*, XXIV, 277 (April, 1943), pp. 126-131; XXV, 294 (September, 1944), pp. 321-328. Also Marin-Sola, O.P., *L'Évolution homogène du Dogme catholique* (2nd ed.; Fribourg, 1924), p. 363.
108. Paul Ortegat, S.J., *Intuition et Religion: Le Problème existentialiste* (Louvain: Éditions de l'Institut Supérieur de Philosophie, 1947), p. 11. For a thorough analysis of Scheler's religious contribution, see Erich Przywara, S.J., *Religions-Begruendung: Max Scheler-J. H. Newman;* and Heinrich Fries, *Die katholische Religionsphilosophie der Gegenwart: Der Einfluss Max Schelers auf ihre Formen und Gestalten* (Heidelberg: F. H. Kerle Verlag, 1949).
109. Scheler, "Probleme der Religion," *Vom Ewigen im Menschen*, pp. 521-522, 648-654.
110. Scheler, "Lehre von den Drei Tatsachen," *Schriften aus dem Nachlass*, I, 407.
111. Scheler, "Tod und Fortleben," *ibid.*, I, 40-43.
112. Scheler, "Lehre von den Drei Tatsachen," *ibid.*, I, 404.
113. Scheler, "Tod und Fortleben," *ibid.*, I, 5, 6, 39.
114. *Ibid.*, I, 4, 5, 8.
115. *Ibid.*, I, 12, 15, 17, 19.
116. Luke 23:46.
117. Scheler, "Tod und Fortleben," *Schriften aus dem Nachlass*, I, 21-25.
118. *Ibid.*, I, 25-27.
119. Scheler, "Reue und Wiedergeburt," *Vom Ewigen im Menschen*, pp. 52, 6-11.
120. *Ibid.*, p. 12.
121. *Ibid.*, pp. 13-15.
122. *Ibid.*, pp. 15-18.
123. *Ibid.*, pp. 20-21, 51-52; John Henry Newman. *Sermons Preached on Various Occasions* (London: Longmans, Green and Co., 1898), p. 65.
124. *Roman Missal, Exsultet* on Holy Saturday.
125. Scheler, "Reue und Wiedergeburt," *Vom Ewigen im Menschen*, pp. 52-58.
126. *Ibid.*, pp. 44-49.
127. *Roman Missal*, Prayer over the People in the Mass for the Wednesday in the Second Week of Lent.
128. *Bab. Yebamoth* 79a; *The Babylonian Talmud: Seder Nashim* (London: Soncino Press, 1936), Vol. II, p. 535.
129. *Bab. Bezah* 32b; *The Babylonian Talmud: Seder Mo'ed*, Vol. VI/2, p. 165.
130. Scheler, "Vom Sinn des Leides," *Schriften zur Soziologie und Weltanschauungslehre*, I, 108.
131. Louis Ginzberg, *The Legends of the Jews* (Philadelphia: Jewish Publication Society of America, 1938), I, 3; V, 3, note 1.
132. Scheler, "Vom Sinn des Leides,"*Schriften zur Soziologie und Weltanschauungslehre*, I, 60.
133. *Ibid.*, I, 65.
134. *Ibid.*, I, 65, 66, 70.
135. *Ibid.*, I, 44-45, 48-52.
136. John 12:24-25.
137. Scheler, "Vom Sinn des Leides," *Schriften zur Soziologie und Weltanschauungslehre*, I, 52.
138. *Ibid.*, I, 52, 55, 57.
139. *Ibid.*, I, 58-59.
140. St. Thomas, *In I Metaph.* 3, 55.
141. Coventry Patmore, "Pain," *Mystical Poems of Nuptial Love* (Boston: Bruce Humphries, 1938), p. 109.
142. Scheler, "Vom Sinn des Leides," *Schriften zur Soziologie und Weltanschauungslehre*, I, 72, 73, 77, 82.

143. *Ibid.*, I, 88-89.
144. Diogenes Laertius, *Lives of Eminent Philosophers*, translated by R. D. Hicks (London: William Heinemann, 1925), pp. 203, 205.
145. Scheler, "Vom Sinn des Leides," *Schriften zur Soziologie und Weltanschauungslehre*, I, 90.
146. *Ibid.*, I, 92-93.
147. *Ibid.*, I, 93-94.
148. *Ibid.*, I, 95-96.
149. Prov. 3:12; Wis. 12:2; Ecclus. 30:1. Cf. Heb. 12:6.
150. Job 1:21.
151. Scheler, "Vom Sinn des Leides," *Schriften zur Soziologie und Weltanschauungslehre*, I, 96-97.
152. Matt. 27:46.
153. Scheler, "Vom Sinn des Leides," *Schriften zur Soziologie und Weltanschauungslehre*, I, 97-98.
154. *Ibid.*, I, 98-102.
155. *Ibid.*, I, 102-103.
156. St. Thomas, *Summa Theol.* I, q. 43, a. 5 ad 2.
157. Scheler, "Liebe und Erkenntnis," *Schriften zur Soziologie und Weltanschauungslehre*, I, 131-133; "Vorbilder und Fuehrer," *Schriften aus dem Nachlass*, I, 177.
158. Scheler, "Die christliche Liebesidee und die gegenwaertige Welt," *Vom Ewigen im Menschen*, pp. 129-135.
159. Scheler, "Probleme der Religion," *ibid.*, pp. 680-701.
160. *Ibid.*, pp. 702-703.
161. *Ibid.*, pp. 703-707, 701. Cf. "Die christliche Liebesidee und die gegenwaertige Welt," *Vom Ewigen im Menschen*, pp. 149-160.
162. Cf. Henri de Lubac, S.J., *Catholicisme* (3rd ed.; Paris: Éditions du Cerf, 1941), p. 38; *Catholicism*, translated by L. C. Sheppard (New York: Longmans, Green and Co., 1950), p. 24.
163. Scheler, "Die christliche Liebesidee und die gegenwaertige Welt," *Vom Ewigen im Menschen*, p. 135.
164. Scheler, "Zur Rehabilitierung der Tugend," *Vom Umsturz der Werte*, I, 20.
165. Yves de Montcheuil, S.J., *Mélanges Théologiques*, p. 225.
166. Przywara, *Religions-Begruendung: Max Scheler–J. H. Newman*, p. 10.
167. Scheler, "Soziologische-Neuorientierung und die Aufgabe der deutschen Katholiken nach dem Krieg," *Schriften zur Soziologie und Weltanschauungslehre*, III/1, 78.
168. Scheler, "Vom Wesen der Philosophie und der moralischen Bedingung des philosophischen Erkennens," *Vom Ewigen im Menschen*, p. 183.
169. Scheler, "Vorrede," *Schriften zur Soziologie und Weltanschauungslehre*, III/1, vii.
170. Scheler, "Probleme der Religion," *Vom Ewigen im Menschen*, pp. 567 ff., 432.
171. Scheler, "Die christliche Liebesidee und die gegenwaertige Welt," *ibid.*, pp. 167, 125.
172. Scheler, "Probleme der Religion," *ibid.*, p. 504.
173. Newman, *Apologia pro Vita Sua*, chap. 5; Scheler, "Probleme der Religion," *Vom Ewigen im Menschen*, pp. 502-503.
174. Scheler, *ibid.*, p. 690.
175. Scheler, "Mensch und Geschichte," *Die Neue Rundschau*, XXXVII, 2 (July-December, 1926), pp. 453-454.
176. Exod. 3:14.
177. Scheler, "Probleme der Religion," *Vom Ewigen im Menschen*, pp. 461-462.
178. Scheler, *Die Stellung des Menschen im Kosmos* (Munich: Nymphenburger Verlagshandlung, 1947), p. 84; *Bildung und Wissen* (Frankfurt a. M.: Verlag G. Schulte-Bulmke, 1947), p. 37.
179. Scheler, "Probleme der Religion," *Vom Ewigen im Menschen*, pp. 434, 503.
180. *Ibid.*, p. 297.
181. Nicolai Hartmann, "Max Scheler," *Kant-Studien*, XXXIII (1928), p. xv.

182. Scheler, *Die Stellung des Menschen im Kosmos*, p. 52.
183. Von Hildebrand, "Max Scheler als Persoenlichkeit," *Zeitliches im Lichte des Ewigen*, p. 384.
184. Scheler, "Probleme der Religion," *Vom Ewigen im Menschen*, p. 723.
185. Scheler, *Der Formalismus in der Ethik und die materiale Wertethik*, pp. 224 ff.
186. Cf. *supra*, p. 196.
187. T. S. Eliot, *Murder in the Cathedral* (New York: Harcourt, Brace and Co., 1935), pp. 83-84.
188. Private communication from Mrs. Maerit Furtwaengler-Scheler, Heidelberg.
189. Private communication from Dr. Rudolf Sobotta, Bonn.
190. Von Hildebrand, "Max Schelers Stellung zur katholischen Gedankenwelt," *Zeitliches im Lichte des Ewigen*, p. 363.
191. Von Hildebrand, "Max Scheler als Persoenlichkeit," *ibid.*, pp. 386-387.
192. Private communication from Dom Paulus Gordon, O.S.B., Beuron.

PAUL LANDSBERG, DEFENDER OF HOPE

1. Paul Ludwig Landsberg, *Die Welt des Mittelalters und wir* (Bonn: Friedrich Cohen, 1922), p. 7.
2. St. Augustine, *De Civit. Dei* XIV, 9, 4 (PL 41:415).
3. Roland Marwitz, "Der junge Landsberg," *Hochland* XL, 2 (February, 1948), p. 165.
4. *Ibid.*, pp. 164-169.
5. Landsberg, "Le Problème moral du Suicide," *Esprit* XV, 128 (December, 1946), pp. 815-817.
6. Stefan George, *Der Stern des Bundes* (Berlin: Georg Bondi, 1914), pp. 22, 79; *Der Siebente Ring* (Berlin: George Bondi, 1909), p. 32; *Stefan George, Poems*, translated by C. N. Valhope and E. Morwitz (New York: Pantheon, 1943), pp. 129, 213.
7. St. Thomas, *De Ver.* II, 2.
8. Wis. 11:21; Landsberg, *Die Welt des Mittelalters und wir*, pp. 12-13.
9. Landsberg, *ibid.*, pp. 13-14. Cf. St. Thomas, *Summa Theol.* I, q. 65, a. 2.
10. Landsberg, *ibid.*, pp. 14-15. Cf. St. Thomas, *Summa Theol.* II-II, q. 101, a. 1.
11. St. Augustine, *De Gen. contra Manich.* I, xxiii, 40 (PL 34:192-193); St. Thomas, *Summa Theol.* III, q. 1, a. 5; a. 6 ad 1.
12. St. Augustine, *De Civit. Dei* XVIII, liv, 2 (PL 41:620). Cf. XVIII, i (PL 41:559).
13. *Ibid.*, XI, 18.
14. Landsberg, *Die Welt des Mittelalters und wir*, p. 15.
15. St. Augustine, *De Civit. Dei* XII, 13, 18 (PL 41:360-362, 367-368).
16. Rom. 6:9-10.
17. Cf. C. N. Cochrane, *Christianity and Classical Culture* (New York: Oxford University Press, 1944), pp. 245-246, 483-485.
18. Landsberg, *Die Welt des Mittelalters und wir*, p. 16.
19. Cf. Mark 12:30-31.
20. St. Augustine, *De Civit. Dei* XV, 22 (PL 41:467).
21. Cf. St. Thomas, *Summa Theol.* I-II, q. 1, a. 8.
22. Landsberg, *Die Welt des Mittelalters und wir*, pp. 17-18.
23. St. Thomas, *Summa Theol.* I, q. 1, a. 8 ad 2.
24. Landsberg, *Die Welt des Mittelalters und wir*, pp. 18-20.
25. *Ibid.*, pp. 21-22.
26. Gertrud von Le Fort, "The Holiness of the Church, III," *Hymns to the Church*, translated by M. Chanler (Copyright 1942, Sheed & Ward, Inc., New York), p. 23.
27. St. Augustine, *Enchiridion* I, 117 (PL 40:286).
28. St. Augustine, *In Epist. Joh. Tract.* VII, 8 (PL 35:2033).

29. St. Thomas, *Summa Theol.* I, q. 2; Landsberg, *Die Welt des Mittelalters und wir,* pp. 22-23.

30. James 2:26; Landsberg, *ibid.*, pp. 23-25.

31. St. Augustine, *Contra Epist. Manich.* I, v, 6 (PL 42:176).

32. Landsberg, *Die Welt des Mittelalters und wir,* pp. 26-27.

33. Cf. St. Thomas, *Summa Theol.* I-II, q. 2, a. 8; Landsberg, *ibid.*, pp. 27-28.

34. Landsberg, *ibid.*, pp. 28-30.

35. *Ibid.*, p. 31.

36. St. Augustine, *Conf.* XIII, 7, 9 (PL 32:847-849).

37. Landsberg, *Die Welt des Mittelalters und wir,* pp. 33-35.

38. *Ibid.*, pp. 35-38.

39. *Ibid.*, p. 39.

40. *Ibid.*, pp. 39-41.

41. *Ibid.*, pp. 41-42.

42. *Ibid.*, pp. 47, 53.

43. *Ibid.*, pp. 53-54.

44. St. Augustine, *De Doct. Christ.* I, xxvii, 28 (PL 34:29); Landsberg, *ibid.*, pp. 54-55.

45. Landsberg, *ibid.*, pp. 56-57. *Monastic Breviary*, Monday at Lauds. Cf. *The Small Hymn Book, The Word-Book of the Yattendon Hymnal,* edited by Robert Bridges (Oxford: B. H. Blackwell, 1914), No. 29; Matthew Britt, O.S.B., *The Hymns of the Breviary and Missal* (New York: Benziger Bros., 1936), p. 56.

46. Landsberg, *Die Welt des Mittelalters und wir,* pp. 76, 119-120.

47. Alfred von Martin in *Literaturblatt der Frankfurter Zeitung,* August 17, 1923.

48. Heinz Monzel in *Das Neue Ufer,* literary supplement of *Germania* (Berlin), August 8, 1924.

49. Sange in *Literarisches Zentralblatt fuer Deutschland* (Leipzig), January 6, 1923.

50. Sudhoff in *Mitteilungen zur Geschichte der Medizin und der Naturwissenschaften,* Vol. XXIII (Leipzig, 1924).

51. Karl Wick in *Luzerner Vaterland,* May 16, 1924.

52. Karl Fleischmann in *Neue Zuericher Nachrichten,* July 13, 1924.

53. Hermann Hesse in *Vivos voco* III, 1/2 (July and August, 1922).

54. Anton L. Mayer-Pfannholz in *Hochland,* Vol. XX (June, 1923).

55. Friedrich Muckermann, S.J., in *Der Gral,* October, 1922, pp. 29-31.

56. Max Weber, "Die Wirtschaftsethik der Weltreligion," introduction; "The Social Psychology of the World Religions," *From Max Weber: Essays in Sociology,* translated by H. H. Gerth and C. Wright Mills (New York: Oxford University Press, 1946), p. 269.

57. Landsberg, *Wesen und Bedeutung der Platonischen Akademie* (Bonn: Friedrich Cohen, 1923), p. 91, note 1.

58. Cf. Ulrich von Wilamowitz-Moellendorff, *Platon* (Berlin: Weidmannsche Buchhandlung, 1948), p. 263; *Der Glaube der Hellenen* (Berlin: Weidmannsche Buchhandlung, 1932), Vol. I, pp. 303-304, note 1. St. Augustine, *Sermo CXCIV,* 3 (PL 38:1016). Landsberg, *Wesen und Bedeutung der Platonischen Akademie,* pp. 56-57, note 1.

59. Plato, *Phaedo,* 67.

60. Landsberg, *Wesen und Bedeutung der Platonischen Akademie,* pp. 62-63.

61. Gal. 2:20; Landsberg, *ibid.*, pp. 52, 53-54, note 4.

62. Landsberg, *ibid.*, pp. 96-99.

63. Landsberg, "Kirche und Heidentum," *Hochland* XXI, 1 (October, 1923), p. 57.

64. *Ibid.*, pp. 58-59; St. Augustine, *Serm. de Script.* LXXXVIII, 5 (PL 38:542).

65. Landsberg, *ibid.*, pp. 59-63.

66. St. Augustine, *De Gen. ad Litt.* VIII, xxvi, 48 (PL 34:392).

67. Unpublished memoir by Dr. Rudolf Sobotta, Bonn.

68. Landsberg, *Einfuehrung in die phi-*losophische Anthropologie (Frankfurt am Main: Vittorio Klostermann, 1934), pp. 143, 164, 142-143, 145, 121.

69. *Ibid.*, pp. 135, 133, 137.

70. *Ibid.*, pp. 133-134; Plutarch, *Plutarch's Lives,* translated by B. Perrin (London: William Heinemann, 1928), p. 469.

71. *Ibid.*, pp. 33-36.

72. *Ibid.*, p. 16.

73. *Ibid.*, pp. 17-19.

74. *Ibid.*, pp. 92, 199, 193.

75. *Ibid.*, pp. 32, 33, 39.

76. *Ibid.*, p. 115; John 14:6.

77. *Ibid.*, p. 112.

78. This and all other excerpts from Landsberg's diary are from an unpublished manuscript.

79. Matt. 8:20.

80. St. Benedict, *The Holy Rule,* chap. 53; Matt. 25:35.

81. Friedrich Nietzsche, *The Genealogy of Morals,* III, 8.

82. 1 John 3:20.

83. David Gascoyne, "Lachrymae," *Poems 1937-42* (London: Nicholson and Watson, 1943), p. 3.

84. Landsberg, "Réflexions sur l'engagement personnel," *Esprit,* November, 1937, pp. 179-197.

85. John 8:31-32.

86. Matt. 18:3.

87. Voltaire, *Dictionnaire philosophique,* IV, 63.

88. Landsberg, *Die Erfahrung des Todes* (Lucerne: Vita Nova Verlag, 1937), pp. 4-9.

89. *Ibid.*, pp. 10-12.

90. *Ibid.*, p. 13.

91. *Ibid.*, pp. 14-16.

92. 1 Cor. 15:54-55; Landsberg, *ibid.*, pp. 16-19.

93. Landsberg, *ibid.*, pp. 20-22.

94. *Ibid.*, pp. 23-24.

95. *Ibid.*, pp. 25-28.

96. Charles Baudelaire, "Mon Coeur Mis A Nu," *Oeuvres* (Paris: Bibliothèque de la Pléiade, 1940), II, 665.

97. Landsberg, *Die Erfahrung des Todes,* pp. 28-30.

98. *Ibid.*, pp. 30-31.

99. *Ibid.*, p. 39.

100. *Ibid.*

101. See Martin Heidegger, *Sein und Zeit* (*Jahrbuch fuer Philosophie und phaenomenologische Forschung,* Vol. VIII; Halle: Max Niemeyer, 1927), pp. 231-267.

102. Landsberg, *Die Erfahrung des Todes,* pp. 41-43.

103. *Ibid.*, pp. 43-44.

104. *Ibid.*, pp. 44-46.

105. Rom. 5:5; Landsberg, *ibid.*, pp. 46-49.

106. Gabriel Marcel, *Être et Avoir* (Paris: Fernand Aubier, 1935), p. 117; *Being and Having,* translated by K. Farrer (Boston: Beacon Press, 1951), p. 80.

107. *Ibid.*, p. 55; *ibid.*, p. 41.

108. Marcel, *The Philosophy of Existence* (London: Harvill Press, 1948), p. 16.

109. Marcel, *Être et Avoir,* pp. 139-140, 138, 135, 114, 109-110, 115, 110, 108-109, 116; *Being and Having,* pp. 97, 95-96, 93, 78, 75-76, 79, 76, 74-75, 80.

110. Is. 43:1.

111. St. Paschasius Radbertus, *De fide, spe et caritate* II, 1 (PL 120:1437).

112. St. Thomas, *Summa Theol.* II-II, q. 19, a. 9 ad 1.

113. Dante, *The Divine Comedy: Paradiso,* XXV.

114. Richard Crashaw, "For Hope," *The Verse in English of Richard Crashaw* (New York: Grove Press, 1949), pp. 226, 227.

115. Gerard Manley Hopkins, "That Nature is a Heraclitean Fire and of the comfort of the Resurrection," *Poems of Gerard Manley Hopkins* (New York: Oxford University Press, 1948), p. 112.

116. St. Augustine, *Conf.* IV, 4 (PL

32:697); Landsberg, *Die Erfahrung des Todes,* pp. 50-53.
117. St. Augustine, *Conf.* IV, 6 (PL 32:697).
118. Landsberg, *Die Erfahrung des Todes,* pp. 53-54.
119. St. Augustine, *Conf.* IV, 6 (PL 32:697).
120. *Ibid.,* IV, 6 (PL 32:697-698).
121. Landsberg, *Die Erfahrung des Todes,* pp. 55-56.
122. Horace, *Carm.* I, 3, 8.
123. St. Augustine, *Conf.* IV, 6 (PL 32:698).
124. *Ibid.,* IV, 7 (PL 32:698).
125. Epicurus, *Epicurus, The Extant Remains,* translated by C. Bailey (Oxford: Clarendon Press, 1926), p. 85; Lucretius, *De rerum natura* III, 830, 885-886; cf. Cyril Bailey, *Titi Lucreti Cari* (Oxford: Clarendon Press, 1947), I, 345, 347.
126. Landsberg, *Die Erfahrung des Todes,* pp. 69-70.
127. *Ibid.,* pp. 71-72.
128. Plato, *Phaedo,* 63-68.
129. Landsberg, *Die Erfahrung des Todes,* pp. 61-68.
130. St. Augustine, *Conf.* I, 6 (PL 32:663-664).
131. *Ibid.,* XI, 21 (PL 32:819); Landsberg, *Die Erfahrung des Todes,* pp. 88-89.
132. Rainer Maria Rilke, *Duino Elegies* (New York: W. W. Norton & Co., 1939), p. 71.
133. St. Augustine, *Conf.* I, 1 (PL 32:661); Landsberg, *Die Erfahrung des Todes,* pp. 89-91.
134. St. Augustine, *ibid.,* I, 5 (PL 32:663).
135. Landsberg, *Die Erfahrung des Todes,* pp. 91-94.
136. Henry Corbin, "Pour l'anthropologie philosophique: Un Traité Persan inédit de Suhrawardi d'Alep (d.1191)," *Recherches Philosophiques,* Vol. II (Paris: Boivin et Cie, 1932-33), pp. 375-376.
137. St. Bonaventure, *Itinerarium Mentis ad Deum* VII; Landsberg, *Die Erfahrung des Todes,* pp. 87, 95-97, pp. 131-132, note 72.
138. Matt. 25:21; St. Augustine, *Conf.* IX, 10 (PL 32:774-775).
139. St. Teresa, *The Life of the Holy Mother Teresa of Jesus,* in *The Complete Works of St. Teresa of Jesus,* translated by E. Allison Peers (New York: Sheed & Ward, 1949), Vol. I, pp. 190, 297-298, 269; *Interior Castle, ibid.,* Vol. II, pp. 253-256. Landsberg, *Die Erfahrung des Todes,* pp. 98-99, 103-107.
140. Landsberg, *ibid.,* pp. 107-109.
141. Rom. 2:29.
142. Job 14:5.
143. Is. 40:31.
144. Cf. Heb. 6:19, Knox translation.
145. From Landsberg's unpublished diary.
146. Landsberg, "Le Problème moral du Suicide," *Esprit,* XV, 128, p. 815.
147. *Ibid.,* pp. 817-820.
148. Cf. Acts 2:1-12.
149. Eph. 4:13.
150. St. Augustine, *Sermo CLXIII,* 3 (PL 38:890).
151. St. Augustine, *De Unit. Eccl.* I, i, 4, 14 (PL 43:393,400).
152. Emmanuel Mounier, "Paul-Louis Landsberg," *Esprit,* XIV, 118 (January, 1946), p. 156.
153. Pierre Klossowski, in an Introduction to Landsberg's "Les Sens spirituels chez Saint Augustin," *Dieu Vivant,* No. 11 (1948), p. 84.
154. Mounier, "Paul-Louis Landsberg," *Esprit,* XIV, 118, pp. 155-156; and private communications from other of Landsberg's friends.
155. *Roman Missal,* Blessing of Palms.
156. From *Rheinischer Merkur,* April, 1948.
157. John 11:25-26.

MAX PICARD, POET OF THE HUMAN FACE

1. "Substanzverlust," *Seele* (Munich, December, 1949), XXV, 12, p. 376.

2. Osee 9:7.
3. Drawn from Max Picard's letters.
4. Karl Pfleger, "Max Picard, der Seher," *Schweizer Rundschau,* 1948/49, no. 4/5, p. 1.
5. From a letter by Picard to Henry Regnery, July 17, 1948.
6. Matthias Claudius, "Ueber einige Sprueche des Prediger Salomo," *Der Wandsbecker Bote* (Zurich: Manesse Verlag, 1947), p. 94.
7. Picard, *Expressionistische Bauernmalerei* (Munich: Delphin-Verlag, 1922), pp. 16, 19-21, 24-26.
8. Heinrich Schlier, as quoted in Picard, *Das Menschengesicht* (Munich: Delphin-Verlag, 1929), p. 11.
9. As cited by Stanley Godman, "Max Picard: The Man and His Work," *Dublin Review* (Spring, 1949), no. 445, p. 27.
10. Private communication from Picard.
11. Rev. Johannes Mumbauer, *Hochland* (April, 1930), XXVII, 2, p. 94.
12. Quoted by Karl Wick in *Vaterland* (Lucerne), June 4, 1948, p. 1.
13. Gen. 3:8.
14. Gen. 1:27.
15. Picard, *Das Menschengesicht,* pp. 13, 16, 17; *The Human Face,* translated by Guy Endore (New York: Farrar & Rinehart, 1930), pp. 3, 6, 7.
16. *Ibid.,* pp. 19-21; *ibid.,* pp. 9-11.
17. *Ibid.,* p. 24; *ibid.,* p. 14.
18. *Ibid.,* pp. 25-28; *ibid.,* pp. 15-18.
19. Claudius, "Taeglich zu Singen," *Asmus omnia sua secum portans, oder Saemmtliche Werke des Wandsbecker Bothen,* III Theil (Hamburg: Beym Verfasser, 1777), p. 128.
20. Picard, *Das Menschengesicht,* p. 29; *The Human Face,* pp. 19-20.
21. *Ibid.,* p. 30; *ibid.,* pp. 20-21; *Die Grenzen der Physiognomik* (Erlenbach-Zuerich: Eugen Rentsch Verlag, 1937), p. 85.
22. Picard, *Das Menschengesicht,* pp. 33, 39, 40; *The Human Face,* pp. 23-24, 29, 30.
23. *Ibid.,* pp. 46-47, 68 18; *ibid.,* pp. 37-39, 59-60, 8.
24. *Ibid.,* pp. 59, 63, 66; *ibid.,* pp. 50, 54, 57.
25. Claudius, "Antwort an Andres auf seinen letzten Brief," *Asmus omnia sua secum portans,* p. 64.
26. Picard, *Das Menschengesicht,* pp. 150, 156-161; *The Human Face,* pp. 145, 150-158.
27. *Ibid.,* pp. 152-153, 14; *ibid.,* pp. 147-148, 4.
28. *Ibid.,* pp. 217-218, 220; *ibid.,* pp. 215-216, 219. Søren Kierkegaard, "The Unchangeableness of God," translated by D. F. Swenson, in *A Kierkegaard Anthology,* edited by Robert Bretall (Princeton: University Press, 1947), pp. 481-482.
29. Picard, *Das Menschengesicht,* p. 223; *The Human Face,* p. 221. Cf. Louis Ginzberg, *The Legends of the Jews* (Philadelphia: Jewish Publication Society of America, 1938), V, 239.
30. Gen. 18:32.
31. John 14:9.
32. St. Thérèse, "Cantique à la sainte Face," *Histoire d'une Âme* (Fribourg: Librairies de l'Oeuvre de Saint-Paul), pp. 334-335; *Soeur Therese of Lisieux, The Little Flower of Jesus,* edited by T. N. Taylor (New York: P. J. Kenedy & Sons, 1922), p. 427.
33. Picard, *Die Flucht vor Gott* (Erlenbach: Eugen Rentsch Verlag, 1934), pp. 11-12; *The Flight from God,* translated by M. Kuschnitzky and J. M. Cameron (Chicago: Henry Regnery Co., 1951), pp. 1-2.
34. *Ibid.,* pp. 12-18; *ibid.,* pp. 2-9.
35. *Ibid.,* pp. 21-23; *ibid.,* pp. 10-13.
36. *Ibid.,* pp. 23-31; *ibid.,* pp. 13-21.
37. *Ibid.,* pp. 44-50; *ibid.,* pp. 34-41.
38. *Ibid.,* pp. 91-95; *ibid.,* pp. 79-85.
39. *Ibid.,* pp. 54-55; *ibid.,* pp. 45-46.
40. *Ibid.,* pp. 54-55; *ibid.,* pp. 45-46.
41. *Ibid.,* p. 79; *ibid.,* pp. 68-69.
42. *Ibid.,* p. 80; *ibid.,* pp. 69-70.

43. *Ibid.*, pp. 80, 82, 84-85; *ibid.*, pp. 70, 72, 75.
44. *Ibid.*, pp. 82-87; *ibid.*, pp. 73-78.
45. *Ibid.*, pp. 138, 139, 130, 119, 183; *ibid.*, pp. 127, 128, 118-119, 107, 170.
46. *Ibid.*, pp. 190, 110-111; *ibid.*, pp. 179, 100-101.
47. Francis Thompson, "The Hound of Heaven," *Poems of Francis Thompson* (New York: D. Appleton-Century Co., 1932), p. 77.
48. Picard, *Das Flucht vor Gott*, pp. 195-198; *The Flight from God*, pp. 181-185.
49. St. Augustine, *In Epist. Joann. ad Parthos* VI, 3 (PL 35:2021).
50. Gen. 3:9; 4:9; Apoc. 3:20.
51. Is. 65:2; Rom. 10:21.
52. Luke 19:10.
53. Picard, *Das Flucht vor Gott*, p. 81; *The Flight from God*, p. 71. Charles Péguy, "Sleep," *God Speaks*, translated by Julian Green (New York: Pantheon, 1945), pp. 21-23.
54. Picard, *Die Grenzen der Physiognomik*, pp. 13-14.
55. *Ibid.*, pp. 14-15.
56. *Ibid.*, pp. 15-18, 23-24.
57. *Ibid.*, pp. 139-140.
58. *Ibid.*, pp. 90-91.
59. *Ibid.*, pp. 49-56.
60. *Ibid.*, pp. 27-28.
61. *Ibid.*, pp. 125-127.
62. *Ibid.*, pp. 179-180.
63. *Ibid.*, pp. 183-184, 154, 175-176. Cf. *Das Menschengesicht*, p. 76; *The Human Face*, p. 68.
64. *Ibid.*, pp. 163-164.
65. *Ibid.*, pp. 85, 98-99.
66. Picard, *Hitler in Uns Selbst* (Erlenbach-Zuerich: Eugen Rentsch Verlag, 1946), pp. 68-71; *Hitler in Our Selves*, translated by Heinrich Hauser (Hinsdale: Henry Regnery Co., 1947), pp. 78-81.
67. *Roman Ritual*, Rite of Baptism of Adults.
68. Picard, *Hitler in Uns Selbst*, pp. 205, 42; *Hitler in Our Selves*, pp. 208-209, 54.
69. Coventry Patmore, "The Wedding Sermon," *Mystical Poems of Nuptial Love* (Boston: Bruce Humphries, 1938), pp. 4-5.
70. Picard, *Die unerschuetterliche Ehe* (Erlenbach-Zuerich: Eugen Rentsch Verlag, 1942), p. 13.
71. *Ibid.*, pp. 14-19, 22-23.
72. *Ibid.*, pp. 29-30.
73. *Ibid.*, pp. 37-42, 49.
74. *Ibid.*, pp. 55-58.
75. *Ibid.*, pp. 58-62.
76. *Ibid.*, pp. 77-79.
77. *Ibid.*, pp. 82-83, 86-87.
78. *Ibid.*, pp. 90-91, 95-96.
79. *Ibid.*, pp. 119-127.
80. *Ibid.*, pp. 131-140.
81. Tob. 8:7-9.
82. Tob. 7:15.
83. Picard, *Hitler in Uns Selbst*, pp. 13-16; *Hitler in Our Selves*, pp. 27-29.
84. *Ibid.*, pp. 23-25; *ibid.*, pp. 35-37.
85. *Ibid.*, pp. 31-33; *ibid.*, pp. 43-45.
86. George Orwell, *Nineteen Eighty-Four* (New York: Harcourt, Brace and Co., 1949), pp. 211-218.
87. Picard, *Hitler in Uns Selbst*, pp. 34-37; *Hitler in Our Selves*, pp. 45-48.
88. *Ibid.*, pp. 37-41; *ibid.*, pp. 49-52.
89. *Ibid.*, pp. 43-47; *ibid.*, pp. 55-58.
90. *Ibid.*, pp. 48-56; *ibid.*, pp. 64-67.
91. *Ibid.*, pp. 57-68; *ibid.*, pp. 67-78.
92. C. S. Lewis, *That Hideous Strength* (New York: Macmillan Co., 1947), pp. 417-418.
93. Picard, *Hitler in Uns Selbst*, pp. 79-89; *Hitler in Our Selves*, pp. 89-99.
94. Friedrich Hoelderlin, *Hoelderlin Gebot und Erfuellung* (10th ed.; Ebenhausen bei Muenchen: Wilhelm Langewiesche-Brandt, 1944), p. 20.
95. Picard, *Hitler in Uns Selbst*, pp. 118-120; *Hitler in Our Selves*, pp. 125-127.
96. *Ibid.*, pp. 95-97; *ibid.*, pp. 105-106.
97. *Ibid.*, pp. 107-111; *ibid.*, pp. 114-118.

98. *Ibid.*, pp. 132-139; *ibid.*, pp. 138-145. Bossuet, *Discours sur L'Histoire Universelle* (Paris: Librairie Hachette et Cie, 1898), pp. 296-298.
99. Picard, *Hitler in Uns Selbst*, pp. 155-158; *Hitler in Our Selves*, pp. 161-164.
100. *Ibid.*, pp. 160-169; *ibid.*, pp. 166-174.
101. *Ibid.*, pp. 170-172; *ibid.*, pp. 175-177.
102. *Ibid.*, pp. 193-195; *ibid.*, pp. 197-199.
103. *Ibid.*, pp. 214-215; *ibid.*, pp. 217-219. Cf. Margaret Seaton Wagner, *The Monster of Duesseldorf: The Life and Trial of Peter Kuerten* (New York: Dutton, 1932).
104. Picard, *Hitler in Uns Selbst*, pp. 178-182; *Hitler in Our Selves*, pp. 183-186.
105. *Ibid.*, pp. 182-186; *ibid.*, pp. 187-190.
106. *Ibid.*, pp. 235-236; *ibid.*, pp. 237-239.
107. Ezech. 18:1-4.
108. Picard, *Hitler in Uns Selbst*, pp. 236-237; *Hitler in Our Selves*, pp. 239-240.
109. *Ibid.*, pp. 238, 247-251; *ibid.*, pp. 240, 249-253. Cf. Ginzberg, *The Legends of the Jews*, I, 179.
110. Picard, *ibid.*, pp. 241, 257-258, 260-263; *ibid.*, pp. 243, 255-256. Strangely, the English translation omits Picard's meditation on poverty.
111. *Ibid.*, pp. 270-272; *ibid.*, pp. 264-267.
112. *Ibid.*, pp. 274-278; *ibid.*, pp. 269-272; Picard, *Zerstoerte und unzerstoerbare Welt* (Erlenbach-Zuerich: Eugen Rentsch Verlag, 1951), p. 240.
113. Private communication.
114. Picard, *Die Welt des Schweigens* (Erlenbach-Zuerich: Eugen Rentsch Verlag, 1948), p. 15.
115. *Ibid.*, pp. 15-16, 11-12.
116. *Ibid.*, pp. 12-13.
117. *Ibid.*, pp. 18-19, 21, 23.
118. *Ibid.*, pp. 20, 22, 23.
119. *Ibid.*, pp. 25-26.
120. *Ibid.*, pp. 28-30.
121. John Keats, *The Poems and Verses of John Keats*, edited by John Middleton Murray (New York: Macmillan Co., 1949), p. 365.
122. Picard, *Die Welt des Schweigens*, pp. 30-31.
123. *Ibid.*, pp. 32, 68-69, 93-96.
124. *Ibid.*, pp. 63-66, 54, 57.
125. *Ibid.*, pp. 67, 179, 188-189, 192, 199, 200-201.
126. *Ibid.*, pp. 205, 207, 217, 242-243. Kierkegaard, "For Self-Examination Proposed to This Age," *For Self-Examination and Judge for Yourselves! and Three Discourses 1851*, translated by Walter Lowrie (Princeton: University Press, 1944), p. 71.
127. Picard, *Die Welt des Schweigens*, pp. 230-236.
128. *Ibid.*, pp. 238-239.
129. 2 Cor. 12:4.
130. Dante, *The Divine Comedy: Paradiso*, I, translated by L. G. White (New York: Pantheon, 1948), p. 129; Picard, *Die Welt des Schweigens*, pp. 240-241.
131. Picard, *ibid.*, pp. 241-242.
132. Gabriel Marcel, "Max Picard, ou le retour à l'original," *La Nef* V, 46 (September, 1948), p. 29.
133. Private communication.
134. Private communication.
135. Jer. 31:31-33.

EDITH STEIN, WITNESS OF LOVE

1. G. K. Chesterton, *What's Wrong with the World* (New York: Sheed & Ward, 1942), pp. 151-152.
2. Cf. S. Thoma Angelica Walter, *Seinsrhythmik: Studie zur Begruendung einer Metaphysik der Geschlechter* (Freiburg im Breisgau: Herder, 1932), p. 67.
3. Edith Stein, *Das Ethos der Frauenberufe* (Augsburg: Verlag Haas und Grabherr, 1931), pp. 9-11. Goethe, *Iphigenie auf Tauris*, Act V, Scene 3. Henry Thode, *Der Ring des Frangipani* (Frankfurt am Main: Heinrich Keller, 1895), p. 95; *Frangipani's Ring*, trans-

lated by J. F. C. L. (London: John MacQueen, 1900), p. 2.
4. Stein, *Das Ethos der Frauenberufe*, pp. 12-13.
5. *Ibid.*, pp. 11-12.
6. *Ibid.*, pp. 13-14, 25-26.
7. Orrick Johns, "The Door," *Wild Plum* (New York: Macmillan Co., 1926), p. 18.
8. Stein, *Das Ethos der Frauenberufe*, pp. 15-21.
9. *Roman Breviary*, Hymn at Terce, translated by John Cardinal Newman.
10. Stein, *Das Ethos der Frauenberufe*, pp. 21-22, 27. S. Teresia Renata de Spiritu Sancto, *Edith Stein* (5th ed., Nuernberg: Glock und Lutz, 1950), pp. 105-106.
11. John 17:19. S. Teresia Renata, *Edith Stein*, p. 90.
12. Cf. *The Authorised Daily Prayer Book*, with a translation by Rev. S. Singer (London: Eyre and Spottiswoode, 1920), p. 258.
13. Cf. Lev. 16:7-10, 15-22.
14. S. Teresia Renata, *Edith Stein*, pp. 20-21.
15. *Ibid.*, pp. 22-25, 37-39, 63-64.
16. *Ibid.*, pp. 33, 67, 20, 66.
17. Ps. 126:1.
18. S. Teresia Renata, *Edith Stein*, p. 22.
19. *Ibid.*, pp. 62, 67, 51-52.
20. *Ibid.*, p. 65; private communication from Mrs. Anna Reinach.
21. Is. 24:16.
22. Richard Crashaw, "The Flaming Heart, upon the Book and Picture of the Seraphical Saint Teresa," *The Verse in English of Richard Crashaw* (New York: Grove Press, 1949), p. 210.
23. S. Teresia Renata, *Edith Stein*, pp. 70-71. Cf. Donald Nicholl, "Edith Stein: Philosopher, Carmelite and Martyr," *Life of the Spirit* III, 35 (May, 1949), p. 502.
24. Crashaw, "A Hymn to the Name and Honor of the Admirable Saint Teresa," *The Verse in English of Richard Crashaw*, p. 206.
25. Private communication from Dr. Hedwig Conrad-Martius, Munich.
26. Crashaw, "Our Lord in His Circumcision to His Father," *The Verse in English of Richard Crashaw*, p. 50.
27. Private communication from Dr. Conrad-Martius.
28. Ps. 112:3.
29. Matt. 22:21. Stein, "Eine Untersuchung ueber den Staat," *Jahrbuch fuer Philosophie und phaenomenologische Forschung*, Vol. VII (1925), pp. 117-118.
30. Stein, "Beitrage zur philosophischen Begruendung der Psychologie und der Geisteswissenschaften. Erste Abhandlung: Psychische Kausalitaet," *Jahrbuch fuer Philosophie und phaenomenologische Forschung*, Vol. V (1922), p. 76.
31. "Hierusalem My Happy Home," an anonymous Poem from a Catholic Commonplace Book, in *Recusant Poets*, edited by L. I. Guiney (New York: Sheed & Ward, 1939), Vol. I, p. 281. Nevile Watts, editor of *Love Songs of Sion* (New York: Benziger Bros., 1924), surmises that it is probably by Francis Baker, priest and recusant, c. 1560 (p. 159).
32. 1 Thess. 5:16-17.
33. S. Teresia Renata, *Edith Stein*, p. 82.
34. Erich Przywara, S.J., "Thomas von Aquin deutsch," *Stimmen der Zeit*, CXXI, 11 (August, 1931), p. 385.
35. Stein, *Des hl. Thomas von Aquino Untersuchungen ueber die Wahrheit* (Breslau: Otto Borgmeyer, 1931), Vol. I, pp. 30-33.
36. *Ibid.*, pp. 89, 110.
37. Ecclus. 24:32; Phil. 4:3; Apoc. 3:5; 13:8; 20:12; 21:27; 22:19; Luke 10:20.
38. Stein, *Des hl. Thomas von Aquino Untersuchungen ueber die Wahrheit*, Vol. I, pp. 127-129, 158, 176-177, 189-190.
39. *Ibid.*, Vol. II, p. 44.
40. John Henry Cardinal Newman, *Certain Difficulties Felt by Anglicans* (London: Basil Montagu Pickering, 1876), Vol. II, p. 249.

41. Newman, *Sermons Preached on Various Occasions* (London: Longmans, Green and Co., 1898), pp. 64-65.
42. St. Thomas, *De Ver.* XVI, 2; XXIV, 10 ad 11; XXI, 1, 4, 5.
43. Stein, *Des hl. Thomas von Aquino Untersuchungen ueber die Wahrheit*, Vol. II, p. 512.
44. S. Teresia Renata, *Edith Stein*, p. 104.
45. Richard Rolle, "Love Is Life," version by Alfred Noyes, in *The Golden Book of Catholic Poetry*, edited by Noyes (New York: J. B. Lippincott Co., 1946), p. 432.
46. Cf. Matt. 5:48.
47. Stein, "Grundlagen der Frauenbildung," *Stimmen der Zeit*, CXX, 6 (March, 1931), pp. 416, 423-424.
48. S. Teresia Renata, *Edith Stein*, pp. 73, 135.
49. *Ibid.*, p. 143.
50. *Ibid.*, pp. 145-146, 127.
51. St. John of the Cross, "Songs of the Soul in Rapture," *The Poems of St John of the Cross*, translated by Roy Campbell (New York: Pantheon, 1951), p. 13.
52. S. Teresia Renata, *Edith Stein*, p. 146.
53. *Ibid.*, pp. 141-142, 152-154. Cf. Col. 3:9-10; John 21:18; Matt. 11:30; Ps. 132:1.
54. *Ibid.*, pp. 186-188. Cf. Ps. 118:116.
55. St. John of the Cross, "Spiritual Sentences and Maxims," no. 25, in *The Complete Works of Saint John of the Cross*, translated by E. Allison Peers (Westminster, Maryland: Newman Bookshop, 1945), Vol. III, p. 244.
56. Stein, "Das Gebet der Kirche," *Ich lebe und ihr lebet* (Paderborn: Bonifacius-Druckerei, 1937), p. 69.
57. *Ibid.*, pp. 81,80; cf. Rom. 8:26. St. Teresa, *Way of Perfection*, translated by E. Allison Peers (New York: Sheed & Ward, 1949) in *The Complete Works of St. Teresa of Jesus*, Vol. II, p. 5.
58. Stein, *ibid.*, pp. 75-76. Cf. Lev. 16:17, 12-13.
59. Ps. 121:1.
60. Matt. 26:26-28.
61. Stein, "Das Gebet der Kirche," pp. 70-71.
62. 3 Kings 19:10.
63. St. Augustine, *De Civit. Dei* VIII, 8 (PL 41:233).
64. Phil. 3:13.
65. St. Augustine, *De Trin.* XV, 12 (PL 42:1073-1074).
66. Stein, *Endliches und Ewiges Sein* (Freiburg im Breisgau: Herder, 1950), pp. 34-37.
67. James 1:17; Stein, *ibid.*, pp. 43-44.
68. *Ibid.*, pp. 46-52.
69. Martin Heidegger, *Sein und Zeit*, Vol. 8 of *Jahrbuch fuer Philosophie und phaenomenologische Forschung* (Halle: Max Niemeyer Verlag, 1927), p. 266.
70. Acts 17:28.
71. Stein, *Endliches und Ewiges Sein*, pp. 53-59. St. Augustine, *In Psalm. CXXXIV*, 6 (PL 37:1742-1743); Exod. 3:14,15.
72. John 3:36.
73. Cf. Ps. 26:10; Is. 49:15; 66:13; 1 John 4:8.
74. Stein, *Endliches und Ewiges Sein*, p. 57; S. Teresia Renata, *Edith Stein*, p. 99.
75. Stein, *ibid.*, pp. 61-66.
76. John 1:1; Stein, *ibid.*, pp. 99, 64, 101-103.
77. Cf. John 1:3-4; St. Thomas, *Summa Theol.* I, q. 18, a. 4.
78. Col. 1:17.
79. Stein, *Endliches und Ewiges Sein*, pp. 103-111; St. Thomas, *De Ver.* II, 5.
80. Stein, *ibid.*, pp. 333-335.
81. *Ibid.*, pp. 336-339, 344.
82. *Ibid.*, pp. 342-344.
83. *Ibid.*, pp. 344-345, 398-408. St. Augustine, *Solil.* II, vi, 9 (PL 32:889).
84. St. Augustine, *De Trin.* XIII, 20; IX, 12; X, 12; VIII, 10; IX, 2 (PL 42:1035-1036, 972, 984, 960, 961). Cf. St. Thomas, *Summa Theol.* I, q. 93, a. 5, 6, 7.

85. Stein, *Endliches und Ewiges Sein*, pp. 412-420, 426-428. Gerard Manley Hopkins, "Margaret Clitheroe," *Poems of Gerard Manley Hopkins* (New York: Oxford University Press, 1948), p. 162.

86. *Ibid.*, pp. 425-426.

87. *Ibid.*, pp. 421-422.

88. John 7:38.

89. Stein, *Endliches und Ewiges Sein*, pp. 421, 410.

90. John Donne, "Hymn to God my God, in my Sickness" and No. II of the "Holy Sonnets," *The Poems of John Donne* (London: Oxford University Press, 1938), pp. 368, 322; Stein, *ibid.*, pp. viii, xi, 12, 474.

91. St. John of the Cross, "Songs between the Soul and the Bridegroom," *The Poems of St John of the Cross*, p. 25.

92. John Milton, *Paradise Lost*, Book IX (Cambridge: University Press, 1934), Vol. I, p. 256.

93. St. John of the Cross, "Songs between the Soul and the Bridegroom,"*The Poems of St John of the Cross*, p. 17.

94. Stein, *Kreuzeswissenschaft* (Louvain: Éditions Nauwelaerts, 1950), pp. 226-228.

95. Stein, *ibid.*, pp. 33-34. St. John of the Cross, "Songs of the Soul in Rapture," *The Poems of St John of the Cross*, pp. 11, 13.

96. Stein, *ibid.*, pp. 40-48; St. John of the Cross, "Songs of the Soul in Rapture," "Songs between the Soul and the Bridegroom," *ibid.*, pp. 11, 21.

97. St. John of the Cross, "Songs of the Soul in Rapture," *ibid.*, p. 11.

98. Stein, *Kreuzeswissenschaft*, pp. 240-241.

99. "Edith Stein," *Gloria Dei*, Vol. VI, No. 1, p. 58.

100. Cf. 1 Cor. 1:23-24.

101. Crashaw, "The Hymn of the Holy Cross," *The Verse in English of Richard Crashaw*, p. 175.

102. S. Teresia Renata, *Edith Stein*, pp. 92, 142, 151.

103. *Ibid.*, pp. 197, 196, 192, 201.

104. *Ibid.*, pp. 190, 191, 206.

105. Matt. 10:23.

106. S. Teresia Renata, *Edith Stein*, pp. 193, 204, 201, 208-209.

107. *Ibid.*, pp. 210-215, which quotes from Dr. Stokman, O.F.M., *Het verzet van de Nederlandsche Bischoppen tegen National-Socialisme en Duitsche Tyrannie* (Utrecht, 1945).

108. S. Teresia Renata, *Edith Stein*, pp. 216-220, which quotes from *De Tiyd* of August 3, 1942.

109. "In Christus' Voetstappen zijn zij getreden," *De Heraut van het Heilig Hart* (January, 1947), pp. 9-15. Private communication from Father Franciscus Stratmann, O.P., Ghent. See also S. Teresia Renata, *Edith Stein*, pp. 229-231.

110. Gertrud von Le Fort, "Te Deum," *Hymns to the Church*, translated by M. Chanler (Copyright 1942, Sheed & Ward, Inc., New York), p. 52.

111. *Ibid.*, pp. 216-218, 222-223, 226-227.

112. *Roman Breviary*, Vespers hymn in Passiontide.

113. S. Teresia Renata, *Edith Stein*, pp. 227-228, 233-234.

114. Matt. 16:24.

115. S. Agnella, quoted in a letter to Edith Stein's godchild, Mrs. Hedwig Spiegel, New York City.

116. Gen. 12:1; Exod. 3:4; 1 Kings 3:10.

Index

Christ, 23, 35-9, 40, 47, 50-3, 56-7, 75-6, 87-9, 91-2, 95-6 119-20, 126-7, 131-4, 136, 142, 147-55, 159, 165-6, 177-8, 185-90, 201-2, 205, 208-9, 213, 220-2, 230, 232-3, 239-40, 246-7, 250-2, 255-7, 273-4, 282-3, 287-9, 295-6, 312, 316-7, 323, 331, 337-8, 341, 343-51, 355, 361-2, 364, 371-2
Christianity, 25-7, 34-6, 47, 56-7, 121, 147, 165-6, 178, 186-9, 219, 305-6
Christian Science, 185
Church, the, 37-9, 40-3, 45, 47, 92, 141, 177-8, 189-92, 208-10, 218, 222-3, 257-9, 322, 335, 337, 349-50
city, the, 280
civilization, 41, 178-9
classical languages, 7, 257, 305, 318
Claudel, Paul, 142
Claudius, Matthias, 264, 269, 272
clothing ceremony of Carmel, 347-8
common good, the, 153
common sense in mystics, 30, 366
Communism, 202, 299
community, 57, 155, 191, 211, 250, 338
competition, 160-1, 224
Comte, Auguste, 43, 154
concentration camp, 229, 254, 259-60, 370-1
condescension, 20-1, 148-50, 193, 293
confidence, 115-6, 143, 204-5, 208, 269
conscience, 81, 177, 342-3
consciousness, 10, 80-1
contemplation, 72, 153, 197, 210-2, 216, 339
continuity, 229, 296, 305-6
contrition, 175-8, 298
conversion, 81-2, 112-3, 179, 223, 227, 301
courtesy, 150
Crashaw, Richard, 76, 114, 246-7, 336-7
Cratylus, 76
creation, 2, 5, 32, 44, 47, 113-4, 216, 222, 224, 227, 271-2
cross, the, 31, 289, 335, 344, 347, 361-5, 370-1
crucifixion, the, 57, 148, 186, 287
Curtius, Ernst Robert, 197
cubism, 306

D

Dante, 246, 267, 320
"dark night," the, 30-1, 362-4
Darwin, Charles, 19, 201, 225-7
Daubert, Johannes, 100
Daumier, Honoré, 289
da Vinci, Leonardo, 21, 170
death, 27-8, 56, 121, 172-5, 181, 208, 237-54, 269, 286, 288, 311, 343, 354
de Jong, Archbishop Johan, 367-9
de Montcheuil, Yves, S.J., 192
Descartes, René, 61
determinism, 9, 13, 176-7
devil, the, 92-3, 230, 267, 270, 296, 366
dialectical theology, 283
Dilthey, Wilhelm, 141
Dionysius the Areopagite, 48
discipline, 215, 217, 328-9
discontinuity, 296-309, 313

Donne, John, 93, 361
Dos Passos, John, 306
Dostoyevski, Feodor, 153, 273, 277
"doublethink," 298
Doumic, René, 7-10
dreams, 279, 284-5
Dryden, John, 113, 120
Duns Scotus, 361
durée, 4-5, 263, 299
Duse, Eleonora, 273

E

Eastern thought, 35, 211, 215
Eckhardt, Meister, 212
economics, 280-1
ecstasy, 30, 253, 342
Edman, Irwin, 2
education, 34, 82, 306, 318, 346
egalitarianism, 155
élan vital, 19-20
Elias, 351
Eliot, T. S., 26, 196
empathy, 332
empiricism, 5-6, 45
Enlightenment, the, 51, 57, 230
engagement, 234-6
Epictetus, 184-5
Epicurus, 70, 249
essences, 80-5, 136, 355-6
eternal law, the, 110-1
eternity, 4, 269, 273, 277, 285
Eucharist, the, 76, 120, 142, 219, 337, 350-1
Eucken, Rudolf, 141
evidence, 65, 69-70
evolution, 4, 17-9, 81-2, 121, 157, 162, 164, 167, 201, 204, 224-7, 276, 286, 292-3
exile, 229
existentialism, 248-9
experience, 5-6, 15-16, 26, 35, 122-6, 223, 237-8, 252
expressionism, 264-5

F

face, the, 267-74, 283-9
faith, 75, 91-3, 121, 129-30, 136-7, 152, 169, 208-9, 213-4, 231-2, 274-6, 320, 342, 354-5, 359
family, the, 295-6
fall of man, the, 38, 103, 177-8, 191, 193, 206, 221, 241-2, 267, 287, 314, 361-2
fascism, 219, 230
fate, 187-8, 231
fear, 168, 246
feminism, 326
Fessard, Gaston, S.J., 259
Fichte, Johann Gottlieb, 62, 307
finality, 20, 203-5
flight from God, 274-83
forgiveness, 80-1, 87, 177, 314
fortune, 321-2
Francis of Assisi, St., 30, 139-40, 149, 205, 220
Franciscan ideal, the, 215-6
Frangipani, Countess Apollonia von, 327
freedom, 10-13, 17, 206-7, 212, 236, 344

Freud, Sigmund, 183, 226, 296
Furtwaengler-Scheler, Maerit, 142, 196-7

G
Galileo, 203
Gascoyne, David, 233
generosity, 20-1
Genesis, 44, 267
Genghis Khan, 235
genius, the, 164-6
George, Stefan, 202
Gide, André, 266
Gilson, Étienne, 43-4
God, 2-4, 15, 29-34, 44, 47-8, 72-5, 86-91,
   103, 109-11, 114, 118, 121-3, 127-31,
   136, 143-4, 147-8, 150-1, 153, 155, 158,
   160, 162-72, 177, 188-90, 193, 203-4,
   210-14, 226, 231-2, 236, 246, 264-5,
   267-74, 276-9, 281-3, 312-3, 316,
   320-1, 330, 340-2, 354-5, 360
Goethe, 57, 65, 145, 170, 183, 327
Gogh, Vincent van, 284
goodness, 20-1, 160, 168, 288, 343-4
gospel, the, 26, 40, 42, 47, 110-1, 209
Gospels, the, 51, 90, 209, 213
grace, 13, 21, 36, 90, 112-3, 149, 154-5,
   202, 207, 224, 227, 236, 251, 329,
   344-5, 360
graphology, 284, 303
Greek language, the, 305, 318
Greek thought, 25, 35, 89, 110, 147-8, 184,
   187, 220, 250, 288-9, 305-6
Greene, Graham, 262
Gruenewald, Matthias, 287
Guardini, Romano, 192, 259
guilt, 142, 155, 178, 185, 212, 226, 231

H
habit, 12
Handel, Georg Friedrich, 119
happiness, 89, 161, 168, 179, 184, 187-8,
   236, 256
Hartman, Nicolai, 194
Hautecombe, Benedictine abbey of, 259
Haydn, Franz Joseph, 119
heaven, 109-10, 211-2, 251-2
Hebrew style, 267
hedonism, 183-4, 187-8
Hegel, George Wilhelm, 62, 70, 164, 204,
   307
Heidegger, Martin, 54, 93, 243-4, 307, 340,
   354, 356
"heir of heresy," 222-3
hell, 212-3, 251-2, 267
Heraclitus, 76
heretic, the, 191, 222
hero, the, 164-6, 184
heroism, 23, 36
Hesse, Hermann, 217
hierarchy, 158-61, 180, 203-4, 209, 213-4,
   307
higher criticism, 51-5
Hildebrand, Dietrich von, 89, 115, 117,
   122, 140, 192, 198
history, 26, 81, 84, 164, 178, 204-5, 208,
   221, 228, 234-6, 312-3, 316

Hitler, Adolf, 26-7, 230, 232-3, 289-90,
   297, 299, 302, 305-7, 309, 312-3, 366
Hoelderlin, Friedrich, 273, 302
hope, 168, 208, 244-8, 283, 311-4, 370
Hopkins, Gerard Manley, S.J., 76, 246,
   359
Hopster, Father, S.V.D., 368
Hufnagel, Alfons, 86
humanitarianism, 32, 150-4
humility, 142, 168, 215, 246, 268
humor, 267, 270
Husserl, Edmund, 49-97, 100, 141, 332-3,
   335, 340, 348, 361
Husserl, Malvine, 97
Huxley, Aldous, 34-5
hysteria, 279

I
"I," the, 11, 154, 227, 250, 344, 353-4,
   358-9
idealism, 9, 62
ideas, Platonic, 74, 85
imagination, 213-4
immortality, 15-17, 27-8, 121, 127-8, 172-
   5, 243
impressionism, 266
Incarnation, the, 36, 57, 75-6, 148, 193,
   204, 219, 288-9, 293, 316, 320
Indian thought, 183
individualism, 211
infallibility, 51, 152
"inner castle," the, 149, 358-9
insanity, 30, 279, 309
instinct, 160-1
intellect, the, 73-4, 78, 190-1, 328-9, 339,
   342
intelligence, 28
intentionality, 59-62
intimacy, 130-1
intuition, 77, 85
Isaac Israeli, 72
Israel, 25-6, 36, 57, 89, 110, 146-7, 178,
   186, 191, 204, 221, 239, 305, 350,
   371-2
Israel, the Seven an authentic voice of,
   13, 34, 43-5, 56, 68, 89, 112, 127, 134,
   138, 178-9, 253-4, 274, 323, 331,
   337-8, 345, 351, 357, 365, 371-2

J
Jaegerschmidt, Sr. Adelgundis, O.S.B., 90,
   93-6
James, William, 42
Jaurès, Jean, 8
Jewish legends, 179, 273
Jews, the, 101, 131, 218, 263, 345, 365
Joan of Arc, St., 30
Job, 186, 253-4
John of the Cross, St., 6, 229, 347-9,
   361-4, 367
John the Baptist, St., 6
Johns, Orrick, 329
Journet, Msgr. Charles, 46
joy, 116, 186, 212, 216, 348, 355-6
Joyce, James, 306
Julian of Norwich, 91
Julius Caesar, 273

393